"Taking an expansive view of immigration policies and practices beyond immigration law, this book is a valuable contribution to specialists interested in the history of immigration into the United States. It shows the complexity of the internal debates in the United States over immigration policy, as well as the role of Mexican diplomats and agents in these debates."
—JÜRGEN BUCHENAU, *Pacific Historical Review*

"Draws on significant research in both U.S. and Mexican archives to provide original analysis of an early and little-known episode in the history of immigration as an issue in the relationship between the two countries. . . . For historians of U.S. foreign policy, this book also provides a fascinating early case study of an executive branch effort to avoid having constraints placed by Congress on its ability to conduct foreign relations."
—HALBERT JONES, *Hispanic American Historical Review*

"In his rich and nuanced study Montoya examines immigration both as a transnational phenomenon and—critically—as a diplomatic issue between states. Rigorously researched, this timely history shows that immigration policy is best addressed not with walls but through diplomacy."
—JULIA F. IRWIN, author of *Making the World Safe: The American Red Cross and a Nation's Humanitarian Awakening*

"This carefully researched and elegantly crafted book provides timely lessons on the importance of building and sustaining bilateral diplomatic relationships across the Mexico-U.S. border. Montoya's new analysis of early twentieth-century legislative practices reminds us that marginalized immigrants have always been central to the discourses and practices of state sovereignty and nation formation."
—MARK OVERMYER-VELÁZQUEZ, editor of *Beyond la Frontera: The History of Mexico-U.S. Migration*

"Timely and pathbreaking. . . . With a focus on diplomacy and politics from the mid-1920s to the early 1930s, *Risking Immeasurable Harm* sheds new light on U.S.-Mexican diplomatic developments as they relate to controversies over quotas, racism, sovereignty, and immigration restriction. This important book reveals how and why diplomacy factored centrally in the failure of congressional attempts to restrict Mexican migration, even as the United States implemented draconian cuts to overall immigration."
—CHRISTOPHER MCKNIGHT NICHOLS, author of
Promise and Peril: America at the Dawn of a Global Age

RISKING IMMEASURABLE HARM

RISKING IMMEASURABLE HARM

IMMIGRATION RESTRICTION
AND U.S.-MEXICAN DIPLOMATIC
RELATIONS, 1924–1932

Benjamin C. Montoya

University of Nebraska Press
Lincoln

© 2020 by the Board of Regents of the University of Nebraska. All rights reserved.

The University of Nebraska Press is part of a land-grant institution with campuses and programs on the past, present, and future homelands of the Pawnee, Ponca, Otoe-Missouria, Omaha, Dakota, Lakota, Kaw, Cheyenne, and Arapaho Peoples, as well as those of the relocated Ho-Chunk, Sac and Fox, and Iowa Peoples. ∞

First Nebraska paperback printing: 2024
Library of Congress Cataloging-in-Publication Data
Names: Montoya, Benjamin C., author. | University of Nebraska Press.
Title: Risking immeasurable harm: immigration restriction and U.S.-Mexican diplomatic relations, 1924–1932 / Benjamin C. Montoya.
Other titles: Immigration restriction and United States Mexican diplomatic relations, 1924–1932
Description: Lincoln: University of Nebraska Press, 2020. | Includes bibliographical references and index.
Identifiers: LCCN 2019035096
ISBN 9781496201294 (Hardback)
ISBN 9781496238863 (Paperback)
ISBN 9781496219862 (ePub)
ISBN 9781496219879 (mobi)
ISBN 9781496219886 (PDF)
Subjects: LCSH: United States—Emigration and immigration—Government policy—20th century. | Immigration enforcement—United States. | United States—Relations—Mexico.
Classification: LCC JV6455 .M665 2020 | DDC 325.7309/042—dc23
LC record available at https://lccn.loc.gov/2019035096

Set in ITC New Baskerville by Laura Buis.

For Elias, Matty, Isla, and Aunt Pat

"The United States, smiling or angry, its hand open or clenched, neither sees nor hears us but keeps striding on, and as it does so, enters our lands and crushes us. It is impossible to hold back a giant; it is possible, though far from easy, to make him listen to others; if he listens, that opens the possibility of coexistence. Because of their origins (the Puritan speaks only with God and himself, not with others), and above all because of their power, the North Americans are outstanding in the art of the monologue: they are eloquent and they also know the value of silence. But conversation is not their forte: they do not know how to listen or to reply."

—OCTAVIO PAZ, *The Other Mexico*

Contents

List of Illustrations	xi
Acknowledgments	xiii
Introduction	1
1. The Basis for the Quota Drive against Mexico: Winter 1924–Fall 1927	19
2. Singling Out Mexico for Restriction: Winter 1927–1928	65
3. International Pressure against the U.S. Effort to Restrict Mexican Immigration: Spring 1928	101
4. The Advantages, Disadvantages, Risks, and Rewards of Immigration Restriction: Fall 1928	125
5. The U.S. Senate Passes a Quota on Mexico: Winter 1929–Spring 1930	167
6. Administrative Restriction, Repatriation, and the Demise of the Quota Effort: Summer 1930–Winter 1932	205
Conclusion	243
Epilogue	255
Notes	261
Bibliography	303
Index	319

Illustrations

Tables

1. House Committee on Immigration and Naturalization hearing on Mexican immigration, late February 1928 — 79
2. Mexico's statistics on Mexican immigration and repatriation vs. U.S. statistics on the same, 1920–1925 — 94
3. Number of visas issued in month of December, 1926–1929 — 188
4. Percent of visa refusals vs. total number of applicants, 1929 — 188
5. Decline in Mexicans' visa applications, May 1928–December 1929 — 188
6. Nationwide repatriation to Mexico from the United States, October 1930–June 1932 — 221
7. Nationwide repatriation from the United States to Mexico, 1930–1934 — 222
8. Visas issued to Mexican nationals, FY1927–1928, FY1929–1930, FY1930–1931 — 228
9. Mexican immigration to the United States following passage of 1924 immigration act — 229

Graph

1. Rates of emigration and repatriation from Piedras Negras and vicinity — 218

Acknowledgments

This book would not have been possible without the help of many. A great deal of thanks must go to Thomas W. Zeiler, a great scholar and a great friend. His guidance, diligence, patience, forthrightness, and humor were instrumental in helping me formulate and finish this project. Also, I wish to thank Joseph A. (Andy) Fry, a valued mentor and friend, who tirelessly edited my manuscript. He has long been a role model to me, and I continue to rely on his professional advice.

The love and care of my family contributed greatly to the completion of this project, especially from my wife, Haley Dove Montoya, and my mother, Susan Montoya. Words fail to capture how they both saw me through instances of doubt, exhaustion, and stress. Their support was tireless; their confidence in me unwavering. When I look over these pages, I am reminded of the countless hours they allowed me to work; I think of the many head-in-hands moments they talked me through. I am fortunate to have them both in my life.

This book is dedicated to four people. To my son, Elias Benjamin Montoya, who was born during the earliest days of this project (2013); to Matthew Joseph Montoya, my half brother, who died as this work was written (2015); to my daughter, Isla Dove Montoya, who was born as I revised this work into a book (2017), and to my aunt, Patricia Ann Barrett, who died during the last stages of this project's completion (2019). I hold each of you close.

Risking Immeasurable Harm

Introduction

Diplomatic pressure prevented congressional efforts to curb Mexican immigration to the United States during the late 1920s and early 1930s. In contrast to the successful restriction of southern and eastern European immigration a few years before, fears of disrupting recently mended relations between the United States and Mexico undercut efforts to extend an immigration quota to the Western Hemisphere. This attempt to legislatively restrict Mexican immigration failed, in part, because the need to preserve harmonious relations with Mexico overrode the need to bar the entry of its citizens.

History and a shared border have long marked U.S.-Mexican relations as exceptional, in part due to the issue of immigration. Geographic proximity and a large, unregulated border allowed for regular—if often contentious—contact between the two nations. A widening disparity of wealth and political stability between the two countries gave the relationship an asymmetrical quality not typical of the gaps in power between the United States and Canada, its northern neighbor. While the United States witnessed sustained economic and geographic growth during the nineteenth century, Mexico struggled to fight off Spanish autocracy, balance neo-royalism with fledgling federalism after independence, resolve a civil war between conservatives and liberals, and defend itself from foreign invasion—first by the United States and later by France. Close proximity served to exacerbate this asymmetry by creating vast opportunities for wealth for American investors, who flocked to Mexico to develop industries ranging from minerals to cotton. Finally a shared border obliged the United States and

Mexico to negotiate a wide range of issues that marked their diplomatic relationship as distinct from others: border creation and adjustment, cross-border Indian raids, water rights, agricultural products, livestock, fisheries, trade zones, drugs, and smuggling (whether of illicit goods or illegal aliens).[1]

Immigration became a diplomatic issue between the United States and Mexico during the first decades of the twentieth century. Along a two-thousand-mile border, in the midst of the unclear distinction in identity between "American" and "Mexican," immigration was a distinct feature of relations with Mexico that the United States shared with no other country.[2] Immigration became a potent issue because of its very nature—the movement of people and the notion of sovereignty. Thus, as historian George Grayson notes, in the history of United States and Mexican relations "immigration, unlike oil, investments, or agricultural products, directly affects human beings whose activities demand and command the attention of leaders on both sides of the [border]."[3] Immigrants as individuals had a great deal of agency in the evolution of the history of U.S.-Mexican relations, and it is undeniable that the movement of people—whether voluntary or coerced—has effected how home and host countries relate. Therefore immigration has been a central issue that animated U.S.-Mexican relations from the nineteenth century to the present. Since immigration is by its nature a transnational process, it is debatable whether it lends itself to bilateral consideration, or whether it should be subject to the unilateral enforcement of a host country's immigration laws.

Immigration blurs a nation's sovereignty. Controlling access to one's country is a universally recognized attribute of sovereignty in the international political system.[4] Indeed the American restrictionist effort discussed in this book represented an attempt to protect national sovereignty against the porousness of international borders and the influx of foreigners. Historian Mai Ngai describes how a desire to reinvigorate the centrality of state sovereignty explains the global proliferation of immigration restriction after World War I. The war simultaneously destabilized and entrenched nation-state boundaries, ushering in an inter-state system based on

Westphalian sovereignty, which sanctified the integrity of the territorial nation-state and the principle that no nation can interfere in the affairs of another.[5] This Westphalian sense of sovereignty changed how nations regulated immigration. Rigid border controls, passports, and state restriction on entry and exit became the norm for governing immigration. In this context the United States Congress's effort to legislate restriction was part of a global trend.[6] It was this renewed Westphalian spirit that ostensibly justified American policymakers in viewing U.S. immigration as a purely domestic matter. Yet how do we account for those opponents of an immigration quota for Mexico, many of whom agreed with a Westphalian sense of state sovereignty?

The answer lies in the contradictory ways U.S. policymakers, diplomats, and consular officials viewed immigration generally, and *Mexican* immigration specifically. If a Westphalian notion of state sovereignty was resurgent after World War I—at least for U.S. officials—it competed with an internationalist vision of diplomacy promulgated by President Woodrow Wilson. While many government officials were opposed to Wilson's international vision, there were aspects of Wilsonianism that were retained to face diplomatic problems throughout three successive Republican administrations in the 1920s. These tenets of Wilsonianism included a belief in upholding international law and spreading democratic values throughout the world (either through diplomacy or Republican trade policies), a recognition that the world was moving toward greater interdependency, and the expansion of U.S. enterprise after the war and the nation's transformation into a prime creditor that precluded any reversion to isolationism.[7] The three secretaries of state from 1921 to 1933—Charles Evans Hughes, Frank Kellogg, and Henry Stimson—were particularly influenced by Wilsonianism. They attempted legally and morally to bind the world through the rule of law with disarmament and peace treaties.

"Administrative restriction," or U.S. consular officials' efforts to curtail the entry of Mexican migrants into the United States by enforcing existing immigration laws, fits squarely into the internationalist framework espoused by the Republican secretaries of state.⁸ Administrative restriction, admittedly rooted in Westphalian terms, was a legal solution to the Mexican immigration problem of the United States. The process precluded the need for the United States Congress to pass restrictive legislation that would have risked harming U.S.-Mexican relations and signal an isolationist resurgence in diplomatic thinking.⁹ Existing U.S. immigration laws were not specifically prohibitive toward Mexican migrants; therefore the Mexican government took far less issue with them than with American efforts to enact a quota. Administrative restriction accomplished what many U.S. policymakers and politicians desired but only thought possible through a restrictive quota: a sharp curtailment of Mexican immigration to the United States. An added benefit of administrative restriction was that it did not undercut U.S.-Mexican relations. Coupled with the economic crisis of the Great Depression and a consequent repatriation crisis, administrative restriction helped to defuse the controversy over the quota drive by shifting the onus of immigration restriction from the nation to the individual. By restricting immigration in this way, the U.S. consular service in Mexico lessened the quota's offense to Mexicans. By curbing drastically the rate of recorded immigration into the United States, administrative restriction seemed to preclude the need for a quota and satisfied many Americans' desires for reduction in Mexican immigration. American prejudice was no less vituperative toward Mexicans; however, the sharp curtailment of Mexicans' presence within U.S. society diverted national attention from the issue. Nonetheless, as late as 1932 some congressmen continued their efforts to impose a quota on Mexican immigration. For them, Mexicans—like Asian and (southern and eastern) European immigrants before them—were a social menace to the United States and should be legislatively barred from entering the country.

Opponents of legislative restriction of Mexican immigration asserted that a quota would harm U.S.-Mexico relations. The U.S. State Department, for example, took a leading role in opposing a quota. But it was not simply American diplomats who feared the diplomatic effect of a quota; Mexican officials and the Mexican press also applied great pressure against any notion of restricting their nation's northward immigration. Mexicans followed quota debates in Washington and reacted strongly to what they viewed as American prejudice toward Mexico's immigrants. U.S. advocates of restriction were often undeterred by warnings that a quota on immigration could harm U.S.-Mexican relations. They insisted that immigration law was solely a domestic affair and that congressional debate on the matter should not be swayed by diplomatic concerns. Even as many quota opponents ostensibly accepted this interpretation of immigration law, they did argue that any type of legislative restriction on Mexican immigration would poison U.S.-Mexican relations, which had only recently recovered from a decade of revolutionary turmoil in Mexico.

Historians have asserted that Mexican immigration was spared from legislative restriction for economic reasons, namely, the need to provide cheap labor to industries in the southwestern U.S. states. While the economic explanation is not wrong, it fails to recognize other contemporary reasons why the United States chose to keep its borders open to Mexican immigration. Economic concerns do not explain why the period of the most intense lobbying for quotas coincided with the height of economic prosperity in the United States during the 1920s. By the time the real effects of the Great Depression had begun to set in across the United States, Mexican immigration figures were sinking to historic lows, even though quota efforts continued into the 1930s. Administrative restriction had achieved the drop in immigration. This policy alternative was implemented for the diplomatic objective of preserving U.S.-Mexican relations while simultaneously diminishing the entry of Mexican migrants into the United States that many Americans desired. The Great Depression encouraged the departure of Mexicans to Mexico, but it did not curtail their entry into the United States. Administrative restriction did that.

Understanding the importance of Mexican immigration for the history of U.S.-Mexican relations requires more than noting the peaks and troughs of the American business cycle. Immigration must be cast in the context of diplomacy between the United

States and Mexico. This book will show how immigration was an issue of distinct bilateral importance for U.S.-Mexican relations, even though each nation differed in its motivations and prescriptions. Differences were clear in how the United States debated immigration generally and how Mexico focused on immigration specifically; in the solutions developed to handle both nations' demands; the effects on U.S. foreign relations; and the ways the United States had to negotiate its interests vis-à-vis foreign governments. Such differences illuminate the distinct nature of U.S.-Mexican relations. Despite an asymmetrical power relationship between the United States and Mexico, the U.S. government was forced to assess the interests of the Mexican government in ways that it did not consider distant European and Asian nations. It was not a relationship of equals, but it was a relationship that obliged the United States to consider immigration. Even when American policymakers rebuffed international pressures—whether Mexican or hemispheric—to adjust its immigration policy, the U.S. government was forced to consider the effects its domestic debate on the quota would have on its bilateral relations with Mexico.

In a broad sense, the U.S. debate over restriction of Mexican immigration during the 1920s and early 1930s was a conflict between a Westphalian notion that national sovereignty should be protected from the influx of foreigners and a Wilsonian vision of liberalism, free trade, and negotiation that encouraged the harmonization of diplomatic relations. Despite a robust U.S. restrictionist effort, Mexico was not placed on the list of quota nations. Mexican immigration did not escape restriction, however; administrative restriction is proof of that. Yet to understand why the U.S. Congress did not pass legislative restriction on Mexican immigration to the United States, it is necessary to show how internationalist sentiment—evident in statements by secretaries of state, consular officials, the American press, and especially the Mexican government and press—defeated any campaign to bar Mexican immigration to the United States. In this regard Mexican immigration was distinct. Westphalian ideology justified the spate of legislation from 1917 to 1924 that would effectively bar the entrance of immigrants into the United States for generations. In the case of Mexican immigration, however, the Wilsonian vision of maintaining amicable foreign relations triumphed over state sovereignty. The exceptional nature of U.S.-Mexican relations explains this divergence. This exception demonstrates not only the importance of Mexican immigration to the history of United States foreign policy but also, and most significant, immigration's effect on U.S.-Mexican relations.

Fear and disdain have greeted generations of immigrants to the United States since the earliest days of the republic. Immigrants, whether coerced or persuaded to go to the United States, were always welcomed for the labor power they brought. Since its colonial period, the United States had enjoyed an abundance of land but suffered from a shortage of labor. The rapid growth of the U.S. economy during the first 150 years of the republic would have been impossible without the labor of slaves in cotton fields, Slovaks in steel mills, Jews in textile plants, Italians in construction, Chinese in railroads, and Mexicans in agriculture. With great economic growth came burgeoning political prestige. The inchoate new republic had the means to pay down debts, generate revenue, and lay the basis for a viable state thanks to the constant supply of labor that answered the entrepreneurial demand of the United States.

Like previous immigrant groups, a complex set of push-pull factors led Mexicans to migrate northward. Mexicans were pushed to the United States because of the monopolization of tillable lands, economic depression, and sociopolitical revolution. The United States pulled in Mexican migrants because it offered higher wages, more work, and a stable society. Mexicans were distinct from other immigrant groups in their relative ease of access to the United States. The world's most-vibrant economy by the turn of the twentieth century was just across the border. Once work had been completed and wages had been earned, home was just back across the border.

Yet there was a great contradiction between the constant and robust demand for labor—which many U.S. citizens considered fit only for destitute immigrants because of meager wages and deplorable working conditions—and the reaction to immigrants in U.S. society. In short the United States wanted immigrants' labor, but it did not want immigrants. Of course, Americans disagreed among themselves about immigration. Business groups profited handsomely from the constant supply of immigrant labor, while nativist groups believed immigrants threatened U.S. society. This contradiction lay at the heart of an effort by the U.S. Congress to place a quota on Mexican immigration during the interwar period.

"Immigration" is a historical term that needs unpacking. First, this book will approach the movement of people rather than the immigrants themselves. The paucity of sources revealing immigrant voices precludes a sustained treatment of how they may have considered their actions amid the broader diplomatic debates over immigration. Second, it is not clear how migrants—as individuals—played a direct role in shaping U.S.-Mexican relations. As a whole unit with a political and social impact, however, they did have a real effect on diplomacy. Third, I will pay attention to demographic distinctions among Mexican migrants where the sources permit. Mexican immigration was comprised of a heterogeneous mix of Mexicans. Unfortunately, in many cases, we can only speculate on the reasons why many chose to migrate to the United States and from what social background they derived.

Immigration is not an abstract historical term but rather represents a series of racial, social, economic, and cultural forces that have diplomatic consequences.[10] Immigration policies of a host country often reflect that particular nation's vision of who belongs to the body politic, who can be assimilated, or who should be excluded.[11] Host countries also conceptualize their immigration policies to complement the need for foreign labor. And immigration policy can be a tool of foreign policy, as in the case of admission preferences for immigrants from the Eastern bloc during the Cold War.[12]

Immigration carries an even more practical importance for sender nations. Immigration challenges internal state-building projects because of the difficulty in administering a portion of the population that has departed. Efforts to cultivate national prestige and solidarity and attempts to (re)produce a cultural community are also difficult for nations that witness their citizens immigrating to other countries.[13] These challenges were especially acute for Mexico during the 1920s and 1930s, as it tried to build a revolutionary nationalism among Mexicans after ten years of revolution that destroyed the Porfirian political system. Conversely immigration can be a boon for sender nations since the immigration of citizens can relieve a glut in labor supply and divest the nation of sources of political unrest.

Mexico benefitted from both of these aspects of immigration. This left Mexican officials, the press, and the populace ambivalent about immigration.[14] On one hand the nation was relieved to be rid of excess workers and political dissenters; on the other hand the nation was embarrassed at its inability to provide work for all its citizens and to quell internal unrest. Ultimately it was American debates over the restriction of Mexican immigration to the United States that clarified Mexico's foreign policy approach to its immigration. The singular offense posed by a quota on Mexican immigration caused Mexico's leaders to protest United States immigration policy and to attempt to steer the debate away from outright legislative restriction. Far from an abstract historical concept, immigration had real consequences for U.S.-Mexican relations.

It is difficult to quantify how many Mexican migrants stayed in the United States after emigrating and for what duration. For example, Frank Bean states that 728,000 Mexicans emigrated to the United States between 1901 and 1930, with 63 percent of those migrants entering the United States after 1920. George Sánchez estimates that approximately double that number—one and a half million Mexicans—migrated to the United States between 1900 and 1930. So there is a clear disparity in numbers.[15] However, there is some consistency to the numbers of Mexicans *in* the United States from the late nineteenth century to the 1920s. David Gutiérrez asserts that there were approximately 103,000 Mexicans in the United States in 1900, up from 78,000 in 1890 and marking a 66 percent increase from 1880. Elliott Barkan contends that 103,393

Mexicans resided in the United States in 1900. Gutiérrez argues for an approximate figure of 222,000 in 1910, Barkan pitches for 221,915. For 1920, Gutiérrez approximates the number at 478,000; Barkan estimates 486,418. A disparity is apparent between Gutiérrez and Barkan when discussing 1930 figures: Gutiérrez estimates 639,000, while Barkan estimates "more than six times" the 1900 figure (or 620,358).[16]

While exact figures for total Mexican immigration to the United States up to 1930 are difficult to ascertain, the numbers do indicate the rapid acceleration of Mexican immigration to the United States from the Porfiriato to the immediate postrevolutionary years. Also, figures are important for demonstrating the demographic weight of immigration relative to Mexico's total population. Finally, immigration statistics can give us a sense of why U.S. policymakers became alarmed about the rate of Mexican immigration to the United States by the 1920s and why they sought legislative restriction to curb it. Douglas Massey estimates that by the outbreak of the revolution in 1910, 18,000 Mexicans were emigrating to the United States annually. By 1919 that figure had reached 29,000. During the 1920s the annual rate of Mexican immigration to the United States skyrocketed to 49,000.[17]

During this rapidly accelerating immigration, Mexico's population was recovering from a decade of revolution. This caught the attention of many Americans who thought the Mexican population was dwindling and that its migrants in the United States were concentrated in the southwestern states. Figures on the admittance of legal Mexican immigration give a sense (albeit a limited one) of how the increased visibility of Mexicans in U.S. society played a role in inciting anti-Mexican sentiment during the 1920s.[18] According to Barkan and Bean, about 459,000 Mexicans entered the United States legally during the 1920s. This occurred at a time when southern and eastern European immigration and Asian immigration to the United States fell by over 76 percent and by over 70 percent, respectively (because of immigration restriction legislation that will be discussed later).[19] This figure of *legal* migrants comprised 3.2 percent of Mexico's population. Sánchez, no doubt keeping in mind the famously unquantifiable rate of illegal Mexican immigration to the United States during this time, believes a tenth of Mexico's population was lost to immigration north.[20]

Not surprisingly U.S. and Mexican leaders were concerned about immigration during the 1920s, especially after the passage of the Johnson-Reed Act of 1924, which established a permanent quota on immigration to the United States. In some respects immigration statistics are irrelevant. Instead the *perception* of a Mexican migrant labor force flocking to the United States was enough for many Americans to advocate for the restriction of Mexican immigration. For Mexico, whether one in ten Mexicans were heading north or not, the perception of impoverished citizens fleeing to another country for livelihood seemed to demonstrate Mexico's weakness and nationalist shortcomings and its inability to rebuild itself after years of revolutionary upheaval. When U.S. leaders began to consider placing a quota on Mexican immigration after 1924, it sparked a diplomatic debate that destabilized recently mended relations with Mexico.

In recent years students of U.S. foreign relations have reemphasized the internal factors that determine the ways in which the United States relates with other nations. According to Robert McMahon, the history of U.S. foreign relations is Janus faced. On one hand it is a national history that focuses on the internal forces within the U.S. state and society that shape its foreign policy. On the other hand it is an international history that focuses on "the external forces that influence and constrain the U.S. encounter with the wider world."[21] While it is critical to understand how U.S. policymakers responded to the external stimuli of immigration and adjusted their diplomatic responses accordingly, a key objective of this book gauges how domestic debates in the United States over a quota on Mexican migration, and the Mexican reaction to that debate, determined diplomatic relations with Mexico. Like McMahon's treatment of U.S. foreign relations, U.S. immigration policy is Janus faced: it is formulated in accordance with domestic initiatives and yet often elicits international responses.[22]

Two recent studies remind us that immigration is not simply a domestic issue. Meredith Oyen, in her 2007 dissertation on migration and U.S.-Chinese relations, argues that a nation's immigration laws "are not merely domestic policies, but can have long-reaching affects [sic] on how countries relate to one another."[23] Erika Lee and Judy Yung, in their discussion of Angel Island (the western port of entry near San Francisco, California, for immigrants to the United States), show a world on the move and the making of "[the United States] as both an inclusive nation of immigrants and an exclusive gate-keeping nation."[24] By showing how restrictive legislation on immigration was implemented at Angel Island, Lee and Yung demonstrate that U.S. immigration law had real international consequences. Immigrants could be barred from entering the United States; undesirable aliens could be deported for fear that they were likely to become public charges.

An instructive example of the diplomatic importance of immigration comes from a scholar of Mexican foreign relations. Friedrich Schuler argues that historians of Mexican diplomacy tend to separate foreign relations history from Mexican domestic issues. The external and internal exist in isolated vacuums. Such an approach, Schuler believes, is a misrepresentation of Mexico's diplomatic history. He argues that scholars of Mexican foreign policy should conduct "integrational, horizontal research" that connects foreign relations with domestic issues in Mexico.[25] This book responds to this call to blend internalist and externalist approaches into an understanding of immigration's effect on U.S.-Mexican relations.

By and large, scholars of United States diplomatic history do not provide much direction on how immigration affected U.S.-Mexican relations before World War II. Some historians situate their work in material terms (oil, debts, investments, jobs, etc.); others focus primarily on relations during the Mexican Revolution; while still others discuss U.S.-Mexico relations in the context of America's broader geopolitical concerns.[26] The historiography shows that Mexico was able to exert its influence abroad and protect its interests locally vis-à-vis the United States. While the United States exerted an influence on Mexico that no other nation lived under, this power did not preclude Mexico's ability to defend itself diplomatically. As my treatment of the immigration debate demonstrates, Mexico protected its interests in the face of American hegemony. Conversely, while many Americans would have preferred otherwise, U.S. leaders could not disregard completely the perspectives of their Mexican counterparts on the matter of immigration restriction. U.S.-Mexican relations were too important for that. Asymmetry was not synonymous with hegemony in the diplomatic relationship between Mexico and the United States.

Historians, political scientists, and sociologists of immigration have given more attention to how immigration influences U.S.-Mexican relations. And yet they, like diplomatic historians, tend to only analyze Mexican migration history of recent decades. A series of studies from the 1980s offers a superficial understanding of immigration's big picture to the deeper context of U.S.-Mexican relations. These analyses (some of them citing incorrect chronology for restrictions on immigration) seem episodic, giving minimal attention to how immigration affected diplomacy.[27] The United States began restricting Mexican migration before the onset of the Great Depression, through administrative restriction, in response to congressional pressure. This periodization of restriction of Mexican migration is also flawed because it presumes that economic factors decisively determined the pressure for restricting Mexican migration. Instead the drive to curb Mexican migration came in the midst of a larger context. Many U.S. policymakers believed Mexicans should have been added to the class of restricted migrants to the United States in the mid-1920s. That this was not done reveals the extent to which diplomatic considerations shaped the debate over the restriction of Mexican immigration.

Some scholars have employed methodologies that inform my approach. Christopher Mitchell and contributors to *Western Hemisphere Immigration and United States Foreign Policy* provide valuable insights into how immigration is simultaneously an internal, national, and international issue by arguing that the U.S. immigration policies—even those primarily responding to internal social and political concerns—are often interpreted in migrant-sending nations as elements of U.S. foreign policy.[28] Jaime Aguila, one of the few historians who directly links Mexican immigration and diplomacy, seeks to internationalize American history and culture by comparing U.S. and Mexican immigration policy before 1929. He argues that a more accurate assessment of U.S.-Mexican relations comes only by analyzing Mexican emigration to the United States.[29] However, Mitchell et al. only analyze migration to the United States after 1960, and Aguila argues that the U.S. government was aloof to the matters of Mexican migration, claiming that the government left it to local and state authorities to resolve. Also, Aguila claims issues of migration and repatriation—often in the midst of economic recessions—had no noticeable effect on Mexican relations with the United States and that the legality of migrants' status in the United States had no effect on the "health of relations" between the two countries. In fact both the U.S. and Mexican governments were deeply concerned about the issue of migration.

Donna Gabaccia and Deborah Cohen have also examined facets of the connections between immigration and diplomacy. Gabaccia probes how foreign relations shaped the lives of immigrants in the United States but does not show how immigration affected foreign relations between specific nations. Cohen, who addresses the bilateral debate over the Bracero program, utilizes a much different periodization and concentrates on labor negotiations.[30]

Immigration historian Mark Reisler offers a previous account of the effort to place a quota on Mexico. His analysis corroborates two of the key points made in this book: first, that race—not economics—was the driving force behind restrictionists' efforts to curb Mexican immigration; and second, that the State Department implemented administrative restriction when other efforts to quell the quota effort failed, and that its effectiveness in curbing Mexican immigration precluded the need for a quota on Mexico.[31]

Reisler's account, however, fails to consider the full breadth of the quota debate and the international ramifications the prospect of immigration restriction had for U.S. diplomatic relations. Reisler argues that the quota debate effectively ended in 1930, when a bill to restrict Mexican immigration failed to reach the House floor for a vote.[32] While it is true that the quota was stymied in Congress after it passed the Senate in May 1930, and that there was credible speculation that President Hoover would have vetoed the measure, there was every reason to believe the bill would have made it into law during successive legislative sessions. The nation was in the throes of its worst economic depression since the 1890s and immigration restriction was considered a method by which to relieve the U.S. labor market. It was not a foregone conclusion to congressional and State Department figures in 1930 that the quota effort would eventually fail. Only by following the course of the quota effort to its end can we understand why its proponents were unable to pass a legislative measure to restrict Mexican immigration.

Moreover, by only considering the quota effort in domestic terms, Reisler fails to show why Mexico was threatened by the quota, how that animosity animated State Department efforts to defuse the crisis, and how the prospect of immigration restriction had relevance for contemporary, international debates on immigration and U.S. relations with other states regarding the issue. An examination of Mexican archival materials informs a more extensive and inclusive analysis. First, substantial Mexican opposition to the quota preceded 1930. Second, Mexican opposition to the quota was not attributable simply to the racist rhetoric that underlined American restrictionists' efforts. Rather, Mexico opposed the quota because it believed U.S. legislators disregarded the Mexican government's national goals for development, which included the curtailment of its own immigration, and contradicted the spirit of amicable relations by refusing to negotiate bilaterally a solution to the immigration problem. And third, the quota debate occurred within a context of international conferences that considered how to regulate immigration vis-à-vis a state's right of national sovereignty, while also protecting the rights of immigrant-sending nations and immigrants themselves. These multilateral discussions applied pressure to the ways in which American officials formulated U.S. immigration law and provided venues where Mexico—and other countries—could oppose immigration restriction measures of the United States.[33]

A historical treatment of immigration shows us that states, and especially the borders that separate them, still matter. Immigration history demonstrates the centrality of the nation-state and the importance of state power. Borderlands historiography argues that state borders and the "contact zones" between nations are not static or rigidly defined, but rather malleable and negotiated. While that is true, a history of immigration shows that the state is still capable of flexing power when enacting and enforcing restriction laws that encourage or discourage flow of migrants.[34] This book will discuss not only the state's ability to restrict the inflow of migrants (e.g., administrative restriction) but also the *perceived* power of the state to restrict the inflow of migrants. Mexican officials and the press would not have protested the American debate over legislative restriction on Mexican migration so vehemently if they believed the United States lacked the power to enforce such legislation. Also, the practical relevance of borders for state power is revealed by the limitations on Mexican foreign policy options once the nation's citizens had emigrated north. Mexico could not manage its external population for the simple fact that it was no longer within its jurisdiction. Instead coercion (disallowing Mexicans from leaving Mexico), incentives (offering land to those migrants who repatriated from the United States), external nation-building (cultural campaigns sponsored by Mexican consulates in the United States to sustain a sense of Mexican national identity among migrants), and protest (of American treatment of Mexican migrants) were some of the only tools available to Mexican policymakers when challenging the disparity of national power between the United States and Mexico. "Emigrants are in another state's grip," historian David Fitzgerald states, "so governments of countries of emigration [e.g., Mexico] must develop creative ways to manage citizens abroad, preserve their national loyalty, and extract their resources." The diplomatic tools described above are largely symbolic since governments do not have the power to use force against citizens abroad.[35] Finally, it will be shown that

Mexicans based their decision to migrate on the likelihood of apprehension in the United States. Illegal immigration will be a constant subtheme of Mexicans' movement northward, as legal requirements—especially administrative restriction—had real effects in curbing Mexican migration.

Chapter 1 of this book focuses primarily on domestic U.S. debates and identifies why Mexican immigration mattered for American policymakers and pinpoints when these domestic debates assumed international importance for Mexico and the rest of the Western Hemisphere. The second chapter shows how the quota debate developed in Washington during the spring of 1928 and how Mexican observers reacted to the debate. If the United States were to place a quota on Mexican immigration, Mexico's policymakers believed, diplomatic relations would be affected negatively. The third chapter places that domestic debate within an international context and demonstrates how multilateral discussions about immigration were construed as a threat to Congress's sovereign right over U.S. immigration policy. Chapter 4 describes legislative attempts to restrict Mexican immigration and asks how the pro-quota movement justified its efforts in the face of domestic and diplomatic blowback. The fifth chapter addresses how the enforcement of existing immigration law by the U.S. consular service in Mexico (what was termed "administrative restriction") was diplomatically preferable to the quota, and why the Mexican government did not protest it with the vehemence it brought to the quota debate. Chapter 6 discusses how the restriction effort died in the midst of diminished immigration numbers because of administrative restriction, the Great Depression, and repatriation. The conclusion addresses how this first wave of Mexican immigration to the United States set precedents that informed later debates between the two countries on immigration.

1

The Basis for the Quota Drive against Mexico

Winter 1924–Fall 1927

A brief history of U.S.-Mexican relations up to the late 1920s reveals the importance of bilateral debates over immigration during the nineteenth and twentieth centuries as well as highlights the pressures effecting the immigration issue. Relations between the two nations had, by 1890, reached a level of mutual amicability. By the start of the 1890s Porfirio Díaz had been president of Mexico for over a decade. Foreign development was thriving in Mexico; the Mexican economy was booming; and Díaz's government had gotten a handle on Mexico's foreign debt. The internal peace that underlined this prosperity in Mexico made Díaz a much-lauded leader by his American and European counterparts. Mexico and the United States cooperated to quell cross-border banditry and Indian raids. In 1898 the two countries raised the status of their diplomatic legations to embassies, and Mexico hosted the Second Pan-American Conference in 1901–1902.[1] Economic prosperity also brought diplomatic stability. As Mexico modernized, it emerged as a force, albeit a secondary one, in international and hemispheric relations for the first time since its wars of independence.

Despite this *Pax Porfiriana*, there were internal problems that undermined Mexico's stability and jeopardized U.S.-Mexican relations. By the turn of the twentieth century Mexicans had grown tired of Díaz's clientalist regime. For thirty years, Díaz had secured his government by influencing the appointment of state governors, approving candidates for the national congress, dispensing patronage to friends, developing a rotation policy in the military command structure, controlling the courts, subsidizing the press, and cultivating the support of the church.[2] Landowners and caudillos sought a greater say in government policy, especially regarding the high rate of foreign investment and ownership of Mexican land and resources. The Mexican populace desired to play an effective part in Mexico's political process; they wanted to elect their leaders from the community instead of seeing outsiders appointed by Mexico City with their prime qualification being loyalty to Díaz. Campesinos protested their displacement from land as the Díaz government gave concessions, subsidies, franchises, and lands to foreign investors and enterprises that hoped to develop Mexican resources.[3] The financial panic of 1907 aggravated many of these brewing tensions and seemed to augur the end of Díaz's regime. Mexico's economy suffered because of its dependency on the American economy. The economic growth that had characterized the Díaz years before 1900 came to an end. Government income declined, foreign debt increased, prices soared (especially for corn, wheat, and beans, staples of most Mexicans' diets at the time), consumption decreased, labor was cut back, and wages declined.[4] Revolution was in the offing.

While internal structural problems in Mexico would soon lead to revolution, U.S.-Mexican relations had never been better than during the last years of the Porfiriato. Such issues as the use of Magdalena Bay by the U.S. Navy, the border dispute involving el Chamizal, and certain differences over policy toward Central America did not disrupt these amicable relations. What concerned U.S. leaders by the end of the first decade of the twentieth century was the political stability of Díaz's government. Suspicion was mutual, as *revoltoso* movements proliferated against Díaz, many of which established safe bases in the United States. Díaz suspected American motives for not clamping down on these cross-border threats to his regime, although U.S. law precluded such action, a precedent Díaz had benefitted from directly when he staged his own coup attempt against the Mexican government in 1875. Despite these mutual suspicions, the United States government had no incentive to promote Díaz's demise. The prosperity of many U.S. investments and holdings in Mexico depended on national stability.[5]

The veneer of centralized power broke down quickly after the outbreak of revolution in November 1910. In less than six months Díaz surrendered power and fled Mexico. Between 1911 and 1915 U.S.-Mexican relations were in limbo as American policymakers supported governments, caudillos, and rebel groups it thought capable of reestablishing stability in Mexico. During these years—as revolution caused economic crisis, social disorder and civil struggle, hunger, and epidemics across Mexico—the diplomatic problem for the United States was deciding which faction to negotiate and cooperate with in order to restore order in Mexico, create a new national government, and secure U.S. interests.[6]

By the time the Constitutionalists brought a modicum of national stability to Mexico after 1915, the United States found an awkward ally in Venustiano Carranza. Ostensibly leading a loose alliance of revolutionary factions against the militaristic government of Victoriano Huerta, Carranza, the self-declared "First Chief" of the revolution, worked hard to establish a stable government that paid its bills, destroyed the remnants of Porfirian power, and protected its interests vis-à-vis the United States. Nationalism infused Mexican relations with the United States to an unprecedented extent. While Porfirian diplomacy had tried to minimize U.S. presence and influence in regions like Central America, Carranza established a foreign policy that questioned the motives of American hegemony and challenged the place of U.S. interests in Mexico.

The 1917 Constitution and the Carranza Doctrine recalibrated U.S.-Mexican relations. The constitution invoked Mexican nationalism and subordinated individual property rights to the nation.[7] Article 27, which allowed for the expropriation of privately owned property and for the nationalization of mineral resources, lay at the nationalist heart of the 1917 Constitution.[8] If implemented it would have repudiated the established global power structure, Western capitalism, and the Anglo conception of property rights.[9] For the United States the most troublesome issue in its relations with revolutionary Mexico during Carranza's presidency was Mexico's nationalistic interpretation of the new constitution. This took precedence over Mexican neutrality during World War I, the violence still affecting some regions of the country, compensation for damages to foreign property during the revolution, and the resumption of payments on foreign debt.[10]

In response to U.S. protests over Article 27, the Mexican government promulgated the Carranza Doctrine, which depicted Article 27 as an affirmation of Mexican sovereignty that took precedence over foreign claims of property rights. Although less meaningful in real diplomatic terms, the Carranza Doctrine represented a Mexican nationalist challenge to U.S. hegemony in Latin America and demanded a reformulation of the asymmetrical relationship between the countries. Carranza's declaration had several components. In sum the Doctrine decried foreigners who sought to attain a predominant position in the national economy in relation to native residents; it argued for judicial equality among *all* American states; it denounced the Monroe Doctrine as constituting interference into the domestic affairs of Latin American countries; it hoped to establish a relationship of true solidarity among Latin American nations based on the principle of nonintervention; it called for treaties and alliances between Latin American nations and any other countries that aligned with their interests; and finally, it asserted control over national resources and promoted industrialization as the best ways to secure independence. Despite the declaration's attempt to foster Latin American solidarity in the face of U.S. hegemony, however, Carranza remained isolated in his efforts to rebuke U.S. influence in Mexico and Latin America.[11]

The implications of Article 27 were enormous for it challenged the European and American understanding of property ownership that gave the owner inalienable control over all resources above and under the soil. Article 27 did not completely eradicate the notion of private property, but it did modify it and nationalize it. Private individuals could buy land but not the subsoil. Only Mexican citizens could own land and obtain concessions to exploit the subsoil. Foreigners could own private property, but only if they gave up extraterritoriality protections (or the protection of their native governments).[12]

The U.S. government was alarmed by Article 27 because it threatened to deprive U.S. petroleum companies of the subsoil concessions they had received during the Porfiriato and the massive profits they gained from oil exploration since the early 1900s. Aside from vigorous lobbying by petroleum companies in Washington to protect investments valued at more than $500 million, the U.S. government's chief concern over Article 27 was the growing demand for oil within the United States. The United States imported virtually no Mexican oil until the first major Mexican oil well came into production in 1904. By the end of the decade Mexico was only producing 1 percent (3.6 million barrels) of the world total. Oil production ramped up dramatically during the revolutionary years, however. Protected by private security forces from the violence and pillage affecting the rest of Mexico, U.S.-owned oil companies were producing 157 million barrels annually, or 24 percent of the world total. Eighty percent of this oil was being exported to the United States to feed the country's growing car culture.[13]

In fact it was U.S. interest in raw materials throughout Latin America during the 1910s that illuminates another reason why Washington was concerned about Article 27, namely, the U.S. economy's insatiable demand for industrial raw materials. First, U.S. oilmen sought other bonanzas in petroleum, especially after promulgation of Mexico's 1917 Constitution. Colombia drew heavy U.S. oil investments, growing from less than $4 million in 1913 to $30 million in the early 1920s. Between 1917 and 1921 Venezuela's U.S.-led oil boom grew by over 90 percent from 121,000 barrels to over a million barrels. But U.S. business set its sights beyond oil. Copper and iron drew massive U.S. investments into Chile during the 1910s. Overall, U.S. investment in Chile grew from $15 million in 1912 to over $100 million by the early 1920s, nearly all of it in mining. By the end of the decade there were 423 million dollars' worth of U.S. investments in Chile.[14]

In the context of burgeoning U.S. investments throughout the region, then, Article 27 held dangerous implications. If U.S. property and investments were subject to the laws of Mexico and could not be protected by home governments, a principle known as the Calvo Doctrine, then what would stop other Latin American nations from following suit? This fear of Article 27 explains why both the Wilson and Harding administrations refused to recognize the governments of Venustiano Carranza and Álvaro Obregón from 1917 to 1923. Even after the United States officially granted recognition to the central government in Mexico City, the prospect of a dependent nation restricting property ownership frightened U.S. policymakers because of the precedent it might set for other Latin American nations that hosted large amounts of U.S. foreign investment dollars. In a telegram to Secretary of State Frank Kellogg in April 1926, U.S. Ambassador to Mexico James Sheffield argued for a tough stance toward Mexico. Over 40 percent of total U.S. investments abroad were in Latin America by the mid-1920s. If the United States showed any "weakness in our attitude [toward Mexico] it is certain to be reflected almost immediately in other foreign countries."[15]

Negotiations over Article 27 consumed U.S.-Mexican relations from 1917 to 1923. When Mexican president Álvaro Obregón sought to normalize relations with the United States after 1920, the Harding administration demanded guarantees of foreign property rights—essentially asking Obregón's government to abrogate Article 27. Obregón balked at the demand; to have abandoned Article 27 would have undermined his government's efforts to gain legitimacy among Mexicans. Consequently the United States withheld diplomatic recognition of Mexico's revolutionary government. A diplomatic standoff between the United States and Mexico took place for the next three years. Finally an amicable *agreement* was concluded during 1922 and 1923, under which Mexico would not retroactively enforce Article 27 as long as U.S. petroleum interests performed "positive acts" of developing their leases. The two sides also established a general claims commission and a separate commission to assess specific damages from the revolution, through which the Mexicans agreed to pay cash for any expropriated property greater than 4,400 acres while the Americans agreed to accept

Mexican bonds for expropriations of smaller acreage. The United States then officially recognized Obregón's government. In early 1924 the first U.S. ambassador in more than five years arrived in Mexico City. Such agreements were unofficial and never constituted a formal international treaty. The agreement was not presented to the congress of either country, and the agreement's execution depended solely on the goodwill of both nations. With the "Bucareli agreement" the United States relaxed its other demand for a treaty on foreign property rights.[16]

Obregón's staunch defense of Article 27—at the expense of nonrecognition by the United States—between 1920 and 1923 demonstrated a diplomatic tenacity that Porfirian predecessors had never displayed toward the United States. While Mexico was economically weak and socially fractured by the long revolution, Mexican leaders of the following decades voiced a nationalistic spirit that sought to minimize U.S. hegemony over Mexico. Economically they grudgingly accepted that Mexico would have to depend on U.S. goodwill, investment, and debt purchases to rebuild their country. Diplomatically, however, Mexico would not surrender its interests for the sake of maintaining good relations with the United States. The revolution destroyed Porfirianism and the harmonious tone that had characterized U.S.-Mexican relations since the 1880s. In its place came a more-centralized state that espoused a revolutionary nationalism that underlined relations with the United States after 1923.

Beginning with Carranza, but especially after 1920 when revolutionary violence largely subsided, Mexico's revolutionary leaders recast the nature of Mexico's sovereignty. Despite its proximity to the United States, Mexico was able to retain a striking degree of political and economic separation. Considering the problems of ending revolutionary violence, moving toward political stability, and beginning the process of centralization and regularization of government functions, the Mexican government was adept at managing internal problems concomitant to its always-difficult relationship with the United States.[17] When the United States challenged Mexican laws, historian Daniela Spenser argues, it rejected both the essence of Mexico's legitimacy and its sovereignty. Mexico's international position and legitimacy were determined by its desire to carry out policies that were "independent of the powerful, dominant, and absorbing northern neighbor." Submission to U.S. interests was anathema to Mexican leaders. Even though the Mexican state power was fragile in the wake of the revolution, the government had to remain committed to a revolutionary program, at least publicly, because Mexicans demanded it. The state owed its existence to the *perception* that it was based on, and was implementing, revolutionary ideals. To maintain this legitimacy the Mexican government could not follow "a course of loyalty towards the United States."[18]

Despite the agreements from 1922 and 1923, problems over Article 27 soon reignited between the two nations. Frank Kellogg, the new and inexperienced U.S. secretary of state, followed advice from lower-level State Department officials who believed a tough stance should be taken against the new government of Plutarco Elías Calles in Mexico City. Calles, Obregón's handpicked successor, assumed the Mexican presidency in December 1924. He was intent on consolidating political control within the central government. Toward this end Calles promulgated anticlerical laws, favored labor unions, and worked to implement agrarian reform. U.S. oil companies were threatened when Mexican federal judges loyal to Calles began handing down decrees against them, despite the Bucareli agreement. U.S. officials were soon accusing Mexico's new president of Bolshevik proclivities.[19] State Department officials argued to Kellogg that Calles was delaying when it came to settling claims and that the Mexican government was threatening to seize subsoil ownership rights from U.S. petroleum interests.

James R. Sheffield, the U.S. ambassador to Mexico from 1924 to 1927, was convinced that Calles was trying to build a socialist state in Mexico. Sheffield viewed Calles as sympathetic to Soviet Russia. Calles, Sheffield wrote, believed "economic laws could be altered by statute and directed by force." Sheffield believed Calles was antagonistic to foreign interests and influences in Mexico and that he sought to nationalize major Mexican industries, notably oil. Calles viewed confiscation of foreign-owned property as a legitimate policy and wanted to officially recognize the Confederación Regional Obrera Mexicana (CROM), a federation of labor unions in Mexico, which Sheffield interpreted as further proof of the Mexican president's socialist inclinations.[20]

Much of this antagonism toward Calles was rooted in racism and disdain among State Department officials toward Mexicans. The department officials who advised Kellogg on Mexico—Francis White, Franklin Mott Gunther, Stokely W. Morgan, and Dana G. Munro—routinely referred to Mexicans as backward, intellectually infantile, illiterate, prone to violence, and inherently undemocratic.[21] This sentiment was typified by James Sheffield. Mexico was not a white nation, Sheffield argued. The great majority of Mexicans were mestizo; only a small percentage of them were pure white. Illiteracy was one of the "greatest menaces" preventing the nation's progress—"it is stated that from 70 to 80% of the people can neither read nor write." By their Indian nature, Sheffield argued, Mexicans were docile and uninspired—"centuries of oppression have broken [their] spirit and destroyed [their] ambition[.]"[22]

In 1925 the Calles government sought to enact provisions from Article 27. Foreigners were debarred from holding frontier or coastal land, from retaining a majority interest in a real estate company, and from acquiring freehold rights to subsoil deposits. This was more than an effort of Mexican economic nationalism by Calles. He was not opposed to U.S. investment into the Mexican economy, especially in the fledgling automobile industry. But, as historian Alan Knight states, oil was the "perennial, politicized enclave industry." As long as U.S. petroleum companies were spared from the full application of Article 27, the "chronic ulcer" of subsoil rights festered and affected each aspect of U.S.-Mexican relations.[23]

Driven by pressure from U.S. investors and the denigrating perspectives from his lower-level officials, Kellogg ratcheted up tensions with Mexico in June 1925 when he declared in a press release that the U.S. government would continue to support and recognize Calles's government so long as it protected American lives, rights, and property and complied with its international engagements and obligations. Ominously Kellogg concluded by saying that the "government of Mexico is now on trial before the world." Calles responded immediately with a press release of his own, saying that the United States threatened Mexican sovereignty. Soon after this terse exchange of press releases, Calles's government enacted a new petroleum law that reiterated the substance of Article 27, that freehold rights on oil-producing soil would be converted from land held in perpetuity to fifty-year leases, as long as "positive acts" had been performed prior to May 1917, and that the Calvo Doctrine would be reinstated, which would strip foreign property owners of their extraterritoriality rights.[24]

In the midst of this struggle over Article 27, U.S.-Mexican tensions were exacerbated by a dispute over Nicaragua. A series of rigged elections during the 1910s guaranteed that that client state always had a president amenable to U.S. interests, namely, in reliable debt servicing and in honoring foreign claims. Another rigged election in 1924 precipitated a crisis in Nicaragua that resulted in a coup that brought to power a Liberal who wanted to roll back U.S. presence in the country. U.S. Marines were deployed to Nicaragua in August 1925, having only left in January of that same year after the Coolidge administration judged that they were no longer needed there: Nicaragua's claims had been paid, its finances put in order, and its foreign relations stabilized. By the fall of 1925 U.S. forces had reoccupied Managua and placed a conservative favorite into the presidency.[25]

The Nicaraguan regime was weak, not from internal rivals, but rather from its neighbor, Mexico. According to the U.S. State Department, the Mexican government had designs to establish regional hegemony over Central America's states and therefore offered assistance to Nicaraguan opponents to the U.S.-backed regime in Managua.[26] Such Mexican involvement in Nicaragua was anathema to U.S. policymakers, and there was even talk of intervening into Mexican affairs.

Despite pressure on the Coolidge administration, from U.S. property owners in Mexico and U.S. senators and congressmen, to militarily intervene in Mexico, cooler heads prevailed in Washington. In late January 1927 the Senate unanimously approved a resolution urging arbitration of U.S. differences with Mexico. And while the U.S. government continued to oppose the Calvo Doctrine, in April 1927 President Coolidge publicly expressed a desire to ease tensions with Mexico. Months later Coolidge backed up his desire to work with the Calles government by sending a new ambassador, Dwight W. Morrow, to Mexico City in October 1927.[27]

Morrow had been close to Calvin Coolidge since their undergraduate days at Amherst College. He was a banker who had spent the previous fifteen years as a partner at J. P. Morgan. In contrast to many career diplomats in the State Department, Morrow was disenchanted with the notion—promoted since at least the time of Theodore Roosevelt—that the United States could intervene into the affairs of nations of the Western Hemisphere to protect U.S. interests. A few years before becoming ambassador to Mexico, Morrow expressed his misgivings about U.S. involvement in Cuba: "of course the government of Cuba has been and is very bad. It is possible, yes, it is probable, that the United States might run Cuba much better. As I get older, however, I think I become more and more convinced that good governance is not a substitute for self-governance. The kind of mistakes that [the United States] would make in running Cuba would be different from those that the Cubans themselves make, but they would probably cause a new kind of trouble and a new kind of suffering."[28]

Whereas Morrow's predecessor James Sheffield was stubborn, Morrow was flexible. While Sheffield was resolute and antagonistic (even suspicious), Morrow was pragmatic and conciliatory. Such an approach to Calles quickly produced results by settling the issues that had hampered U.S.-Mexican relations from the past decade. Within a matter of weeks Morrow had found a solution to the oil issue, by convincing Calles that it would not violate principles of Mexican economic nationalism to abandon a strict enforcement of Article 27 upon U.S. petroleum companies. Consequently the Mexican Supreme Court, even while maintaining the principle of state ownership of subsoil rights, relaxed the declaration of the

Calvo Doctrine and withdrew the fifty-year limitation on foreign owners of Mexican property. In short the Bucareli agreement was revived. By giving respect toward Mexican sovereignty, Morrow dispelled socialist accusations of Calles and showed that the Mexican president wanted to keep his country linked to the world of U.S.-led capitalism.[29]

Calles had his own incentives for calming tensions with the United States. A revolt was taking place in southcentral Mexico against his anticlerical laws and the nation's economy was sliding into recession. But the ratcheting down of the oil issue also coincided with the black sticky stuff's diminishing importance to the Mexican economy. Mexico's oil production in 1927 was a third of what it had been in 1921. For many U.S. petroleum companies, which were already spreading their attention to nations such as Colombia and Venezuela, the profits of Mexican oil were not worth the high political risk incurred in extracting it from the ground. Even for Calles the political toxicity of oil was increasingly incongruent with the profitability of it. In 1921 petroleum contributed 6.9 percent of Mexico's gross national product (GNP) and 22.4 percent of government income. By 1927, Calles's third year in office, those respective figures were 2.6 percent and 8.3 percent.[30]

In addition to brokering détente between the United States and Mexico over the oil issue, Morrow played an instrumental role in resolving a church-state conflict that tore at the fabric of Mexican society. What became known as the Cristero Rebellion was a conflict between the state and the Catholic Church that was precipitated on August 1, 1926, when Mexican bishops suspended public worship nationwide in a protest against anticlerical measures by the Mexican government, which sent out revolutionary schoolteachers to secularize education and required the registration of priests with federal authorities. Public worship services did not take place for the next three years. According to Morrow "there was a condition of acute unrest" in Mexico. The Mexican army crushed the initial rebellion in late 1926–early 1927. The Cristeros were not powerful enough to overthrow the Mexican government or decisively resist the army; the government did not have a sufficiently large and effective army to quell the rebellion.[31] There then followed two and a half years of indecisive guerrilla warfare, characterized by brutal excesses on both sides, from looting and raping to the massacre of civilians and the execution of prisoners.[32] Acts of terrorism occurred toward the nation's highest officials, such as when President-elect Obregón was assassinated by a religious fanatic on July 17, 1928. Soon thereafter a train on which President Emilio Portes Gil was traveling was bombed by religious rebels. The rebellion, as late as the spring of 1929, had about 10,000 rebels in arms. In May 1929, just before a final peace settlement took hold, 1,200 fighters were killed on both sides in the church-state conflict.[33]

Even before he officially entered his new post in October 1927, Morrow met with a liberal American Catholic priest, John J. Burke, who was the general secretary of the National Catholic Welfare Conference. Eventually Morrow was able to arrange a meeting between Burke and President Calles on April 4, 1928, after which both sides formulated their official positions for peace through letters; Morrow drafted Burke's letter. Burke proposed the resumption of religious worship if President Calles would make a declaration that it was not the purpose of the constitution and laws, nor his personal purpose, to destroy the identity of the Church. Also Burke asked that the central government confer with the authorized head of the Church in Mexico before applying subsequent anticlerical laws. Calles's letter agreed to accommodate all of Burke's requests.[34] The following month, on May 17, 1928, Burke met again with Calles and Morrow, who arranged and attended all of these meetings. This time Burke was accompanied by Archbishop Leopoldo Ruiz y Flores of Morelia, the person who had made the public declaration to cease worship back in the summer of 1926. Calles reportedly had to be convinced by Morrow to allow Ruiz to attend the meeting. At this meeting agreements that had been made the previous month were confirmed, and correspondence was sent to Rome for papal approval. Rome dragged its feet in endorsing the peace proposals, however. It hoped to bide time for a better settlement. Catholic leaders in Mexico were hostile to Calles's government and were opposed to any accommodation with it. Such views influenced Rome's position on the matter.[35]

Peace became more viable after the turn of the year. Pressure from the Catholic laity in both the United States and Mexico, the latter of whom had gone without sacramental rites—baptism, marriages, burials—for nearly three years, obliged Catholic leaders to seek peace. By March 1929 it was clear that the rebellion was dissipating. During the spring of 1929 Mexican prelates were issuing public statements promoting peace and order, condemning violence, urging respect for the government, and encouraging a common effort to reconstruct the nation.[36] This propaganda was essential in convincing religious rebels to lay down their arms. Also, the Mexican government, now led by a new president, Portes Gil, had every incentive to end the Cristero war. A new rebellion had broken out in the north in March, over disagreements regarding the presidential succession.

In May 1929 government and religious authorities in Mexico made public statements expressing their desire for peace. Notably President Gil declared that the Catholic Church as an institution was not involved in the military uprising (a dubious, but necessary, claim). Gil and Archbishop Ruiz met on June 8, 1929, to formally negotiate peace. Morrow once again took a direct role in the process of accommodating both sides by drafting the peace statements that both figures were to make public. Less than two weeks later Rome approved the peace proposal and the Cristero Rebellion came to an official end, even though sporadic violence would continue well into the 1930s. Public worship resumed. Morrow played an instrumental role in ending the church-state conflict.[37]

A turning point toward a détente in U.S.-Mexican relations occurred in late 1927. A large part of this shift was attributable to the arrival of Dwight Morrow to Mexico City as the new U.S. ambassador in October. James Sheffield's racism toward Mexicans generally and hostility toward Calles personally did much to aggravate tensions between the United States and Mexico. In a letter from October 1927 imparting advice to the new ambassador, Sheffield wrote that he got the best results with the Mexican government when he was "firm" and made them "understand that you mean what you say." Any attempt at modification or compromise with Mexicans, Sheffield warned Morrow, "is looked upon by them as weakness." Such a duplicitous nature explains why Mexico often gets "the better of us" in diplomacy.[38] By contrast Morrow brought no conceit to his role and accepted Mexican leaders for how they were instead of how the U.S. government believed they should have behaved.

Calles described to the Mexican nation what a difference a year of Morrow's ambassadorship had made in U.S.-Mexican relations during his presidential farewell address on September 1, 1928. As recent as 1927, Calles stated, relations between the two nations were "indecisive, subject to a lengthy controversy, and marked by deplorable acts which injured our commerce and hindered our peaceful development." Now, after the span of a year, Mexico is "free of any annoying difficulty" with the United States. Thanks to an "agent of concord, of good will and lofty views" (Morrow), the issues that were previously "disquieting and ominous" to peace between the two nations had been expeditiously resolved. The lesson from these "advantageous results," Calles argued, demonstrated that "it is easier for peoples and governments to understand each other for mutual cooperation by friendly procedure and by respect which leave unharmed the ideals and decorum of nations."[39]

Just as 1911 marked a descent into years of chaos and acrimony for U.S.-Mexican relations, 1927 was a turn toward a better relationship. It would never be as close as seen during the Díaz years, and U.S. leaders would periodically have to deal with Mexican leaders employing anti-U.S. rhetoric to demonstrate their revolutionary nationalist credibility. After 1927, however, both governments had enough common interests to keep relations stable. This détente would carry through the 1930s, with brief moments of tension such as in 1938 when the Mexican government (finally) followed through on a revolutionary commitment to nationalize the oil industry. By the 1940s, the relationship turned positively friendly, as both nations participated in a common front against

Axis aggression (a significant wartime boost in the U.S. consumption of Mexico's raw materials also helped).[40]

It was this new détente in U.S.-Mexican relations, fragile and fledgling in the late 1920s, that was at stake when U.S. restrictionists contemplated restricting Mexico's northward immigration. When U.S. policymakers began to debate a quota for Mexican immigration during the mid-1920s, Mexico's leaders were equipped—even obliged—to protest the effort. Although in some respects powerless to address the root of the problem (i.e., Mexicans' desire to migrate to the United States), Mexico's leaders did not hesitate to criticize immigration restriction of its citizens as an affront to U.S.-Mexican relations. Vague references to the debate's threat to U.S.-Mexican relations are not so amorphous when one considers the heated conflicts over oil and property rights between 1917 and 1927. The racist justifications used to defend calls for a quota on Mexican immigration were more than a threat to the nationalist identity of Mexicans; they threatened to undermine the relatively amicable relations that had been painstakingly reconstructed between the United States and Mexico by 1927.[41]

Mexican Immigration to the United States, 1890–1924

For generations Mexicans had established corridors of immigration that took them to the mines and agricultural fields of the Mexican north and the American Southwest. Immigration complemented seasonal work patterns that had been established since colonial times. Mexicans often pursued migratory work to supplement seasonal, land-based work in Mexico; the work ebbed and flowed in tandem with economic shifts and growth on both sides of the border. Mexican immigration, whether within Mexico or north to the United States, followed a discernable pattern. Many of the Mexican migrants who settled in the United States had first settled in Mexico's northern states. They had come from rural regions to a town or city within Mexico before they crossed the international border. This immigration process often included a degree of coercive pressure. Migrants from Mexico's western-central states—Aguascalientes, Guanajuato, Jalisco, Michoacán, and Zacatecas—pushed many small farmers, miners, and other workers of the Mexican north (e.g., Chihuahua) toward the United States in search of better wages. The gradual northern ascent was dictated by wage rates. By the turn of the twentieth century the Mexican border states had become the major point of departure north to the United States for migrants. Additionally Mexican immigration had a circular quality that distinguished it from immigration patterns of other migrant groups entering the United States, with the possible exception of Italians.[42] Mexican men migrated north to engage in seasonal labor and then returned south for a few months or years. Economic circumstances often re-initiated the circular pattern.[43] Close proximity to Mexico allowed many migrants to return south with relative ease. The social process of Mexican transnational immigration was maintained through interpersonal connections and was well established by the 1920s.[44] As the United States considered restriction of Mexican immigration after World War I, more was at stake than just diplomatic relations with Mexico. Ways of life and labor patterns were threatened by the enforcement of border restriction policies.

While Mexican immigration north preceded the enforcement, even the establishment, of a fixed United States–Mexico border, a discussion of Mexican immigration in the midst of Porfirian development and the Mexican Revolution reveals why American policymakers of the 1920s sought to curb Mexican immigration to the United States. The economic growth experienced in Mexico during the Porfiriato was part of a larger hemispheric trend during the last decades of the nineteenth century. Beginning in the 1870s oligarchical Latin American governments stabilized their countries and the region. These governments fostered export-led growth and sought trade and investment with the United States and Europe. A type of neocolonial economic relationship with the United States and Europe was established as Latin America opened itself to foreign goods and capital. In contrast to Africa, Latin America required no imperial subjugation. Latin Americans produced raw materials and agricultural commodities for industrializing Europeans and consuming Americans in return for capital and finished goods. Countries like Mexico focused on producing cheap exports. Mexico developed export markets in rubber, hides, coffee, minerals, cattle, and vegetables.[45] The development of such industries often meant acquiring farmland from campesinos. According to historian John Mason Hart, the Porfirian land enclosure process was a crucial step in Mexico's capitalist development. From the late 1870s to the 1890s the peasantry lost most of its land and "was driven increasingly to participate in new hacienda-based export-oriented commercial agriculture and industrial activity."[46] By 1910, 90 percent of Mexican campesinos were without land.[47] Also, Díaz's government rented or sold land cheaply to foreign investors who had the capital to develop Mexico's resources for the market. More than 27 percent of Mexico's land surface, or 130 million acres, came into the possession of American owners alone.[48]

During the Porfiriato, foreign investment in Mexico centered on railroads, mining, and petroleum. Díaz's government believed railroads held the key to Mexico's prosperous future. Despite fears that foreign control over railroad construction and ownership would result in the dominance of the national economy by foreign interests, railroad construction proceeded at a frantic pace during the last quarter of the nineteenth century.[49] Díaz's government abetted this process by giving foreign developers subsidies, land grants, compulsory labor, tax exemptions, and waiving customs duties.[50] Most rail lines were focused on trade with the north, instead of internal development, and created the conditions for Mexico's economic dependence on the United States.[51] Five trunk lines connected U.S. ports of entry on the border to the Mexican interior. Railroads connected Mexico City with the mineral-producing regions of the north and with the major entrepôts at Nogales, El Paso, Eagle Pass, and Laredo.[52]

Before 1884, Hart argues, the lack of railroad transportation in Mexico inhibited foreign investment in mining. As railroad construction exploded, foreign (especially American) investment in mining grew apace. Díaz's government assisted this rapid development by abolishing state taxes and protective mining codes during the mid-1880s, which had inhibited foreign investment in the past. In 1884 American companies were working over forty mining concessions; by 1892 that figure had increased to 2,382. In 1896 the number of mining properties totaled 6,939, with the great majority owned by Americans. Between 1896 and 1900 the number of mines more than doubled; by 1904 the total of active mining concessions was 13,696. The mining industry extracted silver, copper, lead, coal, and zinc.[53]

Petroleum was a latecomer to the list of mineral resources being developed commercially in Mexico. Foreign oilmen rushed to develop Mexico's oil industry after 1900, as the world market demand for petroleum increased dramatically during the 1890s. By 1910 over 290 foreign enterprises were active in Mexico, with some of the largest companies including Standard Oil, the Texas Oil Company, and the Mexican Petroleum Company, all American corporations. The foreign development of Mexico's oil industry was the most egregious display of neocolonialism. Despite the growing government revenues as a result of increased petroleum production, Hart argues, the success of the industry offered virtually no social or political benefits to Mexico or its citizens. "Rather, as an enclave economy," Hart states, "the revenues it provided eased the need for reform in agriculture and industry that otherwise would have been necessary in order to generate an internally dynamic economy capable of providing the government with funds and power." Additionally the zones of economic growth were limited to the areas directly involved in production, and the surrounding territories "were afflicted with displacement and dire poverty."[54]

The foundation for Mexican immigration to the United States can be found in the consequences of Porfirian development. The petroleum industry did nothing to foster a national economy that produced jobs and increased wages. Foreign companies added to the woes of Mexicans by acquiring 553,000 acres of land for the development of their mining enterprises. Mining also drew workers away from the fields of central and southern Mexico, leading to a shortage of labor in those parts of the country and—especially after the economic downturn of 1907—an oversupply of labor in the Mexican north. Historian Ramón Eduardo Ruiz estimates that 150,000 internal migrants settled in Chihuahua and another 75,000 settled in Sonora between 1895 and 1910. Many of these internal migrants, who left rural villages for mining camps, would flock to the United States in search of work during the coming decades.[55] Railroads were most responsible for a continuous stream of immigration from Mexico to the United States. Ruiz states that as railroad construction entered the Mexican countryside, "it upset land prices, exacerbated an already inequitable pattern of land distribution, disrupted the old political and economic balance in many states, and increased the disparity between rural and urban Mexico." The use of peasants in railroad construction encouraged the internal immigration of Mexicans, first to the Mexican north and then, eventually, to the United States.[56] José A. Valenzuela, the Mexican consul at San Antonio, reported in October 1926 that most Mexicans in his district worked on the railways and that the railroad companies of the area (the Great Northern and the Southern Pacific) employed Mexicans exclusively because no other worker was willing to work for such meager wages: "Not even negros are willing to work for such little money."[57]

Northern Mexico, specifically the states of Coahuila, Chihuahua, and Sonora, was particularly representative of Porfirian development. The removal of the Apache threat and the advent of railroads set the stage for immigration into the Mexican north. Both Americans and Mexicans flocked to the region, the former as investors, landowners, railway workers, managers, and technicians; the latter as migrant workers from central and southern Mexico who came to labor in the mines, smelters, foundries, breweries, textile factories, ranches, and cotton farms. By the turn of the century Coahuila, Chihuahua, and Sonora were the most-economically developed states of Mexico. The highest wages in Mexico were earned in these three states. Literacy was more than double the national average: 35 percent in Sonora compared to 15 percent in Chiapas, Guerrero, and Oaxaca to the south. In Sonora foreign-owned mining operations transformed Cananea, formerly a town of 100 in 1891, into the largest city in Sonora by 1906 with a population of 25,000. By 1910 Sonora was the center of Mexico's mining boom, exporting 26 million pesos' worth of ores, most of which was copper. Haciendas in Sonora planted corn, wheat, and garbanzos for export. From 1895 to 1909 the economic development of Chihuahua had annually attracted nearly 10,000 newcomers. The value of the state's mineral production grew from 7 million pesos in 1899 to over 23 million pesos by the eve of the revolution. Likewise, Torreón in Coahuila, once a sleepy town, was transformed into a commercial depot of 35,000 people after the Central and Internacional railways were linked there. *Hacendados* along the Río Nazas in Coahuila cultivated cotton for export and for sale to the republic's textile mills. Over 23 percent of all U.S. capital in Mexico was invested in these three states.[58]

There were at least two drawbacks to the Mexican north's massive economic development during the Porfiriato: an oversupply of labor in the north and a "great divergence" between the socioeconomic development of Coahuila, Chihuahua, and Sonora and the rest of Mexico. Both drawbacks are important for understanding what drew Mexican migrants to the United States. The advent of the railroad, historian Juan Mora-Torres argues, and railroad construction in Mexico during the 1880s sparked the biggest population shift in Mexico in centuries. First the railroad accelerated patterns of immigration from Mexico's center to the north, with most of these internal migrants coming from the western-central states of Mexico, the only part of the country that had an oversupply of labor. Railroad construction and maintenance employed many of these internal migrants. Easier transportation north and a relative abundance of opportunity, buttressed by the "gobbling up" of public lands by railroads and surrounding haciendas, soon created an oversupply of landless migrants who were bound to a life of wage labor.[59] The massive amount of foreign capital that poured into the northern states, its integration with the U.S. economy, and the inflow of internal migrants fostered a modernization of the Mexican north that came at the expense of the rest of Mexico as internal immigration north unbalanced the national labor supply. Labor needs went unmet in the Mexican center—

the most-densely populated part of the nation—while they were in surplus in the north. Elsewhere, development in one state, town, or village came at the expense of development somewhere else. By the last decade of the Porfiriato the problem of oversupply of labor had become a nationwide phenomenon. The neocolonial model of economic modernization that had made the state solvent (and dependent) on export-led growth, and the people displaced by removal from their land, had gone from a regional miracle distinct to Mexico's north to a nationwide trend. Up to the year 1900 Mexico's population had kept pace with the labor demands of Mexican development. During the 1910s, however, the Mexican economy expanded more rapidly, and this expansion coincided with a dramatic increase in Mexican immigration to the United States.[60]

The highly mobile mass of impoverished Mexican rural workers was drawn to the booming U.S. economy. The southwestern U.S. states were integrated into the national economy during the late nineteenth and early twentieth centuries, largely because of mining and agriculture, generating a demand for low-wage labor.[61] Just as railroads drew migrants from central Mexico to the north, so railroads drew Mexican migrants to the United States. The dramatic railroad growth worked in tandem with an agricultural boom throughout the American Southwest from the 1880s to the 1920s. Commercialization of agricultural land in Mexico displaced much of Mexico's rural labor force. These migrant wage earners found ready employment in the railroads and then relied on railroads to seek other wage-earning opportunities. Concomitantly, in the United States, the commercialization of agriculture displaced small farmers and demanded low-wage earning migrants. Ultimately what continued drawing Mexican migrants north to the United States was the promise of better wages than they earned in Mexico.[62]

Mora-Torres's discussion of a "geography of Mexican wages" demonstrates the imbalance of Mexico's economic development during the Porfiriato. Wages were always better in the north because of the economic modernization described above. Common laborers earned an average of 23¢ (U.S. wages, 1900) a day in Mexico's interior. In Ciudad Juárez, a Mexican migrant could earn 88¢, while that same migrant could earn anywhere from $1 to $1.50 across the border.[63] Consequently the populations of the northern states increased at the expense of Mexico's central states. But economic modernization that undergirded Mexican immigration patterns did not end at the United States–Mexico border. U.S. states such as Arizona were to Sonora what Chihuahua was to Jalisco. In short, the closer to the United States, the better the wage.[64] Combined with the insatiable labor demand of the U.S. economy—of which Mexico's northern economy must be seen as a primer from the point of view of the Mexican migrant—and the peonization of Mexican labor during the Porfiriato, the conditions were ripe for a massive influx of Mexicans into the United States during the early twentieth century.

Considering years of contentious diplomacy between the United States and Mexico during the nineteenth century, a striking feature of the Porfiriato was the lack of agitation in U.S.-Mexican relations. Still, Díaz's government was not indifferent to the risk of economic dependence on the United States as it invited foreign investment into Mexico. Particular fear focused on the railroads, as many Mexicans worried that railroads leading north would facilitate U.S. commercial domination and eventually result in Mexico's loss of (more) national territory. Regardless Díaz's regime never wavered in its emphasis on economic growth and its conviction that foreign capital and technology were essential to Mexican development. By the end of the Porfiriato in May 1911, Mexico was economically dependent on the United States.

Norteamericanos dominated transportation, communications, mining, petroleum, investments, technological transfer, and the import-export trade. When the years up to 1910 saw the decline of Porfirian prosperity—demand for Mexican exports began to diminish after 1900, aggravated by the ill effects of the U.S. Panic of 1907—the "hazards" of this economic dependence on the United States became apparent and quickly removed the veil of Díaz's legitimacy.[65] Socially constructed corridors of immigration, coupled with the paradoxically complementary effects of neocolonial development—which demanded a landless, wage-earning labor force created by the displacement of campesinos from land for centralized industries to concentrate on growing products for the export-led economy—fostered the conditions for mass immigration from Mexico to the United States.

By the start of the Mexican Revolution, the Porfirian model of neocolonial economic development had created a transnational low-wage labor force that relied on cross-border immigration for survival. Mexico's economic dependence on the United States and the power of its economy was a triple curse for Mexican migrants: a booming export-led economy in Mexico had displaced many rural workers and forced them into wage labor; Porfirian economic dependence on the United States made Mexico—and impoverished Mexicans in particular—vulnerable to market fluctuations, increasing the likelihood of immigration north in search of work; and the promise of higher wages in the United States almost guaranteed that many Mexicans would migrant north to earn wages they could never earn in Mexico.[66]

The political stability that had underlined Porfirian development between the 1870s and the 1900s collapsed during the Mexican Revolution. For Díaz this meant a loss of power; for many Mexicans, who had experienced economic instability for decades, life in Mexico became almost completely untenable. According to historian Tim Henderson, the years of revolution (1910–1917) marked the start of substantial immigration from Mexico to the United States. Migrants fled violence, disease, starvation, and inflation. Agriculture, especially in the Mexican center, where most of Mexico's migration originated, was virtually destroyed. Historians Linda Hall and Don Coerver estimate that approximately one and a half million people fled Mexico's revolution for the United States during the 1910s. Mexicans crossed as legal immigrants, "temporary" workers, refugees, and illegal aliens. Many of them would spend some years in the United States, even settling permanently in states such as Arizona and Texas. While most of the migrants came from Mexico's lower classes, there were also immigrants from the upper and middle classes who had to abandon their property and personal possessions. During the mid-1920s the former ambassador to Mexico, James Sheffield, lamented in his journal about the end of the Porfirian belle époque in Mexico City. "The revolution had wrought great changes in the social life of Mexico City. The old Spanish and Mexican families had lost much of their property through confiscation and destruction and were *persona non grata* with the Mexican officials. The charming and brilliant society of the Díaz period was merely a memory[.]"[67] For many Mexicans immigration was the only alternative to the dangers and uncertainties of the revolution.[68]

While the Mexican Revolution was the catalyst for large-scale Mexican immigration to the United States and serves as the immediate background for immigration patterns of the 1920s, the revolution merely worsened established socioeconomic tensions in Mexico that encouraged immigration. Hall and Coerver show that we cannot separate economic factors from political factors when explaining Mexican immigration during the revolution. The push-pull tension simply ramped up during the 1910s. The promise of economic opportunity in the United States was buttressed by political stability there, while revolutionary violence exacerbated the displacement and impoverishment caused by Porfirian development policies—giving almost a double push to migrants.[69] This push-pull scheme does not give credence, however, to the simplicity behind Mexicans' decisions to migrate. The booming Porfirian economy uprooted many Mexicans from their lands; economic dependence on the United States made Mexicans susceptible to market fluctuations that they were less equipped to weather since they were wage dependent. The United States was a magnet for wage-dependent migrants because of its promise of higher pay. Add the Mexican Revolution, with the political instability it imposed on Mexico's economy, and one can see that the story of Mexican immigration to the United States up to the 1920s resembles less a push-pull model than a trail of inevitable desperation and poverty. Historian Alan Knight estimates that over 170,000 Mexicans entered the United States between 1910 and 1919; if a modest allowance for illegal immigration is considered, he adds, the figure of immigration could easily touch 250,000. The majority of these migrants were destitute, having left a nation embroiled in revolution, plagued by food scarcity, and rife with disease.[70]

Since the early twentieth century, Mexican immigration had been overwhelmingly a migration of labor. Some workers were documented, but many others were not. During the Great War, the United States allowed Mexican laborers into the country on a "temporary" basis only, to regulate their movement back into Mexico at the end of the work season. In this respect the U.S. Congress was trying to find a middle ground between labor needs of the American Southwest and social pressure to restrict Mexican immigration to the United States.[71] Mexican immigration to the United States was well established by 1917, when the revolutionary violence began to subside, the United States entered World War I, and American legislators began to debate immigration restriction.

United States society was not static during the years of economic development and revolutionary turmoil in Mexico. Great economic growth in the decades after the American Civil War expanded industries; these industries relied on cheap migrant labor. Expanding economics brought social change. The United States was a focal point for global immigration. Waves of "new" migrants flocked to the United States beginning in the 1880s. During the last years of Díaz's presidency in Mexico, millions of immigrants were entering the United States, predominantly from eastern and southern Europe.

Americans had always been ambivalent about the presence of immigrants. Historically a process of acculturation seemed to resolve many of the racial tensions that newly arrived immigrants to the United States encountered.[72] From the 1880s on, the problem with the "second" great wave of immigrants to the United States was their seeming inability or, even worse, their lack of desire to assimilate into American society. According to historian Matthew Frye Jacobson it was the profound foreignness of European and Asian immigrants that bothered Americans most about their growing presence in the nation. Americans were uncomfortable with the fact that the nation's great economic success was bound to the foreign worker. Immigration was part and parcel of economic prosperity.[73] Many Americans worried about the effect on the United States of the teeming masses of immigrants entering the country. The decades between the end of the American Civil War and the end of World War I witnessed an escalating doubt among Americans about the desirability of continued immigration.[74]

Anti-immigrant organizations arose in response to what was increasingly viewed as the undesirability of this new strand of immigrant. The American Protective Association (APA), founded in 1887, advocated for the limitation of numbers and types of immigrants entering the United States. The APA had over two million active members by the 1890s. Founded in 1893 the Immigration Restriction League (IRL) tapped into the growing demand among Americans that the entry of immigrants into the United States be restricted. Based in Boston and comprised of northeastern Brahmins such as Prescott F. Hall, R. D. Ward, John Fiske, and Henry Cabot Lodge, who believed the nation was unable to assimilate the mass of new immigrant groups, the IRL—in contrast to other restriction groups—laid particular stress on the racial dimension of immigration instead of relying on the economic arguments that most immigration opponents, such as the American Federation of Labor (AFL), utilized.[75] Between 1893 and 1918 the IRL moved beyond the advocacy of a vague set of prides and prejudices that have been called an "Anglo-Saxon Complex," and toward what Jacobson calls a "fully eugenic program concerning questions of racial pedigree, national character, and the proper role of the state in tending the biological make-up of its population." By 1910, Jacobson continues, IRL members like Prescott Hall not only embraced "eugenics"—or the biological engineering of the body politic—but situated "the entire discussion of the immigration question in a language of 'desirable' versus 'useless' races, the important national work of 'breeding,' and the statistical averages for this or that race's possessing this or that trait."[76] In addition to the APA and the IRL, other prominent anti-immigration organizations included the Sons and Daughters of the American

Revolution, the Junior Order of Mechanics, the Patriotic Order of the Sons of America, and the Ku Klux Klan. In particular the American Federation of Labor advocated immigration restriction as well as racial segregation in craft unions. According to historian Alan Dawley the AFL was motivated by a combination of nativist prejudice and a "misguided" theory of low-wage "races" whose unfair competition needed to be kept out of the U.S. labor market.[77] Although this period was characterized by powerful strains of nativist thinking, American industry never reduced its demand for cheap labor. Additionally, many Americans took pride in the openness of the United States to foreign, oppressed peoples.[78]

Beginning in the 1880s (with restriction legislation against Chinese migrant workers and the entry of contracted foreign labor), but especially after the turn of the century, the United States formulated an immigration policy that focused on the suitability and quantity of immigrants arriving in the United States.[79] This debate initially focused on European immigrants and revolved around the perception that eastern and southern European immigrants were less desirable than those from northwestern Europe. Restrictionists used several tactics to regulate immigration: literacy tests, eugenic and racial specifications for admission, and quotas allocated to different nations.[80]

Before the 1920s restrictionists proposed literacy as the best criterion for curbing immigration to the United States. Indeed groups like the IRL believed literacy was indicative of a race's suitability for immigration into the United States.[81] The 1917 immigration act raised the bar for immigrants seeking entry into the United States. In the effort to assimilate America's multiple immigrant groups, literacy efforts were considered one of the chief ways to Americanize the immigrant. With literacy came citizenship; with citizenship came racial acceptance, or "whiteness." When the Americanization campaign failed in its effort to refashion immigrants into American citizens, illiteracy became synonymous with nonwhiteness.[82]

The first literacy bill was introduced in Congress in 1895, where both houses quickly passed it, but President Grover Cleveland vetoed it in 1897. In his veto message President Cleveland declared that the best reason given for the literacy test was the necessity of protecting America's population from "degeneration" and preserving national peace from imported turbulence and disorder. "I cannot believe," Cleveland stated, "that we would be protected against those evils by limiting immigration to those who can read and write in any language." In Cleveland's opinion it was infinitely safer to admit immigrants who, though illiterate, "seek among us only a home and opportunity to work than to admit one of those unruly agitators and enemies of governmental control." "Violence and disorder do not originate with illiterate laborers," Cleveland argued; rather, illiterates are "the victims of the educated agitator."[83]

In 1906 legislation was introduced that included both a literacy test and an English-language requirement for naturalization. Nativist groups were joined by labor unions in advocating this new policy, as unions were increasingly wary of the economic threat to their wages and working conditions ostensibly posed by unrestricted immigration. Business leaders opposed the new law, seeking to avoid any limitation on new and cheap labor sources.[84]

This Basic Naturalization Act of 1906 created a joint Congressional and Presidential Commission to study the impact of immigration. Reporting its findings in 1911, the commission—named after its chairman, Congressman William Dillingham of Vermont—recommended a literacy test, exclusion of unskilled laborers unaccompanied by families, and the levy of a head tax "so as to make a marked discrimination in favor of men with families." Congress again passed a literacy test in 1912, and it was vetoed, this time by President William Taft. The literacy test was passed once more in 1915, and rejected yet again, now by President Woodrow Wilson. Wilson justified his veto by arguing that a restriction like the literacy test, had it been adopted earlier in the nation's history, "would very materially have altered the course and cooled the humane ardors of our politics."[85] All three presidents were convinced that the United States needed immigrants for economic development and that it had a sacred obligation to serve as a refuge for immigrants.[86] But with war looming, as German U-boats sank U.S. merchant marine ships and as many Americans believed the proliferation of foreign-born peoples constituted a danger to the nation, support for immigration restriction enabled Congress to override Wilson's veto.[87]

On February 5, 1917, the same day Mexico ratified its new constitution, Congress passed the Immigration Act of 1917. The act followed many of the Dillingham Commission's recommendations: an $8 head tax was to be levied for each alien entering the country, and "vagrants," "paupers," contract laborers, those likely to become public charges, and persons whose passage was paid by another person or a corporation were all excluded from entering the United States. Finally, the act barred from admission any illiterate alien.[88] The act was the first action by the U.S. Congress in almost forty years to place substantive restrictions on immigration into the United States. For Mexican migrants specifically, this new law outlawed circular immigration and obliged many migrants to settle permanently in the United States.[89]

The 1917 act was barely in effect when the Bureau of Labor, responding to pressure from labor-short employers in the American Southwest, attempted to reduce restrictions.[90] Until 1917 the U.S. Immigration Service was not greatly concerned with Mexicans entering the United States, as most of them were not excluded by law and crossing the border was largely a formality. The 1917 act, however, had the immediate effect of removing much of the immigration that otherwise would have been legal. The law banned all forms of solicitation of immigrant workers outside the United States and immediately depressed the number of Mexicans crossing into the Southwest. The curbing of Mexican immigration threatened to choke off a valuable cheap labor supply for American business. Proponents of Mexican immigration included Chambers of Commerce, the Farm Bureau, railroad corporations, and virtually all agricultural growers in the American Southwest. These groups insisted that any regulation of Mexican immigration would cause severe labor shortages and ruin many business enterprises.[91] Businesses of the American Southwest had so thoroughly relied on

Mexican labor to harvest cotton (for example) that immigration restrictions would be nothing short of economic disaster for the region. As one Texas cotton grower stated to the House Committee on Immigration and Naturalization in April 1921, "In our country, cotton is made within a period of four to five days; whenever it matures it opens in the same time. You have got to hold 50 to 75 Mexicans. . . . What would you do? Just exactly what we do. You would have somebody there who would not sleep. You would not let the Mexicans leave."[92]

Agricultural groups pressured Secretary of Labor William Wilson to suspend the provisions of the new immigration law. On May 23, 1917, just three months after the law was passed, Secretary Wilson invoked the "Ninth Proviso" of that act, enabling him to permit the emergency admission of temporary workers by relaxing the new head tax, literacy requirement, and ban on contract labor.[93] In what was later known unofficially as the "first" bracero program, about a quarter of a million Mexicans entered the United States under the terms of the waiver between 1918 and 1920. Immigration continued to the American Southwest because U.S. employers considered it beneficial and necessary to the health of the economy and hence to the stability of the nation.

When Secretary Wilson rescinded the temporary admission program after the end of the Great War, agricultural growers renewed their protest that they would be unable to operate without Mexican labor. Pro-grower congressmen once more pressured the labor secretary to extend the program indefinitely. Reluctantly Wilson agreed to extend the program until 1920.[94] Southwestern employers remained consistent critics of efforts to restrict the free flow of Mexicans across the border. By 1920, as a result of southwestern employers' consistent demands for exemptions from U.S. immigration laws, the flow of Mexican migrants to the United States had become "torrential."[95]

The temporary suspension of certain provisions of the 1917 act provoked a storm of protest from southwestern nativists, patriotic societies, labor unions, eugenicists, and congressmen who challenged Secretary of Labor Wilson's authority to suspend restrictions enacted by Congress. Representative John Burnett (D-AL), the chair of the House Committee on Immigration and Naturalization, was bothered that the exemption of Mexican immigration from the restrictions of the 1917 act would create a "slippery slope." "If you have the right to suspend the law in such cases," Burnett wrote to Secretary Wilson, "then you would also have the right to suspend the law admitting millions of people from the Barred Zone of Asia as laborers on the Pacific Coast, or to admit hundreds of thousands of European laborers to work in the coal mines and great manufacturing enterprises of the East."[96] Immigration restrictionists also argued that most Mexicans did not return to Mexico, took jobs from white people, lowered the U.S. standard of living, and compromised the purity of the Anglo-Saxon race. Restrictionists' fundamental concern was the fear of losing control of their culture, of having it transformed by the presence of an alien and nonwhite "other."

During the postwar period, popular U.S. opinion began to push for immigration restriction. By 1920–1921 many Americans had lost faith that immigrants could be remade into citizens. Beliefs set in that inborn racial traits precluded an immigrant's ability to assimilate. This view, that immigrants were racially flawed and inferior, was powerful, widely held, and contributed to immigration restriction laws.[97] This angst largely lay in the belief that the 1917 immigration law had failed to weed out immigrants considered unfit for citizenship and who posed a danger to the nation. Just a few years after its passage, the Immigration Act of 1917 was considered a failure by many nativists, labor leaders, eugenicists, and politicians. While it refined the prerequisites for American citizenship, it did not establish an upper limit on annual immigration. Also the resumption of large-scale immigration after World War I demonstrated the literacy test's inefficiency in restricting the entrance of supposedly undesirable aliens into the United States. During the postwar years the restrictionist movement shifted its support to a quota system as the best means to curtail immigration.[98]

The subsequent Quota Act of 1921 codified this shift in restrictionists' focus. The act reaffirmed all the previous restrictions on "excluded groups" as established by the 1917 immigration act; but it added one important feature: a quota that would determine an annual limit of immigration from immigrant-sending nations. The central basis for establishing each country's quota under the 1921 law was a 3 percent limit on the foreign-born population as present in the United States according to the 1910 census data. The new quota laws dramatically reduced immigration from more than 23.5 million people between 1880 and 1920 to fewer than 6 million during the following forty-five years. The chief purpose of this legislation was to shift the weight of immigration to the United States from poorer nations of southern and eastern Europe in favor of immigration from northwestern Europe. Passage of the 1921 act was a triumph for restrictionists as Congress accepted the nativist axiom that a wise immigration policy must not only limit the total number of newcomers but also discriminate among prospective immigrants on the basis of racial characteristics.[99]

The U.S. Labor Department's exemption of Mexican immigration ended in 1922, largely in response to the postwar recession of 1921–1922 that put a temporary halt to the flow of Mexican migrants. While labor demand for Mexican migrants recovered by 1923 as the U.S. economy rebounded, Mexican migrants now faced an increased head tax, and each entrant who crossed the border legally was subjected to a humiliating process of delousing. Beginning in the early 1920s, significant numbers of migrants entered the United States illegally to avoid the strictures of American immigration law.[100] The 1921 quota act, however, did not include Mexico in its list of quota-restricted nations. Consequently the legislation had the unintended consequence of boosting immigration from Mexico, from less than 1 percent of the total to 8.7 percent.[101]

As the expiration date for the 1921 quota act approached (June 30, 1924), Secretary of Labor James Davis predicted "the greatest inundation of foreigners" to the United States if Congress failed to renew the "three per cent law" of 1921 or pass new, related legislation.[102] Davis feared that many of the millions of immigrants were unassimilated. He, and like-minded restrictionists, believed the presence of foreign hordes within the United States could only spell disaster for "American ideas and ideals, customs, manners, government, economics, business, labor, art, religion, and education."[103]

The congressional debate over extending the 1921 act was followed internationally. When the 1890 census was proposed to replace the 1910 census as the gauge by which immigration quotas would be set for each nation, the international response was swift. Acknowledging Congress's right to limit, even suppress, immigration, the Romanian chargé d'affaires ad interim expressed his government's disappointment that such a restrictive measure could become law, especially considering that its "disguised purpose . . . is not only the reduction in the total number of admissible immigrants, but more particularly the practical elimination of immigration from southern and southeastern Europe, including Roumania." Immigration from northern and northeastern Europe would hardly be affected by the use of the 1890 census as a basis for the quota, the Romanian chargé argued, whereas the quota for his country would be reduced "to a wholly negligible figure" of approximately 10 to 15 percent of the existing one. Such a restrictive measure, the chargé concluded to Charles Evans Hughes, U.S. secretary of state at that time, could only leave a painful impression on Romania and would undermine the United States' "determined opposition and aversion to discriminatory policies."[104] Based on similar protest from the Italian Embassy, Secretary Hughes, in a letter to Albert Johnson, the chairman of the House's Committee on Immigration and Naturalization, urged that the committee would be able to establish some quota basis "which will be proof against the charge of discrimination."[105]

At the end of 1923, when it seemed clear that a more-restrictive quota would be placed on European immigration, Secretary Davis advocated extension of the quota to the Western Hemisphere. This communication was made public in the press in early January 1924. International critics responded quickly. The Salvadoran chargé d'affaires ad interim, on the day Davis's proposed quota amendment was made public, sent a letter to Secretary Hughes stating that such a measure concerned his government because it seemed "inconsistent with the special policy followed by the [U.S. government] towards [*sic*] the other republics of America, a policy which has always manifested itself in acts which show that the relations of the United States with its sister republics are above all inspired by the strong ties of interest which are born in neighborhood."[106] Likewise the Cuban ambassador to the United States wrote to Hughes saying such a restriction could affect commercial relations between Cuba and the United States. The offense to Cuba posed by restrictive legislation on its immigrants to the United States would be disproportionately grievous, since few Cubans migrated to the United States.[107] Secretary Hughes was quick to oppose the quota proposal for the Western Hemisphere, saying that any restriction on immigration would be resented by Latin American nations and that such anger could be harmful to U.S. economic relations with the region.[108]

The 1917 and 1921 immigration acts defined the acceptability of immigrants to the United States. First, the 1917 act equated illiteracy with undesirability. Second, the 1921 act used race to decide which immigrants were acceptable. This was the first piece of immigration legislation to utilize a quota-based system for the number of entrance visas given to nations around the world. The Immigration Act of 1924 (also known as the Johnson-Reed Act) continued the quota-based system and made it even tighter. While the 1921 act allowed a 3 percent annual quota for nations based on the total of each nation's immigrant population in the United States by 1910, the 1924 version set a 2 percent annual quota based on the 1890 census of the United States. The 1924 act reduced the total number of immigrants from quota-based countries to 15,000.[109] "To illustrate," a *New York Times* article stated that "if there were in the United States in 1910, 100,000 Finlanders, the number of immigrants who might be admitted from Finland in any given year would be 3,000." The 1921 act applied to Europe, the "Near East" (Turkey, Persia, Mesopotamia, and Arabia), Africa, Australia, and New Zealand. It did not apply to Asian nations—most of which were already barred by previous legislation—or Western Hemisphere countries such as Canada or Mexico.[110] "Washing-

The Basis for the Quota Drive

ton," the article continued, "considers immigration the most vital *nonpolitical* problem which [the United States] has to face." Interestingly the same article argued that, in spite of official denials, "the question [of immigration] is also political, though not in the sense that [political] platforms will be built upon it."[111]

Until 1924 Mexican immigration was just one of many immigration streams entering the United States. Not many Mexicans entered the United States compared to immigrants from southern and eastern Europe. Also Mexican immigration was localized to the American Southwest, a fact that diminished its nationwide recognition. And Mexican immigration was circular. Mexican migrant communities, with some exceptions, such as El Paso and Los Angeles, had fluid populations. By 1927 this relative isolation of Mexican immigration ended. The drastic curtailment of European immigration cast into sharp relief the continued existence of cheap Mexican migrant labor in the United States. The symbiosis between diminishing European immigration numbers and growing Mexican immigration heightened U.S. attention to Mexico's migrants and undergirded discussion over extending the quota to Mexico.

Diplomatically changes arose as well. Application of a general immigration restriction law over regions and groups of nations precluded any sense of collective protest from sender nations abroad. To be sure, individual nations regretted U.S. quota restrictions, but protests that such legislation was discriminatory fell flat. U.S. policymakers could, and did, claim that application of restrictive legislation was in accordance with the exigencies of domestic considerations and that no foreign nation could reasonably expect to sway how the United States set its immigration policy.

This triumph of Westphalian isolationism regarding immigration policy was complicated by the post-1924 American effort to extend the restrictive quota to Mexican immigration. The tone and subject of the debate, the objective sought, and the resulting controversy could not be construed as anything other than discriminatory by Mexico's leaders. American responses that U.S. immigration policy was a purely domestic matter fell on deaf ears in Mexico, which only heard that the Mexican migrant was unfit to enter the United States. Finally, the diplomatic slight posed by the prospect of immigration restriction prompted Mexico to protest the effort to an extent that immigrant-sending nations of Europe did not in 1924. Arguably the drive to place a quota limit on Mexican immigration would have been successful if Mexico had been included among the list of barred nations in the Johnson-Reed Act. After 1924, however, the discriminatory nature that such a proposal posed to Mexico, in tandem with the distinctive, if problematic, nature of U.S.-Mexican relations, doomed the quota extension effort to failure.

The remainder of this chapter, which covers winter 1924 to fall 1927, will focus primarily on domestic U.S. debates and identify when Mexican immigration became a problem that seemed to require a solution. The chapter will end by pinpointing when these domestic debates took on international importance—thereby identifying why immigration became a diplomatic concern between the United States and Mexico.

Immigration from the Western Hemisphere was not added to the list of quota nations in 1924 for fear of disrupting Pan-American relations. Almost immediately restrictionists regretted that Mexican immigration had not been included in the quota-based system. The increasingly larger Mexican immigration to the United States during the years after passage of the Johnson-Reed Act reinforced this misgiving. Newspaper and consular reports from 1924 to 1927 described a constant and growing stream of Mexican immigration to the United States. Many emigrated despite the Mexican government's efforts to dissuade them through accounts of the high cost of living in the United States, the scarcity of work there, and the mistreatment of migrants by American officials. What primarily drew migrants, the American consul at Torreón stated in 1925, was the promise of higher wages in the United States. A migrant, for example, could earn nearly $7 a day in an Arizona mine while similar work in Mexico could only yield $1. According to the consular official, "it is little wonder that there is a continued effort

[by] laborers to migrate to the United States, where the work will be no harder, hours no longer, living [slightly] higher, but wages more than double." Most of these migrants did not intend to settle permanently in the United States, the consular official concluded. Instead migrants aimed to earn a sufficient amount of money, return to Mexico to "display [their] acquired wealth" to countrymen, and then to return to the United States to earn more, once they had "enjoyed this distinction and [have] lived up [their] funds."[112]

Demand for Mexican labor grew in the United States during the mid-1920s. Businesses of the American Southwest contracted much of this migrant labor, in spite of U.S. immigration law barring such activity. In contrast to quota restrictions that had begun to curtail immigration from southern and eastern Europe, there was no legislation to halt such a stream from Mexico. Indeed, by mid-1927, Mexican immigration was taking the place of Italy as the source of the greatest amount of non-English-speaking immigration to the United States. Most other streams of immigration from southern and southeastern Europe were drastically reduced or even reversed by 1927. The latter occurred when the number of immigrants returning to their countries from the United States exceeded those seeking entrance into the United States. The quota-based system of the 1924 immigration act was working. But Mexican immigration, unhindered by U.S. immigration restriction legislation, not only continued but grew during the mid-1920s. The *New York Times* estimated that Mexican immigration trebled between 1924 and 1927, with the yearly average of entrants being 47,261.[113]

As seen during the revolution of the 1910s, internal troubles in Mexico during the 1920s played a large part in initiating Mexican immigration north. An important example of the internal unrest that sparked immigration was the Cristero Rebellion. This church-state conflict (described in depth above) produced outright rebellion in the west-central states of Mexico from 1926 to 1929. The locus of the rebellion by Catholic, antigovernment partisans—most of whom were rancheros, small farmers, and cattle ranchers—

was the part of Mexico that had sent the most migrants north for decades.[114]

The Cristero Rebellion took a heavy toll on central Mexico. Almost half of rural Mexicans who lived in the region were affected by the war. Agricultural production fell by over 30 percent. Regional disparities initiated under the Porfiriato were exacerbated by the rebellion. The Mexican north continued to grow economically and, consequently, attract migrant workers from the south. Rural Mexicans left Mexico's center for the north to flee violence and scarcity for peace and opportunity.[115] The rebellion, in short, precipitated immigration from Mexico to the United States according to established patterns. People were not only leaving hamlets but also abandoning villages and small towns, beginning the immigration path north.[116]

While the Cristero Rebellion was largely a regional phenomenon, the Mexican national economy began to falter in 1926, preceding the economic downturn that would begin in the United States three years later. Between 1926 and 1932 demand for Mexican products declined, output fell, profits disappeared, and investments vanished. In this sense political unrest in the Mexican center was indicative of social unrest across Mexico as unemployment, labor strikes, peasant revolts, and army rebellions against the government proliferated. Some historians suggest that twice as many Mexicans migrated to the United States during the 1920s as during the 1910s.[117]

The perennial reason for Mexican immigration north was the booming U.S. economy. What was distinctive about U.S. demand for migrant labor during the latter half of the 1920s, however, was that it paralleled a sharp curtailment of European immigration. American observers of the Mexican labor market recognized this correlation immediately. As the commercial attaché in Mexico reported to the Department of Commerce in March 1924, a "steady stream" of immigration from Mexico to the United States was abetted by the restriction of European immigration.[118] A year after the 2 percent quota took effect, the *New York Times* reported a 68 percent net reduction in immigration to the United States.

Such a decline in immigration showed that the quota was not only immediately effective, but that it had cut immigration "to a greater degree than was expected during the first year of its operation." The chief source of migrant labor for the United States came from Mexico.[119] Reports for the following year indicated a continuation of the trend: Mexican migrant labor was replacing unskilled European immigrant labor in the United States.[120] By the second year of the 2 percent quota restriction, the net gain of immigration from the Western Hemisphere, particularly Mexico, exceeded that from Europe. This development, one reporter noted, "is certain to create *new interest* in the question of whether numerical restriction should be placed on immigration from Mexico and other nearby countries." On racial grounds, the writer stated, the restriction against Mexico would be needed since most Mexican migrants are of "Indian blood"—as opposed to the "purer" racial stock of Latin countries to the south—and were not likely to assimilate to U.S. society. On economic grounds, however, the fact that Mexican immigration was growing indicated that American business needed the labor.[121]

By spring and summer of 1927, calls resurfaced for a restrictive quota on Mexican immigration to the United States. One of the main reasons for this renewed effort was Mexicans' increased visibility within U.S. society. The commissioner of immigration of the Port of New York stated in May 1927 that he was "astounded" at the marked increase of Mexicans in the United States. He urged an extension of the quota law to Mexican immigrants; otherwise the United States would suffer from the influx of these undesirable immigrants.[122] A month later the New York Chamber of Commerce adopted a resolution to extend the restrictive quota to all immigration from the Western Hemisphere. It was "illogical and inequitable," the Chamber declared, "to apply the quota system to the countries of Europe whence the bulk of our population has been derived and leave wide open our gates" to immigrants from the Western Hemisphere.[123]

The New York Chamber of Commerce's resolution raised difficult questions about the quota law and Mexican immigration.

If the 1924 quota was put into place to curb the inflow of immigrant labor to big cities in the East, the Chamber asked, then why was cheap migrant labor allowed to flow freely to the Southwest? If racial homogeneity of the United States was the goal of the quota, then what was the point of curbing southern and southeastern European immigration if such an action augmented the presence of Mexicans within the United States? The most difficult question was what to do about other Western Hemisphere nations and their immigration if the restrictive quota was extended to include Mexico.[124]

Since the 1917 immigration act, restrictionists had chafed at the exemptions and loopholes allowed to Mexican migrant labor on behalf of industries in the American Southwest. From the restrictionists' point of view the Mexican migrant was just as dangerous to the racial, cultural, and social integrity of the United States. After 1924 restrictionists argued that the reasons put forward by southwestern businesses for the continued immigration of Mexicans to the United States—that migrants were docile, apolitical, and likely to return to Mexico after temporary seasonal work periods or contracts had transpired—became the very points for excluding Mexican immigration to the United States. Restrictionists believed Mexicans were unassimilable. They argued that continued leniency of U.S. immigration policies toward Mexico would create a new race problem in the United States.[125] The American Eugenics Society warned, "Our great Southwest is rapidly creating for itself a new racial problem, as our old South did when it imported slave labor from Africa." Also a report of the House Committee on Immigration and Naturalization warned against "the creation of a race problem that will dwarf the negro problem of the South; and the practical destruction, at least for centuries, of all that is worthwhile in our white civilization."[126]

For decades southwestern employers and their lobbyists had successfully fended off such restrictionists' attempts to bar Mexican immigration to the United States, even as restriction laws were placed on immigrants from other nations. Employers countered retrictionists' arguments by insisting that Mexican labor was safe because migrants were pliable and apolitical. Immigration advocates stated that Mexicans would do the stoop labor Americans would not and that they were ideally suited for such work. Finally, advocates tried to calm public angst over Mexico's immigration north by pointing to the temporary nature of Mexicans' presence within the United States. Like homing pigeons Mexicans always returned to Mexico and so were not a menace to U.S. institutions.[127]

Opposition to the renewed call for a quota was immediate. The El Paso Chamber of Commerce, which called a conference of Southwest agriculturalists and manufacturers in November 1927, sounded the familiar refrain against a quota on Mexican immigration. Southwestern industry, the delegates declared, would receive a "staggering blow" if Mexican immigration to the United States was curbed. The resultant labor shortage would force southwestern businesses to seek American workers in other parts of the country. The result would be highly disruptive to the American labor market. Moreover Mexicans were ideally suited to the nature of work in the American Southwest. Other laborers would not work in the conditions of the Southwest. Even if alternate workers were found, the numbers needed for stoop labor would be difficult to procure. Mexican migrants were not only accustomed to the work but were able to fulfill southwestern businesses' demand because of close proximity to Mexico. For the sake of the regional and national economy, Mexican immigration to the United States should not be restricted.[128]

What was distinct about the opposition to the quota effort was Mexico's response. Mexican opposition to the proposed quota took on a diplomatic dimension in the wake of the Johnson-Reed Act. Mexico decried American insistence that immigration policy was a purely domestic matter, citing the discriminatory implications of a quota. Couching the quota debate in diplomatic terms converted U.S. immigration policy into foreign policy and situated the effort to extend the quota to Mexico as a central issue in U.S.-Mexican relations.[129]

Historically the Mexican government had been ambivalent about immigration. On one hand it viewed immigration as a national disgrace because it was a sign that Mexico could not meet the needs of its own people. Mexico's inability to provide sufficient work for all of its citizens was embarrassing, while accounts of migrant abuse by American employers and border officials were infuriating. The Mexican government often criticized migrants as traitors who sought work abroad instead of working to build the nation.[130] On the other hand the Mexican government looked favorably upon the "safety valve" effect of immigration to the United States, which stated that immigration was a necessary evil for Mexico since it relieved the nation of the unemployed and kept political agitation at bay. Every migrant who left Mexico was one less unemployed (and frustrated) citizen with whom Mexican leaders had to contend.[131] Despite this ambivalence the Mexican government generally tried to restrict immigration north. Both internal and external factors hampered such efforts. Internally there was a disparity between the Mexican government's warnings against the travails of immigration and its ability to prevent the departure of its citizens north. Externally the booming U.S. economy and the effects of the Johnson-Reed Act undermined Mexico's effort to stem the tide of its immigration.

Attempts to dissuade Mexicans from migrating to the United States had begun during the last years of the Porfiriato, when Mexican federal and state authorities ordered county governments to stop issuing travel documents to U.S.-bound workers. Propaganda and pamphlets were disseminated to towns, cities, and villages and through the press to inform Mexicans of the abuse their co-nationals faced in the United States. Such efforts were largely ineffective, however, because many migrants were illiterate.

Constitutional considerations also complicated the Mexican government's response to immigration. Article 11 of the 1857 Constitution (in place until 1917) established the freedom of exit from and travel within Mexico. The Constitution of 1857 made it illegal for the federal government to curb the transnational immigration of its citizens, and Mexico City's historically problematic administration of its northern border also precluded any efforts to stop immigration. Article 123 of the Constitution of 1917, in an effort to protect its workers abroad while acknowledging the prevalence of Mexican immigration, restricted the exit of migrants unless they possessed signed labor contracts detailing wage rates, hours of work, and provisions that (American) employers would pay repatriation costs. Article 123, historian David Fitzgerald notes, was contradicted by the U.S. ban on entering the United States *with* a labor contract. Therefore, after 1917, Mexican migrants were breaking the law of at least one country when they migrated: leaving Mexico without a labor contract violated Mexican constitutional law; leaving Mexico with a labor contract broke U.S. immigration law. Instead of offering a degree of protection for its citizens in the United States, Mexico's 1917 Constitution only made migrants more vulnerable by guaranteeing that some facet of their immigration was illegal.[132]

An important change occurred in Mexican immigration policy after 1917. Mexico's government had always, to the extent it was able, tried to assist its citizens abroad. The revolutionary nationalism that was born out of the Mexican Revolution justified, even obliged, the government to extend its protection of its migrants in the United States.[133] This increased protection manifested itself in repatriation assistance to migrants. Repatriation was often done to spare Mexicans from deportation. After World War I the Carranza government feared the prospect of massive deportations of Mexican workers no longer needed in U.S. industries. Carranza funded a repatriation drive as a preemptive measure to avoid the humiliation of seeing thousands of Mexicans deported. Obregón instituted similar efforts during the postwar recession of 1921–1922, when nearly 160,000 Mexicans were repatriated.[134]

During the mid-1920s, as American restrictionists began to agitate for an extension of the immigration quota to Mexico, the Mexican government renewed its efforts to stem the tide of Mexican immigration to the United States. Mexico's 1926 immigration law put into federal hands the enforcement of Article 123's clause requiring a labor contact for immigration. By placing the Ministry of Foreign

Relations in charge of monitoring immigration, the government of Plutarco Elías Calles hoped Mexicans would be dissuaded from migrating north. Calles's government also encouraged Mexicans to return to Mexico by continuing to fund repatriation efforts and by sponsoring propaganda campaigns that warned against migrating. Finally, federal officials tried to curtail immigration by subjecting Mexican travelers on U.S.-bound trains to document searches and by offering Mexicans material incentives, such as land and subsidized travel, to repatriate.[135]

Despite these efforts Mexican immigration continued at an increasing rate during the mid-1920s. The tide was pushed along by internal unrest in Mexico, Mexico's economic stagnation after 1926, and the draw of the booming U.S. economy. Federal efforts were also undermined at the local level. County governments had incentives to keep migrants moving north. Local officials in the Mexican center issued travel documents to political rivals, while their counterparts in the Mexican north encouraged immigration to the United States as a way to relieve the glut of labor symptomatic to that region.[136] By 1927 officials in Mexico City were lamenting the loss of human capital to the United States. An *El Universal* editorial from May 1927 captured the sentiment of many Mexicans when it stated that Mexico's "greatest affliction is the outpouring of its greatest energy source, its people. . . . The Mexican government should not allow Americans to restrict Mexican citizens from entering the United States, but should instead restrict its citizens from leaving for the United States."[137] The Mexican government would continue efforts to curb Mexican immigration north, and the challenge would continue to be insurmountable.

After 1927, as Americans debated a quota for Mexican immigration, Mexico's policymakers applied diplomatic pressure as a way to protect its migrants traveling north to the United States. Grudgingly accepting that many Mexicans were choosing to migrate, the quota debate provided an opportunity for Mexican leaders and critics of immigration to defend national interests by decrying the discriminatory implications of U.S. restrictions on Mexican immigration. Diplomacy was seemingly the only way that Mexican leaders could exert pressure or influence the issue of immigration. Socially Mexico was fractured by a decade of revolution. Building revolutionary nationalism required a vast store of legitimacy that postrevolutionary governments either lacked or struggled to attain. Economically the prosperity of the U.S. economy—and the transnational dependence of migratory labor on that economic growth, and vice versa—almost guaranteed the failure of Mexico City's administrative measures to curb Mexican immigration to the United States. Diplomatically, however, Mexican leaders could protest the effect that a quota on Mexico's immigration would have on U.S.-Mexican relations. Mexico's leaders could claim that the peculiar relationship between the United States and Mexico, and the interconnectedness of their economies, would be endangered by a quota. Mexican leaders could state that the racial undertones of the U.S. debate over a quota for Mexico contradicted the United States' role as a leading nation in hemispheric relations among American states. Finally, the quota debate in the United States gave Mexico's leaders the chance to display to its citizens how they defended their migrants against the abuse and prejudice of U.S. society. Mexican leaders, for the sake of their own domestic and international credibility, used diplomacy to defend their migrants in ways that policy measures could not.

2

Singling Out Mexico for Restriction

Winter 1927–1928

By 1928 American restrictionists were campaigning hard to place a quota on Mexican immigration to the United States. This effort encountered domestic opposition, not only from southwestern employers but also from the U.S. State Department and the Mexican press and government. The twin pressure of domestic and international opposition made it difficult for restrictionists to argue that immigration policy was a matter solely for domestic debate. Opposition from the State Department and Mexico demonstrated that by the late 1920s immigration was an issue that had international currency and that was perceived to have very real consequences for U.S.-Mexican relations.

The precedent for immigration restriction had already been established by the late 1920s. American lawmakers had been considering a restriction of Mexican immigration for the better part of a decade by 1928. Mexico's migrants had been spared restriction because of southwestern industries' labor demands during the world war and economic recession. What was different about the debate during the late 1920s was the economic prosperity of the United States and the potential diplomatic consequences of a quota on Mexico. By the late 1920s the United States economy was doing well. Consequently some Americans believed the need for foreign labor was as great as ever, especially in the wake of immigration restriction toward European countries. Well-worn arguments for the necessity of immigration continued to hold their appeal as the U.S. economy witnessed year after year of growth.

Economic prosperity did not help the restrictionists' argument. Since the need for immigration was just as great as it had been in previous years, and the supply of immigration from Europe had been drastically curtailed after 1924, there was less economic incentive for the restriction of Mexico's immigration. Instead restrictionists relied on racial arguments against Mexican migrants to promote a quota against Mexico. The booming economy and the Immigration Act of 1924 helped quota advocates to a certain degree. The regulation of cheap labor from Europe increased the demand for Mexican migrants in the U.S. economy, but the augmented presence of Mexicans within U.S. society brought with it nationwide attention to the rapid acceleration of Mexican immigration to the United States after 1924. By the latter half of the 1920s Americans were increasingly concerned about the social costs of the insatiable economic demand for Mexican labor. Restrictionists tapped into this anxiety by pointing to the supposed racial inferiority of Mexicans as justification for placing an immigration quota on Mexico.

The stabilization of U.S.-Mexican relations by the late 1920s made a quota problematic. Quota opponents argued that such a restriction would damage U.S.-Mexican relations. Predictably business groups—as they had done for decades—decried immigration restriction as a hazard to economic productivity. What was distinct about quota debates during the late 1920s was the State Department's active opposition to legislative restriction of Mexican immigration. The department consistently opposed all congressional efforts to regulate immigration from the Western Hemisphere, asserting that diplomatic and trade relations would be disrupted as a result. When such region-wide efforts to regulate immigration were stymied, some congressmen called for a quota on Mexico alone. As the Latin American nation that sent the most immigrants to the United States, Mexico was the obvious target for any type of legislative restriction. The singling out of Mexico for restriction only intensified the State Department's opposition to the quota. They argued that regulating Mexico alone among all other nations of the region would bring national embarrassment on the Mexican people, poison U.S.-Mexican relations, and threaten U.S. diplomacy with the rest of Latin America. The State Department sought to undermine the call for a quota on Mexico by promoting immigration statistics that seemed to show a predominant trend of repatriation among Mexican migrants. These efforts were flawed for multiple reasons, the chief among them being illegal immigration. It was hard to rely on numbers showing that more Mexicans left the United States than entered it when consular officials could not provide an accurate number of how many Mexicans entered the United States illegally. The inability to quantify the extent of illegal immigration alarmed restrictionists and caused them to redouble their attempt to place a quota on Mexico's immigration.

Numerous bills and resolutions to amend U.S. immigration laws were introduced at the Seventieth Congress when it convened in December 1927. The measures ranged from proposals to stop immigration for fixed periods of time (e.g., ten years), to proposals to stop all immigration. The House Committee on Immigration and Naturalization, chaired by Rep. Albert Johnson (R-WA), who was a staunch advocate for immigration restriction and one of the cosponsors to the 1924 immigration act, sifted through more than one hundred such measures. Among the handful of proposals the committee considered most promising was the application of the quota laws to nations of the Western Hemisphere, particularly Mexico.[1] The proposed extension of a quota to the Western Hemisphere, debated during passage of the Johnson-Reed Act in 1923–1924, was abandoned to preserve amicable diplomatic relations and profitable trade between the United States and other American nations. After 1924, however, the growing rate of Mexican immigration to the United States and the increasing presence of Mexicans within U.S. society, both real and perceived, reinvigorated restrictionists' efforts to apply the quota to the Western Hemisphere, and at the very least to Mexico. In a public address on February 14, 1928, Johnson predicted that the current Congress would amend U.S. law to suspend Mexican immigration.[2]

For twenty years, between 1913 and 1933, Albert Johnson was the congressional champion of the restrictionist cause. Before entering Congress he made his reputation as a small-town newspaper editor who staunchly opposed organized labor, particularly the Industrial Workers of the World. Elected to Congress as an arch restrictionist, Johnson chaired the House Committee on Immigration and Naturalization from May 1919 until he left office in March 1933. During that time he mobilized the restrictionist lobby for the passage and enactment of the 1921 quota law, introduced nationality quotas and absolute limits for immigrants, and cosponsored the 1924 immigration act. By that year, historian Desmond King states, Johnson had become the "éminence grise" of American immigration policy.[3]

Beginning in late February 1928 the House Committee on Immigration and Naturalization and the Senate Committee on Immigration and Naturalization, chaired by Sen. Hiram Johnson (D-CA), held hearings on the restriction of immigration from the Western Hemisphere. It became clear early in the hearings, even if committee members and witnesses did not always admit it openly, that the crux of the debate was about placing a quota on Mexican immigration. The hearings focused on answering four fundamental questions: Where would the necessary labor come from for southwestern agricultural businesses if Mexican immigration was restricted? How many Mexicans returned to Mexico? And of those who remained in the United States, how many constituted a "social menace"? And, finally, how would a quota on Mexico reverberate throughout Latin America?[4] These economic and social concerns harkened back to earlier prejudice and discrimination concerning Mexican immigration.

To these core issues quota advocates and opponents added additional arguments between the early 1920s and 1928. First, restrictionists believed there was no point in restricting immigration from southern and eastern Europe if Mexicans were allowed to enter freely into the southwestern United States. Second, quota opponents argued that immigration restriction was unnecessary because most Mexicans did not reside in the United States permanently and so posed no social risk. Finally, what was different from similar debates a few years earlier was the consideration of how the restriction of Mexico's immigration could have negative effects on U.S.-Mexican relations. Thus diplomacy emerged as a prominent factor in the debate over a quota. Additionally restrictionists justified a quota by pointing to Mexicans' low standard of living, their inferior racial quality when compared to other immigrants, their poor physical condition, their illiteracy, and their susceptibility to disease. They stated that Mexican migrants' cheap labor was driving white farmers off their land and that most Americans in the Southwest wanted Mexican immigration curbed. Finally, restrictionists believed that most Mexican migrants did not return to Mexico but instead resided permanently in the United States.[5]

Restrictionists emphasized that Mexicans' racial inferiority necessitated a quota on Mexico's immigration. Henry Ward of the Immigration Restriction League (IRL) voiced this belief in testimony before the House Committee on Immigration and Naturalization on February 21, 1928. Ward began his testimony by reading to the committee a statement from the IRL about Mexican immigration. The statement provided a sense of the alarm with which restrictionists viewed Mexican immigration by the latter half of the 1920s. Restrictionists saw a horde of undesirable immigrants entering and spreading throughout the United States. The most concerning aspect of the Mexican immigration problem was that it was unclear how many Mexicans were entering the United States. Legal, recorded immigration by Mexicans, the IRL believed, was only "a small proportion" of the total Mexican immigration northward.

> The situation as to Mexican immigration is very serious. Not only is this influx very large, but it is certain to increase. From the States along the Mexican border, Mexican laborers are rapidly spreading northward and eastward. They are in Colorado; in Minnesota and other Northwestern States; in Illinois; in the Pennsylvania steel mills; on the railroads all through the Middle West. But little can be known definitely as to the annual Mex-

ican immigration, for the number of legally admitted is but a small proportion of the total [*sic*].⁶

Ward argued that Mexican immigration of all kinds was undesirable. When asked by committee member Rep. George Schneider (R-WI) to compare the problems of Mexican and Canadian immigration, Ward argued that race comprised the chief difference between the two immigration streams:

> Ward: "Mexico will create a great race problem, and we should give that consideration first. . . . We have, I think, a definite problem in regards to the Mexicans so far as the future citizenship of our country is concerned. The Canadian problem is not so important as the Mexican problem."
>
> Rep. Schneider: "You do not consider Canadian immigration as undesirable?"
>
> Ward: "No; I certainly do not. . . . Mexicans are certainly the least desirable of all immigrants."⁷

Rep. John Box (D-TX) was the most vocal of restrictionists opposing Mexican immigration. From east Texas Box represented constituents in cotton-growing districts who faced stiff competition from cotton growers in the Southwest who employed cheap Mexican migrant labor.⁸ Box deemed Mexicans a hazard to U.S. institutions and ideals. By the late 1920s Box had been trying to stop Mexican immigration for a decade. As a member of the House Committee on Immigration and Naturalization, he had a ready forum for his views. He had adamantly opposed the exemption of Mexican immigration from the 1917 and 1921 immigration acts. Box scoffed at the temporary work contracts given to migrants in southwestern industries between 1917 and 1922. Opponents of the restriction of immigration believed the temporary presence of Mexicans in U.S. society would defuse the debate over restriction. For Box, however, it was the very temporariness of contract labor that was most dangerous. Between scarce institutional resources to administer the border (the U.S. Border Patrol was not founded until 1924) and southwestern industries' insatiable need for cheap labor, there was a high probability of Mexicans "getting away" and surreptitiously staying in the United States. Since the U.S. Immigration Service did not have the means to enforce the return of temporary Mexican labor, Box argued, Mexican immigration should be barred completely.[9]

Box tirelessly continued his effort to restrict Mexican immigration, even though his proposals continually failed throughout the 1920s.[10] He saw himself as the "voice of the people," as a man of the common people who wished to defend the nation against wealthy capitalists and foreign hordes. He believed his arguments for a quota on Mexican immigration represented the views of Americans across all strata of U.S. society.[11] By 1928, after years of failure, Box and like-minded quota advocates had gained nationwide appeal as Americans turned their attention to Mexican immigration in the wake of the Johnson-Reed Act. A sample of patriotic societies and organizations that supported Box's restrictionist efforts included the following: Sons of the American Revolution, United Spanish War Veterans, Junior Order of American Mechanics, Immigration Study Commission, Immigration Restriction League, California History and Landmark Club, Order of White Citizens of America, Public School Defenders of California, American Defense Society, and the American League of Good Will.[12]

Box reiterated many of his past points for restricting Mexican immigration in front of the House Committee on Immigration and Naturalization in late February 1928. He argued that Mexicans were bad for public health (often illiterate and diseased), bad for public order (many Mexicans were criminals and they disproportionately filled southwestern prisons), and their presence in U.S. society had sparked a new race problem. In 1928 Box added two new points to his well-worn arguments: that the quota-based immigration regime established in 1924 would break down if Mexico were not added to the list of restricted nations, and that the current never-ending stream of Mexican migrants would eventually nullify the credibility of U.S. immigration laws.[13] If a quota was not placed on Mexico, the "North" would not continue to endure a quota law that cut off its labor while keeping a cheap source of labor open to the "South." Moreover the continued influx of Mexicans—Box proclaimed that up to 150,000 Mexicans entered the United States each year, both legally and illegally—would fundamentally reshape U.S. society. When asked if a quota would harm diplomatic relations, Box responded that no foreign country should dictate U.S. immigration policy. Moreover good relations with Italy and Japan were proof that U.S. immigration policy did not have to damage U.S. relations with other countries.[14] Box and other restrictionists devoted little attention to the potential diplomatic consequences a quota on Mexico's immigration would have for U.S.-Mexican relations. For them immigration policy was purely a domestic matter. Foreign nations were expected to accept the United States' right to regulate immigration.[15]

Most quota opponents agreed with restrictionists' assertion that U.S. immigration policy was solely a domestic matter. Many of these opponents also backed the 1924 law and its restriction of European immigration. Interestingly, however, these same figures believed that a quota on Mexico would spell disaster for agricultural industries reliant on Mexican labor and would risk damaging U.S.-Mexican relations. The first reason was the standard response of immigration advocates used against pleas to restrict Mexican immigration. The second reason was distinct to the discussion about immigration restriction after 1924.[16]

Opponents of Mexican immigration restriction continued to rely on the arguments they had successfully deployed for decades: that Mexicans were docile and apolitical (not likely to organize, demand higher wages, or work limited hours), law abiding, non-diseased, likely to return to Mexico once seasonal work was complete and willing to do the stoop labor even the most "down and out" Americans were unwilling to do. Points raised by Fred Bixby of the California Cattle Raisers' Association typify these arguments against a quota on Mexican immigration. First, Bixby argued that Mexican migrants supplied much-needed labor to southwestern industries. "We have no Chinamen, we have no Japs," Bixby stated. "The Hindu is worthless; the Filipino is nothing, and the white man will not do the work." Second, Bixby argued that despite propaganda to the contrary, Mexican laborers were not prone to crime, diseased, or troublesome. "The Mexican is not the kind of man who would indulge in the tactics practiced by the [Industrial Workers of the World (IWW)] or any similar organization. The Mexican is quite unassuming and will work as hard as he can as long as he has to do so. He is extremely loyal; he is not dirty; he is not diseased; he is not any worse than half the white men." Third, Bixby believed Mexican migrants were preferable racially to other types of migratory labor, namely, that of African Americans.

> We do not desire the colored people [in the Southwest]. We do not like the cotton-picking type of colored people in our part of the country. We shipped in a few years ago when we first began planting cotton at Bakersfield two and three trainloads of Southern cotton-picking type colored people. They were most unsatisfactory from the very start. We were not accustomed to that sort of labor and to a degree the production of cotton was given up because of the fact that the labor was unsatisfactory. A Mexican in our part of the country is a better citizen and a better employee than the colored man.[17]

While immigration restriction was good generally, Bixby added, it was a bad idea to place a quota on Mexico and would only harm relations with that nation. Besides, Bixby concluded, quota restrictions were unenforceable because of shortages in money and personnel to guard the border. Some opponents of the quota added that Mexicans were physically endowed to do the stoop labor in hot temperatures.[18]

Discussion of restricting immigration from the Western Hemisphere also included the question of how a quota could affect U.S. relations with other American nations. While quota advocates waved off this question by stating that immigration policy was a domestic matter, quota opponents argued that immigration restriction would be bad for U.S. foreign relations. In early January 1928 the House Committee on Immigration and Naturalization heard the testimony of Dr. John D. Long of the U.S. Public Health

Service and chief quarantine officer of the Panama Canal Zone. He recounted to the committee how, during a Pan-American Sanitary Conference the previous October held in Lima, Peru, several state representatives asked him about the possibility that the United States would pass an immigration quota for Latin America. "I told them that I had no personal knowledge in the matter at present," Long stated, "but that it would not appear to be the policy to adopt a quota system, particularly in view of the fact that the immigrants from Latin America are relatively small in number, *with the possible exception of Mexico.*" The Latin American representatives responded "that they sincerely hoped that the quota system would not be adopted because they could not take it otherwise than as an insult." In addition to the national affront inherent in an immigration quota, Long continued, Latin Americans believed their "pride would be seriously wounded" if a quota were placed on the Western Hemisphere, since it would classify their nations with Asia, from where immigration was considered totally undesirable by U.S. immigration law.[19]

Rep. John Garner (D-TX), one of John Box's staunchest opponents, testified before both committees on immigration and argued against a quota extension to Mexico. Garner believed a quota would be "disastrous." Not only would it cut off a much-needed labor supply, but it would also harm relations with Mexico. He argued that applying a quota to Mexico alone among other states of the Western Hemisphere would cause resentment among Mexicans.

> You could not apply the quota to Mexico and leave it open to Central and South America and Canada without [offending Mexico], and you will not ameliorate anything of the kind by any diplomatic methods you might proceed upon.... If we undertake to apply a quota restriction to Mexico and we do not apply it to Canada also, I do not know what reason we can give that will be satisfactory to a proud people and a people who feel that their honor has been impinged by our legislation.[20]

During his testimony before the Senate Committee on Immigration and Naturalization on February 27, 1928, Garner asked the committee about what difference there would be between a quota on all American nations and one on Mexico alone: "If you apply the quota to Mexico alone and admit similar people from Central America and South America, can you explain to [Mexicans], who are, I will say, a part of the people contrasted with Central and South America?" Sen. David Reed (R-PA), the other cosponsor to the 1924 immigration act, asked Garner if he thought a quota law on Mexican immigration would offend Mexico. Garner's reply was a direct retort to some quota advocates' claims that Mexico could not take umbrage at what other nations had accepted in 1924.

> Rep. Garner: "Would you not think [Mexico would take offense]? I will ask you to answer the question you are asking."
> Sen. Reed: "It did not offend Great Britain."
> Rep. Garner: "But if you had selected Great Britain alone and applied a quota to it, what would Great Britain have said?"[21]

A week later, on March 5, 1928, Secretary of State Frank Kellogg appeared before the Senate Committee on Immigration and Naturalization to address the quota issue. He opposed the extension of the quota to the Western Hemisphere. Such a measure, he believed, would "adversely affect the present good relations" between the United States and the other American nations. The risk to trade and amicable relations would be disproportionate to the negligible number of immigrants who entered the United States from Central and South America, Kellogg argued. The extension of the quota would "be interpreted by [Latin Americans] as a radical departure from the traditional policy of the United States towards Latin America and as evidence of unwillingness to continue to regard them as equal and neighbors having common problems, interest, and aims." Such legislation risked stoking anti-American feeling throughout Latin America and would risk retaliatory immigration restrictions against Americans who sought investment opportunities and work across the region.

Kellogg opposed a quota on Canada and Mexico as well, the two American nations with the highest rates of immigration to the United States. It was unnecessary to apply a quota to Canada, he stated, because it was "a country made up of people so closely allied to the people of the United States by blood, by speech, by habits of thought, and by industrial interest." Regarding Mexico, the improvement of relations with Mexico was "a source of considerable satisfaction to [the U.S.] government. . . . The interests of the United States in Mexico are of such importance that no action prejudicial to their advantage should be undertaken without a most careful weighing of the possible consequences." A quota, Kellogg argued, whether on all American nations, on only Canada and Mexico, or on Mexico alone, would "seriously injure" U.S. relations with the region. The potential risk a quota posed to diplomatic harmony between the United States and other American nations made the issue of immigration restriction a matter of "great national importance as far as the foreign policy of the United States [was] concerned." Economic justifications for a quota, he concluded, should be considered secondary to the diplomatic consequences of immigration restriction.[22]

W. W. Husband, assistant secretary of labor, immediately followed Kellogg's testimony. Whereas the State Department largely opposed any restriction on Mexican immigration for diplomatic reasons, the Labor Department advocated the extension of the quota to Mexico for economic reasons. Indeed it was Secretary of Labor James Davis who helped to initiate the call to extend the quota to Mexico a few years earlier. Husband, on behalf of the Labor Department, called for a "reasonable limit" on immigration from the Western Hemisphere. When pressed by the committee to define a reasonable limit, Husband stated that the 2 percent quota would be too harsh. Instead he advocated a restriction proposal that favored a quota on immigration from the Western Hemisphere that reflected 10 percent of the resident population in the United States in 1890, with a maximum quota of 2,000 for each American nation. Chairman Johnson pressed Husband further, asking him if he believed a 2 percent quota should be extended to Mexico specifically among all nations of the Western Hemisphere. Husband responded "no," saying that the crux of the issue was to determine how to restrict Mexican immigration without discriminating against Mexico. "It is a peculiar sort of thing we would be asked to do," Chairman Johnson rhetorically asked in reply to Husband, "a perfectly futile thing in reference to 18 countries and not give offense to Mexico in telling her to reduce her immigration?"[23]

Mexican leaders echoed the assertion that an extension of the quota to its immigration would undermine U.S.-Mexico relations. They were not opposed to restriction for economic reasons. In fact Mexico City believed restriction could complement goals to curtail the outflow of Mexican workers to the north. Instead the prejudicial rhetoric that underlined the quota debate in the United States, plus the thinly veiled attempt to restrict Mexican immigration alone among all other American nations, rendered the prospect of immigration restriction anathema to Mexican policymakers.

Francisco Suástegui, the commercial attaché to the Mexican Embassy in Washington, explicated many of these points of opposition to the quota. Suástegui attended congressional hearings on Mexican immigration and reported "points of interest" from testimonies at those hearings to the Mexican ambassador to the United States, Manuel Téllez. These reports are important for two reasons. First, they provide a Mexican perspective on congressional discussions regarding the prospect of restricting Mexico's immigration. Second, the points detailed by Suástegui give a sense of what concerned Mexican officials about the quota debate.

Suástegui attended House Committee on Immigration and Naturalization hearings on Mexican immigration during the latter half of February 1928. He highlighted testimonies from both quota advocates and opponents. His record of the hearings reflects many of the reasons why restrictionists opposed Mexican immigration and why others opposed the quota. The overlap of his accounts and other documentary records that describe the same hearings suggest that Suástegui was likely in the audience when John Box described Mexicans as illiterate, diseased, and criminal, and when Box argued that Mexican immigration would likely lead to a new race problem in the United States if it was not curbed by a quota. Suástegui was also probably present when Henry Ward of the IRL described Mexicans as the worst kind of immigrants and asserted that the mass of illiterate peons from Mexico had penetrated every section of the United States, not just border states of the Southwest. Suástegui likely witnessed the testimonies of quota opponents like Fred Bixby, who argued that Mexican labor was essential to southwestern industry and that Box's comments about Mexicans were fallacious: instead of illiterate, diseased, and criminal, Mexicans were docile, healthy, hardworking, and loyal. Finally, evidence suggests that Suástegui recorded John Garner's testimony before the House Committee on Immigration and Naturalization (days before Garner gave similar testimony in front of the Senate Committee on Immigration and Naturalization); Suástegui deemed Garner a *defender* of Mexicans in his report to Téllez, since Garner argued that a quota on Mexico would hurt U.S.-Mexican relations and harm Mexicans' national pride.

Suástegui's notes on the congressional hearings reflect many of the reasons restrictionists used to justify a curb on Mexican immigration: that Mexicans posed a racial problem for the United States (table 1: A2, A3, A7, A11, B2, B3, C1, C4); that Mexican immigration would undermine the U.S. labor market, even the U.S. standard of living (A1, A12); that employers hurt the nation by hiring cheap Mexican labor (A5, A14); that Mexican immigration was not just a regional problem of the American Southwest but a nationwide problem; and that despite employers' assurances to the contrary, Mexicans did not return to Mexico but instead wandered the United States in search of work, oftentimes becoming public burdens (A9, A10, A16, C3).

In addition to these reasons was a fear that Mexican immigration would alter the socioeconomic balance of agricultural districts in the United States (A4, A8, A13, A15, B4, B5, B6, B7, B8, B9, C2). Suástegui recorded predictions that Mexicans would displace white

Table 1. House Committee on Immigration and Naturalization hearing on Mexican immigration, late February 1928

Points of Interest	A. February 21, 1928 (morning session)	B. February 21, 1928 (afternoon session)	C. February 23, 1928	D. February 24, 1928
1.	Mexican laborers bring down living standards and increase discontent among workers	The quota system of immigration restriction on other nations is useless when immigration from Canada and Latin America is not restricted by the quota	Many Mexican workers join the IWW	Production costs would increase if Texas farmers were unable to depend on a steady supply of Mexican labor
2.	Compared to Canadian immigrants, who are able to assimilate easily, Mexican immigrants are unassimilable to U.S. society	97 percent of Mexico's population (15,000,000) is comprised of ignorant *peons*, and it is this stratum of Mexican society that sends migrants northward; Mexicans of the upper class do not migrate	The cause of overproduction in cotton in the Southwest is the Mexican worker	Mexicans are peaceable, hardworking, and generous people
3.	Mexicans do not make good citizens	The *peon* class of migrants is harmful to the United States as it introduces inferior elements into society, and the inability of these *peons* to assimilate establishes differences in the character of the population	Mexicans do not return to Mexico because of fear of revolution	Mexicans are not prone to crime; they are less prone to crime than American workers

Singling Out Mexico for Restriction

Points of Interest	A. February 21, 1928 (morning session)	B. February 21, 1928 (afternoon session)	C. February 23, 1928	D. February 24, 1928
4.	Mexicans are ruining the small farmer	The agricultural output of the nation is excessive; prices are low and the problem is getting more serious because of the increase its [*sic*] creating in an ever-growing class of exploitable labor	Mexicans reproduce at such a rate, under conditions that are less sanitary than is normal in the United States, that they will gradually constitute the great majority of the Southwest's population	Mexicans earn good salaries and are not subjected to miserable wages
5.	Only those who demand cheap labor oppose a law restricting a curb on Mexican immigration; only large agricultural interests (*latifundistas*) defend Mexican workers	This [see above] will with time result in a depopulation of the countryside by our small farmers and American wage earners, to be replaced by Mexican workers living alongside the large commercial farmers (*latifundistas*) who employ them	Mexicans live in better economic and hygienic conditions than [John] Box states; Box exaggerates the extent of misery and disease among Mexicans	In El Paso, where Mexicans constitute more than half of the population, Mexicans live well, their children attend school, and the economic situation is good

6.	Only Mexicans will do the work needed by Southwestern industries	Fruit producers in California only employ Mexican *peons*; American workers are forced to travel to all parts of the country to find work	A quota would hurt the national pride of Mexicans, would complicate U.S.-Mexican relations, and would require a great expenditure to enforce such restriction
7.	Mexicans are dirty and diseased	The number of American men without work is higher than in past years	There is plenty of work in Texas for Mexicans
8.	Negros have been forced out of Texas because of competition from Mexican workers	Illinois and Pennsylvania report highest rates of unemployment since the war	Mexicans reside in Texas only temporarily and then return to Mexico. Better wages would resolve the agricultural problem of the region
9.	Mexicans are not only in the border states but have also "penetrated" all other parts of the country; between legal and illegal entrants there are 2 million Mexicans in the United States	There are 4 million people out of work in the United States, or 10 percent of the nation's working population	

Points of Interest	A. February 21, 1928 (morning session)
10.	Fewer Mexicans return to Mexico than before; when they finish work in the Southwest they "penetrate" further into the country by migrating to large industrial centers
11.	There will be a racial problem in the United States comparable to that of slavery that brought the civil war, and (later) a reliance on cheap labor from Europe, unless a quota is implemented; millions of Mexicans are now in the United States
12.	If Mexican immigration continues it will drag down wages for all workers in the United States; businesses that employ American laborers will be undercut by employers of cheap Mexican labor. "The level of American life will be replaced by the Mexican."
13.	The internal immigration of Mexicans within the United States exacerbates the need for Mexican immigration, since many Mexicans migrate to cities seeking better wages, creating a constant demand among American farmers for cheap Mexican labor
14.	Construction companies will often lay off American workers so they can hire Mexicans for lower wages
15.	Certain parts of Texas have been abandoned by Americans and replaced by Mexicans
16.	Employers will often contract Mexican labor with the condition that they will guarantee the return of Mexicans to Mexico once the work is done. The reality is, however, that employers do not comply with such stipulations; migrants wander the country seeking work, they are often arrested for vagrancy, and, after a month or two serving in public works, they become dependent on charitable services and constitute a social problem

Source: As recorded by Francisco Suástegui, commercial attaché of the Mexican Embassy, Washington DC. "Asuntos de interes, Febrero 21 de 1928, sesión de mañana," 2 pages; "Asuntos de interes, Febrero 24, 1928, 10.40 a.m.," 1 page; "Asuntos de interes, Febrero 21, 1928, sesión de la tarde," 2 pages; "Asuntos de interes, Febrero 23, 1928, 2.10 p.m.," 2 pages, AHSRE:LEG 772, exp. 5 (all emphases added).

and black laborers and that consequently American workers—not Mexican migrants—would have to wander the country in search of work. In this sense restrictionists saw in unregulated Mexican immigration a stifling of Jeffersonian liberty, in which the freedom to till one's own land was sacred. Agricultural centers would be Mexicanized in the scenario where Mexicans replaced American workers. Commercial farmers (*latifundistas*) would live alongside a mass of cheap migrants, from whom they extracted labor for their plantations. Such fears made a strong case for a quota on Mexican immigration.

Suástegui informed Téllez regarding testimonies from quota opponents, notably from Reps. John Garner and Claude B. Hudspeth (D-TX), both of whom defended commercial farmers' reliance on Mexican labor in Texas and downplayed the racial danger Mexicans posed to U.S. society. In a statement he would reiterate before the Senate Committee on Immigration and Naturalization four days later (see above), Garner argued that a quota on Mexico's immigration to the United States would offend Mexicans, complicate U.S.-Mexican relations, and require a great expenditure for border enforcement (C6). Garner also took this opportunity before the House Committee on Immigration and Naturalization to state that John Box's denigrating remarks about Mexicans were exaggerated (C5). Claude Hudspeth, of El Paso, argued similar points during his testimony before the House Committee on Immigration and Naturalization. He stated that Mexicans were decent, hardworking people who fulfilled labor demand for southwestern business. Without Mexicans, Hudspeth argued, production costs would increase for Texan farmers (C7, C8, D1–D5).

Representative Garner suggested alternatives to the proposed quota. First he called for a measure to allow Mexican immigrants only to the American Southwest, where they were most needed, and to prohibit them from migrating to any other part of the country. He also suggested that Mexican immigrants be allowed to enter the United States under strict conditions that obligated employers to return Mexicans to Mexico when their work contracts were complete.[24] During the early part of the decade, Hudspeth proposed a similar measure to Congress to restrict Mexican immigration. Congressional opposition to the Hudspeth resolution of 1920 shows why Garner's suggestion for a temporary worker program was rejected and gives a sense of why U.S. lawmakers were apprehensive about establishing temporary labor agreements with Mexico in the years before World War II.

In early 1920 the House Committee on Immigration and Naturalization heard a joint-house resolution relating to the temporary admission of illiterate Mexican laborers. Hudspeth was the main sponsor of the measure. The "Hudspeth resolution" proposed to suspend the provisions that barred the importation of foreign contract laborers (the Foran Act of 1885) and the denial of entry to illiterate aliens (stipulated by the 1917 immigration act) and to waive the $8 head tax. While calling for the admission of illiterate aliens, Hudspeth's resolution sought only to allow contracted Mexican laborers into the United States on a temporary basis for one year. After their time of service expired, all laborers were to report back to their ports of entry to repatriate to Mexico. Finally, the resolution stipulated that only Mexicans were permitted to enter the United States as contract laborers and to benefit from the proposed exemptions to U.S. immigration law.[25]

Members of the House Committee on Immigration and Naturalization criticized Hudspeth's resolution for making no definite provision to repatriate Mexicans after their labor contracts were fulfilled. Also, they believed that waiving the head tax would encourage a disproportionate number of Mexican migrants into the United States and that the temporary inflow of Mexican workers would not satisfy American industry's insatiable labor demand. Finally, the House Committee on Immigration and Naturalization objected to the Hudspeth resolution because there was no administrative institution in the United States that could, first, curb the desertion of temporary laborers and, second, apprehend migrants who broke their contracts and prevent them from wandering the country in search of work. The Border Patrol was not established until 1924. Implicit in all criticisms of Hudspeth's resolution was the fear of a permanent mass of illiterate Mexican immigrants who, once in the United States, would be hard to extricate. The presence of illiterate aliens, critics contended, represented a menace to the American nation.[26]

The crux of Hudspeth's resolution was the stipulation that Mexican migrants would only reside in the United States *temporarily*. Defending his proposed measure, Hudspeth stated that it was only an "emergency resolution" to serve temporary labor needs and "to save millions and millions of dollars' worth of property to the people of the United States." This aspect of the resolution was meant to protect the nation from illiterate aliens. Hudspeth believed Mexicans were an inferior race. Nonetheless, as his testimony eight years later before the House Committee on Immigration and Naturalization confirmed, Hudspeth also believed Mexican labor was indispensable to southwestern industry. Any threat that undesirable Mexicans posed to U.S. society could be alleviated, Hudspeth proposed, by an immigration measure that restricted the duration of a Mexican laborer's residence in the United States. "If I believed by bringing these people in you were going to permanently increase the Mexican population [along the southwestern border]," Hudspeth stated before the House Committee on Immigration and Naturalization, "I would say keep them out"; however, he reiterated, the committee could trust that these temporary laborers would not form a permanent addition to the U.S. population. He went so far as to say that "90 percent of them will go back as quick as they get sufficient money."[27] Responding to the issue of desertion by temporary contract laborers, Hudspeth stated that "there is no certainty of keeping them; you have to take that chance of them getting away from you after they are here."[28]

It was the transient nature of this contract labor—the chance of them "getting away"—that disturbed restrictionists most and formed the basis of their opposition to Hudspeth's call for a temporary worker program. John Box, then in his first congressional term, led the fight against the Hudspeth resolution. For Box and his supporters, the need for cheap labor was trumped by the danger illiterate Mexicans posed to U.S. society.

Box developed a multipoint argument against the Hudspeth resolution. First, the U.S. government would have to create an institution or department that would ensure that Mexican laborers did not shirk their contracts. An inherent dilemma to this writ would be separating Mexican Americans—who had the legal right to reside in the United States—from Mexican immigrants—who were not considered fit for American citizenship.[29] Second, the illiteracy of these immigrants made them undesirable for naturalization. Referring to the process of hiring migrant workers in Mexico for temporary work in the United States, Box stated that any people who can be "corralled and bought are not the stuff good Americans are made of."[30] Third, the injection of undesirable aliens into U.S. society would negatively affect the American nation. The Hudspeth resolution will "fill the country with undesirable people and underpaid labor and help to create here an underworld, wretched and dangerous," Box stated; the presence of illiterate contract laborers would "put an element in American life which is certainly not American in character."[31] Fourth, temporary contracted labor violated U.S. immigration law, which since the 1880s had forbidden the importation of foreign contracted labor to the United States.[32] Fifth, and most important, the enforcement of temporary contracts for undesirable aliens was untenable because the Immigration Service did not have the wherewithal to track down and apprehend Mexican immigrants who deserted and "scatter[ed] over the country and [were] lost among their racial kindred."[33] To build a department that would regulate temporary admission of Mexican contract labor, Box argued, would require a "vast and expensively organized force" to check and follow Mexican laborers, "as they come in tens or hundreds of thousands, and scatter throughout the interior." "Such a system," Box believed, "would break down because of its administrative impossibility. . . . The system would in the long run be ruinous in its effects upon the country."[34]

Eight years later, members of the House Committee on Immigration and Naturalization were no less opposed to any measure that would compromise U.S. immigration law in favor of maintaining a steady flow of cheap migrant labor from Mexico to the American Southwest. To Garner's first suggestion of cordoning off parts of the United States where Mexican immigration could be allowed, Albert Johnson stated that it was impossible to establish an "imaginary line" and that such a measure would give other sections of the country incentive to demand exemptions to U.S. immigration laws that complemented their labor needs.[35]

On February 17, 1928, days before he attended the congressional hearings on Mexican immigration, Suástegui composed a letter to Téllez that captured the main aspects of the immigration problem for Mexico. His argument anticipated many of the objections raised by other Mexican officials against the quota later in the year as Congress took concrete steps to curb Mexico's immigration. Suástegui believed that Mexican immigration would continue until structural changes in both national economies (but especially Mexico's) were realized, that a quota would offend Mexico and undermine its diplomatic relations with the United States, and that bilateral negotiations on immigration restriction was the only path toward a long-term solution to the problem of Mexican immigration.

Suástegui argued that Mexican immigration, both legal and illegal, represented two economic realities: first, that Mexico could not provide enough employment for all of its workers; and second, that there was not enough labor in the American Southwest to satisfy the demand of industry and agriculture. These two factors would perpetuate Mexican immigration, Suástegui wrote, until Mexico developed its internal industries to an extent that most Mexican workers were employed. For Suástegui, no measure to solve the problem of Mexican immigration would succeed unless the Mexican economy was modernized.[36]

Next Suástegui stated that the quota would offend Mexico. Already "anti-Mexicans" had created a "dangerous environment" for Mexicans in the United States. Mexicans, especially those who migrated illegally, were vulnerable to arrest, castigation, and deportation. These anti-Mexican measures were often state-led, Suástegui wrote. If Congress passed a quota on Mexican immigration, the insult to the Mexican people would be complete. The only way in which the Mexican government could respond to such a "humiliation" would be to pass retaliatory measures against American immigration to Mexico. In this scenario Suástegui suggested that Mexico place more stringent prohibitions on the employment of foreigners in industries like oil, mining, or agriculture. Such retaliatory immigration policies, Suástegui argued, would cause "profound hatred" between the two countries and disrupt their business relations.[37]

Finally, Suástegui stated that while Mexico wanted to curtail its immigration to the United States, it must seek to bilaterally negotiate such a limitation. These negotiations should be held in tandem with the development of Mexico's internal industries. Otherwise, if a quota was established without a mutual agreement between both nations, then it would be taken as "a grave offense of significant consequences" by the Mexican government. Suástegui predicted that if the United States unilaterally imposed a quota on Mexican immigration before Mexico had sufficient chance to develop its economy, then it would be impossible for Mexico to curb the flow of its workers northward.[38] Not to mention the prospect that immigration restriction risked provoking a hatred between the two countries that would poison their economic, cultural, and political relations, so recently restored since the Mexican Revolution.[39]

Consistent with Suástegui's letter to Téllez, the Mexican government sought to find a solution to the immigration problem through bilateral negotiations throughout the late 1920s and early 1930s. These efforts were never reciprocated by the United States; Washington believed any bilateral or multilateral discussions about U.S. immigration policy would undermine Congress's sovereign power to make immigration law. Aside from unofficial talks between American and Mexican delegates at international conferences during the spring of 1928, Mexico was unsuccessful in its efforts to resolve the immigration issue through negotiations with the United States. Failure to discuss common interests on immigration restriction perpetuated the quota effort and endangered the fragile stability of U.S.-Mexican relations during the late 1920s.

Immigration became an issue of national prestige for Mexican officials as the U.S. Congress began to debate the extension of the quota to Mexico in February 1928. Based on a conversation with Genaro Estrada, the Mexican foreign minister, Dwight Morrow, the U.S. ambassador to Mexico, reported that Estrada believed a U.S. bar on Mexico's immigration would cause "considerable feeling" on the part of the Mexican people, especially if the quota were applied only to Mexico of all the Latin American nations. Even though the restriction of immigration would have economic value for the Mexican government, since it would work toward the government's goal of restricting its immigration, such action by the United States would offend Mexicans.[40]

On March 5, 1928, the same day that Frank Kellogg testified against the extension of the quota to Mexico, former Mexican president Álvaro Obregón addressed immigration. He argued that each Mexican laborer in the United States produced more than he consumed. From this perspective there was no logic behind restricting Mexican immigration to the United States because of the wealth Mexican laborers produced. Obregón believed a restriction of immigration would be economically advantageous for Mexico. It would keep laborers in the country who could work on development projects utilizing the nation's natural resources. In time Mexico's land-reclamation projects could provide "remunerative work for all Mexican laborers and so take advantage of those noble and generous efforts which are now benefitting foreign lands [i.e., the United States] where our emigrants are well exploited and badly treated." While there were economic incentives for the United States to restrict Mexican immigration, Obregón concluded, imposing immigration restriction on Mexico "would be depressing and hurtful to national sentiment."[41]

The Mexican government had for decades been concerned about the condition of its citizens abroad and decried tales of their harsh treatment in the United States. For many officials, accounts of mistreatment were especially egregious for Mexican labor in the southwestern industries of the United States. "The Mexican immigrant is now a serious social problem for the authorities of

[Mexico]," the Mexican consul in San Antonio, Texas, told *El Universal* in July 1927. The Mexican migrant

> is made a victim of all kinds of injustice and spoliation; entire families work for months and months only to be mistreated at the end of that time, expelled from the place in which they live, and without receiving a single cent as recompense for their labors. These [migrants] become a public burden and are looked upon without pity or commiseration by the inhabitants of [the United States]. They came from Mexico to escape poverty, only to fall into a state a thousand times worse and more painful.[42]

The failure of the Mexican government's various attempts to stem the tide of immigration northward persuaded many officials to instead put their efforts toward the protection of migrants abroad. Past attempts by Venustiano Carranza's government to dissuade migrants from going north, often by pointing to the rampant prejudice and exploitation that awaited them in the United States, largely failed because migrants relied on information from friends and family about the opportunity in the United States that was absent in Mexico. The embarrassment and consternation caused by the growing rate of Mexican immigration to the United States was partially assuaged by attempts to protect migrants abroad.[43] Mexican consulates took the lead role in protecting migrants in the United States. Álvaro Obregón's government actively encouraged consulates to expand efforts to protect Mexican citizens in the United States. Consulates played a central role in fostering links between Mexico City and migrants by sponsoring cultural programs that helped maintain migrants' Mexican identities. While Mexico's relationship with its migrants had always been ambivalent, during the 1920s the government began to view them as important economic assets since they had learned work techniques that were essential to the nation's development. Thus convincing migrants to repatriate to Mexico became a central goal of the Mexican government's immigration policy.[44] Nonetheless Mexico was unwilling to regulate its immigration. Morrow reported to the State Department on February 10, 1928, that government officials informed him that they did not intend to implement a law or regulation that would restrict the immigration of its citizens northward.[45]

The Mexican press, which keenly followed U.S. debates about restriction of Mexican immigration, echoed Mexican officials' feelings about the quota. Like the government, the press favored a curb on immigration northward since it would work toward domestic goals of stopping the outflow of laborers. Mexican observers, however, were not willing to accept the quota on Mexico if it was predicated on migrants' "alleged low standards of living."[46]

For years the Mexican press had decried immigration. Newspapers argued that the best Mexican labor was attracted to the United States by the lure of high wages and improved living conditions and that Mexican migrants were treated badly and were unduly subject to vagrancy laws in the United States.[47] Beginning in 1928, though, major newspapers such as *Excelsior* and *El Universal* argued that a quota on Mexico would undermine U.S.-Mexican relations. The press rejected as a "puerile argument" quota advocates' statements that the proposed legislation did not intend to establish racial differences. Mexican observers believed that the recently improved relations between the United States and Mexico would be undermined by any action of "American officialdom which would tend towards emphasizing the so-called Mexican inferiority."[48]

Many Mexicans were confused by the U.S. debate to restrict Mexico's immigration. On one hand American business groups stated that Mexican migrants were indispensable to southwestern industries in the United States and that Mexicans did not present a racial problem in the United States because of their "roving temperament" or likelihood to return to Mexico. On the other hand American congressmen portrayed Mexican migrants as dangerous to U.S. society because of their racial inferiority. Most Mexican observers of the U.S. quota debate concluded that racism underlined the call for the restriction of Mexican immigration. Despite repeated claims that Mexicans were taking jobs away from Americans, one *Excelsior* editorialist stated, the real reason such legislation has been proposed is because Mexicans are not white.

Mexicans, the editorialist wrote, resented the Box bill and other similar measures to restrict Mexico's immigration north because it represented "race prejudice and antagonism" that contradicted the "much-heralded spirit of friendship and cooperation" between Mexico and the United States.[49] Until Mexico had developed its internal industry to such an extent that migrants will not have to leave the country to find work, the editorialist concluded, Mexicans should cease migrating to the United States out of a sense of national dignity.

Mexican observers of the quota debate in the United States took some comfort in the fact that Frank Kellogg and the U.S. State Department opposed efforts to restrict Mexico's immigration. "It is recognized here," an American correspondent reported from Mexico City, "that [Kellogg] appreciates the immeasurable harm which might result in international relations by such legislation."[50]

Kellogg certainly recognized the harm an immigration quota would have for U.S.-Mexican relations, and during the first half of 1928 he tried to devise a way to defuse the increasingly heated quota debate. Days prior to his testimony before the Senate Committee on Immigration and Naturalization, Kellogg sent a telegram to Morrow in Mexico City describing his opposition to a quota extension on Mexico. He explained how he planned to counter demands for immigration restriction by showing how "a large proportion of Mexicans entering the U.S. return to Mexico." This strategy was Kellogg's initial attempt to quell calls for a quota on Mexico. Utilizing a point made by American opponents to the quota—that most Mexican migrants return to Mexico at the end of seasonal work—he hoped immigration statistics would show that Mexicans' presence in U.S. society was temporary and transitory, and, therefore, posed no fundamental danger to the United States. Kellogg believed that if statistics could bear this trend out then there would be no need to extend the quota to Mexico. The quota was a disproportionate response to the "problem" of Mexican immigration, he argued. It was unnecessary to risk harming relations with Mexico with a quota when the problems posed by

Mexican immigration were not permanent. Kellogg first asked Morrow to confirm State Department figures for Mexican immigration to the United States. These statistics showed that more migrants returned to Mexico than stayed in the United States. Morrow confirmed State Department figures and provided statistics from the Mexican Immigration Service for total Mexican immigration and repatriation between 1908 and 1926: 627,535 Mexicans migrated to the United States while 963,026 returned.[51]

A few weeks after his testimony before the Senate Committee on Immigration and Naturalization, on April 18, 1928, Kellogg lamented to Morrow that there was widespread sentiment in the United States favoring the restriction of Mexican immigration. It was a common belief among Americans, Kellogg wrote to Morrow, that the Mexican population in the United States was increasing rapidly because of immigration and that a quota was necessary to stop it. Many policymakers advocated for a quota as well: Secretary of Labor Davis, much of the Labor Department, and most members of the congressional committees on immigration and naturalization pushed for such a restriction. Kellogg feared that if one of these committees reported favorably on a quota extension to Mexico, then the proposal would likely pass Congress and become law.[52] The repatriation figures Morrow provided, however, gave Kellogg hope that there was still an instrument by which the perceived presence of Mexicans in U.S. society could be dispelled. Kellogg's second step was to ask the consulate general to compile a complete survey of the latest Mexican immigration data. If it were possible to show that the actual increase of the Mexican population in the United States had been negligible, Kellogg hoped, then there would be no need for a quota on Mexican immigration.[53]

The consulates relied on figures provided by the Mexican Immigration Service and reported that the process by which the institution registered migrants was effective and that the immigration statistics provided by it were "fairly accurate." There were several reasons why American consular officials relied on Mexican, and not U.S., immigration data. First, it was not obligatory for Mexicans to register with the American immigration offices when they departed the United States. By contrast it was compulsory for Mexicans returning from the United States to register with Mexican immigration offices. This difference was explained by the fact that American immigration officials were concerned primarily with the number of immigrants entering the United States, as opposed to those departing.[54] There were several other reasons why Mexicans registered in larger numbers when they returned to Mexico from the United States: Mexican law mandated the compulsory registration of both immigrants and emigrants upon (re)entering Mexico, illegal entry into Mexico carried the risk of being considered a revolutionary and an enemy of the Mexican government, there was no fee to reenter Mexico and no delay was involved (as there was when entering the United States), and it was "troublesome and costly, and unnecessary" to reenter Mexico illegally since there was not in the United States a comparable social network that facilitated illegal immigration as there was in Mexico.[55]

A table provided by the Mexican government illustrated the disparity between Mexican and American statistics on repatriation. Mexican statistics not only showed fewer immigrants entering the United States, but they also logged more Mexicans returning to Mexico. According to Mexican sources, 27 percent fewer Mexicans (272,735 of 376,985) entered the United States between 1920 and 1925 than U.S. statistics reported. Most important, this data stated that over 451,000 more Mexicans repatriated during the same period than were recorded by the United States (489,748–38,740); a net increase of 92 percent.[56]

Table 2. Mexico's statistics on Mexican immigration and repatriation vs. U.S. statistics on the same, 1920–1925

	Mexican: Immigration	Mexican: Repatriation	U.S.: Immigration	U.S.: Repatriation
1920	50,569	64,620	68,392	11,154
1921	9,165	106,242	46,794	7,902
1922	33,180	50,171	30,295	7,500
1923	80,793	85,825	75,988	3,901

1924	57,269	105,834	105,787	3,572
1925	41,759	77,056	49,729	4,711
Totals	272,735	489,748	376,985	38,740

Source: Manuel Gamio, "Quantitative Estimate of Mexican Immigration to the United States," AHSRE: LEG 761, exp. 1, 8.

Manuel Téllez, the Mexican ambassador to the United States, passed along this data to the House Committee on Immigration and Naturalization in order to "bring to light certain important discrepancies" in the statistics available on Mexican immigration.[57] The ambassador was trying to persuade the committee that the Mexican immigration problem was overblown by demonstrating to U.S. congressmen that more Mexicans returned to Mexico on an annual basis than U.S. immigration statistics recorded. Such a correlation, he hoped, would make a quota on Mexican immigration unnecessary and spare Mexico the national embarrassment of immigration restriction.

A U.S. Visa Office report comprising immigration statistics from various American consulates throughout Mexico showed a dominant trend of repatriation among Mexican migrants, seemingly confirming Téllez's argument to U.S. congressmen.[58] Whereas 297,934 Mexicans migrated north from the reporting consular districts between 1922 and 1926, 409,909 Mexicans returned to Mexico through the same districts and during the same years. The report also gave nationwide figures for Mexican immigration from 1908 to 1926: 1,049,220 migrants returned to Mexico from the United States while only 702,255 Mexicans migrated north during the same period.[59] These statistics helped Kellogg's strategy to defuse the quota debate. They demonstrated that up to three-quarters of all Mexican migrants in the United States would, eventually, return to Mexico.

Yet the problematic nature of quantifying Mexican immigration soon became clear as other American consular officials in Mexico reported repatriation statistics to the State Department. The first glaring problem with quantifying repatriation numbers was the fact that many migrants were not counted as they left Mexico. Of those posts that were able to provide information on the number of Mexicans migrating north, most of the data only went back as far as June 1926, when Mexican immigration officials—in accordance with the Mexican Immigration Law of 1926—began tracking the number of Mexicans who migrated to the United States.

A second problem with accurately counting Mexican migrants was inadequate personnel within the Mexican Immigration Service and a lack of institutional knowledge. The American consul at Nuevo Laredo reported that, despite confident claims by the local Mexican immigration chief that Mexican repatriation had increased markedly from 1926 to 1927, the entire staff of the local Mexican immigration office was new to its post and had no knowledge—"either by experience or from records"—to corroborate this estimation. Additionally the same consular official (who had been in place since 1922) believed that as many as 10,000 Mexicans repatriated through the district without being recorded by Mexican immigration officials.[60]

A third problem was that distinct social, economic, and geographic features of consular districts throughout Mexico made the tabulation of a uniform immigration trend across Mexico impossible. Immigration patterns in Agua Prieta, Sonora, for example, undermined the argument that most Mexicans who migrated to the United States would return south. In contrast to other districts, the local consul reported that the "peculiar geographic situation" of Agua Prieta reduced Mexican immigration to a minimum and made it relatively simple for local immigration officials to tally rates of immigration. Also, data was easy to produce and corroborate because Douglas, Arizona, was the sole port of entry into the United States for Mexican migrants. Finally, low rates of economic growth in local industries—mining, agriculture, and livestock—elicited low labor turnover and gave Agua Prieta a stable population. The town, then, was a crystal-clear prism through which the true trend of Mexican immigration revealed itself. The people who migrated to the United States, the consul wrote, "do so for the purpose of seeking employment and *if this is found these individuals settled [in the United States] and do not return to Mexico."* Contrary to other consular reports, which stated that between 68 and 73 percent of all migrants returned to Mexico from the United States, the report from Agua Prieta argued that only 2 to 3 percent of Mexicans returned to the south permanently, while up to 50 percent of migrants who repatriated eventually returned to the United States to live.[61]

A fourth problem behind quantifying Mexican immigration involved what American consular officials called "repeats." This term referred to Mexicans who had legally migrated to the United States, returned temporarily to Mexico, and were recorded as return migrants by the Mexican Immigration Service. Upon a subsequent (re)departure to the United States, having emigrated at least once in the past (and especially considering Mexican immigration officials gave far less attention to migrants leaving Mexico as opposed to those returning to Mexico), repeat migrants ordinarily did not obtain another immigration visa, nor were they recorded by Mexican immigration officials, unless their stay in the United States exceeded six months. American consular officials believed incidents of repeats were frequent along the U.S.-Mexico border as migrants went north for seasonal work and returned at the end of the season, often during the course of one calendar year.[62] It was not uncommon for the Mexican Immigration Service to record, unknowingly, migrants' multiple re-crossings as separate instances of repatriation to Mexico. The case of repeats called into question the very validity of repatriation figures.[63]

The final, and most important, problem behind counting migrants was illegal immigration. The "surprisingly large balance" in favor of returning Mexicans, Vice Consul George Winters reported to the State Department in May 1928, could have been explained by the fact that a large number of migrants entered the United States illegally. Winters estimated that annually between 20,000 and 50,000 migrants avoided getting checked by both Mexican and American immigration services. Winters explained that when migrants returned south they entered Mexico legally; migrants were duly recorded by the Mexican Immigration Service as having returned, "there being no need for evading the [Mexican Immigration Service] since it is understood that departing aliens are rarely questioned."[64]

Mexicans migrated illegally for various reasons. Most Mexican migrants were completely ignorant of the stipulations of U.S. immigration law. Even if they were aware of the legal requirements to enter the United States, many Mexicans had difficulty satisfying such stipulations. For example, most migrants were illiterate, which legally barred them from entry into the United States. The disparity in economic development between the United States and Mexico also played a role in the peonization of Mexican workers. Skilled workers in Mexico would be considered unskilled in the United States because of their ignorance of English and their inability to operate modern agricultural and industrial machinery. Mexicans also chose to migrate illegally because of the time and expense associated with legal immigration. Long periods (often days at a time) of waiting in line at border posts and the process of meeting the bureaucratic stipulations for legal entry represented a loss of earnings for many Mexicans. Also, the sum required by coyotes to get migrants across the border was usually smaller than the $18 consular fee and head tax required of each Mexican to enter the United States. Finally, Mexican laborers who were previously contracted out for work in the United States were barred from entering the States legally, so they would cross the border illegally.[65]

Thus many Mexicans found it was easier to migrate illegally than to seek legal entry into the United States. *Enganchistas* (or labor contractors, often in the employ of American business) contracted them out for work when they were still in Mexico; coyotes helped them across the border; and southwestern business had a ready economic demand for Mexicans to supply. While Mexicans risked deportation if caught in the United States illegally, the promise of higher wages and flaccid rates of deportation facilitated a constant stream of illegal Mexican immigration. In the end, Americans' racial animosity toward Mexicans underlined illegal immigration. Americans, by viewing migrants as poor and ignorant foreigners who threatened the tenets of U.S. society, treated Mexicans as poor and ignorant workers. Discouraged from migrating legally, Mexicans relied on illegal channels for immigration instead. As migrants outside the bounds of legal protection, Mexicans were vulnerable to abuse by enganchistas, coyotes, border guards, and employers. Ironically such vulnerability showcased the undesirability of Mexicans and confirmed American racism against Mexico's citizens.[66]

The picture of repatriation changed completely if estimates of illegal immigration were taken into account. Low illegal immigration estimates would have matched the repatriation rate or even exceeded it. The high estimate of illegal immigration would have decisively altered the trend of Mexican immigration from a predominant pattern of repatriation to a predominant pattern of immigration.[67] Before estimates of illegal immigration were factored in, it was possible to argue that migrants returned to Mexico at higher rates than they migrated to the United States. This statistical argument brought solace to both sides of the quota debate. American restrictionists took comfort in the fact that the Mexican population in the United States was gradually dwindling; opponents took comfort because the disproportionate rate of return seemed to preclude the need for a quota. The debate was transformed, however, as one attempted to account for illegal Mexican immigration. Quota opponents could not prove that Mexican immigration was not a growing problem, and quota advocates reinforced their call for restricting Mexico's immigration.

The unquantifiable nature of Mexican immigration undermined Kellogg's hope to resolve the quota debate. Repatriation figures, while initially convincing, were simply unreliable in the face of inconsistent tabulation methods by Mexican immigration officials, peculiar local conditions in different consular districts, "repeats," and the unknown scale of illegal immigration. The specter of tens of thousands of Mexicans crossing the border illegally only animated further restrictionist calls for a quota on Mexico. It was clear by mid-1928 that a better solution to the immigration problem was needed. Illegal immigration discredited any attempt to quantify the number of Mexicans crossing into and out of the United States. And the reliance on repatriation figures actually reinforced restrictionists' argument for a quota: if it was impossible to know how many Mexicans entered and left the United States on an annual basis, all the more reason to bar Mexican immigration outright.

3

International Pressure against the U.S. Effort to Restrict Mexican Immigration

Spring 1928

During the first half of 1928, as American congressmen discussed the merits of a quota on Mexico, the United States sent delegations to attend two conferences that were convened, in part, to consider the international ramifications of immigration. American delegates to the Sixth Pan-American Conference and the Second International Conference on Emigration and Immigration were instructed to not participate in any discussions that might imply that the power over U.S. immigration policy lay with any political body other than Congress. No nation directly challenged U.S. sovereign power over its immigration policy at these conferences, and in some cases these gatherings reaffirmed a nation's sovereign power over its immigration policy. Nonetheless Latin American nations, including Mexico, approved measures that countermanded immigration policies that were considered discriminatory toward other nations of the Western Hemisphere. More directly, the conferences offered a venue in which Mexico could advocate for a bilateral solution to its immigration problem with the United States. Mexican policymakers also wished to curb Mexico's immigration northward, while they simultaneously protested the racist justifications offered by U.S. policymakers in their calls for a quota on Mexican immigration. American consuls reported this confluence of goals to Washington, and comprehensive bilateral talks on the matter could have taken advantage of this common interest. However,

Congress's dogged defense of its sovereign right over immigration policy, demonstrated by the American delegations' guarded impartiality at the conferences, stymied such efforts.

The Sixth Pan-American Conference and the Second International Conference on Emigration and Immigration represented an international recognition that immigration problems could not be resolved unilaterally. Rather they required bilateral or even multilateral cooperation. In this regard international discussions of immigration seemed to counter U.S. congressmen's efforts to solve the Mexican immigration problem by placing a quota on Mexico. Additionally the spirit of cooperation that these conferences promoted called attention to the potential diplomatic consequences of restrictive immigration legislation that was founded on the undesirability of another nation's citizens.

During the 1920s Italy and Japan had set a precedent for challenging what was considered by both nations as the racial prejudice and social discrimination that characterized U.S. immigration policy. According to Frank Kellogg, up to the 1920s immigration to the United States was "practically unlimited" and excited little comment from international circles. The Immigration Act of 1917 was regarded as a "natural and normal expression" of national sovereignty. The 1921 quota act and, especially, the Immigration Act of 1924 changed this. "It immediately became to the interest of immigration countries," Kellogg stated, "to endeavor to have immigration questions regarded as a matter of international concern and as a subject for international discussion."[1]

Italy proposed and hosted the First International Conference on Emigration and Immigration in Rome in 1924. In the April 1923 conference invitation to the U.S. State Department, the Italian government argued that while the immigration "phenomenon" affected all nations differently, the problem of immigration had "a fundamental importance, to every nation. Those countries most clearly concerned with immigration "see clearly the necessity of a common effort" that could "lead . . . to direct agreements and to a coordination of action with regard to immigration." Concerned nations should endeavor to "reach a practical solution" to the problems of immigration and should "bring forth suggestions which may prove most valuable in leading to an efficient international regulation of this complex question."[2]

Interestingly the Italian Embassy was quick to qualify that the conference would only discuss immigration in "strictly technical," not "diplomatic," terms. Instead the conference would focus on formulating "principles which may serve later as a basis for general or particular international conventions to be stipulated, or of administrative agreements which the various governments could enter into for the respective services." The Italian Embassy suggested that the conference agenda include the following: "transportation of emigrants," "hygiene and sanitary services," "*cooperation* among immigration and emigration services of various countries," "*assistance* to emigrants at the port of embarkation, of immigrants upon their landing and of the emigrated on the part of private institutions," "means to adapt immigration to the labor demand (labor information service, employment agencies, colonizations)," "development of *cooperation* and mutuality among emigrants," and "*general principles* that should govern immigration treaties."[3]

The Italian Embassy's concession to not discuss immigration in diplomatic terms was not enough to prevent the State Department's quick defense of U.S. immigration policy as a domestic matter only. In defense of U.S. policy, Kellogg wrote that the "reception of immigrants within the United States is regarded wholly as a domestic matter, and the exclusive authority of Congress must be recognized. Consequently, when participating in a conference of the proposed nature, certain restrictions, obviously, would be incumbent upon any American delegates." Despite the qualification that the conference would only discuss immigration in technical terms, State Department officials recognized how the proposed talking points, featuring words and terms such as "assistance," "cooperation," and "general principles," represented a blurring of the line between domestic policy and international concession. Within a year of Kellogg's reply to the Italian Embassy, the United States passed the 1924 immigration act, which significantly curtailed immigration from southern and eastern Europe and completely barred Asian immigration.[4]

Japan protested what it viewed as racial prejudice that underlined the restriction of Asian immigration with the passage of the 1924 act. Like Mexico, Japan had been spared from formal immigration restriction for the first two decades of the twentieth century. Since 1908, in accordance with its "Gentlemen's Agreement" with the United States, Japan had regulated its immigration to the United States. The Japanese government agreed that it would greatly decrease the number of immigrants by restricting the issuance of passports. The agreement, according to historian Izumi Hirobe, was a face-saving measure for Japan: "it was imperative that Japan, eager to assert its equality with the Western powers, be able to preserve its honor."[5]

Anti-Japanese sentiment had been surging in the United States since the 1890s in tandem with the growth of the Japanese immigrant population along the Western Seaboard. The movement to curb Japanese immigration centered in San Francisco, California, and was spearheaded by the Japanese and Korean Exclusion League, which was founded in May 1905. In large part, Hirobe shows, the Gentlemen's Agreement, brokered between 1907 and 1908, was the result of both governments attempting to resolve diplomatically what had been viewed up to that point as a local issue.[6] Despite this intergovernmental agreement, local animosity toward Japanese immigrants continued to grow throughout the 1910s and 1920s. By 1923 anti-Japanese measures began appearing at the congressional level. A clause barring all Japanese immigrants from entry into the United States was inserted into an immigration bill proposed in the 68th Congress, which convened in December 1923. Worried that the bill, if passed, would disturb U.S.-Japanese relations, the State Department and Japanese Foreign Ministry worked to abort the clause. The Japanese Foreign Ministry sent frequent letters of protest to the State Department, and the State Department pledged its full support in opposition to the bill. This protest culminated in April 1924 with a letter to Charles Evans Hughes from Masanao Hanihara, the Japanese ambassador to the

United States, appealing to the Senate not to include the clause, which would totally prohibit Japanese immigration.[7]

> The manifest object of the [exclusion clause] is to single out Japanese as a nation, stigmatizing them as unworthy and undesirable in the eyes of the American people . . . [the exclusion clause] in apparent disregard of the most sincere and friendly endeavors of the Japanese Government to meet the needs and wishes of the American Government and people, is mortifying enough to the Government and people of Japan. . . .
>
> Relying upon the confidence you have been good enough to show me at all times, I have stated or rather repeated all this to you very candidly and in a most friendly spirit, for I realize, as I believe you do, the grave consequences which the enactment of the measure retaining that particular provision would inevitably bring upon the otherwise happy and mutually advantageous relations between our two countries.[8]

According to Hirobe the vehemence of Japan's opposition to the exclusion laws was based on the racial prejudice that underlined it and the betrayal of past U.S.-Japanese agreements on immigration. Japan felt the immigration question had been settled by the Gentlemen's Agreement of 1907–1908. More importantly Japan chafed at the racial implications of the law. "In Japan," Hirobe argues, "the total ban of Japanese immigrants to the United States in 1924 was interpreted as a rejection of Japan, made exclusively on the grounds of race, by the existing world order, controlled by the Western nations. The Japanese interpreted this to mean that no matter how hard Japan tried to cooperate with the United States, they would never be treated as America's equal."[9]

Japan did not challenge the United States' sovereign right to formulate immigration policy, though it did assert that such an exclusionary law threatened to undermine harmonious relations between the two countries.[10] Rather the Japanese government protested "the fact that discriminatory immigration legislation on the part of the United States would naturally wound the national susceptibilities of the Japanese people." A formal letter of protest from the Japanese government to the State Department less than a week after the 1924 immigration act was signed into law on May 26 explicated this argument.

> It is, perhaps, needless to state that international discriminations in any form and on any subject, even if based on purely economic reasons, are opposed to the principles of justice and fairness upon which the friendly intercourse between nations must, in its final analysis, depend. To these very principles the doctrine of equal opportunity now widely recognized, with the unfailing support of the United States, owes its being. *Still more unwelcome are discriminations based on race.*[11]

According to the Japanese ambassador to the United States, the Gentlemen's Agreement was formulated "for the purpose of relieving the United States from the possible unfortunate necessity of offending the natural pride of a friendly nation." Nonetheless, the immigration law including the clause to bar Japanese immigration passed Congress in April 1924. President Calvin Coolidge signed the Johnson-Reed Act the following month, believing the need to protect the sovereignty of immigration policy overrode any concerns about international sentiment regarding the law.[12]

Japanese citizens boycotted American goods, American society, and Christian churches in reaction to the exclusion law; they mutilated the U.S. Embassy flag and glorified as a hero a student who committed suicide on the steps of the U.S. Embassy in Tokyo out of protest. Editorial invective against the United States continued for years after 1924. According to a contemporaneous account, the exclusion of Japanese immigration infected every aspect of U.S.-Japan relations, and to the average Japanese citizen, relations with the United States were clouded by the 1924 act.[13]

That act also endangered relations with Mexico, and four years after it was enacted, it posed, once again, a challenge for American diplomats. As the quota debate in the United States heated up from February 1928 on, the State Department found itself in an unenviable position. On one hand it had to balance legislative sovereignty over immigration policy with the increased demand for a bilateral agreement, or at least negotiations, on immigration from the Mexican government. On the other hand the State Department hoped to temper the prejudicial language and discriminatory nature of the quota debate because of the need to preserve amicable relations with Mexico.

Kellogg, during his testimony before the Senate Committee on Immigration and Naturalization, argued that consular reports made clear that Latin American nations would not only resent the application of a quota on their immigration but that these states would also protest the extension of the quota to Mexico, even if the rest of the hemisphere were not subject to similar immigration restriction.

In gathering this information Kellogg had not consulted the Mexican government on their views about a quota—much less pursued bilateral negotiations on the matter with Mexico. He did not do so because he believed United States immigration policy was a domestic matter.[14] In this respect he was typical among all U.S. policymakers who debated the extension of the quota to Mexico. Kellogg's defense of United States immigration policy as exclusively domestic policy was clearly defined in his instructions to American delegations to the Sixth International Conference of American States (the Pan-American Conference) and the Second Conference on Emigration and Immigration. Both conferences took place in Havana, Cuba, between January and April 1928, at the same time that Congress heard arguments on whether to extend the restrictive quota to nations of the Western Hemisphere. These conferences present a distinct venue in which immigration was discussed at the international level, as well as a focus on American delegates' stubborn defense of immigration policy as domestic policy.

Kellogg found ample precedent for defending the sovereignty of U.S. immigration policy. At the Assembly of the Interparliamentary Commercial Conference at Rio de Janeiro in September 1927, Sen. Joseph T. Robinson (D-AR) responded to proposals advanced by the Italian delegates regarding control of Italian emigrants on foreign soil. After describing the long history of open immigration to the United States, Robinson stated that after 1920 the United

States found it necessary to pass legislation to curb immigration. Such domestic policy, Robinson acknowledged, did conflict with a sovereign nation's duty to protect its people abroad.

> We understand that under the principles of international law as commonly and generally accepted, every nation has the right if it chooses to exercise its power to exclude immigrants or admitting them to define the conditions under which they shall or may be admitted, and we understand that the principle of law is in conflict with the right of the country of origin to control the destiny of the immigrant after he has taken his place in a foreign land among strangers.

Nonetheless, Robinson argued, while legislation that restricted another nation's immigration risked causing international discord, the United States subscribed to the tenet that when an immigrant left his native country "to seek residence and citizenship under a new flag and in a strange land," he submitted himself to the authority of the host country and the laws of that land.[15] "A perusal of the foregoing," Kellogg instructed the American delegation, should leave no doubt about the U.S. government's position, which held that immigration was solely a domestic matter, "representing as it does the exercise of a sovereign right" and the exclusive authority of Congress.[16]

Kellogg highlighted this precedent of defending immigration policy as domestic policy as the American delegation prepared to attend the Pan-American Conference in January 1928.[17] Any international influence on the formulation of domestic immigration policy would undermine the sovereign rights of the United States. Accordingly, Kellogg stated, the delegation should be careful not to be drawn into any discussions or resolution votes that would tend to weaken this sovereign principle: the delegates should "be prepared to combat such a tendency by clear and unequivocal statements based on the historic position of the United States."[18]

At the Sixth Pan-American Conference international immigration matters were discussed, under the rubric of Economic Problems and "International aspects of immigration problems."[19]

Enrique Hernández Cartaya, of the host delegation, suggested the session address the problems of immigration by focusing on the legal and social protection of immigrants. Additionally he proposed that bases be established that would promote the organization of immigration streams, which would take into account "diverse national needs." By the very nature of immigration, Cartaya argued, such measures required multilateral consideration. In the short term, he believed, bilateral treaties on immigration could help establish precedents, until international law had the time to evolve to adequately handle the "transcendental phenomenon" of immigration. Additionally Cartaya recommended that measures be established to regulate intercontinental immigration in order to protect and guarantee labor markets and to ensure domestic security and order within nations.[20] Cartaya's suggestions were reflected in the final measures adopted by the fifth commission and passed along to, and subsequently accepted by, the Second Conference on Emigration and Immigration.

Three points stand out from Cartaya's address: first, the call to protect immigrants in host countries; second, the belief that immigration problems required bilateral negotiation and, eventually, multilateral mediation; and third, the domestic regulation of immigration. In some respects the second suggestion contradicted the third. This contradiction was not noted at the time. And the final principles established by the Sixth Pan-American meeting and confirmed by the Second Conference on Emigration and Immigration acknowledged a nation's sovereign right to regulate immigration while also recognizing that international cooperation was necessary to fully address the problems posed by immigration. For Latin American states, sovereignty and international cooperation were not mutually exclusive endeavors. Indeed for some delegates at these two conferences, hemispheric solidarity over immigration matters was a means to protect each nation's sovereignty over the regulation of its immigration.

The conference's following final points embodied this dual Latin American perspective. First, that conferences on immigration and emigration "cannot ever impose" on an American nation measures that tend to "subtract" that nation's jurisdiction over its emigration policy. Second, that there be equality of civil rights between nationals and foreigners in host countries, and so that "the quality of the free man" be recognized in each immigrant, there should be equal protection of rights and human dignity toward all immigrants, the protection of which *can justify* "any offense" of the sovereignty of the nation. Third, that American nations reserve the right to examine the advantages of the entrance of current immigration into its territories, *from other continents*, adjusting the mode of procedure according to its economic, social, and political interests.[21]

Lindolfo Collar, Brazil's delegate, elaborated. Regarding the first, he said that this was "an American principle that all representatives of the New World can accept and must defend. I am certain that if we come together and present a [united] front," then this principle would be accepted by delegates to the Second Conference on Emigration and Immigration. On the second point he stated that the "principles contained in this amendment are peaceful for America. In the constitution of Brazil there is no established difference between the rights of nationals and foreigners. Brazil shelters and protects the foreigner equally, in regards to the civil rights [enjoyed] by nationals; and if a country has in its constitution a principle so liberal as this, then of course [that nation] can and must adopt the [second] principle," within the exercise of its sovereign right over immigration matters. Collar connected the third point to the development of the first. "If emigration countries reserve the right to fix and examine the conditions within which they can abandon the emigrants of their countries, no one can deny us the right that we, the American nations, fix the rules and principles that are most suitable to determine the conditions in which we must admit [immigrants]." Finally, Collar ended on a note of solidarity. "I insist to all the American nations represented here that they must group together and show a [united] front of the greatest strength and firmness," when presenting these "fundamentally essential" points to the Second Conference on Emigration and Immigration. For its part, Collar stated, Brazil was committed to upholding the amicable relations between and the solidarity among the American nations.[22] Collar's call for hemispheric solidarity was reflected in the final versions of the three points adopted at the conclusion of the Second Conference on Emigration and Immigration in mid-April 1928.

The Mexican delegation presented another, related, set of principles on immigration at the Sixth Pan-American Conference. These principles were eventually accepted by the Second Conference on Emigration and Immigration. First presented on January 24, 1928, by Mexican delegate Salvador Urbina, the measures were approved by the fifth commission on February 7 and passed along to the Second Conference on Emigration and Immigration. After defining an *emigrante* and an *inmigrante,* the Mexican proposal's three main points called for the following:

> The governments must not permit the exit of an emigrant without first having established the following contracts
> i.) a transportation contract for work that guarantees that the emigrant is conducted to the place of work, and that the conditions in the workplace are hygienic, safe, and comfortable.
> ii.) a work contract that guarantees that the same emigrant is given the means to return to their place of origin after their contract is completed.
>
> The governments, in addition to the stipulated guarantees above, should pronounce the necessary protective measures in favor of the emigrant, and in favor of the immigrant from the port of entry to the place for which they have a contract to work.
>
> The immigrant must enjoy the same rights and legal guarantees of the country to which the immigrant has entered, with exception to the political rights [distinct to the nation], [host nations] *may never pronounce* measures of any nature that tend to place the immigrant in a legal situation or in fact inferior [position] to that of nationals.

> The government of a country which solicits emigrant labor must establish laws that comply with the measures expressed in the second point, namely, that work and transportation contracts are fulfilled.[23]

Like representatives from other Latin American nations, the Mexican delegation endorsed legal equality between aliens and nationals. The Mexican proposal moved beyond Cartaya's position by calling for greater accountability from emigrant-receiving nations to fulfill work contracts, to guarantee immigrants' safety while residing in host countries, and to ensure that emigrants had the means to return to their home nations once labor contracts had been completed. Interestingly the Mexican proposal had less to say directly about nations' sovereign rights over immigration vis-à-vis the protection of workers abroad; nonetheless the measures formulated by Mexico were no less radical, as shown by the third point, which stated that the necessity of immigrant protection should not be curbed by national laws.

By calling for nation-by-nation accountability for the rights and protections of immigrants, Mexico took for granted the transnational nature of immigration. Indeed each of the measures proposed by Brazil and Mexico implied *at least* bilateral, if not multilateral, efforts to protect immigrants in the midst of a demand for their labor. This set of principles on immigration demonstrated how Mexico viewed the immigration problem during the first half of 1928, as the U.S. Congress debated the merits of a quota on Mexican immigration. Regional neighbors affirmed Mexico's proposals to resolve problems of immigration by approving the Mexican proposal at both the Sixth Pan-American Conference and the Second Conference on Emigration and Immigration.[24] Such an affirmation represented a hemispheric challenge to the unilateral nature of U.S. immigration policy.

Kellogg reiterated Congress's sovereign right over U.S. immigration policy two months later as the U.S. delegation prepared to attend the Second Conference on Emigration and Immigration.

After instructing the delegation to make clear to the conference that immigration was a matter of U.S. domestic policy, Kellogg directed the delegation to "take no action inconsistent with the attitude and prerogatives of the Congress of the United States in this connection or in any way committing the government of the United States." As with the Pan-American Conference a few weeks before, Kellogg excluded U.S. participation in any discussion or voting that risked implying that immigration policy was anything other than the domain of sovereign states.

The second convening of the Conference on Emigration and Immigration took place in Havana, Cuba, between March 31 and April 17, 1928. Over forty nations from Asia, Europe, and Latin America attended the gathering.[25] True to the word of the Italian Embassy in 1924, the conferences on immigration and emigration largely discussed the issue in technical terms. The principal question before the conference, the American delegation reported, was the manner and means "whereby international consideration of the problems of immigration and emigration could best be conducted."[26] The proceedings regarding immigration were separated into five commissions. The first commission discussed the transport and protection of the emigrants, as well as hygiene and sanitary services. Assistance to the emigrated—"cooperation, insurance, systems of mutual insurance"—was discussed by the second commission. The third commission, importantly, discussed the "adoption of measures in order to adapt immigration to the labor necessities of immigration countries," as well as international cooperation between the immigration and emigration services. The fourth commission discussed general principles of immigration treaties. And the fifth commission discussed the resolutions of the first conference in Rome and how they could be expounded upon by the second meeting.[27]

By the conference's second convening the U.S. government had grown accustomed to deflecting calls to discuss immigration internationally. Most of the U.S. delegates took turns defending the sovereignty of U.S. immigration policy. Several examples illustrate this point. As the slate of officers was assigned the day before the conference began, Undersecretary of Labor W. W. Husband was offered the chance to act as the chairman for the third commission. Husband declined the offer because he believed the position would conflict with the "nature of his instructions" to defend the sovereignty of Congress's immigration policy powers. After the first meeting of the fifth commission on April 3, Henry Carter, the State Department's plenipotentiary at the conference, wrote to the commission *rapporteur* that "the fundamental position of the United States is that control of immigration is a matter of purely domestic concern, representing the exercise of a sovereign right, and that, as far as the United States of America is concerned, the authority of its Congress in immigration matters is exclusive." Toward the end of the first commission's final meeting on April 9, Dr. John D. Long, of the U.S. Public Health Service, stated that the delegation of the United States "did not vote either for or against any of the motions nor took any part in the discussions that have taken place, all because the Government [*sic*] of the United States understands that immigration questions come within the province of the Congress of the United States and that if any other line of conduct had been taken, a limit might have been put upon that exclusive authority held by the Congress of the United States in the matter."[28]

The U.S delegation was right to see an international aspect to the conference that at times, while perhaps only indirectly, suggested that immigration issues transcended unilateral solutions. The final program of the conference, and the nations that agreed with the final points, demonstrated a transnational desire to cooperate in order to resolve questions and problems of immigration. Final resolutions of the third and fourth commissions are of particular note. Under the heading "Adoption of measures in order to adapt emigration to the labor necessities of immigration countries; International cooperation between the emigration and immigration services," the third commission adopted measures that suggested doing various things. The first measure regarded the professional selection of emigrants before they left their country of origin. This measure was advanced in order to minimize conflict between skilled and unskilled workers in host countries.[29] A second measure put forth a temporary worker scheme, in which workers living in the border regions would be allowed to enter the host country. By restricting the movement of these workers within the host country, this measure hoped to preclude conflict over immigration between nations.[30] The commission propounded a third measure that stipulated that public and private organizations should coordinate the recruitment and placement of emigrants into jobs and that such a process should be conducted under the surveillance of both nations. This proposal was meant to establish between countries a regular exchange of information about the conditions of work and the availability or need for laborers, as well as prevent the dangers of immigration and the illicit profit of private recruiting agents.[31] The commission also proposed that countries develop agreements to facilitate the settlement of uncultivated lands, a plan meant to promote the mutual cooperation between nations to make fallow land productive while responding to a glut of migrant labor.[32] Fifth, a measure was discussed to promote efforts toward stemming illegal immigration.[33] Finally the commission aimed to fix a "reasonable" term before which regulatory measures on immigration were enforced. In the words of the third commission, "considering that the *unexpected restrictions* on immigration and emigration *cause serious damages* to persons who have made preparations to travel and have left their jobs," this sixth measure suggested an easing-in period before which a nation's immigration legislation would restrict the movement of emigrants and immigrants.[34] In a similar vein the fourth commission to the conference—focused on general principles of immigration treaties—put forth a measure to guarantee effective equality in pay, working conditions, and the application of laws regarding work safety and social security for foreign workers who reside *legally* in a host country. According to the measure the unequal treatment of foreign workers was harmful not only to the workers themselves but also to the interests of emigrant-sending nations.[35]

Of greatest importance, the conference accepted a declaration of principles passed along for consideration by delegates to the Sixth Pan-American Conference a few weeks before. The first principle stated that conferences on emigration and immigration, **whether they be among nations from the Western Hemisphere or abroad**, "cannot ever impose" on an American nation measures that tend to "subtract" that nation's jurisdiction over its emigration policy. The second principle ensured that the equality of civil rights between nationals and foreigners in host countries and "the quality of the free man" be recognized in each immigrant and that there should be equal protection of rights and human dignity toward all immigrants, the protection of which *can justify* "any **limitation**" of a nation's sovereignty. Third, that American nations reserve the right to examine the advantages of the entrance of current immigration into its territories, *from other continents*, adjusting the mode of procedure according to its economic, social, and political interests.[36]

All these measures envisioned bilateral or multilateral cooperation on immigration. Implicit in this international dialogue and delegations' approval of the measures was a belief that immigration was a problem that required an international solution. National sovereignty, to be sure, was not directly challenged at these proceedings, but the talks and argued-upon recommendations sought a middle way between a nation's domestic right over immigration policy and the international ramifications of immigration. Whether such a middle way represented a risk to national sovereignty was not discussed directly at the conference. For the U.S. delegates, judging by their nonactions at the conference, any kind of middle way would have compromised Congress's sovereign power over immigration policy. Such a unilateral approach, while it limited dangers to national sovereignty, also limited the range of options available for resolving immigration problems.

Article 5 of the fourth commission raises some interesting points about how Latin American nations envisioned the balance between sovereign rights over domestic immigration policy, regional solidarity over immigration matters vis-à-vis non-American nations, regional exceptions to national restrictions on immigration, and the protection of immigrants in host countries. This article was previously discussed by the Third Commission of the Pan-American Conference in January and February 1928, passed along to the Second Conference on Emigration and Immigration for consideration, and subsequently approved by participating national delegations. The second part of Article 5, which suggested that the violation of a common respect and protection of rights and human dignity by a host nation could justify the limitation of that nation's sovereignty, seems to contradict the first part of the same article, which defends an American nation's right over its own immigration policy. The third part of Article 5 seems to advocate a nation's right to regulate (read: restrict) the inflow of immigrants as it sees fit. Yet the qualification that only immigration "from other continents" is covered seems to prevent Latin American states from passing restrictive immigration legislation aimed at its neighboring nations of the Western Hemisphere.

It is not clear from the conference proceedings how immigrant abuse would be reprimanded or how Latin American states would defend their sovereign rights in relation to European or Asian immigration while at the same time expecting exemptions from immigration restriction from within its own region. Nor is it clear what administrative body would have enforced the protection of immigrants' human rights against a sovereign state power or overseen the harmonization of regional immigration standards. While these clauses raise many questions, they demonstrate a chief theme of discussion about immigration at both the Sixth Pan-American Conference and the Second Conference on Emigration and Immigration in Havana between January and April 1928: the transnational recognition of the need to protect immigrants and a balance between a nation's sovereignty over its immigration policy and a regional exemption to immigration restriction.

The U.S. trepidation about discussing the domestic matter of immigration at the international level must have been confirmed when the Mexican delegation introduced a proposal to disallow any quota on immigration between American nations. According to the Mexican proposal, "None of the American [nations] can place obstacles on the immigration and emigration of other [nations] or limit it to a determined number of citizens" from the nation of origin. The measure was originally proposed by El Salvador's delegation to the Sixth Pan-American Conference and appended to the fifth commission's final act along with the Mexican proposal and a list of other measures for discussion at the Second Conference on Emigration and Immigration on February 7, 1928. In contrast to the Mexican proposal, which received a unanimous vote of approval from the fifth commission, the Salvadoran measure received a slim majority (9 yays:6 nays) from delegates to the Sixth Pan-American Conference. Henry Fletcher of the U.S. delegation, which abstained from voting on whether to forward the proposal to the second conference, stated that if there was no unanimity in the commission on the measure, then it would be "dangerous" to portray the proposals as espousing principles shared by all countries of the Western Hemisphere. Fletcher also took the opportunity to reiterate the U.S. delegation's resolve not to enter into a debate on this or any other related matters since its government viewed matters of immigration as domestic concerns that only Congress could resolve.[37]

The Salvadoran proposal was initially presented by the Mexican delegation to the fourth commission (which discussed general principles of immigration treaties) of the Second Conference on Emigration and Immigration on April 11, 1928. It is not clear from the documentary record why Mexico's delegates presented the measures instead of El Salvador's. Three days after its initial presentation the Mexican delegation struck the proposal; yet at the conference's concluding plenary session on April 17, the proposal was resurrected. "After heated discussion," the proposal was tabled for discussion at the Third Conference on Emigration and Immigration, scheduled to take place in Madrid, Spain, in 1932. During this and other debates related to immigration, the U.S. delegation responded as it was instructed by Kellogg—with passivity and a reiteration that immigration was a matter of each sovereign state's domestic policy.[38]

The U.S. delegation must have been equally uneasy when Manuel Gamio, a member of Mexico's delegation and a person widely considered to be the contemporary expert on Mexican immigration, presented a study that suggested ways in which to resolve the immigration problem between the two countries. While there is no direct evidence to indicate how W. W. Husband and his colleagues received the report, there is information that suggests that they were sympathetic to some aspects of the analysis, at least to Gamio's opposition to a quota on Mexican immigration. In a telegram to Mexico City summarizing the conference, Carlos Trejo y Lerdo de Tejada, the chairman of the Mexican delegation, reported to Husband the reasoning that had contributed to the quota on Mexico not being passed during the current year. For their part, Trejo y Lerdo implied, the U.S. delegation tended to oppose the quota's adoption. Husband's stance on the quota confirms the testimony he gave five weeks before, on March 5, 1928, before the Senate Committee on Immigration and Naturalization. While his testimony waffled between support for a general quota on Latin America (but one that was less harsh than that proposed by congressmen) and opposition to a quota on Mexico alone (since that would be construed as national discrimination), Husband and his colleagues were obliged to follow Kellogg's directions to defend U.S. immigration policy as a strictly domestic matter that was not open to international debate. Such a diplomatic stance countered the prospect of official bilateral talks about the quota issue and the immigration problem. Trejo y Lerdo's letter shows that at the Second Conference on Emigration and Immigration, U.S. and Mexican officials did discuss the quota privately. This dialogue, however, was not recognized officially. Trejo y Lerdo concluded his telegram by stating that the great majority of delegations to the conference supported Mexico's proposals and that most Latin American nations showed "enthusiastic solidarity" with Mexico.[39]

Manuel Gamio's report on "Some suggestions towards a solution of the problem of Mexican immigration to the United States" is revealing in two ways. First it indicates larger themes Gamio discussed in his studies of Mexican immigration during the latter half of the 1920s. Second, and more important, it demonstrates how Mexican officials pressured their American counterparts to view the immigration problem as a transnational problem that required a bilateral, not a unilateral, solution. Gamio called for the restriction of permanent Mexican immigration to the United States, the organization and encouragement of transitory/temporary emigration, and the repatriation of permanent immigrants from the United States to Mexico.[40]

According to Gamio, it was imperative that U.S. immigration law be amended to permit the entrance of *contracted* temporary laborers, that employers be obliged to honor conditions of their work contracts with Mexican laborers, and that those employers pay for transportation from the border to the site of labor and for the return.[41] Such measures would not only favor temporary emigration over permanent immigration, thereby promising to reduce permanent immigration, but they would also counteract laborers' tendency to move on to other parts of the United States when they had no work and no means of subsistence. Instead laborers could return to Mexico where living was cheaper. Additionally, Gamio believed, U.S. immigration law should permit the entrance of illiterate Mexican migrants. He argued that it was unnecessary for temporary laborers to know how to read and write and that their failure to meet such criteria of U.S. immigration law often led to the abuse of Mexican migrants. Gamio predicted that if his proposed measures were adopted, labor needs could be adjusted to complement the regions that lacked workers, in the quantity required, and with little negative effect on the American labor market.[42]

Gamio asserted that permanent immigration was bad for both nations: in the United States permanently settled immigrants competed with native workers and became the root of other social disputes; in Mexico permanent immigration represented a permanent loss of the nation's best workers. The encouragement, regulation, and control of temporary labor to the United States could satisfy the transitory labor needs of that country and avoid the problems that came with permanent immigration. Mexico could also benefit from such restriction, Gamio continued, when laborers brought back to Mexico their skills in modern agriculture and industry.[43]

It was even possible, he believed, that such measures could preclude the need for a quota. If U.S. immigration law were relaxed in regard to Mexican migrants, then the permanent immigration stream would shift into a temporary labor stream and the permanent immigration population in the United States, and all the ire it caused, would dwindle. In other words Mexicans would have no need to immigrate permanently if U.S. immigration law were more amenable to their satisfying the labor demand from American businesses. Eventually, Gamio concluded, the adoption of his suggestions would reduce the great migratory movement that had occurred during the previous years.[44]

The "united acceptance" of these three proposals and their "coordinated application" during the next few years, Gamio predicted, would prevent the "irreparable damages" that would ensue from the "sudden" establishment of an immigration quota on Mexico. Gamio argued that the solution to the immigration problem required the work and common agreement of both countries and that their actions must be coordinated. Such a solution necessitated an international commission comprised of various agencies—notably the foreign ministries and labor departments, but also business groups and labor unions—from both countries.[45]

Obviously the suggestion that the United States not only work bilaterally with Mexico but also adjust its immigration law to forge a solution to the immigration problem was unacceptable for U.S. policymakers. At root here was a conflict between the essentials of Westphalian nationalism and the contemporary sprout of Wilsonian diplomacy. Unilateral approaches to solving the immigration problem by applying a quota to Mexico risked harming U.S.-Mexican relations. Yet bilateral negotiations for a solution to the same problem risked truncating American policymakers' understanding of national sovereignty. Amicable relations with Mexico were necessary for cross-border peace, regional harmony, protection of private property abroad, payment of foreign debts, satisfaction on claims, and Pan-American solidarity. But the Wilsonian bent that would have urged American policymakers to preserve these amicable relations by seeking a long-lasting and bilateral solution to the immigration problem was impeded by a Westphalian urge to protect the sanctity of national sovereignty. Consequently demands for a quota on Mexico would continue irrespective of their effects on U.S.-Mexican relations.

Officially the United States brooked no attempt to discuss its immigration policy at the international level. A few months after the Second Conference on Emigration and Immigration, Kellogg declined the invitation for U.S. participation at the next meeting: "In view of the very definite manner in which the Congress has exercised [its sovereign authority over immigration matters], particularly in the passage of the Immigration Act of 1924, and considering the fundamental division of opinion on the subject of immigration at [the last conference], this Government is constrained to state that in its view *no useful purpose* is served by such conferences."[46] Consequently the United States played only a passive role in conferences that recognized the international importance of immigration. American delegations confined their efforts to continuously declaring the sovereign right of U.S. immigration policy.

American intransigence toward international discussions of immigration did not occur in a vacuum, nor were these conferences isolated events. The 1920s witnessed a whole host of international conferences that discussed the problems of immigration and the forging of several treaties between nations to help resolve bilateral issues related to immigration. Considerable attention was given to the problems of immigration by the Conference of the Interparliamentary Union in Bern and Geneva in 1924, the Interparliamentary Conference on Commerce in Brussels in June 1924, and the Federation of Unions of the Society of Nations during its meetings in 1924 and 1926. In June 1926 the Universal Congress of Workers in London studied immigration problems. The Association of International Law, during its sessions in Buenos Aires in 1921 and Stockholm in 1924, was occupied with questions of nationality and expatriation in connection with matters of immigration. In February 1923 several countries, including Argentina, Brazil, Canada, Chile, and Cuba, met in Paris to consider ways in which to provide protection for immigrants. And the International Association for Social Progress, organized in Basel, gave continuous attention to immigration matters. Additionally several bilateral treaties between Latin American and European states demonstrated that there was successful international dialogue regarding problems of immigration. Brazil brokered immigration treaties with Portugal in September 1919, Italy in October 1921, and Great Britain in July 1922. Argentina and Belgium established an agreement in September 1922, while Argentina negotiated a treaty with Spain two months later regarding work accidents. As this activity shows, during the 1920s there was a growing acknowledgment in the international community that bilateral and multilateral attention and agreements were necessary to resolve the problems posed by immigration.[47]

Unofficial meetings between the Mexican and American delegations at the Second Conference on Emigration and Immigration was the closest both nations would come to brokering a bilateral treaty on immigration before the 1940s. The focus on reiterating their sovereign rights over immigration policy represents a missed opportunity by U.S. policymakers to solve the problem of Mexican immigration during the late 1920s. If the State Department had consulted the Mexican government, it would have found that Mexican officials did not feel markedly different about immigration from their American counterparts. Mexico City had attempted to curb Mexican immigration north for decades. If restriction advocates in the United States had not been so focused on preserving the domestic sanctity of U.S. immigration policy, they might have recognized that they and the Mexican government had a common interest—namely, the curbing of Mexican immigration. Instead the social and racial prejudice used by restrictionists to justify the extension of the quota to Mexico alienated Mexican leaders and precluded any mutually designed framework for restriction.

Despite U.S. insistence that immigration policy was domestic policy, immigration became a matter of diplomatic concern during the 1920s. This does not mean diplomatic pressures always influenced the shaping of immigration policy, though in some cases, such as in Mexico, it did. Instead after the 1920s, U.S. policymakers had to consider how domestic immigration policies affected relations with emigrant-sending countries. Often the economic climate and a foreign nation's power shaped how U.S. policymakers set immigration policy. In the case of Mexico, however, the sovereign right to formulate immigration policy was not wholly immune to the exigencies of diplomatic relations.

4

The Advantages, Disadvantages, Risks, and Rewards of Immigration Restriction

Fall 1928

The Pan-American solidarity of the spring of 1928 delayed congressional efforts to place a quota on Mexican immigration. Yet restrictionists sustained their campaign during the rest of the year. Their efforts seemed to be rewarded when the Senate Committee on Immigration and Naturalization reported a measure to restrict Mexican immigration in December 1928. In contrast to earlier proposals for a quota on Latin American immigration, the bill focused specifically on Mexico. Restrictionists, while they hoped all Western Hemisphere nations would eventually be added to the list of quota-restricted countries, focused their efforts on at least extending the quota to Mexico since that country sent the most Latin American emigrants to the United States. And restrictionists were alarmed by what they saw as a growing permanent Mexican population within the United States.

The sudden legislative success of the quota measure in December 1928 set off a diplomatic crisis between the United States and its southern neighbor when it ignited a firestorm of rhetoric in Mexico denouncing the discriminatory nature of U.S. immigration law. For Mexicans immigration was a chronic socioeconomic problem that required a structural remedy. The most common solution proposed was the development of national industries that would relieve the glut of laborers in Mexico. If internal development projects were allowed to take root, Mexican leaders and journalists argued, then the problem of immigration would dissipate. Migrants, it was believed, would no longer find it necessary to migrate when ready work was available in their home country. In this regard most Mexican observers favored some kind of U.S. restriction on Mexican immigration. These restrictions would further Mexico's goal of maintaining its labor force; however, it was the nature of the quota debate, which cast Mexicans as racially inferior, and the proposed end of that debate, recommending immediate curtailment of Mexico's immigration northward, that angered Mexicans and fueled their opposition to the American effort to place a quota on Mexico. Moreover the sudden stoppage proposed by a restrictive quota struck Mexican observers as heavy-handed and unjustified. Migrants, Mexican officials stated, were only responding to the labor demand from industries throughout the United States. To restrict the movement of Mexicans who were simply seeking work failed to account for the role American employers played in the immigration problem. Instead, Mexican observers believed, the United States should recognize the value of Mexican labor and acknowledge its role in developing the American economy. Most important, Mexican analysts of immigration argued, U.S. leaders should consider how a sudden halt in Mexican immigration would destabilize Mexico by burdening it with an oversupply of labor.

Mexicans recognized that Americans had been contending for immigration restriction for decades by the 1920s. Until then, one of the most common arguments employed against immigration had been the economic one: that cheap migrant labor negatively affected the U.S. labor market. In the wake of the Johnson-Reed Act's passage in 1924, such arguments were used against Mexican immigration, especially by groups like the American Federation of Labor. A subtle change occurred in the 1920s, as the United States enjoyed one of its most prosperous decades on record. After 1924 what primarily drove the call to restrict Mexican immigration were arguments for racial ascription rather than economic necessity. Restrictionists believed Mexicans were racially inferior and a hazard to U.S. society and its institutions. It was this racial justification for a quota that precluded any bilateral solution to the immigration problem. Racism and restrictionists' insistence that immigration policy was solely a domestic matter undermined amicable relations between the United States and Mexico.

In the midst of this debate over the quota, the State Department tried to devise a way to restrict Mexican immigration without harming relations with Mexico, while still satisfying and persuading them to abandon their quota plans. Starting in early 1929 American consular officials throughout Mexico began enforcing existing U.S. immigration laws so as to gradually roll back the tide of Mexicans to the United States. *Administrative restriction* would succeed where the previous strategy of relying on repatriation figures had failed. By strictly enforcing U.S. immigration law toward Mexico's migrants, the State Department removed the exemptions that had spared Mexican immigration from restriction during the past decades. The strategy of using repatriation figures to show that Mexican immigration was not a permanent problem had failed because immigration statistics were unreliable. Administrative restriction worked because of its neutral position within the quota debate. The State Department could be seen as simply enforcing existing U.S. immigration law instead of discriminating against Mexican migrants. Secretary of State Frank Kellogg had sided with quota opponents when he tried to defuse the debate with repatriation statistics. The enforcement of existing U.S. immigration laws allowed him to begin to quell the debate without appearing to take one side over the other.

Administrative restriction worked because it had something for everybody. For American restrictionists, administrative restriction would curtail the growth of the Mexican population within the United States. For Mexican leaders, administrative restriction aided their socioeconomic goals by curbing Mexico's immigration northward, but without the blatant, underlining racist rhetoric that suffused the quota effort. Administrative restriction benefitted American employers but was much more problematic for Mexican immigrants. Consular enforcement of U.S. immigration laws only affected those Mexicans who sought a visa to enter the United

States legally; it did nothing to stem the tide of illegal immigration. Arguably administrative restriction may have abetted illegal immigration since legal entry into the United States became more difficult. Only the onset of the Great Depression reversed the illegal and temporary streams of Mexican immigration. Administrative restriction slowed legal immigration; the Great Depression curbed illegal immigration. American employers, then, suffered no shortage of Mexican labor. Conversely, however, while the demand for work across the border remained high for Mexicans, administrative restriction reinforced the illegality of surreptitious immigration. This enhanced illegality made migrants more susceptible to abuse by *coyotes* and *enganchadores*, to exploitation by American employers, and to the physical dangers of transnational immigration.

On December 14, 1928, the Senate Committee on Immigration and Naturalization unanimously approved a proposal to extend the restrictive quota to Mexico. The proposal was dubbed the "Harris bill," after its sponsor Sen. William J. Harris (D-GA), who, like John Box of Texas, represented constituents who wanted to reduce or eliminate competition from cotton growers in the Southwest who were employing Mexican laborers.[1] The Harris bill was similar to the Box bill before the House Committee on Immigration and Naturalization, which called for an extension of the quota to all Western Hemisphere nations. The difference between the bills was that the Senate Committee on Immigration and Naturalization amended the Harris bill to apply to Mexico only. The committee did this in part because immigration from other Latin American nations was negligible compared to that from Mexico. More important, however, was that the modification of this bill and its recommendation to the Senate demonstrated that the real problem of immigration from the Western Hemisphere concerned Mexico only. This focus on Mexico did not go unnoticed, nor was it taken lightly by either the State Department or Mexico. On the same day that the Senate Committee on Immigration and Naturalization passed the Harris bill, Secretary of State Kellogg sent a telegram to the U.S. Embassy in Mexico City, reporting that a first step had been taken to place Mexico on the same restrictive basis as Europe. Kellogg, in an effort to calm the Mexican government about the quota, urged the embassy to remind Genaro Estrada, Mexico's foreign minister, that the bill had to clear several legislative hurdles before it became law.[2]

The Harris bill represented a shift in restrictionists' approach to the extension of the quota. Instead of trying to cover the entire hemisphere with the quota, restrictionists believed it was more feasible to extend it to Mexico only. For many quota advocates Mexico was the main culprit in the immigration problem anyway, and it was the presence of Mexican migrants, above all other immigrant groups, that posed the biggest menace to U.S. society after the restrictions of 1924.

Secretary of Labor James Davis and Sen. David Reed (R-PA) typified the restrictionists' focus on Mexico. In early December 1928, as the Senate Committee on Immigration and Naturalization discussed the Harris bill, Secretary Davis publicly called for a quota that would reduce Mexico's immigration to the United States by 90 percent, or from 80,000 to 7,000 annually. Davis made no similar proposal for any other nation of the Western Hemisphere. Such action was necessary, Davis argued, to protect the American labor market and to give credence to U.S. immigration laws. Davis argued that wherever Mexican immigration was exempted from restriction, the American worker would be undermined by cheap migrant laborers.[3]

Davis heightened the virulence of the quota debate by arguing that opponents of restriction of Mexico's immigration, namely, employers of Mexican laborers, were not good Americans. According to Davis one of the main features of the immigration problem was the "unpatriotic employer." He believed that most U.S. employers had learned that it was in their best interest to pay laborers a "saving wage." A saving wage, Davis stated, was a wage that would provide "not only the comforts of life but [would also enable] workers to lay something by for the later days when the need of ease has become apparent." By contrast the employer

Advantages, Disadvantages, Risks, and Rewards

who insisted on paying subsistence wages was "out of step in the march of progress." The employer who refused to pay a saving wage, he insisted, was the same employer who opposed restrictive immigration laws, because such laws would prevent the employer from obtaining emigrant labor that was willing to work for less than the American worker. For Davis U.S. employers who opposed the quota were unpatriotic because they placed their private interests before "the interests of the whole nation from which [the employer] has derived [his] entire prosperity."[4] To the pro-quota restrictionist argument, Davis added the assertion that American employers were culpable in the immigration problem and their use of migrant labor had an unhealthy ideological taint.

While Secretary Davis blamed U.S. employers for the problem of Mexican immigration, Senator Reed cited the precedent of exempting Mexican migrants from U.S. immigration laws as the reason why a quota was necessary. Unlike John Box, Reed readily acknowledged the futility of stopping Mexican immigration completely. Box treated the quota as a panacea and refused to acknowledge that the same administrative shortcomings that precluded the effective and regular removal of migrants from the United States also blocked a complete ban on Mexican immigration. Reed more realistically recognized that no amount of allocation or personnel would make a quota totally effective. Before the Senate, on the same day that Davis's call for a quota on Mexico was published in American newspapers, Reed declared that if it were possible to guard the border adequately and stop all migrants who attempted to cross, then there would be no need to update or add to the restrictive measures laid out by the 1917 immigration act. Mexican labor was not needed, Reed argued, and so Mexican immigration should be stopped: "But there is no use passing laws we cannot enforce. There is no use making a face at Mexican immigration unless we can actually keep that immigration out down to the point that we set ourselves, and until we guard the border we cannot keep that immigration out."[5]

Reed perceived both a short-term and a long-term problem with Mexican immigration. First, Mexican immigration had benefitted from exemptions to U.S. immigration law to an extent that it was harming U.S. society. Second, the United States did not possess the administrative means to stop migrants from crossing the border. The practical and interim solution to both problems lay in the extension of the quota to Mexico. A quota would end the precedent of exempting Mexican immigration and lay the groundwork for a regime of effective and total immigration restriction. The next step in the process, Reed stated, was the expansion of the Border Patrol, which could stop migrants at the border, and the establishment of facilities that could deport Mexicans who were in the United States illegally. Reed was under no illusion that restrictive legislation would resolve the problem of Mexican immigration immediately, but he was willing to extend the quota to Mexico to establish a comprehensive regime of restriction in U.S. immigration law, while the practicality of regulatory enforcement caught up to the law.[6]

Secretary Davis, Senator Reed, and other restrictionists were concerned about exemptions in the Immigration Act of 1924—specifically section 3, part 2, which seemed to facilitate Mexican immigration. Section 3 of the 1924 act legally defined an "immigrant" for purposes of regulating the movement of such persons. Six exemptions were given to the definition of an immigrant. The second exemption, "an alien visiting the United States temporarily as a tourist or *temporarily for business* or pleasure," was the exemption by which many Mexican migrants were exempted from any immigration inspection. *Temporary* immigration was the taproot of Mexican movement northward. The problem, restrictionists argued, was that many migrants who entered the United States temporarily did not return to Mexico. Davis argued for a quota since thousands of Mexicans were not temporary visitors.

In addition to section 3, part 2, and section 4, part c had exempted Mexico and other Western Hemisphere nations from the restrictive 1924 quota. Tamping down the flow of temporary Mexican labor by removing the first exemption would help stem the tide of Mexican immigration, restrictionists believed, and would serve as an essential first step in removing the second exemption

Advantages, Disadvantages, Risks, and Rewards

and restricting Mexican immigration outright.[7] To realize the success of this strategy, restrictionists needed to ensure that Mexican migrants were not benefitting from any other exemptions to U.S. immigration law and that American consular officials vigorously enforced U.S. immigration laws.

Mexico's reaction to the Harris bill was swift. Responses varied from an understanding that a quota was justified in terms of national sovereignty, to resentment that the United States sought to extend the restrictive quota to Mexico alone. Most Mexicans believed immigration was detrimental to national development; however, they also resented the racism that underlined the American debate to extend the quota to Mexico. Mexican observers chafed at the American effort to restrict a labor supply that had contributed so much to the development of the United States and believed effective enforcement of the quota was impossible. "What would the Western railroads of the [United States] have done," Mexicans asked, "without the influx of Mexican labor which proved so essential to the development in recent years?" Mexicans also questioned, "what would many Western and Southwestern industries do, as well as the Texas cotton growers, without the Mexican assistance, which so often has carried them through a temporary demand for labor?"[8] Mexicans believed no law could resolve the immigration problem. A quota would simply deprive American industry of labor, burden Mexico with an oversupply of labor (and endanger the stability of Mexico itself), and poison U.S.-Mexican relations and U.S. standing with the rest of Latin America.

Excelsior, weeks before the Senate Committee on Immigration and Naturalization passed the Harris bill onto the full Senate, identified the "paradox" of Mexican immigration for both the United States and Mexico. "On the one hand," an editorialist wrote, "there is at work [in the United States an] ethical puritanism . . . which spurns in horror any contamination with races that are without the aristocracy of color and extraction." On the other hand the United States was "belabored by the contrary convenience which would induce [it] to entice the Mexican laborer because there is no other who could perform the extreme labor yielded by our countrymen." If immigration were unpleasant for the United States, the writer stated, it was doubly problematic for Mexico. Many Mexicans were unable to find work unless they migrated, and Mexico must tolerate this loss of labor since it relieved its labor glut. In this sense immigration was a "double-edge sword," that inflicted "deeper and more irreparable" wounds upon Mexico (the "weakened organism") than upon the United States (the "harsh mass of money and pride").[9] Some Mexican observers of immigration believed that a quota would help the nation accomplish its socioeconomic goals for development by keeping more laborers in Mexico. At the same time, many feared that Mexico was not able to provide a "corresponding compensation" to migrants who were accustomed to work in the United States. The denial of entry into the United States and the reduced pay for work in Mexico would "mean the misery of many thousands of Mexican workmen" if the Harris bill became law.[10]

Two Mexican government officials' responses to the Harris bill typified Mexico's opposition to the quota. An official of the Interior Ministry (under which the Department of Immigration oversaw matters related to immigration), "Señor" Salinas, stated that the United States was unjustified in any attempt to extend the quota to Mexico. He criticized American accusations that Mexico had not taken enough "drastic steps" to curb Mexican immigration to the United States. According to Salinas a quota was bad for Mexico because immigration relieved Mexican unemployment, because 90 percent of migrants returned south at the end of seasonal work, and because work in the United States benefited laborers in skills and wealth. In this sense a quota would be a disproportionate response to the temporary and transitory problem of Mexican immigration. A quota would undermine the Mexican economy and increase Mexicans' desire to migrate to the United States. Also, restrictive laws against Mexican immigration would make migrants more susceptible to exploitation.[11]

A month after the Senate Committee on Immigration and Naturalization approved the Harris bill, José Davila, Mexican immigration inspector at Tijuana, gave an address on the immigration problem before the Friends of Mexico conference in Los Angeles, California. First, he stated that restrictionists like John Box unnecessarily incited Americans about the immigration problem by exaggerating the number of Mexicans residing in the United States. Second, Davila argued that regardless of the perception of that figure, which Davila put at one million, it should be recognized that Mexican labor was essential to American industry, especially in the wake of quota restrictions on European immigration. Mexican migrants did the work that other laborers would not or could not perform. The white American worker, Davila argued, was skilled and considered stoop labor beneath him; the American Negro was "utterly unadaptable" to any other climate besides the American South; and urban blacks were "undoubtedly lazy." The Asian immigrant, while tenacious, hardworking, and honest like the Mexican migrant, "was truly an ethnic danger" to the United States and was barred through the "exercise of a right and just nationalism." Therefore, Davila asserted, Mexican migrants were the only reliable foreign labor force left to sustain the continued prosperity of American industry.[12]

In response to accusations that Mexicans were socially unfit—too diseased, slovenly, lazy, and criminal—to enter the United States, Davila argued that Mexican migrants should be paid more. If Mexicans were well compensated, they would not have to rely on public charities and services, would likely save more of their earnings, and would be able to provide for their own needs. For those Americans uncomfortable with the temporary presence of indigent, roving Mexicans in U.S. society, Davila suggested that U.S. employers do more to place migrants in industries that required their labor throughout the year. Continuous employment would benefit the U.S. economy and tamp down the likelihood of migrants becoming public charges after the completion of seasonal work.[13] Finally, Davila argued that the United States was not justified in considering a quota on Mexican migrants when Mexico kept its border open for laborers to migrate northward. Mexico, Davila stated, did not welcome the closing of the safety valve that had, in times of past national troubles, given shelter, protection, and work to many Mexicans. "If a sort of Chinese Wall is to be erected between Mexico and the United States," Davila argued, "it will no doubt be a blow and do harm to Mexico, but it will act as a 'boomerang,' doing more harm to the United States" by cutting off the essential supply of Mexican labor that had built prosperous industries throughout that country.[14]

Like David Reed, Mexicans recognized the impossibility of a quota stopping Mexican immigration completely. Whereas American restrictionists believed a quota was an essential step toward the effective and total regulation of Mexico's immigration, Mexicans thought such a law would expose their migrants to greater exploitation and would represent a national offense to Mexico. Similar to Labor Secretary James Davis's denunciation of unpatriotic employers, Mexican observers cited American business that relied on Mexico's migrant workers as the real transgressors in the immigration dilemma. Adding more restrictive measures to U.S. immigration law would not be enough to deter laborers attracted by the insatiable demand of American industry for workers. While a political division existed between states like Arizona and Sonora, these areas were inextricably linked economically. And denigrating Mexican laborers as undesirable only compounded the problems. John Box and other American restrictionists, Genaro Estrada reported in December 1928, exaggerated the social risk that Mexican migrants represented to the United States. Claims that Mexican migrants eroded the American labor market and displaced small farmers in favor of large agricultural corporations, and that the Mexican population in the United States had grown disproportionately and many migrants were unemployed and burdened public resources, Estrada wrote, had made Mexicans victims of harassment, humiliation, insults, and racial prejudice.[15] Arguments of racial inferiority justified the exploitation of Mexican laborers; adding an un-enforceable quota would expose migrants to further abuse as illegal immigrants.[16]

Mexican leaders searched for solutions to the immigration problem in response to the American debate on the quota and the Harris bill in particular. The short-term goal was to regulate immigration, by educating and protecting their migrants, without shutting off the safety valve of immigration. The long-term goal was to develop internal industries that would end Mexico's chronic underemployment and resolve the problem of Mexican immigration to the United States.

According to the Mexican undersecretary of interior, the Mexican government was envisioning a number of measures to regulate immigration:

1. Coordinating local and federal authorities to inform migrants on U.S. immigration law and requirements.
2. Detaining migrants who do not meet legal requirements to enter the United States or leave Mexico.
3. Refusing railway tickets to Mexicans going to border towns who did not have a visa to emigrate from their local emigration office.
4. Providing lodging, transportation, and banks in border towns for migrants.
5. Securing agreements between the United States and Mexico over the fulfillment of Mexican labor contracts and preventing exploitation of Mexican workers who do not have contracts. Also, establishing a regime that ensures "the most economical, comfortable, and legal" return of Mexicans to Mexico.
6. Diversifying the industries in which Mexicans abroad work, and coordinating where Mexicans can work in other industries and how those migrants—upon returning to Mexico—can apply their skills to the national economy.[17]

Additional measures to regulate immigration and to protect migrants abroad included maintaining lists of U.S. firms that fulfilled their contracts with Mexican laborers, offering reduced rates on railway tickets for those migrants who wished to return to Mexico, and having the Banco de México lead all money exchange systems in border towns.[18]

The regulation of immigration was always considered a stopgap measure until the Mexican economy developed to the level that afforded the great majority of Mexicans work without having to migrate to the United States. None of the measures proposed to control immigration meant to stop it outright. Most Mexican observers believed that the only solution to the immigration problem was structural. Laborers, it was predicted, would no longer migrate when the Mexican economy was sufficiently developed to provide work to most citizens, primarily in irrigation projects to turn fallow pastures into agricultural land. In the meantime a sudden stoppage was impossible and inadvisable. The Mexican government believed an abrupt halt of immigration would aggravate Mexico's underemployment problem and potentially destabilize the nation. Mexican officials hoped immigration regulation would buy time for Mexico's economy to develop, and if such regulatory measures defused U.S. debates over a quota, all the better. In this regard Mexicans were more willing than Americans to let the long-term socioeconomic trends—the same trends that created a demand for immigration in the first place—develop naturally and gradually. Legal intervention with a quota would only bring harm to both the United States and Mexico by depriving the former of labor and overburdening the latter with labor. In the short term, then, the Mexican government proposed measures that would protect its citizens abroad and inform prospective migrants of U.S. immigration laws so they would be less vulnerable to abuse across the border.

Resigning itself to the fact that immigration would happen, however, was not the same as abandoning migrants to their fates in a foreign country. A particular goal behind efforts to inform Mexicans of U.S. immigration law was to reduce illegal immigration. Mexicans who did not report their departure to Mexican immigration officials were unaccounted for and far more susceptible to abuse than migrants who entered the United States legally and, at least in theory, could appeal to the Mexican government for protection. Also, it was believed that illegal immigration had a direct correlation to U.S. immigration law. The more Mexican migrants who entered the United States illegally, the more likely Washington would respond by passing legislation to restrict Mexican immigration.[19]

The Mexican Department of Migration was founded in 1926. It tried to curb illegal immigration through several methods that included suasion, coercion, and interdiction. First, the department promoted radio notices, newspaper articles, and flyers that encouraged potential migrants to stay home unless they were prepared to comply with all the requirements for legal entry into the United States, which included entrance fees, literacy exams, and health inspections. Second, the department planted officers at checkpoints throughout the Mexican north to verify that Mexicans planning to cross into the United States could fulfill U.S. guidelines for legal entry into the United States. At train stations in northern cities such as Matamoros, Nuevo Laredo, Torreon, Saltillo, and Monterrey, officers of the Mexican Department of Migration took migrants off trains to, as historian Kelly Lytle Hernández argues, enforce the provisions of U.S. immigration law. Oftentimes these migration officers would confiscate potential migrants' passports as a way to indirectly control illegal immigration to the United States. Such a method, while it was coercive and unconstitutional (the 1917 Constitution protected citizens' rights to travel outside the national territory), would effectively discourage illegal immigration because without a passport, a Mexican national could not easily prove their right to freely return to Mexico. Finally, the Migration Law of 1926 tried to diminish illegal immigration by coming down hard on people smugglers, or *coyotes*. The law levied a fine of one hundred to one thousand pesos on persons found guilty of attempting to take migrants from Mexico without official inspection and sanction. Also, the law stipulated one- to two-year prison sentences as well as additional fines for smugglers who assisted laborers in crossing the border illegally.[20]

As Hernández argues, "the attempt to enter the United States illegally began by evading the officers of the Mexican Department of Migration." But the bark proved worse than the bite. Mexican efforts to patrol and regulate the border were sporadic and hampered by a paucity of personnel. Tens of thousands of Mexicans were able to illegally cross into the United States, despite their government's efforts to stop them.[21]

In December 1928, the same month that the Senate Committee on Immigration and Naturalization passed the Harris bill, the Mexican Ministry of Foreign Relations (SRE) issued a report entitled "The Migration and Protection of Mexicans Abroad." The document detailed several aspects of the immigration problem: the difficulty of accurately quantifying the rate of Mexican immigration to the United States, past efforts to curb Mexican immigration northward, instances of migrant abuse in the United States, and Mexican consular efforts to protect Mexico's citizens in the United States. Composed by the head of the Migration Service Department in the Interior Ministry, Andrés Landa y Piña, the report urged Mexicans not to emigrate and to contribute to the economic development of Mexico.[22] One of the report's most important sections discussed reasons why many Mexicans preferred to migrate illegally to the United States.

According to the SRE report, there were several reasons why Mexicans migrated illegally to the United States. First, Mexicans found it difficult to meet the requirements of U.S. immigration law. Valid documentation in the form of birth certificates or marriage certificates was hard to produce, and many Mexicans were illiterate. Second, legal entry into the United States was expensive. A Mexican seeking to cross the border had to pay $10, or the equivalent in Mexican gold, to get permission from the local consul to immigrate. Then, an $8 head tax was required in U.S. dollars immediately upon crossing the border. Both fees were applied to each person entering the United States, regardless of age. Coupled with the expense of the trip to Mexico's northern border towns from the interior, the cost of legal immigration was prohibitive for many Mexicans. Third, deprivations suffered by many rural Mexicans during the revolution of the 1910s and rebellions during the 1920s made life in the countryside almost impossible. Fourth, the steady and increased demand for Mexican labor in the United States encouraged many poor, illiterate

Mexicans to migrate illegally. Finally, the contradiction between Mexico's constitutional requirement that Mexicans possess a labor contract before migrating (article 123 of Mexico's 1917 Constitution, and article 72 of the Mexican Immigration Law) and U.S. immigration law that disallowed foreign contracted labor from entering the United States ensured that Mexicans were breaking at least one country's law when they migrated northward for work. *Enganchadores* helped many Mexicans who shirked these contract laws by guiding them to employers who flouted the legal requirements of U.S. and Mexican immigration law.[23]

Mexican officials discouraged illegal immigration in order to relieve its burden on the Mexican treasury. If illegal immigration resembled a broken door for the United States, then illegal immigration resembled a bleeding wound for Mexico, both in terms of the loss of laborers and the cost of funding the repatriation of indigent Mexican migrants from the United States. In his introduction to the report on "The Migration and the Protection of Mexicans Abroad," Genaro Estrada argued that illegal immigration was "prejudicial" to both Mexico and Mexican laborers. Despite the government's efforts to prevent illegal immigration and inform migrants of the troubles they would face in the United States, Mexicans continued to migrate illegally, making themselves vulnerable to disadvantageous work contracts and exploitation, arrest, and labor abuse. There were many cases, according to the report, of labor contracts either being extended or being revised to require new work duties of the migrants, distinct from the labor obligations expressed in previous contracts.[24] Also, Mexican consuls frequently had to press American employers to provide final payments to migrants upon the completion of contracts.[25] Migrants were especially vulnerable to abuse at the end of seasonal work: many did not have the means to return to Mexico and were susceptible to arrest and to deportation for breaking U.S. immigration law. According to Hernández, when Mexican immigrants crossed into the United States without authorization, they entered not as laborers with a set of enforceable protections but as fugitives targeted and chased by the U.S. Border Patrol.[26]

The consequence of this "imprudent migration" that violated the immigration laws of both countries, Estrada wrote, was that the Mexican government had to provide food, transportation, and various other expenses for "many thousands" of its citizens in the United States.[27] Despite the imprudence of illegal immigration, Estrada argued, no other nation but Mexico went to such great lengths to protect its citizens abroad.[28]

Several motives prompted Mexico City's desire to prevent illegal immigration without stopping Mexican immigration entirely. Immigration regulation was an effort by the Mexican government to gain domestic credibility by showing that it attempted to protect its citizens from abuses in the United States without violating migrants' rights to seek work abroad. Also, immigration regulation was meant to foster the work and return of migrants so the national economy could benefit from the skills and training they acquired in the United States. Notably, immigration regulation was meant to continue the flow of legal migrants to the United States to relieve the Mexican economy of its oversupply of labor. Finally, the desire to curtail illegal immigration was rooted in the hope of forestalling a U.S. quota on Mexican immigration.

During the early months of 1929, the Mexican government solicited regional and state-level reports analyzing immigration. Mexican officials wanted to understand why Mexicans migrated, from where they migrated and why, and how regions or states of high immigration were affected by the departure of workers. This information was meant to resolve the "national problem" of immigration. To promote successful internal economic development, the Mexican government deemed it essential that immigration "be reduced to such reasonable limits that the population and economic and social situation of the country not be impaired."[29]

Years before the Mexican government officially proposed studies of immigration, Manuel Gamio conducted extensive research into why Mexicans migrated, from where they migrated, where they resided in the United States, the type of work they did there, the social lives of migrants north of the border, and ultimately

Advantages, Disadvantages, Risks, and Rewards

why the great majority of migrants returned to Mexico. A well-respected anthropologist and sociologist and former undersecretary of education within the Calles government, Gamio produced the most-authoritative study of Mexican immigration during the 1920s. His research influenced Mexican migration policy and he advised state-sponsored repatriation efforts in the 1930s.[30]

Gamio is readily acknowledged as a pathbreaking Mexican anthropologist of his time. Trained at Columbia (MA: 1911; PhD: 1921) under the guidance of Franz Boas, Gamio was, by the 1920s, considered an important figure in American continental archaeology and anthropology. President Plutarco Elías Calles appointed Gamio to the post of undersecretary of education in December 1924. Not long after he accepted the post, Gamio publicly denounced the ministerial corruption tolerated by his immediate superior, Secretary of Education José M. Puig Casauranc. Calles sided with Puig Casauranc and forced Gamio from the government in June 1925. Soon thereafter Gamio left Mexico for the United States. His stellar academic reputation helped Gamio land a contract with the Social Science Research Council (SSRC) in late 1925 to direct a study of Mexican immigration to the United States. The SSRC funded Gamio's research for the next four years.[31]

Gamio believed Mexico's history, economy, and social relations had left Mexicans in a wretched condition. "As an applied anthropologist," historian Arthur Schmidt states, "Gamio regarded scientific research as the essential prerequisite to change the conditions that trapped [Mexicans] in their 'backwardness' and forced migrants to leave their homeland in search of earnings in the United States."[32] Significantly, Gamio challenged prevalent contemporary thinking, which focused on the race of Mexicans. Gamio regarded racial discrimination as an insult that solidified the social castigation migrants faced in the United States. He "stood firm" against a nationwide fear that Mexican migrants were invading the United States and represented a debasement of the racial stock of American society.[33] "There is," Gamio argued, "no scientific basis for an innate inferiority of the Mexican, nothing beyond the dark pigmentation of the Mexican to account for the racial prejudice against him."[34] This empirical approach to the immigration problem was consistent with the methods of his advisor at Columbia, Franz Boas. Boas was a well-known critic of the racist anthropological theories prominent at the time. Instead Boas argued for a form of pluralism in which cultural influences, rather than genetics, mainly determined human behavior.[35]

Days before the Senate Committee on Immigration and Naturalization passed the Harris bill, Gamio, in an editorial for *El Universal*, warned that a quota would damage the political stability of Mexico. According to Gamio the "brusque stopping" of Mexican immigration northward would bring such harm to Mexico that it would negate any advantage either nation would derive from a quota. While other Mexican observers of immigration believed that the sudden halt to immigration could jeopardize national development by burdening Mexico with an oversupply of labor, Gamio took this argument a step further by contending that the restriction of Mexican immigration threatened the very stability of the Mexican state. Mexico, Gamio stated, had no clear picture of how many citizens were unemployed in the nation. While some nations (e.g., England and Germany), had the capacity to provide temporary unemployment insurance to workers, Mexico had no such ability. Consequently unemployed Mexicans who could not rely on a social safety net had to resign themselves to starve, to emigrate, or to rebel against the state. Such socioeconomic problems were largely averted while the safety valve of immigration was open to Mexicans. If that safety valve were closed abruptly, Gamio predicted, 100,000 or more *repatriados*, or Mexican immigrants returning to Mexico from the United States, would swell the ranks of Mexico's unemployed, and they would be forced to take direct action to satisfy their most basic needs. Gamio feared a "revolution of starvation" would immediately follow the passage of a quota law by the U.S. Congress.[36]

Gamio's assertion that American restriction of Mexican immigration endangered Mexico's political stability was not made in a void, as Mexico's internal affairs were problematic during most of the 1920s. Adolfo de la Huerta, who had been Mexico's interim president during 1920, staged a coup attempt against Álvaro Obregón's government between late 1923 and early 1924. The Cristero Rebellion, from 1926 to 1929, did not seek national power per se, yet it did bog down federal forces and revealed the limits of the government's power. Finally, the Escobar Rebellion of March 1929 involved over a fourth of the Mexican army and seized Chihuahua, Durango, Sonora, and Veracruz before it was put down by the Calles government with military equipment provided by the United States.[37]

Gamio agreed with other Mexicans who argued that the immigration problem was rooted in economics.[38] What Gamio articulated better than other observers of Mexican immigration, was that the solution to the problem—just like the phenomenon of immigration itself—necessitated a transnational, bilateral, and "transcendental" response from both the United States and Mexico. For Gamio the United States–Mexico border was not just an international division but rather a great convergence zone between the two distinct peoples of the Western Hemisphere: the Anglo-Saxon and the Latin American peoples. Along the contact zones of Arizona, California, New Mexico, and Texas, it was necessary to study the interracial, cultural, economic, and psychological contacts developing within this "gigantic sociological laboratory" for the purposes of establishing more "human[e], comprehensive and mutually beneficial" political relations between the United States and Mexico.[39]

Gamio's 1926 study of immigration suggested that there was a contradiction between how Americans felt threatened by Mexican immigration and the fact that American business depended on Mexican labor.[40] For their part Mexicans only migrated out of economic necessity; if it were not for the shortage of work, laborers would not leave Mexico. "Beyond a doubt," Gamio argued, Mexican immigration would seriously diminish when Mexico developed its own industrial and agricultural enterprises that supplied work to all its citizens.[41] The economic solution was clear: Mexico must develop to an extent where Mexicans would find it unnecessary to migrate for work, and Americans must reconcile their social abhorrence for Mexicans with the economic need for Mexican laborers.

By diagnosing the socioeconomic causes of immigration in Mexico, Gamio demonstrated that racial justifications for immigration restriction were fallacious. Instead he sought to show how solutions to immigration had to take into consideration the social, demographic, economic, and political factors that caused immigration. By explaining the reasons why immigration happened and from where it originated, Gamio hoped to repudiate the American justification for a quota based on the specious racial arguments that Mexicans were inferior. Analyzing the work habits and productivity of Mexican migrants compared to those of other immigrant groups, Gamio declared that there was no Mexican inferiority that legitimized racial prejudice against them. In this sense Gamio refuted eugenicists who asserted that science explained a racial hierarchy of peoples. Instead Gamio showed that racial prejudice was a cultural phenomenon. Any disadvantages Mexicans suffered from vis-à-vis Americans, such as poverty, illiteracy, slovenliness, were rooted in the distinct economic, social, and political environments experienced both in Mexico and the United States.[42]

Gamio's "Preliminary Report" explained why most of Mexico's migrants fled from the west-central states of Guanajuato, Jalisco, and Michoacán. In this predominantly agrarian region, land had always been owned by a small number of landowners. Low rates of land ownership across the region had created a large peon class. This peon class of laborers was underemployed in their home states and so were forced to migrate for work. The west-central plateau was a highly fertile region with an overabundance of laborers. Aguascalientes, Durango, San Luis Potosí, and Zacatecas also witnessed this paradox and consequently had become emigrant-sending states within Mexico. By contrast relatively few Mexicans from Mexico's northern states migrated northward because that region's underemployment problem was less acute and the working population was more transitory than in the west-central plateau. The Mexican north was often a temporary stop for migrants who would eventually enter the United States to seek work.[43]

Gamio's research revealed the structural problems that underlay immigration. A quota to restrict immigration, he argued, would only exacerbate Mexico's economic underdevelopment and would likely undermine the political stability of Mexico itself. Also, Gamio believed the quota would hurt the U.S. economy and worsen many of the social risks American restrictionists hoped to obviate by barring Mexican immigration.

Gamio argued that there would be several negative consequences to the extension of the quota to Mexico. First, the present permanent immigrant population in the United States would remain indefinitely for fear of not being able to reenter the United States at a later time. Second, while the transitory migrant would not—at least theoretically—be able to enter the United States, thereby helping to resolve the Mexican immigration problem for Americans, the oversupply of labor (or the shutting off of the safety valve) could cause social disorder and conflict in Mexico as many Mexicans— many of whom would migrate for work and become accustomed to the better working and living conditions in the United States— would be out of work and would drag down Mexico's economic progress.[44] Third, American industries, mainly in agriculture, that depended on Mexican labor would suffer in direct proportion to how much Mexico's immigration was restricted. And finally, the quota would not stop illegal immigration and would likely abet it unless the United States were willing to massively expand its border patrol. The quota, then, was bad for both the United States and Mexico. While the problem of immigration may have been economic in origin, it required a solution that was multidimensional in nature: social, cultural, and political.[45]

Two sociological studies of Mexican immigration to the United States conducted by American academics during the mid-1920s contrast sharply with Gamio's research and confirm his belief that racism was an aspect of U.S. society that hampered efforts to develop lasting solutions to the immigration problem. The first study was a survey of race relations along the Pacific Coast between 1924 and 1925. In the fall of 1923, as Congress debated a more-restrictive immigration quota, the Institute of Social and Religious Research (1921–1934) approved a proposal for the *Survey of Race Relations*. While the survey was primarily concerned with Asian immigration, it gave attention to Mexican immigration and serves as an interesting comparison to how Gamio viewed the immigration problem and the racist tension that fed into it.[46]

One of the survey's main objectives was to understand the origin of racial conflict. Social scientists were to serve as lay missionaries in a crusade against racial prejudice. Survey directors stressed the importance of scientific and academic leadership in the project, to forestall any political manipulation, and hoped their objective findings would help inform debates about immigration policies and restriction.[47] In an article describing the findings of the survey, Eliot G. Mears, the initial research director of the project and a professor at Stanford University, argued that exclusion laws toward Asian immigration had "settled practically nothing" regarding the long-term implications of immigration. No matter how justifiable restrictive legislation may have been, Mears stated, "few persons anywhere are worldly wise on the subject of human personal relations, especially when different cultures meet." Mears lauded the "strictly scientific approach" that had been adopted by survey researchers to study issues of race and immigration along the West Coast. "Educated persons," Mears concluded, "experience a sense of relief when they learn of any endeavors, entirely divorced from legislative programs or special formulas, which center about the greatness of fact."[48]

Almost immediately the survey encountered a host of problems: financial shortages, lack of support, and even outright hostility along the West Coast. Also, the survey sought to analyze objectively a topic rife with subjective meaning, during a time when racial ascription was a pressing issue of debate between American lawmakers. The survey was conducted during 1924, as Congress passed landmark legislation on immigration. And finally, the project encountered internal division over the survey's objective. Institute directors were disappointed when the "Tentative Findings" of researchers presented in March 1925 did not speak directly to the effects of the exclusion law on themes of immigration and race relations.[49] Interestingly it was the organization's internal differences over methods and objectives that curtailed the survey's effectiveness. First, the institute and its researchers in the field disagreed on the uses of the findings. Researchers sought to record objectively the nature of race relations along the West Coast, while the institute wanted the survey findings to suggest how restrictive legislation affected race relations between immigrant and native groups. Second, the deep roots of anti-immigrant sentiment along the West Coast limited public enthusiasm for, participation in, and especially material support for the survey. Consequently the survey findings only affirmed the racism of American society that underlined the immigration restriction debates regarding Japan and later Mexico without suggesting constructive ways in which xenophobia could be balanced with bilateral regulation of immigration, much less the harmonizing of race relations.

Nevertheless the survey shows how immigration issues, and the racial problems they fostered, held consequences for international relations. In the context of the debate over Japanese exclusion, American social scientists attempted to gather empirical evidence on how race relations affected the nation and how problems related to them could be resolved through the understanding of that data. The institute hoped to use the scientific data of the survey to reduce racial tensions in the United States between natives and immigrants. The social practices, cultural influences, and economic conditions of the time, historian Eckard Toy argues, made achieving such objectives nearly impossible. Yet despite its failure in its objectives, Toy contends, the survey raised important questions of how international relations, racial conflict, and immigration issues converged.[50] In this sense the survey directors' understanding of immigration was not very different from Gamio's. They seemed to understand that immigration was a multidimensional phenomenon. Where they diverged from Gamio was the inherent belief that problems related to race relations, to which immigration contributed, could be resolved internally through the use of empirical evidence.

The survey produced dozens of field studies and compiled 640 life histories and nearly 6,000 pages of related documents about racial assimilation and social attitudes. Most important, the survey provided a window into American attitudes toward Mexican immigration in the years immediately before Congress attempted to place a restrictive quota on Mexico. The life histories were brief biographical and autobiographical sketches or oral histories, and the data confirmed the survey directors' assumptions about the influence of cultural and racial factors on social conflict.[51]

Survey researchers were asked to focus on the international and interracial factors of the "Mexican situation" in the Southwest. Their criteria for analysis included the following points:

1. How does Mexican immigration affect relations between the governments of Mexico and the United States?
    a. The temporary immigration of seasonal labor?
    b. Does this temporary immigration result in a large permanent reduction of Mexico's domestic labor supply, or does it simply provide employment for the surplus labor element of Mexico?
2. What is the attitude of the Mexican immigrant towards Americans, American ideals, and the United States government?
    a. How far is the immigrant influenced by his new contacts?
    b. Does he approach them in a receptive or an antagonistic spirit?
    c. Do his experiences encourage a desire to become an American citizen, or do they prejudice him against American citizenship?
3. What is the influence of Mexicans in the United States?
    a. Of the educated class?
    b. Laborers who return to Mexico after a considerable stay in the United States?
    c. Laborers who remain permanently in the United States?
4. Data covering cases of American prejudice against Mexicans [as they occurred within various public institutions: churches, schools, etc.].

5. Compare prejudice upon the part of Americans against Mexicans with that against the Japanese, Chinese, Negro and other alien races.
6. What are the relations between non-Anglo-Saxon groups on the Pacific Coast, such as Japanese, Chinese, Negro, etc., with the Mexicans?
7. Collect data as far as possible and give the point of view of the following four groups upon the Mexican problem in California.
    a. The employer.
    b. Labor unions.
    c. The Mexican consul or government official.
    d. The Mexican transient laborer himself.[52]

Researchers reported on various aspects of Mexican immigration: the seasonal distribution of labor among the southwestern states, the agricultural industries in which Mexicans found work, annual immigration figures from 1922 to 1924, the docility of Mexican labor and the low wages for which they worked, and their disproportionate draw on social services.[53] One researcher provided an account of "José" and his immigration story to the United States. Purportedly based on true history, José's story, the researcher believed, represented the immigration experience faced by thousands of Mexicans. First, José went to the American consulate in Ciudad Juarez, where he had to answer a range of questions ("am I crazy? am I sick? am I anarchist? am I bolsheviki?"). After responding "no" to all questions and paying the $10 fee, José crossed the bridge into the United States and was received by U.S. immigration officials, who led him to the disinfecting plant ("It did me no good to tell them that I had taken a bath a few minutes before in Juarez"). After his person and clothes were disinfected, José was vaccinated and inspected by a doctor. José then paid the $8 head tax. Finally, after answering another round of questions ("what is my name? how many years have I? am I married? where I go?"), José was allowed to leave the immigration station.

Next José was lined up and was told "many pretty stories" by labor agents about work opportunities. While other migrants chose to go to California, Arizona, and Colorado, José went to Pennsylvania. During the long train ride there, José was given only crackers and sardines to eat ("Since that time I do not like even the odor of sardines"). José was not allowed to look out the windows of the railcar, in case he planned to escape; and every morning and night he and his fellow migrants were counted "as if we were prisoners." "And I asked myself: 'Is this the land of Liberty?' "

After four days of travel by rail, José arrived in Pennsylvania and was almost immediately put to work on the railroad track. José did not like Pennsylvania ("I felt a cold more icy than that of El Paso"). Everybody gave him curious looks and was afraid to come close. After three months in Pennsylvania, José joined his brother to work in Indiana Harbor, near Chicago. The cold weather there was no better, and José fell ill. Soon thereafter José and his brother returned to El Paso, "where we passed the winter with much hardship."

The following spring José went to pick sugar beets in Colorado and then to California and Arizona to pick cotton. "In your country," José concluded, "I have traveled much and worked much too. It is a good place to make money, sometimes; but not so good to make friends.... After many years, I feel still that my real home is in Mexico, not here. Perhaps later I feel different, but *quien sabe*."[54]

The same researcher who interviewed José argued what he or she believed were the "salient factors" of the Mexican problem. The researcher described southwestern industry's "absolute economic dependence" on Mexican labor, the difficulty of restricting Mexican immigration along the long international border, southwestern businesses' complicity in Mexican migrants' shirking the fees required to enter the United States, the difficulty of assimilating Mexicans to U.S. society, and the Mexican government's "friendly attitude" toward the restriction of its immigration.[55]

Survey researchers reflected how Americans viewed the problems of Mexican immigration as inherently racial. Interviews collected by the survey confirmed many of the viewpoints that Americans had of Mexicans: that they were lazy, docile, and prone to drink, vice, and crime; that they were profligate, diseased, and intellectually infantile. According to historian Clare Sheridan, both quota advocates and opponents used the "common wisdom" of Mexicans' racial inferiority to their advantage. Employers of Mexican labor, who were not inclined to see it curtailed by a quota, argued that Mexicans were childlike and simpleminded; they lived in the present and did not plan for the future. In this regard Mexicans posed no danger to U.S. society. Conversely restrictionists argued that it was Mexicans' indigence that underscored their danger to the American policy. Their status as a "peon caste" would undermine the U.S. labor market and erode the social, political, and economic underpinnings of American nationality.[56]

The views of Dr. Edgar L. Hewitt, an esteemed American archaeologist of the time, confirmed this racist view of the Mexican and contrasted sharply with Gamio's understanding of Mexico's immigration problem. While Hewitt's discussion was concerned primarily with the Indian population of Mexico, the survey researcher believed the data were applicable to the mestizo of Mexico, suggesting a common American insinuation that "Indian" was synonymous with "Mexican." Other derisive terms used to describe Mexicans, and which were often employed during congressional debates of the 1920s regarding Mexico's immigration, were "peon" and "imported pauper labor."

Edgar Hewitt divided his discussion of Mexican social and cultural traits into six categories: "mentality," "social life," "economic life," "industrial life," "esthetic sense," and "moral sense." First, the Mexican was "naturally simple, superstitious and submissive." Hewitt attributed these traits to centuries of coercion under the Catholic Church. Such coercion also helped explain the docility of the Mexican, Hewitt believed. Second, the Mexican was naturally gregarious and tended to align himself into larger groups or communities. Mexicans did not take well to isolation, Hewitt argued. In other words Mexicans were not the stuff of the Protestant work ethic, for the Mexican was not naturally sober or individualistic. Third, the Mexican had no "ingrained sense" of thrift, had no desire to save for the future, and only focused on satisfying his immediate needs. Fourth, the Mexican worked slowly—not out of indolence, Hewitt argued—but out of a certain "innate deliberateness and dignity." Temperamentally, Hewitt added, the Mexican was averse to rapid action. Fifth, the Mexican had a highly developed esthetic sense while materially the Mexican was underdeveloped. Hewitt pointed to pottery as an example. While pottery making had attained a high level of sophistication, he argued, all the pieces and utensils of pottery were made by hand without the use of a pottery wheel. Attempts to replace this esthetic culture with a material one had resulted in inefficiency, Hewitt argued. Last, the Mexican's moral sense was low. This was not due to some innate depravity, but rather "to the sordid conditions to which [the Mexican] has been subjected by his conquerors." Centuries of virtual slavery under the Spanish had eroded the moral sense of the Mexican. Nonetheless, Hewitt concluded, a Mexican's moral sense could be salvaged if he were handled with patience and educated properly.[57]

While Hewitt, like Gamio, believed environment explained much about the Mexican's natural character, unlike Gamio, Hewitt described sociocultural traits of the Mexican that attempted to illustrate the distinct racial difference between Mexicans and Americans. Hewitt did not agree with other critics who argued that Mexicans were lazy, yet he confirmed other accusations that Mexicans were immoral, unindustrious, unsophisticated, and intellectually stunted. By objectively recording Americans' view of Mexicans, the *Survey of Race Relations* only confirmed the subjective racism Americans held toward Mexicans.

Robert F. Foerster, a professor of economics at Princeton University and a promoter of eugenics, compiled another notable sociological study of Mexican immigration in the mid-1920s. Sponsored by the U.S. Department of Labor and published in 1925, *The Racial Problems Involved in Immigration from Latin America and the West Indies to the United States* employed race to determine the desirability of Latin American immigration.[58] Foerster sought to analyze the racial composition of the Latin American states in order to determine whether the infusion of those races into U.S. society via immigration was beneficial or detrimental. The survey addressed all Latin American nations but particularly Mexico. Like Edgar Hewitt, Foerster treated "Indian" and "Mexican" as synonymous terms when he discussed the racial composition of Mexico. The "basic race" of Mexico, Foerster claimed, was either Indian or mestizo. No more than 10 percent of Mexico was composed of white persons, with the great majority of Mexicans deriving from either "pure Indian blood or of mixed Indian blood." Consequently Foerster argued that Mexico was an Indian nation since most Mexicans had at least some degree of Indian blood coursing through their veins.[59]

Foerster then analyzed the likelihood that an Indian race could thrive if it adopted the social, economic, and political trappings of the "white man's civilization" first introduced to the Mexican people by the Spanish. Despite the examples of such notable figures as Benito Juárez and Porfirio Díaz, who were of mestizo origin, the future did not look bright. The active, aggressive, and inventive traits that characterized native peoples in Mexico up to the time of Cortés had been eroded by centuries of Spanish colonization. The Indian population of Mexico had been reduced to indolence and ignorance.

> In industry the Indians occupy the lowest places. They are farm hands, unskilled laborers, mule drivers, factory hands, workers in the mines, sometimes servants. They seem to be men of few wants, apathetic, without ambition, not concerned with the future. Rarely do they own land. They are improvident and prefer to work intermittently, getting into debt with their employers, who thereby are enabled to hold them to their estates. Sometimes a bonus is offered them for a month's continuous employment. In many cases only if there is a surplus of laborers on hand can industrial operations be maintained continuously. They are much given to drinking pulque, an intoxicating liquor.[60]

These Indian characteristics carried over to the mestizo class of Mexican society, Foerster argued. "The mestizos resemble the pure

Indian in many respects. Most are of the peon or labor class. . . . They, too, are given to drinking pulque. Their lives are much determined by custom." Foerster pointed to high rates of national illiteracy to demonstrate Mexican ignorance. These sociological traits boded ill for Mexico's political future. Despite the Mexican Revolution and its democratic struggle against autocratic government, "no effective democracy resting on universal suffrage can come quickly in a country whose population is still so retrograde as the Mexican in the essential prerequisites of democracy."[61]

The last part of Foerster's study considered what the racial history of Latin American nations implied about the desirability of its peoples' immigration to the United States. Foerster assumed Latin American immigration to the United States would increase as American prosperity continued and European immigration was curtailed by the restrictive laws of the 1924 act.[62] From this perspective Foerster argued that it was dangerous to rely on the economic gain through the steady supply of cheap immigrant labor to justify the unregulated continuation of Latin American immigration. "No man is a worker alone," Foerster stated. He believed each immigrant to the United States brought a new "race element or unit" into society and that Latin American immigration introduced "a dubious race factor."[63] Basically, Foerster stated, the desirability of Latin American immigration should be boiled down to one question: "Are the race elements involved therein such as this country [the United States] should today welcome into its race stock?" Foerster's answer was no.

As the taproot of a hemisphere-wide labor exodus to the United States, Mexican immigrants were the least desirable of Latin Americans.[64] Mexicans' unfitness for a place in U.S. society was not based on the lack of need for their labor, Foerster contended, but rather on the racial shortcomings of an Indian nation. Paradoxically, Foerster concluded, the existing U.S. immigration law, which placed European immigration on a quota but did not regulate Latin American immigration, allowed into the United States "a greater proportion . . . of nonwhite [racial] stocks than at any previous time in the history of the Republic."[65]

This comparison of treatments among Manuel Gamio, the *Survey of Race Relations*, Edgar Hewitt, and Robert Foerster demonstrates how race infused the debate over immigration restriction. Racial arguments were a solid foundation upon which the restrictionist movement was built, while rejection of racial prejudice was a central consideration Mexico's opposition to the quota bill. These different perspectives on race, both professional and non-professional, show that discussions over immigration restriction touched on broader themes of national belonging and nationalism. Whether one advocated the protection of the nation from foreign immigrant hordes or the defense of nationals' rights abroad, the immigration quota debate struck at the heart of a country's social, political, cultural, and *racial* integrity.

By the summer of 1928 it was clear to the State Department that quota advocates in Congress were undeterred by arguments that the quota's extension to Mexico would hurt American business and damage U.S.-Mexican relations. The Seventieth Congress had come to an end and restrictionists were not convinced by figures showing a predominant trend of repatriation in Mexican immigration. Various factors undermined the validity of such statistics, but the glaring problem with quantifying Mexican immigration was the illegal entry of migrants into the United States. No one could provide a firm number of how many Mexicans migrated illegally to the United States, but if estimates from American consular officials were to be believed, the claims that most Mexicans returned to Mexico and that the Mexican population in the United States was not growing were dubious. Unless some "other effective means of curtailing Mexican immigration can be proposed," Monnett Davis, the chief of the State Department's Visa Office in Washington believed, it was likely that Congress would pass new immigration restriction legislation on Mexico.[66]

The State Department and consular service did not advocate the "free admission" of a large number of aliens into the United States, yet they did believe any measure to reduce Mexican immigration should cause the least harm to American interests. The

State Department opposed a quota for multiple reasons. First, since Mexico was the only Latin American nation with a high rate of immigration to the United States, a quota would alienate Mexico. Second, a quota would divert the legal stream of immigration to "illegal channels." Third, a quota was unenforceable because the Border Patrol was not robust enough to guard the entire U.S.-Mexico border. And fourth, the State Department believed a quota was unnecessary if existing exclusionary laws were enforced properly. If a "more gradual reduction" of the volume of Mexican immigration could be accomplished by enforcement of existing exclusionary laws, Davis believed, any hazards to Mexican stability from a quota would be precluded.[67]

The State Department, in an effort to obviate the need for a quota on Mexico, proposed *administrative restriction*, or a stricter enforcement of existing immigration laws toward Mexican immigrants. The enforcement of present laws promised at least two benefits. First, quota opponents, such as Secretary of State Kellogg, believed the reduced volume of Mexican immigration to the United States would eliminate the need for Congress to extend a restrictive quota to Mexico. Second, enforcing existing laws could end the precedent of exemption that had been officially and unofficially granted to Mexican immigration since at least the end of World War I. Many restrictionists, such as Senator Reed, believed a quota was justified for no other reason than ending the exemptions extended to Mexican immigrants that European immigrants did not enjoy. For Reed and other like-minded policymakers, the exemption given to Mexico's immigration represented a yawning gap in U.S. immigration law and a disconcerting laxity of the American consular service in Mexico. *Proper* enforcement of existing immigration law, it was hoped, would counter this additional justification for a quota on Mexico.

The first aspect of administrative restriction was the enforcement of existing exclusionary provisions from the 1917 immigration act. These provisions prohibited the entry of any immigrant who was illiterate, likely to become a public charge (LPCs), insane, or diseased. Up to the late 1920s, this was the primary form of exclusion faced by Mexican migrants. In reality consular officials enforced these provisions lightly, and those Mexicans seeking to migrate temporarily were not usually barred from doing so. The second component of administrative restriction was the requirement of a valid passport to obtain the immigration visa necessary for permanent (or more appropriately, non-temporary) immigration to the United States. This was not a new law, but it had almost never been enforced toward Mexican immigrants. This form of restriction was primarily directed at legal immigration and was considered the most effective measure for reducing Mexican immigration.

The quota debate that reached a head in 1928 also inspired a reevaluation of existing immigration laws and how they could be harnessed to address the problem of Mexican immigration. Standards of admissibility had always been "considerably lower" in Mexico than in other parts of the world, particularly Europe. Immigration requirements were relaxed during World War I when Mexican labor was needed, and the standards remained "fairly low" thereafter.[68] As the consul at Ciudad Juarez reported, since the passage of the 1924 immigration act, the State Department requested its consuls be "as easy as possible" on Mexican migrants. A reason for this laxity was the common knowledge that Mexican immigration documentation was often worthless. Birth certificates, medical examination records, and other such documents necessary for immigration were easily obtained from any local official and for a small price.[69]

Nonetheless, consular officials such as Monnett Davis had "little doubt that a strict and literal application" of provisions from the 1917 act would result in curbing the "peon" labor that comprised Mexican immigration. Rigid enforcement included the barring of illiterates and mental incompetents who could not pass spot tests administered at consular offices; better coordination with medical inspectors in border towns to ensure that diseased migrants were not passing as healthy individuals; the restriction of contracted migrants from entering the United States; and the indication that migrants could post a $500 bond in case of unemployment (in accordance with section 21 of the 1917 act).[70] Stricter enforcement of existing exclusionary laws, Davis believed, would face resistance from American business that depended on Mexican labor, but it might curb Mexican immigration sufficiently to preclude the extension of the quota to Mexico.

Enhanced administrative restriction could also require Mexicans to have valid passports for entry into the United States. Up to the late 1920s, consular officials had not required Mexicans to present valid passports as a prerequisite for applying for an immigration visa. Enforcement was so lax that the Mexican government did not issue passports to emigrants proceeding to the United States. During the summer of 1928, however, the State Department ordered consular offices to give immigration visas only to those Mexicans who presented valid passports.

The passport scheme was not without its critics. George Winters, American vice consul in Mexico, believed the passport requirement would disproportionately regulate the most desirable of Mexican migrants and would abet the illegal immigration of those Mexicans least wanted in U.S. society. Winters, like most consular officials in Mexico, opposed the plan to extend the quota to Mexico. He believed a quota would increase illegal immigration because the Border Patrol would not be able to guard the two-thousand-mile border against migrants who shirked quota restrictions. A quota system would also primarily affect the stream of legal immigration that was comprised of "honest" and "more desirable" Mexicans, while abetting the flow of "unscrupulous and undesirable" Mexicans who entered the United States illegally. Passport enforcement would not be a suitable alternative to the quota, Winters argued, because it would perpetuate many of the problems posed by a quota. First, there was the issue of administering the passport scheme. Even if the Mexican government cooperated by restricting the issuance of passports, it was impossible for all would-be immigrants to get passports at the Ministry of Foreign Affairs office in Mexico City. Such a hurdle would encourage illegal immigration. Then if state governments were given power to issue passports, the centralized regulation of passport issuance would become diffuse and corruptible, and there would be little actual limitation of immigration.

Most important was that the passport requirement would encourage illegal and undesirable immigration. The Mexican government would have no incentive to issue passports to citizens who sought to migrate legally to the United States, since most legal migrants were skilled and stable laborers who could contribute to Mexico's economy. Winters stated that an inability to migrate legally might force Mexicans to migrate illegally, alongside those who already entered the United States surreptitiously. Paradoxically the laborers most valued by the Mexican government and found the least objectionable to American restrictionists would bear the brunt of passport restriction.[71]

Instead Winters believed a stricter enforcement of exclusionary laws that pertained to contract labor, LPCs, mental stability, medical examinations, and illiteracy would be the most effective means to reduce immigration numbers. These laws would preclude the need for a quota and improve the quality of immigrants entering the United States. While stricter enforcement might not appreciably prevent illegal immigration, Winters concluded, it would not exacerbate it as the quota was likely to do. The enforcement of existing laws was preferable to a quota because "exclusion would be individual rather than international."[72]

Despite such criticism, passport enforcement became the prime objective of administrative restriction. Although Congress had agreed to table discussions about quota extension as an American delegation attended the Pan-American Conference during the spring of 1928, Secretary of State Kellogg feared Congress would eventually extend the quota to Mexico, or even to all of Latin America. Passport enforcement was meant to prevent this eventuality.[73] Kellogg believed that if Congress extended the quota to Mexico it would be because of a large *recorded* rate of immigration into the United States. Kellogg, then, was "primarily interested in reducing the recorded immigration through a proper enforcement of existing laws and regulations in the hope of obviating the application of quotas to American countries, a measure which I fear would have the most serious consequences upon our relations with Latin America."[74]

The passport scheme's restrictive benefits were manifold. First, it encouraged a bilateral solution to the Mexican immigration problem between the United States and Mexico. The Mexican government could regulate its immigration by selectively issuing passports to those citizens who wanted to migrate. Another bilateral benefit to the passport scheme was that the Mexican government could regulate its immigration without being blamed for restricting the movement of its citizens. The onus of restriction—a required passport for an immigration visa—could be placed on the U.S. government. A second advantage to this approach was that it proposed to decentralize Mexico's immigration regulation by making home immigration office sites of restriction instead of border towns, which were often crowded with expectant migrants who had sold belongings and paid visa fees and transportation costs toward their northward journeys. And finally, the State Department hoped that reduced congestion at the border would have the further effect of reducing illegal immigration. The State Department was aware that Mexico wanted to curb its immigration to the United States, but American diplomats and consular officials were hesitant to propose restriction measures that might alienate the Mexican government and harm U.S.-Mexican relations. Still, the passport plan had to be a workable alternative to a quota; otherwise, the U.S. Congress might extend the quota to Mexico.

Immediately after the Senate Committee on Immigration and Naturalization passed the Harris bill in December 1928, the Mexican government sought a bilateral solution to the immigration problem with the United States. Mexico recognized the U.S. government's right to restrict immigration and did not oppose the passport plan's objective of regulating immigration. As earlier debates on immigration during 1928 revealed, the problem between the two governments was that Mexican leaders hoped to broker a bilateral deal with the United States on the best way to regulate immigration mutually, while the U.S. government rejected all calls for a bilateral conference as a potential infringement on Congress's sovereign right to restrict immigration.[75]

As early as August 1928, the same month that the State Department ordered all consular officials in Mexico to implement the passport requirement, Mexico's foreign minister Genaro Estrada called for a conference between both nations to discuss the various aspects of the immigration problem and to consider the passport scheme. A few months later, after the Harris bill was passed, Estrada feared a quota would create an "unexpected" situation, "the implications of which were not now to be fully foreseen."[76] The Mexican Ministry of Foreign Relations believed the immigration problem was a transnational concern and hoped to be consulted by the U.S. government regarding restriction "in order to secure the most equitable and mutually desirable result."[77] Estrada argued that Mexican immigration should not be regulated in the same way as European immigration because the problem of Mexico's immigration to the United States was "very different" and required an alternative solution rather than the restrictive quota placed on Europe. He believed bilateral negotiations were the best way to establish an effective system of regulation between the United States and Mexico.[78] For its part the U.S. State Department deflected Estrada's calls for a conference and was careful not to engage in any bilateral discussion with Mexico on immigration to avoid any suggestion that immigration policy was an international relations issue as opposed to domestic policy.[79]

The passport approach's invitation of bilateral cooperation was not the same as a concession to negotiate a bilateral solution to the immigration problem. In the midst of reiterating the U.S. Congress's sovereign right over immigration policy to American delegates who attended international conferences that planned to discuss the international importance of immigration, Kellogg was quick to clarify any "misunderstanding" about bilateral efforts between the United States and Mexico to curb Mexican immigration. In a letter to Morrow, Kellogg stated that the enforcement of the passport requirement should not be contingent on the approbation and participation of the Mexican government. Requiring passports for immigration visas would be "purely an administrative measure" toward the enforcement of regulations from the

1924 immigration act. Once the passport approach was effectively enforced by the U.S. consular service, bilateral cooperation with Mexico over the immigration issue would be considered.[80]

Such a multidimensional problem as immigration inevitably had significant consequences for U.S.-Mexican relations. The debate over Mexican immigration and its restriction, which had largely taken place since the end of World War I, became tangible, immediate, and threatening after the Senate Committee on Immigration and Naturalization passed the Harris bill in December 1928. For American restrictionists it was a welcome, long-sought-after, and necessary first step toward the complete restriction of Mexican immigration into the United States. While not all restrictionists were equally optimistic about the quota's chance for success, they agreed on the philosophical underpinnings of a quota extension to Mexico: removing exemptions that allowed the entry of undesirable foreigners, and employing U.S. immigration law to apply uniform, reliable, and effective restriction to all emigrant-sending nations around the world.

Mexican leaders opposed the quota because it risked their long-term goals of national economic development; it rested on a supposition of Mexicans' racial inferiority; and it discriminated against Mexico among all other nations of the region. A sudden halt to immigration northward would disrupt development projects by burdening the Mexican labor market with an oversupply of workers. If national development were given time, Mexican leaders believed, migrants would reverse their course and work in Mexican industries. While many Mexicans understood that a quota was theoretically necessary to protect the American labor market, it was American restrictionists' argument that Mexico should be added to the list of quota-restricted nations because its migrants were racially inferior that prompted Mexican leaders to object to the quota. The United States, Mexicans believed, was well within its right to protect itself through immigration policy, but when that policy endangered the economic and political stability of a neighboring nation, then problems would ensue. In addition Mexicans opposed the Harris bill because they believed it would diplomatically embarrass their nation among other Latin American states.

At root was a fundamental difference between how the immigration problem should be solved. United States policymakers believed the problem could be stopped at the border. Economic arguments by "unpatriotic" employers did not carry much weight for restrictionists who presumed that U.S. society was fundamentally menaced by the presence of undesirable migrant labor. Americans thought a unilateral application of restrictive laws would resolve the immigration problem. Americans assumed immigration was more of a social problem than an economic one by the late 1920s, during the height of postwar prosperity. In contrast Mexicans considered immigration an economic problem that underscored Mexico's social, cultural, and political difficulties. And since the underlying economic phenomenon was that the immigration issue was transnational, it was necessary that the United States and Mexico negotiate to find a bilateral solution. In the meantime Mexican leaders sought to regulate immigration to the extent that its citizens would be protected from the increased strictures of U.S. immigration law, but not to a degree that Mexican immigration northward would be cut off entirely. Mexico's political and economic stability was tied to the safety valve of immigration, and U.S. plans to shut the safety valve with a quota threatened Mexican national peace.

In April 1929 *Excelsior* expressed what many in the U.S. State Department already knew: that a restrictive quota would completely undermine the spirit of Pan-Americanism that had been carefully fostered since the 1890s. While Mexicans conceded that the United States had the right to protect its workers from foreign competition, and in this sense that restriction of European immigration was justified, it was "just" that Mexico and other Latin American nations be spared the quota. The spirit of Pan-Americanism demanded the exemption of Latin America from a restrictive quota. Pan-Americanism, the editorialist wrote, was largely "farcical"; it contained meaningless verbiage and only existed at the discretion of the United States. Nonetheless, the writer continued, the spirit of

Pan-Americanism imposed a "reciprocal obligation" between the peoples and nations of the Americas. To ignore that obligation would be "the height of shamelessness." "Resentment," "distrust," and "spiritual difference" would increase and harm Pan-American solidarity if the United States were to place a quota on Mexico.[81]

5

The U.S. Senate Passes a Quota on Mexico

Winter 1929–Spring 1930

By 1930 it was clear that some type of restriction would be placed on Mexican immigration. Congressional restrictionists continued to push for a quota on Mexico while domestic quota opponents, notably the State Department, pointed to administrative restriction as an alternative method to curb Mexican immigration without incurring diplomatic blowback from Mexico and the rest of Latin America. Interestingly the apogee of the quota drive occurred during the spring of 1930, just as the State Department began to report on the positive results of administrative restriction. The Harris bill, first introduced during 1928, was revived in April 1930 and passed the Senate the following month. This was the closest a measure proposing a quota for Mexican immigration had ever come to becoming law. Mexico vehemently protested the Harris bill, pointing to how restrictionists contradicted American businesses' demand for Mexican labor. Efforts to deter Mexicans from migrating northward were continued by Mexico's government while Mexican observers of immigration continued to argue that a quota could not only harm U.S.-Mexican relations but also harm Mexico itself. The primary argument against the quota was that it discriminated against Mexico, both racially and regionally: racially in that the justification for a quota rested on arguments that Mexicans were inferior and undesirable immigrants; regionally in that the quota effort focused on restricting the immigration of Mexico alone among all other Latin American nations. During the late 1920s some congressional restrictionists hoped to extend the quota to all the Western Hemisphere. Such efforts failed repeatedly as Congress dealt with "consolidated" regional resistance to such immigration restriction. Restrictionists found better success in the spring of 1930, when they focused their efforts on extending the quota to Mexico only. As the Latin American nation with the highest rate of immigration to the United States, Mexico was the obvious target for restriction; the restrictionists hoped that the extension of the quota to Mexico would facilitate their broader efforts to place the entire region under a quota. Racial arguments remained the primary tools restrictionists used to justify extending the quota to Mexico. While such a rationale had always been part of the larger call to restrict Mexican immigration, these arguments were now so sufficiently well received that the Harris bill's passage in May 1930 became a topic of bilateral concern between the United States and Mexico. Coupled with restrictionists' strategy of extending the quota to Mexico alone, the debate over immigration restriction and its potential effects on U.S.-Mexican relations reached a fever pitch in 1930.

Interestingly the arguments that underscored both sides of the quota debate had not changed much by the turn of the decade. In some respects the points made for and against Mexican immigration repeated earlier statements, though they were argued more loudly during 1929 and 1930 as the international economic downturn worsened and as Congress took a major step toward restricting Mexican immigration. Restrictionists defended a quota in racial terms; quota opponents justified themselves by saying that Mexican labor was needed and that such restriction would be bad for diplomatic relations. While 1928 had witnessed a flurry of debate over the quota—Congress hosted hearings on Mexican immigration and considered the initial Harris bill proposal to restrict the immigration from Mexico, and American delegations attended (and abstained from) multilateral discussions about immigration at a pair of international conferences in Havana, Cuba—the quota debate was largely quiescent during 1929. State Department officials took comfort in the success of administrative restriction that, after its implementation in April 1929, had an immediate effect in reducing *legal* Mexican immigration. Nonetheless important arguments about Mexican immigration made during the latter half of the year demonstrated that the quota debate was anything but stagnant. Viewed in the context of congressional actions toward immigration restriction between January and May 1930, such arguments lent new vigor to the points of race, national sovereignty, and diplomatic relations that animated the problem of Mexican immigration. Senate passage of the Harris bill in May 1930 dispelled any notion that the problem of Mexican immigration was dormant or that the quota debate had become redundant.

Mexican immigration to the United States declined during the last months of 1929. Some of this was attributed to the restriction efforts of the Mexican Immigration Service, but American consular officials thought the real decline was attributable to U.S. administrative restriction. Mexican newspapers began to report that support in the United States for a quota on Mexico was waning in light of decreasing immigration numbers and stubborn opposition from U.S. business interests. The American consul at Nuevo Laredo stated that the immigration of laborers through that entry point had practically ceased. Felipe Canales, the Mexican secretary of the interior, even suggested that reports of abuse against Mexicans in the United States were exaggerated and that life across the border was improving for migrants. After a recent visit to the United States, Canales argued that Mexicans had not been arrested because of American animosity or prejudice against them, but rather because migrants had violated immigration laws applicable to all foreigners. Also, Canales opined that many Mexicans in the border region who claimed to be deportees and victims of abuse were merely rejected from migrating because they did not meet the requirements necessary to enter the United States.[1]

Paradoxically Mexican newspaper articles from the same period continued to report the abuses of Mexicans in the United States, and the Mexican consul general, on a trip to the Rio Grande Valley, found prisons overfilled with Mexicans who could not show legal entry. These prisoners were subjected to great suffering: lack of space, and common holding areas for all sexes and all ages. The consul general in San Antonio was purportedly making efforts on behalf of Mexicans who were confined primarily because of their ignorance of immigration laws. On October 16, 1929, *Excelsior* described a case of fifty-six Mexicans rejected and stranded at the border. According to the article the Mexican government planned to take steps to assist them, and sent notice to state governments not to let their citizens migrate northward until they were aware of and compliant with U.S. immigration law.[2]

The Mexican government continued its efforts to dissuade its citizens from migrating northward during 1929. The Interior Ministry issued a pamphlet in August entitled "The Problem of Migration of Mexican Workers and Peasants." The tone of the pamphlet, which was written by Alfonso Fabila, was more polemical than official. The author's background may help explain the narrative tone of his writing. Of peasant heritage, Fabila was radical member of the Casa del Obrero Mundial, Mexico's national labor union. Later he worked for the Ministry of Education where he met Manuel Gamio and became a social scientist with a Marxian bent.[3] Fabila wanted the pamphlet to illustrate the multiple dangers that faced Mexican migrants in the United States. According to Fabila, migrants suffered abuse at the hands of U.S. immigration officials. Migrants also worked long hours in dangerous conditions along roads, in mines, or in factories; they were underpaid for degrading labor; they worked under faulty contracts; they suffered from poor working and living conditions that often bred diseases like tuberculosis; and they were often malnourished and homesick. Some migrants had gone insane and even become suicidal. Mexican laborers also often confronted moral dangers, Fabila continued, whether it was from alcohol or prostitutes. Americans did not welcome Mexicans and resented their presence in the United States. Mexicans had to travel under harsh conditions in hot and cold weather to find work, often sleeping outside in a single car as a whole family. Finally, many migrants were stuck in the United States, unemployed but unable to return to Mexico because of lack of money.[4] In short Fabila argued that immigration was "a real disgrace" ("una verdadera desgracia") for Mexico. Most migrants did not return to Mexico. By recounting the various dangers of immigration, Fabila hoped to prevent this problem that was "continuously bleeding" Mexico.[5] Fabila's work was based on firsthand observations while living in Los Angeles, and copies of it were distributed to Mexican consuls throughout the United States. According to Francisco Balderamma and Raymond Rodríguez, its acceptance and use as a reference source gave the pamphlet legitimacy and "fostered the view that it was an officially approved version of conditions in the United States."[6]

Enrique Santibáñez, the Mexican consul general in San Antonio, gave an equally pessimistic, if less polemical and more official, analysis of Mexico's immigration problem. Between October and December 1929, Santibáñez produced an article series for *Excelsior* that discussed various aspects of Mexican immigration. Santibáñez developed multiple themes throughout his twenty-three articles on Mexican immigration to the United States. Early in the series he argued that the "fenómeno inmigratorio" was not just a national problem for Mexico; instead it was "absolutely necessary" that both the United States and Mexico understand the "bilateral" conditions that underlined immigration and that could help resolve it.[7] Later in the series he argued that Mexico's amicable relations with the United States had only served to impoverish Mexicans and to undermine the "elements" necessary for Mexico's national development. Mexico had become dependent on the United States economically, making Mexicans themselves dependent on work in the United States and vulnerable to abuse when they migrated there.[8] In the same essay Santibáñez argued that Mexicans retarded Mexico's national development when they migrated northward and consumed U.S. products instead of Mexico's goods. He believed immigration represented a permanent loss of the nation's labor force, as migrants who acquired labor skills often did not return to Mexico because they could not command a comparable salary to what they would earn in the United States.[9]

One essay pointed to China and Japan as case studies for how the United States had flouted the interests of emigrant-sending nations. In 1904 the United States unilaterally and indefinitely prohibited the immigration of all Chinese, despite a prior agreement between the two nations that established immigration restriction only for Chinese laborers. While the Chinese government accepted the limitation of its immigration in principle, Santibáñez stated, it did not condone complete prohibition. Additionally, notwithstanding the "Gentlemen's Agreement" between the United States and Japan, which spared the latter the national disgrace of formal immigration restriction, the United States added Japan to the list of quota-restricted nations in 1924.[10]

An important subtheme of Santibáñez's articles was the alleged racial inferiority of Mexicans. Migrants were accused of being diseased, slovenly, criminal, a drag on local wages, and illiterate. While some of these accusations may have been accurate, Santibáñez wrote, American restrictionists should consider the conditions that produced these characteristics. Santibáñez argued that if American quota advocates were to study the immigration problem objectively, "free of the dirt of the Mexican barrios" ("menos suciedades en los barrios mexicanos"), they would see that migrants' social shortcomings were not inherent to their race, but rather were attributable to the social and economic conditions to which they were relegated.[11]

One essay, entitled simply "Racial Prejudice," described how Mexicans were considered an inferior race in the United States. They were mocked, looked down upon, castigated, and forced to live in the most squalid conditions. Santibáñez argued that the racism Mexicans faced was comparable to the conditions faced by blacks in the United States. Consequently Mexicans made no effort to assimilate to U.S. society.[12]

An article by Glenn E. Hoover typified the racism that Santibáñez argued against. Published in *Foreign Affairs* magazine in October 1929, weeks before the onset of what would become the harshest and most-prolonged economic depression in the United States during the twentieth century, Hoover's article demonstrated how race—not economic protection—was the prime motive behind the effort to extend the quota to Mexico.

Hoover, a professor of economics at Mills College in Oakland, California, opened his essay by arguing that the American people were confused generally about Mexican immigration because of confusion about the nature of race. Hoover stated that most Mexicans were "Indians"; as such, they were nonwhite. Yet Mexicans were considered legally white by U.S. immigration officials. Hoover found this perplexing, saying that there was a "tacit but universal understanding among government officials that the biological characteristics of the Mexican people shall be assumed to be what they are not in fact."[13] For Hoover this mischaracterization discounted the racial danger of Mexicans for U.S. society.

Like other restrictionists, Hoover argued that Mexicans were depraved, poor, drunken, illiterate, docile, and superstitious. In short, Mexicans were not fit to enter U.S. society, much less to become citizens of it. Moreover Mexicans only entered the United States to find work, and they did not assimilate because they planned to return to Mexico. Hoover refuted the claim that most Mexicans returned to Mexico by arguing that census records showed clearly an increase in the number of Mexicans living in the United States. Hoover attributed this steady growth of the Mexican population in the United States to illegal immigration; for every Mexican who entered the United States legally, he argued, at least one other entered illegally. For restrictionists like Hoover, illegal immigration undermined any hope that the Mexican population would be kept low by natural repatriation.[14]

There were four key points to Hoover's argument. First, he rejected claims that a restriction of Mexican immigration would harm industries in the American Southwest. While some land may have to lay fallow, he argued, it would be a small price to pay if Mexican labor could be made redundant: "If labor were withdrawn from such lands it should be cause for national rejoicing rather than sorrow."[15] Hoover balked at the anti-quota argument that stated that only Mexicans would or could do the stoop labor required by some southwestern industries. If "conditions are made acceptable," he argued, whites could and would do the work. And Hoover disagreed with the notion that American prosperity in the Southwest was largely attributable to Mexican labor, arguing that up to 1908, Mexican immigration to the American Southwest had been negligible.[16] Second, Hoover asserted that Mexican racial inferiority justified their exclusion. He stated that "competent and impartial observers," such as Dr. S. J. Holmes, a biologist, zoologist, and eugenicist at the University of California, Berkeley, considered the Mexican both physically and mentally inferior to whites. According to Holmes, Mexicans were on par with the American Indian, from whom the "meager contributions . . . to the intellectual life of the nation speaks eloquently for excluding those [Mexicans] who are no better."[17] Third, Hoover argued that while a quota was an "arbitrary method" by which to restrict Mexican immigration, it was "logical" to make uniform U.S. exclusionary laws by extending the quota presently curbing European immigration to Mexico. While any curb on Mexican immigration, especially "paper restrictions," was "futile" in the face of illegal immigration (even if "our entire military forces were concentrated along the border"), Hoover argued, it was necessary to establish a *nationwide* regime to stop illegal immigration. Hoover suggested registration of aliens, or laws prohibiting the employment "of those with visible Indian blood," who could not show they were in the United States legally. "More Indians have crossed the southern border in one year than lived in the entire territory of New England at the time of the Plymouth settlement," Hoover stated. "This movement . . . will have to be curtailed for the same reasons that dictated the Immigration Act of 1924."[18] Finally, Hoover disregarded the warning that a quota could harm U.S.-Mexican relations by arguing that the U.S. government had never felt "obliged" to welcome all races equally. "The control of immigration is a domestic question," Hoover wrote, "and the fears of offending some of those who do business with us in South America should not deter us from making such discriminations as are felt to be in the national interest."[19]

Hoover believed Mexicans posed a social danger to the United States. Failure to take their presence seriously encouraged unwanted racial mixing that would undermine the nation. "If the [Mexican] is considered undesirable as an immigrant and permanent citizen," Hoover concluded, "we ought not to accept him as a mere piece of productive machinery. Immigration inevitably leads to racial fusion; and any nation which regards its immigrants as mere factors of production is laying trouble for itself."[20]

Santibáñez's article series on Mexican immigration attempted to repudiate such racist arguments for a quota. Santibáñez even responded to Glenn Hoover's point regarding the paradox of Mexican whiteness, by pointing to a federal district court decision in Texas that granted Mexicans legal whiteness in 1897. During the fifty years after the end of the Civil War, the federal government left immigration enforcement to states. Naturalization laws passed at the state level were at the center of racial debates in the United States during these years. Federal district courts heard twelve cases in which petitioners appealed for the right to naturalize. Petitioners lost eleven of these twelve cases.[21] The one exception involved a Mexican resident of Texas who sought the right to become an American citizen. In 1897 a federal district court upheld the legal whiteness of Ricardo Rodríguez, a thirty-seven-year-old Mexican immigrant who had resided in Texas for more than a decade, and who sought final approval of his application for naturalization. Local politicians, historian Natalia Molina argues, opposed Rodríguez's petition by citing the racial restriction on citizenship that allowed only whites and blacks to naturalize. However, legal precedent was used to justify Rodríguez's right to become a U.S. citizen.[22]

Judge Thomas Maxey argued in his decision that although Congress did not consider Mexicans to be white, it had negotiated several treaties with Spain and Mexico that gave Mexican nationals and their descendants U.S. citizenship and the right to naturalize. Under none of the treaties with Mexico and Spain, Maxey ruled, did Congress limit citizenship to free whites. Since Congress had agreed to extend citizenship rights to annexed peoples after the Mexican-American War, this privilege also extended to their descendants and subsequent Mexican immigrants. Maxey also declared that since Congress did not explicitly include Mexicans in racial restriction and naturalization laws, Mexicans were allowed to naturalize. "When all the foregoing laws, treaties, and constitutional provisions are considered," Maxey's decision stated, "the conclusion forces itself upon the mind that citizens of Mexico are eligible to American citizenship, and may be individually naturalized." Speaking to Mexicans' nonwhiteness, Maxey declared that "whatever may be the status of the applicant solely from the standpoint of the ethnologist, he is embraced within the spirit and intent of our laws upon naturalization, and his application should be granted."[23] Although the petitioner was illiterate and not knowledgeable about U.S. laws, Maxey concluded that this fact could not disqualify the petitioner from the right to naturalize, since Congress had "not seen fit to require of applicants for naturalization an educational qualification."[24]

The Texas federal district court case *In Re Rodriguez* (1897) confirmed Mexican whiteness. It would be naïve, however, to believe that legal whiteness constituted social whiteness. Nevertheless, *Rodriguez*'s significance lay in the legal inclusion of Mexican immigrants into American whiteness. This technicality granted Mexicans a particular privilege over other migrant groups, namely, that their right to enter was secure. Even when restrictionists attempted to block Mexican immigration twenty years later, declaring that Mexicans' illiteracy demonstrated their unwhiteness, Mexicans' whiteness protected them from these exclusionary efforts and made them a preferable labor force compared to other migrant groups. Racism would certainly compromise the privilege of whiteness for Mexicans. The working conditions and racial prejudice they faced clearly indicated the American belief that Mexicans were inferior. Despite their lesser whiteness, however, their racial acceptability over Asian immigrants (who were completely barred by U.S. immigration law) allowed them across the border. While new laws customarily repealed old laws, Santibáñez contended, since the 1924 immigration act had not been directed toward Mexico, then it should be considered irrelevant to Mexican immigration.[25]

The last article of Santibáñez's series encapsulated many of the themes he had raised previously and provided what he thought necessary to resolve the Mexican immigration problem. Entitled "How it is possible to resolve the immigration problem," the article argued first that Mexican immigration was unnecessary and that the fear and pessimism that underlay it were exaggerated. Second, he stated that both the United States and Mexico had incentives to resolve the immigration problem bilaterally.

Santibáñez believed that the apprehension about Mexico's national stability that justified Mexican immigration was exaggerated. He believed immigration was unnecessary if it were construed as a means to escape Mexico's instability. While there was a definitive link between revolutionary violence and economic conditions in Mexico, Santibáñez stated, revolutionary upheaval rarely harmed the nation as a whole. Rather, Santibáñez argued, violence was sporadic and fleeting, affecting economic conditions in a locale for no more than a few days. What is more, the national impact of revolutionary upheaval had declined from 1911 to 1929. Whereas the revolution inaugurated by Francisco Madero in 1910 witnessed the participation of Mexicans from all strata of society, the most recent conflagration led by General Escobar involved only "a few ambitious political bosses" ("unos pocos jefes ambiosos") and their small cadre of supporters. The national impact of the Escobar rebellion was small, affecting only a handful of northern states.[26] Therefore, Santibáñez contended, it was unnecessary for Mexicans to migrate to flee violence. Not only was it unnecessary; it was harmful to the Mexican state.

Like other observers of immigration, Santibáñez argued that the immigration problem would be resolved by peace and order in Mexico. Unlike other observers, however, Santibáñez deemed migrants culpable in Mexico's chronic instability. Francisco Suástegui, the commercial attaché in the Mexican Embassy during the late 1920s, for example, stated that the immigration problem would be solved once Mexico's government had developed the national economy to the point that Mexicans would no longer need to migrate for work. In this regard Mexico City bore responsibility for the country's immigration problem. By contrast Santibáñez argued that when Mexicans migrated northward in search of employment, they retarded national economic growth and the political strength that stemmed from it. Peace and order would not return to Mexico until all of its citizens made efforts to bring it about. It was reckless to hope that stability would return to Mexico while its citizens sought opportunities abroad. Therefore stemming immigration was the fundamental prerequisite for Mexico's economic reconstruction. To meet this goal Mexicans must overcome their fear of national instability and should stop diverting their productive energies to work that may have seemed more lucrative in the short term but would only degrade them and their nation in the long term.[27]

Next, Santibáñez believed it was in the interests of both nations to broker an agreement ("un acuerdo") that would resolve the immigration problem and facilitate the return of migrants to Mexico. To satisfy the need for Mexican labor, Santibáñez suggested a bilateral regime that would coordinate American business demands to employ Mexicans. Under bilateral guidance Mexican laborers could sign contracts with American employers, and those contracts would end once Mexicans returned to Mexico. His proposal anticipated the system adopted in 1942. Regardless of how both nations resolved their immigration problem, it was "our most profound and fervent hope that the two republics would live and work in the best harmony" ("nuestro más profundo y ferviente deseo es que las dos repúblicas vivan y trabajen en la mejor armonía").[28]

Like other Mexican officials, Santibáñez advocated some type of U.S. curb on Mexico's immigration, and he recognized the sovereign right of the United States to regulate immigration into its country.[29] At the same time, Santibáñez believed the United States must acknowledge that Mexican labor had played an instrumental role in the economic development of the American Southwest.[30] Such a concession, alongside a mutual desire to maintain amicable relations, embodied Santibáñez's belief that a middle ground should be found between U.S. sovereignty and the need to employ Mexican labor. Like other Mexican observers of immigration, Santibáñez opposed all U.S. immigration laws that rested on the racial inferiority of Mexican migrants. Such specious justifications, they believed, countermanded the real and mutual need to employ Mexican labor and undermined the bilateral efforts necessary to resolve the immigration problem.[31]

Both Enrique Santibáñez and Glenn Hoover indicate how Mexican immigration was discussed throughout the latter half of 1929 while Congress was out of session. Their observations, arguments, and proposed solutions provided material for debate during the following spring, when the Senate passed a measure to extend the quota to Mexico.

During the last weeks of 1929, opponents of Mexican immigration criticized the fact that the Western Hemisphere was not restricted under the National Origins Act, which had gone into effect the previous July. Patriotic societies decried the "incomplete and defective" immigration laws that barred the entry of Europeans while they continued to allow the entry of migrants whom restrictionists considered more racially inferior and more harmful to American workers. The quota restriction implemented in 1924 was replaced with a national origins plan that sought to reinforce the "original native [white] stock" of the U.S. population. A special executive board overseen by the secretaries of commerce, labor, and state was charged with determining the national origins of the American population and calculating national quotas to complement the native white population of the United States on the basis of the 1920 census. The analysis concentrated on white immigrants and divided them into two groups: "original native stock" and "immigrant stock." Of the almost 95 million whites enumerated by the 1920 census, 53.5 million were immigrants and 41 million were "native" Americans. Such a disparity alarmed restrictionists. The national origins commission, accordingly, calculated national quota rates that favored immigrants arriving from nations of "original native stock" (e.g., Britain) and discriminated against those nations that did not (e.g., Italy).[32]

In mid-January 1930 Reps. Albert Johnson and John Box presented a joint bill that proposed to drastically reduce immigration from the Western Hemisphere. Like the Immigration Act of 1924, which capped the annual total number of European immigrants at 150,000, the Johnson-Box bill would limit immigration from the Western Hemisphere to 50,000 annually. A month later, as a concession to business leaders who depended on cheap migrant labor, the proposed bill was revised to allow an annual total immigration from the Western Hemisphere at 76,064 instead of 50,000. Johnson predicted leaders of American nations would not complain about his proposed measure because many of those governments wished to stem the influx of their immigrants into the United States.[33]

Almost immediately objections were raised over the possibility of placing a quota on Canada. Americans and Canadians "are so much alike, and share so many common interests," the *New York Times* declared, "that they are in no sense 'foreigners' to each other." While a quota on Canada was objectionable, the same writer noted, it was difficult to see how Canada could be exempted from the quota while immigration from the rest of the hemisphere would be restricted. Addressing Mexico specifically, while the economic value of Mexican labor was undeniable, the writer stated, the "great mass" of migrants was unassimilable because of differences in living standards and traditions. "Yet it would be unequal to restrict Mexicans without placing handicaps on others." It was natural for Mexico to resent the "slur" cast upon its migrants. For these reasons, the editorialist concluded, it would be better to extend the quota to the entire Western Hemisphere.[34]

Despite proposed quota rates that were not expected to affect real rates of immigration from the Western Hemisphere, U.S. neighbors opposed the Johnson-Box bill. Canada was granted the largest allotment of annual immigration by the quota bill: 89 percent or 67,556. Nonetheless Canada objected to any measure that seemed to curb the tradition of free movement between the two nations. Immigration restriction on Canada, the *New York Times* feared, would likely "injure peculiarly delicate and significant interrelations."[35] Latin American nations objected to the Johnson-Box measure because it seemed to reflect a belief that their citizens were racially inferior and unassimilable. Also, such a quota would have gone against Pan-American sentiment and degraded Latin

American nations to the level of Asian countries, which bore the full extent of U.S. immigration restriction law.[36]

In some ways the Johnson-Box bill, while reflecting a genuine restrictionist desire to extend the quota to all nations of the Western Hemisphere (even Canada), was really a veiled attempt to place a quota on Mexico alone. While quotas were proposed for each American nation, most of those quota rates equaled or even exceeded real rates of immigration to the United States. Canada and Latin American nations objected to the spirit of the law, not its proposed practical effect. Only Mexico faced a quota that would cut significantly its actual rate of immigration to the United States. The Johnson-Box bill proposed to cut annual immigration from Mexico to below 3,000, or 4 percent of the total immigration from the Western Hemisphere. Another concession the House Committee on Immigration and Naturalization made to employers in the American Southwest who were dependent on Mexican labor was to establish a sliding scale for the reduction of Mexican immigration. The annual immigration allotment for Mexico would be 11,021 in 1931 (or 14 percent of total immigration from the Western Hemisphere), and 6,961 in 1932 (or 9 percent of total immigration from the Western Hemisphere), until an annual quota rate of 4 percent would be fixed for Mexico in 1933.[37]

The Johnson-Box bill was flawed and diplomatically provocative. By trying to apply a quota to all of the Western Hemisphere—and obviating accusations of specific discrimination against Mexico—the bill invited ire from many parts of the region, notably from nations such as Canada that hitherto had had no cause for complaint against U.S. immigration policy. Conversely, by proposing a quota allotment that so baldly and unequally restricted Mexican immigration, the bill reignited Mexico's argument that a quota would be discriminatory and would risk harming U.S.-Mexican relations.

The maintenance of amicable relations with the rest of Latin America was more than just a theoretical concept for the United States during the 1920s; it was a concrete goal toward which the United States made practical and real efforts. Understanding more of the United States' efforts to foster good Pan-American relations provides a better sense of why various U.S. proposals to place a quota on immigration from the Western Hemisphere were so objectionable to Latin American nations, and to Mexico in particular. The contrast between the Pan-American diplomacy of the United States and its immigration policy also highlights the fine line between the Wilsonian internationalism that underlay many foreign policy decisions made during this period and the Westphalian dictum of sovereignty that guided policymakers' drive to extend immigration restriction to some or all of the Western Hemisphere.

The Fifth Pan-American Conference in spring 1923, held in Santiago, Chile, established a "Treaty to Avoid and Prevent Conflicts between the American States." Later known as the Gondra Treaty, the agreement was meant to foster better hemispheric relations by strengthening the "mutual respect" in their "reciprocal relations" and solidifying the "sentiments of concord and loyal friendship" among the peoples of the region.[38] Proposed by President Baltasar Brum Rodríguez of Uruguay, the treaty was modeled on the League of Nations. Its fundamental points included the "intensification" of inter-American friendship, increased friendly relations with nonassociated nations, "the settlement of every American international conflict by arbitration," and the adoption of measures "to effectively maintain peace."[39] The Gondra Treaty can be construed as a League of Nations for the Western Hemisphere, as it established a system where member states would submit and subject any bilateral or multilateral conflict to the treaty organization for deliberation.[40]

The Johnson-Box bill, for Latin America, seemed to undermine the Pan-American spirit of cooperation typified by the Gondra Treaty. Latin American resentment over the proposed quota helped stymie the bill in committee.[41] Nonetheless by spring 1930 Johnson put aside his own quota proposal and threw his support behind a resurgent measure to extend the quota to Mexico alone. That measure was the Harris bill.

During the early months of 1930 it became clear that a general restriction of immigration from the Western Hemisphere was not feasible. Latin American states opposed the discriminatory implication of a quota law, and Canada believed such a law would needlessly taint close relations with the United States. This "consolidated opposition," to use a phrase from Johnson, from regional neighbors rendered such a proposal unpalatable to American policymakers who valued harmonious Pan-American relations. By spring 1930 restrictionists devised an alternative strategy to curb immigration from the Western Hemisphere. Instead of pursuing a general bill for the entire region, restrictionists proposed extending the quota to individual nations one at a time. The potential benefits to such a strategy was that "consolidated opposition" region-wide would be undercut, and the United States would find it easier to defend its sovereign right over immigration restriction in the face of a single nation's protest.

Mexico was the obvious first target for restriction of a Western Hemisphere nation. It had the highest rate of immigration to the United States among all Latin American countries, and restrictionists had been trying to add Mexico to the list of quota-restricted states since 1924. When the Harris bill was resuscitated in spring 1930 after lying dormant since the last legislative session, it was quickly passed by the Senate on May 13. Its chief appeal over the comparable Johnson-Box bill in front of the House Committee on Immigration and Naturalization was that the Harris bill sought to extend the quota to Mexico only. To be sure, the Harris bill, like the Johnson-Box measure, originally aspired to extend the quota to the entire region. Fear that it would spark "unfriendly feeling" across Latin America caused senators to revise the bill to apply to Mexico alone.[42] Sen. William Borah voiced the only protest against the bill, saying that he disapproved of singling out Mexico for immigration restriction. Albert Johnson, in an address before the American Eugenics Society and the Eugenics Research Association (he was president of the latter organization) shortly before the passage of the Harris bill, committed himself to postponing his previous attempts to extend the quota to all nations of the Western Hemisphere, and instead redirecting his efforts to place a quota at least on Mexico. Past endeavors to place a quota on the entire Western Hemisphere had created "consolidated opposition from too many minorities to be handled just at present. Later we can try for further restriction."[43]

The State Department continued to protest the quota effort in Congress. Two days after the Senate passed the Harris bill, Undersecretary of State Joseph Cotton testified before the House Committee on Immigration and Naturalization. Cotton dismissed a quota as pointless because it would not effectively stop Mexican immigration. Instead, he argued, it would be better to continue relying on administrative restriction to curb the entry of Mexicans into the United States. According to statistics Cotton presented to the committee, administrative restriction had reduced legal Mexican immigration by 37 percent during the first months of 1930 alone. If the stricter enforcement of labor contract laws, literacy tests, and physical examinations were enough to reduce Mexican immigration so significantly, he argued, why extend a quota to Mexico when it would largely be ineffective or superfluous? Also, Cotton stated that a quota on Mexican immigration would complicate—perhaps even undermine—bilateral negotiations on other diplomatic issues such as border disputes and foreign property between the United States and Mexico.

When asked by Albert Johnson if the decline in immigration numbers was attributable to the economic downturn that had begun the previous year, Cotton replied that there was no concrete correlation. Quite the opposite: instead of a diminution in the number of Mexicans applying for entry into the United States, the rate of rejected applications had increased, to a level of 60 to 70 percent.[44] When asked by the committee whether Mexico would object to the Harris bill, Cotton, in ostensible deference to Congress's sovereign right over immigration policy, stated that he would not ask Mexico whether it objected to a bill before Congress. Cotton made his position clear in a reply to the committee chairman, Albert Johnson.

> Rep. Johnson: "We have restricted immigration from Europe, from which fine immigrants came since the establishment

of this country. We restricted that movement. We restricted the European countries but not the countries of the Western Hemisphere. Now, why should Mexico be offended when we take the first step to place countries on this Hemisphere on a quota basis such as applies to European countries?"

Undersecretary of State Cotton: "What is the use of talking about offense? If it will not do any good to put a country on a quota basis, why do it?"[45]

Later in the hearing Johnson stated that Congress was determined to continue with the policy of immigration restriction. While consolidated opposition may have prevented passage of a "sound" bill that restricted the entire Western Hemisphere, Johnson declared, it could be more effective to restrict immigration from the Americas one nation at a time. "After the *Mexican Act* [i.e., the Harris bill] is passed," Johnson stated, "if we get too many laborers from Cuba and other countries of the West Indies, another act will be passed by Congress to tighten up those places." Cotton admitted that Congress could do whatever it saw fit, but reiterated that a quota on Mexico would not stop the immigration of Mexican laborers.[46]

Cotton's testimony also called attention to how a quota on Mexican immigration could complicate other diplomatic issues between the United States and Mexico that required bilateral negotiations. Cotton asked the committee if the proposed benefits of the Harris bill would outweigh the potential cost to bilateral cooperation. Two particular issues required amicable diplomatic relations, El Chamizal and claims. When the Rio Grande River changed course in 1864, it stranded six hundred acres on the U.S. side of the river. Known as the Chamizal, this valuable piece of property near El Paso, Texas, continued to be claimed by Mexico. A treaty was required to settle this dispute and to ensure both sides of the border were protected from future flooding. The second issue involved compensation for damages done to, and confiscation of, American-owned property in Mexico. Most claims for damage originated during the revolutionary period and were estimated at $750 million. Until the late 1920s there had been no bilateral agreement on a neutral member to preside over the arbitration proceedings; some claims had been pending since 1923, and Mexico intransigently defended its right to nationalize property. Bilateral cooperation on such issues as El Chamizal and claims, Cotton argued, could be undermined by the Harris bill. According to Cotton, "the programs in which cooperation between the United States and Mexico—that is, the plans under which the United States and Mexico are expecting to cooperate within the immediate future—are bound to be affected by [immigration restriction] legislation of this kind."[47]

Cotton's testimony before the House Committee on Immigration and Naturalization in May 1930 demonstrated the State Department's continued opposition to any legislation that restricted Mexican immigration. Cotton developed this line further in May 1930 by arguing that immigration restriction policy could undermine diplomatic issues between the United States and Mexico that required bilateral cooperation. Cotton's testimony was important for two additional reasons. First, it discussed how administrative restriction was showing positive results and could serve as a suitable solution to curb Mexican immigration without resorting to a quota. Second, Cotton's appearance before the House Committee on Immigration and Naturalization in May 1930 revealed how American restrictionists had changed their strategy for extending the quota to Mexico. Restrictionists like Albert Johnson believed it imperative to restrict immigration from the Western Hemisphere, yet such efforts were frustrated by "consolidated opposition" from the region. Instead the Harris bill presented an opportunity by which immigration from the Americas could be restricted without facing combined condemnation from multiple countries. By applying the quota to one nation at a time, beginning with Mexico, restrictionists would meet their goal of covering the Western Hemisphere with a quota.

Paradoxically it was this single-nation approach that animated much of Mexico's opposition to the quota. Mexicans resented that their nation was singled out among all the other nations of the Western Hemisphere for restriction. Together with restrictionists justifying a quota on Mexico because of Mexicans' alleged racial inferiority, the proposed application of the quota to Mexico alone was the reason why Mexico's government opposed the quota. The U.S. State Department understood why this double discrimination—both against Mexico as a nation and against Mexicans as a people—was anathema to Mexico. Consequently Kellogg and the State Department promoted administrative restriction as an effective alternative to the quota and as a resolution to the Mexican immigration problem. The stricter enforcement of existing immigration laws did not require the passage of new legislation and avoided restrictionist efforts being construed as a slight against the Mexican state. Also, the enforcement of immigration laws that pertained to literacy, physicality, and work contracts or visas occurred at the individual level, precluding accusations that exclusion was discriminating against Mexicans as a people.

As early as the summer of 1929, administrative restriction appeared to be curbing Mexican immigration. Sen. David Reed, an archrestrictionist for most of the 1920s, repudiated his previous call for a quota on Mexico in light of administrative restriction's apparent success, although he still advocated for a strengthened Border Patrol. To single out Mexico for restrictive measures like a quota, Reed believed, "might have serious international implications and lead to diplomatic as well as legislative difficulties." Not only would a quota undermine amicable relations with "our sister republic," Reed continued, but it would also injure U.S. relations with the rest of Latin America.[48]

In December 1929 John Farr Simmons, chief of the Visa Office in Washington, DC, reported to Congress that Mexican immigration was down by almost 70 percent. By mid-January 1930 William Dawson, general vice consul in Mexico City, reported reductions in the number of visas granted to Mexicans, a decrease in the number of Mexicans applying for visas, as well as the rise in refusal rates of visa applicants.

Table 3. Number of visas issued in month of December, 1926–1929

1926	3,323
1927	3,743
1928	2,587
1929	815

Source: Simmons to Carr, December 12, 1929, NARA, RG 59, 811.111 Mexico/298.

Table 4. Percent of visa refusals vs. total number of applicants, 1929

May: 34.5	September: 50.4
June: 42.0	October: 48.5
July: 44.9	November: 47.1
August: 47.6	December: 52.6

Source: Simmons to Dawson, December 30, 1929, NARA, RG 59, 811.111 Mexico/305.5, 1–3.

Table 5. Decline in Mexicans' visa applications, May 1928–December 1929

	1928	1929	% decrease
May	5,096	4,357	15
June	4,460	3,820	14
July	4,930	3,538	28
August	6,019	3,102	48
September	4,795	2,882	40
October	4,114	2,452	40
November	3,127	1,937	38
December	2,715	1,755	35
Total	32,256	23,843	32

Source: Dawson to Stimson, January 14, 1930, NARA, RG 59, 811.111 Mexico/309, 1–3.

Data from consular districts on the border reported lower rates of visa refusals. William Blocker, the American consul in Ciudad Juarez, reported a visa refusal rate of 36 percent for December 1929, while his counterpart in Nogales, Maurice Altaffer, recorded a refusal rate of 37 percent for all of 1929.[49] The American consul in Nuevo Laredo, Richard Boyce, reported a visa refusal rate of 90 percent. Also, Boyce stated that the overall number of Mexicans going to the border to migrate had decreased. Subsequently, despite a lack of data to prove his point, Boyce believed the rate of illegal immigration was also down.[50] Such reports seemed to show that administrative restriction was working: it not only reduced the official rate of (legal) immigration; it also seemed to have a related effect of reducing illegal immigration. By spring 1930 the State Department reported that Mexican immigration had been reduced to such an extent that it was "no longer a problem." On May 14, the same day Undersecretary of State Cotton gave his testimony before the House Committee on Immigration and Naturalization opposing the Harris bill (which had been passed by the Senate the day before), the State Department reported that administrative restriction had reduced Mexican immigration by almost 77 percent from previous years, "without resort to a numerical immigration quota."[51]

If administrative restriction worked, why did American restrictionists still seek to place a quota on Mexican immigration during the spring of 1930? One answer was the racism inherent to the call for a quota, which was only amplified by the onset of the Great Depression. Another explanation relates to the shortcomings of administrative restriction, namely, that curbing legal immigration intensified illegal immigration. Despite persuasive data and consular reports that extolled administrative restriction's effectiveness, the stricter enforcement of existing immigration laws risked increasing illegal immigration. In this regard both advocates and critics of administrative restriction were wrong. In spring 1928 Frank Kellogg believed Congress would only extend a quota to Mexico if the *recorded* rate of Mexican immigration remained high. The passport scheme was proposed as a way to reduce recorded immigration, thereby undercutting the quota drive. On the other hand George Winters believed the passport scheme would disproportionately restrict more-desirable Mexican migrants and encourage illegal immigration. Instead Winters argued that the stricter enforcement of exclusionary laws that pertained to contract labor, LPCs, mental stability, medical examinations, and illiteracy would be more effective in reducing Mexican immigration.[52]

Both Kellogg and Winters were wrong. Congress, by continuing its efforts to place a quota on Mexico during the first half of 1929, was undeterred by the sharp reduction in recorded Mexican immigration. Aside from Senator Reed, few restrictionists were persuaded that a quota on Mexico was unnecessary. Indeed throughout the fall of 1929 and the winter of 1929–1930, as the Visa Office, consular officials, and State Department reported the positive effects of administrative restriction, Albert Johnson expressed regret to John Farr Simmons that the State Department had not implemented administrative restriction sooner, and gave no indication that he would cease his efforts to place a quota on Mexico.[53] Indeed his actions during the next congressional session demonstrated his unending drive to place a quota on Mexico. By February Simmons and other State Department officials believed "very confidently" that Congress would extend a quota to Mexico.[54]

Administrative restriction, by relying on a stricter enforcement of existing immigration laws to curb Mexican immigration, actually fostered the conditions for increased illegal immigration. Glowing consular reports of the reduction of Mexican immigration and the refusal of visas failed to account for what happened to those Mexicans denied legal entry into the United States. For example, the consular report from Ciudad Juarez that reported a 36 percent visa refusal rate in December 1929 (100:275), alongside a 23 percent visa issuance rate (62:275), neglected to mention what may have happened to the remaining Mexicans who applied for visas that month (113:275, or 41 percent of the total visa applicants at Ciudad Juarez during December 1929).[55]

The American consul at Nogales, Maurice Altaffer, provided a sense of what transpired when Mexicans were refused visas to enter the United States. Altaffer reported that unemployed Mexicans who were turned away at the consulate became burdens to the town. Juan Robles, secretary of the local Chamber of Commerce, told Altaffer that most of the destitute were from Mexico's interior. They traveled to the border region with plans to migrate to the United States but were refused visas by the consulate. According to Robles most of these wayward Mexicans could not afford a return trip home and so remained in Nogales with the hope that "something would turn up." Altaffer believed it "likely" that some of these wayward Mexicans remained in Nogales with intentions to enter the United States illegally. While he was unable to provide definite data, Altaffer argued that "it is probable that the number of persons successful in or attempting illegal entry into [the United States] from Mexico has increased during the last year." Even if only a small percentage of persons refused visas remained in Nogales, Altaffer concluded, it is clear that they will "constitute a problem" since the town cannot provide employment for them.[56]

The case of Elisa Recinos provides an example of how migrants found themselves stuck along the border after failing to enter the United States. Elisa, her husband, and their infant child lived on a farm near Torreón. They migrated to Ciudad Juarez after hearing of the work and better wages there. Once in Juarez, Elisa and her family tried to cross over to El Paso, Texas, but were unable to because they did not have the money to cross legally or illegally. They were then stuck in Juarez: too poor to migrate northward and too poor to return home. Elisa's husband made and sold birdcages in the town plaza, and she begged for money on the streets. They hoped to save enough money to make the trip to El Paso, where they were sure they would find work and a better lifestyle.[57]

Historian Kelly Lytle Hernández provides a sense of what happened to those Mexican migrants who attempted to enter the United States illegally. The U.S. Congress further criminalized illegal immigration by passing the Immigration Act of March 4, 1929, which defined unsanctioned border crossings as a misdemeanor for first-time offenses and a felony punishable by two-to-five years in prison and a fine of ten thousand dollars for second offenses.

Those picked up for illegal immigration were henceforth subject to lengthy jail terms and costly fines prior to their deportation back to Mexico. Within the first year of its enforcement, hundreds of Mexican migrants were convicted of violating the March 4 law.[58]

Altaffer's report demonstrated the shortcomings of administrative restriction. While it had a very real effect on legal Mexican immigration, administrative restriction almost certainly increased illegal immigration. No definite figures are available to demonstrate the extent to which illegal immigration from Mexico to the United States increased after 1929. Mae Ngai suggests that contemporary estimates show that illegal immigration was as high as 100,000 a year throughout the 1920s, but Altaffer's report illustrates how the burden of immigration shifted from the Mexican interior to Mexico's northern bordertowns.[59] Until the early 1920s, when U.S. immigration laws were lightly enforced toward Mexicans seeking to migrate northward, border towns like Nogales were stopping-off points. Migrants, whose journeys often began hundreds of miles to the south, arrived in the north seeking entry into the United States. Most were granted such entry. The border was the entrepôt that connected two streams of immigration: immigration northward and repatriation southward. The circular flow of Mexican immigration was disrupted by administrative restriction, but not ended by it.

To a certain extent the founding of the U.S. Border Patrol in 1924 represented the first spike in Mexicans' circular immigration between the United States and Mexico. Limited personnel and resources, as well as the two-thousand-mile border, prevented the Border Patrol from effectively checking Mexican immigration. Nevertheless the new agency put up a substantial effort in policing the border. Dorothee Schneider explains how the Patrol's main job was to stop all illegal activity in the borderlands, especially smuggling (whether that be of drugs, liquor, or people). But the main task of the Border Patrol was to pursue illegal immigrants. As a result the number of deportations rose dramatically after the mid-1920s. In 1931 alone the Border Patrol arrested and deported over 23,000 people. The Border Patrol saw its mission as preventing border crossings of those designated as racially inferior. As such, border officers focused their efforts on darker-skinned Mexican common laborers (peons). The ease with which these immigrants were deported, Schneider argues, suggests that they were not just poor and unskilled, and therefore unable to be self-supporting workers, but also "racially inferior and incapable of articulating their right to stay in the United States." Illegal immigrants from Mexico were particularly vulnerable to deportation because they were usually identified by local residents as well as by the police or Border Patrol officers during random searches and interrogations.[60] The agency's existence, Natalia Molina argues, "signaled that Mexicans were not welcome in the United States, despite their being exempt from the draconian provisions of the 1924 immigration act."[61]

Despite the Border Patrol's robust effort to regulate immigration, however, administrative restriction played a far greater role in curbing Mexican immigration. Nevertheless the positive results of administrative restriction were limited. It made the border a distinction between different standards of social ascription.[62] Consequently American consulates in Mexico's northern border towns were the sifters through which Mexicans' circular immigration was denied and largely curtailed. A degree of illegality, already in place well before 1929, was added to immigration, as failure to meet guidelines for immigration northward marked potential migrants as "refused." Without the means to return to home districts or without work in a border town, Mexicans often migrated illegally to the United States. This increased degree of illegality made Mexicans even more undesirable in restrictionists' eyes. Far from obviating the need for a quota, administrative restriction exacerbated illegal immigration—the darkest, least quantifiable, most problematic aspect of the Mexican immigration issue.

By the latter half of 1929, Mexican debates about the quota had quieted. Aside from Santibáñez's article series on the immigration issue, which *Excelsior* ran in serial form between October and December, there was little editorial comment on the matter of immigration restriction. Mexican newspapers even seemed to reflect reduced tensions surrounding the issue. *Excelsior* reported that accounts of mistreatment of Mexican migrants in the United States were down and that arrests and deportations were also diminished. *El Universal* argued that rates of illegal immigration had subsided. Both newspapers reflected State Department arguments that held that administrative restriction was curbing Mexican immigration. *Excelsior* desired hopefully in January 1930 that administrative restriction was effective enough to preclude the need for the U.S. Congress to pass a quota on Mexico. In March *El Universal* stated that the State Department believed administrative restriction had decreased Mexican immigration northward by almost 78 percent during the past eight months and that currently only 1,700 Mexicans were entering the United States annually.[63] One reason immigration was down, *El Universal* declared in December 1929, was because many thousands of Mexicans were repatriating. The paper asserted that the return of migrants was due to cold weather conditions, and did not mention economic slowdown in the United States.[64]

By the turn of the year, however, and especially after the Johnson-Box bill was passed by the House Committee on Immigration and Naturalization in mid-January 1930, the Mexican press gave renewed attention to the American debate over the quota. Both newspapers followed congressional hearings on the matter. In February *El Universal*, like the *New York Times*, argued that the Johnson-Box bill, which proposed a quota for all Western Hemisphere nations, would cause "intense resentment" in Latin America and Canada and that Mexico, in particular, "would take exception" to a quota on its immigration.[65] Mexican newspapers became more pessimistic about migrants' fate in the United States as the quota debate in Congress progressed from an effort to restrict immigration from the entire region to an effort to restrict Mexico's immigration alone. Reports of migrant abuse resurfaced; accusations of racial prejudice against migrants rebounded; and accounts of migrants' desperation to repatriate to Mexico proliferated. Both *El Universal* and *Excelsior* devoted considerable page space to describing the alleged desire of many migrants to return to Mexico and the overall misery Mexicans experienced in the United States. "The Mexicans in the United States are anxious to return [to Mexico]," Luis Bustamante, a Mexican journalist in Los Angeles, wrote in *El Universal*.[66]

By May 1930, as the Senate discussed the Harris bill, and would pass it soon thereafter, the Mexican press once again became defensive and cynical about the nature of the U.S. effort to place a quota on Mexico. A sample of prominent newspaper captions demonstrates how the Mexican press opposed the quota.

> "[John] Box continues rude attack upon us. Texas representative hurls insults at Mexicans."
> "Another speech by Box against entry of Mexicans into the United States."
> "Discussion of immigration law continues in United States. Press in certain Latin American countries discusses this important question in editorial pages."
> "Restriction of Mexicans only. Senate of United States approves so-called percentage [quota] system."
> "All may enter except Mexicans."
> "Passage of Mexican quota bill appears certain. State Department to oppose measure as likely to impede existing friendly relations."[67]

Concurrently the Mexican press continued to report on Mexico's growing unemployment problem. The situation was particularly bad in northern Mexico, where there was an increasing mass of deported Mexicans alongside others who wanted to migrate to the United States but who could not meet admission requirements. While Mexico's northern border towns suffered from a labor glut and were burdened by would-be migrants refused admission into the United States by American consulates, regions to the south suffered from a lack of workers as administrative restriction curbed pecuniary benefits of immigration. According to the postmaster in Michoacán, the state suffered from the loss of laborers due to immigration as well as from the drastic drop in remittances due to immigration restriction.[68]

A 1930 *Excelsior* editorial reflected Mexican opposition to the Harris bill. The U.S. Senate, the editorial stated, had given Mexico the unusual distinction of placing its immigration in a special class, "that of the undesirable," amid immigration from all other nations. While every other immigrant could continue to enter the United States, from the "Madagascans, Filipinos, and Moros reared by the estuaries of western islands," to "the hard-headed Brazilians born on the banks of the Amazon," as well as "Bolivian llama-drivers who live on the highest mountain peaks," and "Paraguayans who bathe along the edge of their magnificent rivers," only Mexicans would suffer from the quota. The Harris bill singled out Mexico for "curious exception" among all other Latin American nations. It would be better, the editorial concluded, to abandon all pretense of "goodwill" and call Mexico what the quota demonstrated it to be: "The Most Maligned, Least Favored, and Most Ill-Received Nation" on the continent.[69]

The U.S. Senate's passage of the Harris bill ignited a tirade of editorial comment from the Mexican press. In addition to the editorial described above, *Excelsior* published an article decrying how the Harris bill would place a quota on Mexico only. The editorial stated that the Harris bill "is inimical to Mexico from the mood it signifies and the exception of placing our country on a basis of inferiority as compared with other Latin American races. As such [the Harris bill] is a project both odious and outrageous." Similarly an editorial in *El Universal*, while appreciating the motives behind the Harris bill (namely, the preservation of American national unity and cohesion and the American standard of living), agreed that a quota would cause great injury to the Mexican people. Americans, "who are 100 percent white, as they say," "have no right to catalog us among inferior races and to deny us entry into their country after having taken without pity the last ounce of energy of hundreds of thousands of our compatriots who contributed with their strength, their health and even their blood to cementing that superb structure of North American prosperity from which they obtained not even a modest benefit." Another *El Universal* editorial argued that the quota undermined Pan-Americanism. The Western Hemisphere, the editorialist wrote, had been spared immigration restriction during earlier phases of restriction as "an attempt . . . to restore the word *American* to its rightful continental application." To restrict Mexican immigration would undermine "the last bases" of Pan-Americanism "and all hope for cordial understanding and goodwill among the nations of this new world." Finally, an editorial in *La Prensa* stated that while the United States was well within its right to pass such measures as the Harris bill, Mexico was well within its right to boycott American goods as a way to reciprocate the national slight caused by a quota.[70]

By the summer of 1930 Mexican president Pascual Ortiz Rubio was receiving myriad protests against the Harris bill. Protest letters came from all across Mexico: from Villa Acuña, Balcones, and Parras de la Fuente, Coahuila, in the northeast; from Salina Cruz, Oaxaca, in the south; from Ciudad Durango, Durango, in the west; and from Orizaba and Nogales, Veracruz, on the Gulf Coast to Mexicali, Baja California, in the northwest. Many of these protest letters came from worker syndicates comprised of bakers, dockworkers, day laborers, general workers, and farmers. The local syndicate of workers and farmers of Aljojaca and San Martín Texmelucan, Puebla, sent letters of support to President Ortiz Rubio; workers of Ajalpan, Puebla, protested the Harris bill and committed themselves to support "any attitude the government will adopt to counter such measures." Laborers in Tehuacan, Puebla, argued that the measures passed by the U.S. Senate against "our nationals" greatly affected all Mexican workers' groups, and supported the government to take "measures to counteract this work" ("medidas para contrarrestar esa labor").[71] Such letters demonstrate how immigration was an issue of national concern for Mexicans and that passage of the Harris bill sparked a national outcry against the United States. These letters are also noteworthy for the fact that many of the workers' syndicates that wrote letters protesting the Harris bill were of the same economic class as many of the Mexicans who sought to migrate northward.

Not surprisingly business groups in both nations protested the Harris bill. The president of the U.S. Chamber of Commerce, William Butterworth, urged organization chapters throughout the country to oppose the quota effort. Butterworth reiterated that the Harris bill would not only disrupt the national economy but also diplomatic relations.

> The State Department has frankly told the congressional committees that quota legislation applied to any of the Latin American republics would seriously injure our existing friendly diplomatic and commercial relations with those countries and adversely affect the general economic conditions and prosperity of the United States, through damage to our foreign trade.[72]

On May 25 the Mexican Chamber of Commerce in Ciudad Juarez, Chihuahua, sent a letter of protest to Mexico City, arguing that the approval of the Harris bill by the U.S. Congress "will be a grave moral offense to Mexico which will unfortunately be felt by its national dignity." Workers' organizations in Ciudad Juarez planned anti-quota demonstrations.[73] The American Chamber of Commerce in Mexico City sent protest letters not just to President Ortiz Rubio but also to President Herbert Hoover, Albert Johnson, and to the chairmen of the Foreign Relations Committees in Congress—William Borah in the Senate and Stephen Porter in the House of Representatives. In a telegram to U.S. ambassador Dwight Morrow, the chairman of the American Chamber of Commerce in Mexico City, C. D. Hicks, argued that the quota measure for Mexico was wrong.

> Proposed legislation restricting immigration from Mexico would not only be of no benefit but most unwise [at] this time[;] it will undo some of your good work[;] cordial and friendly relations between our two countries were never better and nothing should be done to affect this amicable feeling[;] such legislation will be inimical to the trade and friendly relations of the two countries[;] to single out Mexico for such legislation will inevitably result in unpleasant consequences.[74]

In a similar telegram to President Hoover, the American Chamber of Commerce expressed hope that the chances of the Harris bill's enactment into law were remote. In the event that the measure should be passed by Congress, the telegram stated, "we respectfully and with deep interest recommend your thoughtful consideration to its veto."[75]

Mexicans considered the Harris bill discriminatory "to the highest degree" and feared that its enactment would harm amicable relations between Mexico and the United States. According to the *New York Times*, Mexican opposition to the Harris bill was unanimous. Observers of immigration saw no potential benefit from the quota that would offset the ill feelings it would engender. Not only would the quota not curb immigration, it was argued by critics, but it would do nothing to help the many impoverished Mexican migrants stranded in the United States.[76] El Paso newspapers declared that the Harris bill was "careless" of Mexico's national pride. According to the *El Paso Evening Post*, passing a quota on Mexico alone would excite justifiable Mexican protest against the quota, since it would cast U.S. immigration policy as discriminatory against Mexicans. It would be better to apply the quota to all of Latin America. This would give Mexico no grounds on which to protest U.S. immigration law. Moreover passage of the bill into law would be futile since the Border Patrol did not have the wherewithal to enforce it. Such "sharply restrictive legislation" would create an "army of waders," who would enter the United States by "wading the . . . [Rio Grande] river instead of crossing the bridges." Cutting off cheap labor from Mexico would only encourage cheap labor immigration from other Latin American countries.[77] Finally, as Manuel Gamio argued again in April 1930, the quota would undermine the long-term structural solution to the immigration problem—Mexico's political stability.

Weeks before the U.S. Senate passed the Harris bill, Gamio contended in a new report on Mexican immigration, titled "Quantitative Estimate, Sources and Distribution of Mexican Immigration in the United States," that the numbers of migrants going to the United States and residing there were exaggerated. The heated debate about Mexican immigration to the United States was primarily based on the belief that the number of Mexicans in the United States was high and growing. Also, it was feared that the allegedly high numbers of Mexican immigrants in the United States would cause "serious" economic, racial, and cultural problems, especially considering the fact that few Mexicans assimilated to U.S. society.[78]

Gamio countered that Mexican immigration was bad for both nations, and to dispel the belief that Mexicans were swarming to the United States, he discussed two predominant streams of Mexican immigration. First, there was the stream of permanent immigration, which was comprised of Mexicans who sought to reside in the United States permanently without intending to return to Mexico. For Mexico these immigrants represented a permanent loss of labor; for the United States permanent Mexican immigration had social and economic consequences, often negative ones.[79] Second, there was the transitory or temporary stream of immigration, comprised of Mexicans who went back and forth between the United States and Mexico seeking work, often on a seasonal basis. For Mexico this stream was detrimental to national development, even as most migrants eventually returned. The instability of the Mexican workforce meant that much of the nation's natural resources remained unexploited. Gamio estimated that this transitory immigration stream regularly deprived Mexico of 9 percent of its workforce. Additionally, Gamio argued, temporary Mexican laborers were often the victims of mistreatment, exploitation, and racial prejudice in the United States. In this sense Mexico not only suffered from a shortage of labor but also from the national disgrace rooted in its inability to defend its citizen migrants. For the United States, while temporary Mexican labor fulfilled an economic demand, it also undermined the American labor market.[80]

Although economics was the main reason why Mexicans migrated northward, Gamio argued, Mexico's political instability had sustained steady rates of immigration throughout the 1910s and the 1920s. Gamio believed immigration spiked during times of political instability: during Francisco Madero's revolution in 1911, the

Constitutionalists' consolidation of power from 1915 to 1916, the fall of Carranza's government in 1920, the de la Huerta rebellion against Obregón's government between 1923 and 1924, and the Cristero Rebellion during the latter half of the 1920s.[81]

In short Gamio argued that the best remedy for the problem of Mexican immigration was Mexico's political stability. This analysis differed from other Mexican commentators' analysis of Mexican immigration. In his earlier reports Gamio had argued that a quota on Mexican immigration risked burdening Mexico with a labor glut and thereby compromising the state's internal security. Unlike Alfonso Fabila, who warned that Mexicans should stop migrating because of the abuse they could endure, Gamio was not suggesting that Mexico's immigration to the United States should stop. While Mexico suffered disgrace because of its citizens' abuse in the United States, Mexican immigration was still necessary. The safety valve of immigration, Gamio argued, spared Mexico the potential social strife caused by a labor glut, relieved the nation of unemployed or underemployed workers, and benefited the country through labor skills migrants brought back to Mexico and the remittances they sent from the United States.[82] Santibáñez argued the opposite. Instead of preserving Mexico's political stability, he believed immigration was perpetuating the country's political instability by retarding national economic growth. Gamio and Santibáñez, however, could both agree that the racial justification for a quota was fallacious and that only bilateral negotiations between the United States and Mexico could bring a permanent solution to the problem of Mexican immigration.

According to an editorial in *El Universal* from May 1930, Gamio's report showed how "unilateral interpretations" of the immigration problem and its solutions were "dangerous."[83] For Mexicans immigration was a national problem with a transnational cause and a bilateral solution. Not only was the quota offensive to Mexico's national pride and the Mexican people themselves; it was reprehensible because it could aggravate the social, economic, and political conditions that underlay immigration. For Mexico immigration was a "hemorrhage" that increased and decreased with the sociopolitical stability of the nation. Each revolutionary upheaval and recovery was exacerbated by the loss of citizens to northward immigration.[84] The quota placed in sharp relief the problems of economic underdevelopment and political instability that burdened Mexico. Immigration was a necessary evil to help maintain Mexico's domestic harmony, and yet it was a blight on the national identity because of the abuses migrants faced in the United States.

For American restrictionists, Mexican immigration was a social hazard that required regulation. Despite the success of administrative restriction throughout 1929, the first year of its implementation, restrictionists continued to seek a quota for Mexico. This was basically a function of U.S. racism, but administrative restriction and the increased illegal immigration contributed to the campaign. As the Great Depression eroded U.S. economic wealth and devastated the American labor market, the quota debate began to change. Some restrictionists continued their efforts to place a quota on Mexico. These efforts were largely redundant in the face of massive Mexican repatriation from 1930 to 1932. Economic reversal and American prejudice combined to coerce Mexicans to return to Mexico. This movement affected more than just recent migrants; in many cases permanent Mexican residents of the United States, and their children who had been born in the States and were American citizens, were coerced into going to Mexico. Repatriation would diminish the call for a quota. Whereas administrative restrictions largely curbed legal immigration, economic downturn undermined Mexicans' incentive to migrate northward. Curiously, despite high unemployment among American workers by the early 1930s, a demand for Mexican workers began to rebound as early as 1932–1933. Put simply, migrants were willing to do work Americans were not—despite economic depression. The racism that transcended data demonstrating Mexicans' high rate of repatriation during the late 1920s and that underwrote continued demands for a quota was the same racism that created a constant demand for the Mexican laborer.

While the Great Depression eased U.S.-Mexican tensions regarding the quota issue, repatriation complicated diplomatic relations between the two countries. Economic stagnation in the United States intensified all the worst features of American racism toward Mexicans, typified by nationwide efforts to send Mexicans back to Mexico. The sudden and massive return of Mexicans forced Mexico's government to divert resources to repatriate its citizens. Mexico City had taken steps to avoid such expenditure; indeed a primary reason it advised its citizens against immigration northward was to avoid the expense of repatriating its indigent citizens stranded in the United States. During the early 1930s, saddled with its own long-term underemployment problem and a recent downturn of unemployment attributable to the Great Depression, Mexico had to dedicate great energies to the repatriation of its citizens. The racism that seemed to motivate U.S. immigration law was now cited as a nationwide American abhorrence toward Mexicans that Mexico City utilized to demonstrate how it protected its citizens. Repatriation worsened the endemic racism that affected U.S.-Mexican relations during the quota debate.

6

Administrative Restriction, Repatriation, and the Demise of the Quota Effort

Summer 1930–Winter 1932

After 1930 the effects of administrative restriction and the Great Depression combined to end the quota debate in Congress. The pressure of unemployment caused many Mexicans to leave the United States during the early 1930s, initiating a wave of repatriation in which hundreds of thousands of Mexican immigrants and Mexican Americans flocked to Mexico. During this same period administrative restriction brought Mexican immigration almost to a complete standstill. For Mexico's workers the stoppage was complete; according to State Department figures, no Mexican common laborers entered the United States legally after the spring of 1930.

This twin pressure of repatriation and administrative restriction rapidly diminished Mexican immigration and Mexicans' presence within U.S. society. Administrative restriction's effectiveness tamped down congressional calls for a quota. Even as efforts to legislatively restrict Mexican immigration continued as late as January 1932, such efforts gained little support in the face of administrative restriction's drastic reduction of Mexican immigration.

While administrative restriction barred the steady flow of immigrants to the United States after it was implemented in March 1929, the repatriation crisis depleted the permanent Mexican population that had established itself within the United States. Mexicans throughout the States chose to return to Mexico because of unemployment. Also, many Mexicans fled to Mexico to escape the social prejudice against them in U.S. society, an animosity that was only heightened by the economic downturn after 1929. In this sense social coercion played as great a role as individual incentive in the repatriation crisis.

And yet, even as Mexicans went to Mexico in great numbers during the early 1930s, many sought to return to the United States soon after their arrival back in Mexico. Mexico, like the United States, suffered its own economic downturn; but Mexico's had its origins in the mid-1920s. The more recent unemployment problem was worsened by the nation's chronic underemployment problem and also by the return of thousands of *repatriados*. Finally, in an example of almost macabre humor, such socioeconomic difficulties were aggravated further by administrative restriction: consular reports show that almost none of the *repatriados* who applied to legally immigrate back into the United States were given permission to do so. With few options and stuck in Mexico's northern border towns, many of these rejected Mexicans chose to enter the United States illegally.

Diplomatically the repatriation of thousands of Mexicans to Mexico and how that movement heightened Mexico's socioeconomic problems was a peripheral concern for the United States. Administrative restriction was viewed as an effective compromise between no restriction on Mexican immigration and the implementation of a quota. For its part Mexico tried to put a good face on the repatriation crisis. The Mexican government hoped that labor skills *repatriados* had acquired in the United States could be applied to the development of Mexico's economy. The government planned resettlement projects, where newly returned *repatriados* would be settled on undeveloped lands. Many of these hopes were dashed by poor administration and meager financial resources.

The Mexican government did not express great opposition to administrative restriction. Despite its restrictive nature, consular restriction was less offensive nationally than the quota would have been. Additionally administrative restriction matched the socioeconomic goals of the government. By keeping common laborers in the country, Mexico was not losing workers. No objection was raised because administrative restriction curtailed permanent immigration, not temporary immigration.

Between 200,000 and 300,000 Mexican immigrants and Mexican Americans repatriated to Mexico from 1930 to 1934. They left the United States because of a lack of work and public prejudice against them. While most *repatriados* left the United States voluntarily, their departure was coerced and abetted. Historian Fernando Saúl Alanís Enciso argues that news of harassment, rumors of local authorities visiting Mexican homes to request immigration documentation, and the general mood of persecution coerced many Mexicans to return to Mexico.[1] Throughout the United States, local governments and railroad companies, which were more than happy to get immigrants out of their midst, facilitated Mexicans' return southward by discounting transportation costs (often by half); more altruistically, local charities provided food, shelter, and information to *repatriados* in need, though there is evidence that even these organizations played a part in pressuring Mexicans to leave the United States.[2] At the same time, local governments enforced immigration laws in such a way that Mexicans preferred to leave by their own accord rather than risk the ignominy of deportation. Historians Francisco Balderamma and Raymond Rodríguez argue that Mexicans "elected to face deprivation in their homeland rather than endure the disparagement heaped upon them in El Norte. . . . In Mexico they might suffer hunger pains, but at least they would be treated like human beings."[3] While there is little evidence to suggest that repatriation directly affected U.S.-Mexican relations, the period during which many Mexicans repatriated reveals how Mexico's government continued to regard immigration (in this scenario, return immigration of its nationals) as a matter of national concern. And how Mexico City prioritized its handling of the repatriation crisis illuminates how it addressed immigration as a diplomatic issue with the United States.

Mexico had encouraged the repatriation of its citizens from the United States since the Porfirian era. In 1908 Díaz's government attended to Mexican nationals deported from the United States during the recession of 1907–1908. During the postwar recession of 1921–1922, Obregón's government supported the repatriation of over 150,000 Mexicans.[4] Mexico City was no less active in assisting the repatriation of its citizens after the onset of the Great Depression in 1929. As in past moments of repatriation, the sudden return of Mexican nationals to Mexico was attributable to unemployment, hunger, deportation, raids by U.S. immigration service officers, and anti-foreigner sentiments within U.S. society. The repatriation crisis took place during the presidencies of Emilio Portes Gil (1928–1930), Pascual Ortiz Rubio (1930–1932), and Abelardo Rodríguez (1932–1934), all of whom took measures to help Mexicans return to their place of origin in Mexico. Mexico's Foreign Ministry (SRE), working through its consulates throughout the United States, took charge of repatriating Mexicans. The Mexican government concentrated on transporting migrants from the border to their towns of origin. The Interior Ministry provided free rail tickets from the border.[5] Railroads were most utilized because they were the cheapest form of transportation.[6]

Mexico City had a political and economic incentive to support repatriation. According to Enciso the Mexican government assumed a patriotic duty to repatriate its nationals; *repatriados* were considered a part of the nation, and the government sought to provide for its destitute citizens abroad. Such efforts reflected well on a government that sought to build credibility with the Mexican populace. At the same time, Mexico City saw in the repatriation crisis an opportunity to meet its socioeconomic goals for the nation. *Repatriados* were viewed as nationals with distinct labor skills that could benefit Mexico. Consequently many *repatriados* were encouraged to settle in new development colonies throughout underpopulated and undeveloped parts of the country. In short the Mexican government supported repatriation on nationalist, humanitarian grounds, but it also expected *repatriados* to help promote the postrevolutionary development of Mexico into an "agricultural, irrigated, colonized, 'racially-improved,' Mexicanized, and sovereign" nation.[7]

Despite Mexico City's best intentions, the repatriation crisis quickly overwhelmed it. Repatriation revealed several problems within the Mexican state. First, Mexico was constrained in its efforts to repatriate its nationals. Government funding was scarce, and the number of Mexicans seeking to repatriate soon outpaced the capacity of Mexican consular authorities. Second, entry ports like Nogales, Ciudad Juarez, Nuevo Laredo, and Matamoros could not accommodate the onslaught of *repatriados*. The small border towns of Mexicali and Tijuana were so encumbered with *repatriados* that the Mexican government sent a formal request to the United States that returnees be routed to other entry points. At the time Tijuana was a dusty town of twenty thousand people that was unconnected by rail or road to the rest of Mexico. The United States subsequently took steps to return Mexicans through larger exit points like El Paso or Nogales.[8] According to Balderamma and Rodríguez, Mexican officials were unprepared for the massive influx of Mexicans seeking entry into Mexico. "Customs facilities, food supplies, housing, medical attention, and railroad transportation creaked, groaned, and in some cases finally collapsed."[9] *Repatriados*, often traveling as families, frequently could not afford rail fare to the U.S.-Mexico border and became stuck inside the United States. The case of Pascual Camarena and his family illustrates this point. After departing for Mexico from Manhattan, Kansas, the Camarenas were unable to afford rail fare from San Antonio to the border. On their behalf the Mexican consulate in San Antonio asked Mexico City permission to provide half the cost of the fare. The government responded by saying that it could not afford such expenditure.[10] In a similar situation the Mexican consul at Galveston, Texas, appealed to American railroad companies to provide drastically reduced fares for *repatriados*, and even requested the local baseball association to host a game that could raise funds for *repatriados*.[11]

In his landmark book, *Troublesome Border*, historian Oscar Martínez describes "floating" Mexican populations, or groups of migrants who sought to enter the United States but were unable to for various reasons. As mentioned in the previous chapter, unemployed laborers were often a burden on Mexico's northern border towns. The problem was particularly acute during the repatriation crisis of the early 1930s, Martínez argues, when as many as 500,000 to one million Mexican Americans and Mexican immigrants were stranded along the border as they awaited transportation to Mexico's interior after leaving the United States. A related floating population phenomenon occurred within the border towns of the American Southwest. Mexicans, in an effort to return to Mexico amid economic depression, could not afford transportation to the border.[12]

Repatriation also aggravated Mexico's unemployment problem. Since the mid-1920s Mexico had been in a period of economic recession and stagnation. According to historians Gil Joseph and Jürgen Buchenau, the most significant reason for the economic crisis was a decline in the export sector, particularly in the value of mineral production. From mid-1926 to mid-1927 the world market price of silver, copper, and other precious metals declined by 20 percent. To make matters worse, foreign-owned petroleum companies divested their holdings from Mexico for fear that they might be expropriated. Between 1924 and 1928 oil production dropped by 65 percent. Commercial agricultural yields also declined. Demand for cotton and henequen, two of Mexico's main export crops, shrank massively after the end of the Great War. As market demand decreased so did employment opportunities: commercial farmers reduced the size of their crops, which reduced the number of hands needed for cultivation, and leaner crop yields demanded fewer workers at processing plants. The year 1929 was a particularly bad agricultural year for Mexico. One-fourth of lands planted never yielded harvests because of drought. Finally, there were declines in yields of corn and beans, the two basic staples of the Mexican diet. In 1933 Mexico produced 30 percent less corn and 22 percent fewer beans than in 1907, the last good agricultural year before the revolution. Between 1928 and 1930 per capita consumption of corn declined by more than a third.[13]

In short the Great Depression hit Mexico more than two years before it did the United States. The nation suffered from capital flight and a monetary crisis. Between 1926 and 1932 per capita gross domestic product (GDP) dropped by almost 31 percent and federal tax revenues declined, even as Mexico's unemployment rate tripled from 1930 to 1932. Half of the miners living in Cananea, Sonora, were unemployed; massive layoffs occurred in Toluca, Mexico State, when the local brewery and several textile mills closed down. In Jalisco, historian Ramón Eduardo Ruiz states, "armies" of jobless men begged for work while the return of Mexicans expelled from the United States worsened the unemployment situation. Already suffering from chronic underemployment since the mid-1920s, Mexico witnessed a sudden rise in unemployment with the onset of the Great Depression north of the border. Consequently Mexico City was unable to fund revolutionary programs in education and public health, as well as efforts to aid the repatriation of its nationals from the United States during the early 1930s.[14]

American consuls in Mexico witnessed the rise in unemployment firsthand and recorded Mexicans' plight. In June 1930 the American consul in San Luis Potosí, G. P. Shaw, reported that many laborers who were normally employed regularly had barely enough for their daily needs.[15] Four months later, in his next quarterly report on the economic conditions in San Luis Potosí, Shaw stated that there was an excess of labor across all branches of industry. The National Railway was laying off workers, as well as were the factories. And those who still had work had seen their wages reduced.[16]

The American consul at Chihuahua reported that unemployment there increased because of layoffs in the mining industry, as well as cutbacks in dam and irrigation projects in the surrounding areas. Farmers were destitute because of poor crop yields, and retail and wholesale firms were reducing their number of employees. Despite the new state governor's intention to study the unemployment situation and to sponsor new public works projects, the American consul continued, the lack of money in the state treasury would likely prevent the fulfillment of such measures. Wholesalers were living "from hand to mouth" and retailers were on the verge of bankruptcy. Wholesalers had an overstock of goods and they did not believe their orders would pick up anytime soon. Retailers were even worse off; the value of the peso had dropped considerably during recent months, while duties on imported goods had forced them to raise prices on all imported articles. And as unemployment had increased, the purchasing power of the people had decreased. These deleterious economic conditions were intensified, the consul stated, by the fact that residents who had disposable income often traveled to El Paso, where prices were lower, to buy clothing, shoes, and other goods. Finally, the consul concluded, few laborers in his district migrated legally to the United States, worsening the unemployment situation in Chihuahua. In this sense the safety valve was not only closed but reversed by repatriation.[17]

W. E. Copley, the American consul at Monterrey, reported in July 1930 that the industrial recession that had begun during the early months of the year continued to negatively affect local industries. Orders and collections were down and, consequently, production and employment were down. Local businesses and laborers awaited with nervous anticipation the result of a dispute between the town's smelter owners and its workers, who demanded at least part of their salaries in the face of the owners announcing a suspension in production.[18] And the American consul at Nuevo Laredo, John Macdonald, reported in September 1930 that wages were low (an average of $1 per day or less) and that there was always an excess of labor. The glut of workers was heightened by the recent harvesting of the local cotton crop.[19]

Finally, Dudley Dwyre, the American consul in Mexico City, provided a nationwide perspective on the growing unemployment crisis in Mexico in 1930, in the midst of the repatriation crisis. According to Dwyre the unemployment situation had become "more serious" during the second quarter of 1930. He attributed the unemployment crisis to the curtailment or suspension of mining activities, adverse conditions in agriculture, general business depression, and, significantly, the return of Mexican laborers from the United States. In Mexico City and the vicinity, he reported, was an "unknown but large" number of unemployed. This mass of out-of-work laborers was exacerbated by the "considerable numbers" of unemployed flocking to the capital from regions where unemployment was worse. Textile mills across the country had appealed to the federal government to suspend production; some mills had shut down entirely. Both scenarios added to the body of unemployed Mexicans. The curtailment or suspension of operations, Dwyre continued, in the mining industry had thrown many laborers out of work in Ciudad Chihuahua, Chihuahua, Pachuca, Hidalgo, and Cinco Minas, Jalisco. Across the country there was a rise in the number of unemployed agricultural workers. A large number of these laborers, who had attempted but failed to obtain work in the United States, had returned to Mexico and had aggravated the nation's unemployment problem. Rumors and press reports stated that the National Railways was contemplating a reduction in operations. Many feared such downsizing would result in additional workers losing their jobs.[20]

Few practical advantages awaited *repatriados* as they returned to Mexico. Many fled poor economic conditions in the United States only to find a worse situation in their home country. The repatriation crisis clearly intensified Mexico's economic woes.

The Spanish-language press reacted quickly to the repatriation crisis, which, according to Balderamma and Rodríguez, was "tailor made for engaging in biting, often vitriolic, Yankee baiting."[21] In addition to *Excelsior* and *El Universal* (Mexico City), *La Opinión* (Los Angeles), *La Prensa* (San Antonio), and *El Heraldo* (San Diego) decried the conditions of repatriation and constantly reported the plight and numbers of *repatriados*. In their critique of the repatriation crisis, the Spanish-language press argued several points: that Mexicans had been instrumental in the development of the U.S. economy, often at the expense of their health and their best years of labor power; that honest and industrious workers were treated inhumanely in U.S. society; and that the repatriation crisis itself was attributable to blatant racism against Mexicans.[22]

In October 1930 *Excelsior* reported that during the previous month 3,385 Mexicans returned to Mexico via Nuevo Laredo, and *El Universal* reported the same month that 25 families were returning daily to Mexico through the same port of entry.[23] In December *Excelsior* reported that 12,000 Mexicans returned to Mexico via Nuevo Laredo between September and November and that 2,695 returned during the first half of December. Robert Frazer, American consul general in Mexico City, had little doubt that the rise of unemployment in the United States was what drove Mexicans to return to Mexico. Also, he reported that the Mexican Department of Interior warned nationals not to migrate north in search of employment, as American authorities were "constantly arresting and deporting" those Mexicans who were unable to find work and were in difficult financial circumstances.[24]

Rates of repatriation accelerated in 1931. In January *El Universal* reported that repatriation was not only affecting the border region. The Mexican consul in New York City was also besieged by Mexicans who wanted to repatriate. The paper also gave an account of American workmen in Terre Haute, Indiana, intimidating Mexican railroad construction workers and forcing those Mexicans to quit their jobs. That same month *Excelsior* stated that a train of 3,000 *repatriados* had left Ciudad Juarez for the interior. The persons on the train were believed to be "entirely destitute" and dependent either on the Mexican government or private organizations for necessities such as food and clothing.[25] By February 1931 the Mexican Immigration Department observed that 60,228 Mexicans had returned to Mexico between January and November 1930.[26] In June *Excelsior* reported that more than 150,000 Mexicans had returned to Mexico from the United States since January. *El Universal* reported that from Houston, Texas, 140 families (about 500 persons) left during the month of May alone.[27] That same summer the *Diario del Norte*, the local daily newspaper in Saltillo, Coahuila, estimated that between 3,000 and 5,000 Mexicans were departing the United States monthly. Almost daily, the newspaper reported, *repatriados* arrived in Saltillo in their cars and trucks, with license plates of several U.S. states, carrying all their household and personal effects.[28]

An editorial from *El Universal* in January 1931 applauded the Mexican government's efforts to assist *repatriados*, while at the same time acknowledging the difficulty of protecting citizens residing in a foreign country. Although measures had been proposed and even enacted to defend the interests of Mexicans in the United States and consulates had gone to great lengths to aid Mexicans, the Mexican government's hands were tied. It could not watch over the security of its citizens in a foreign country; neither could it demand privileged treatment for its citizens in the United States. Instead Mexico "must content itself to requesting for its citizens temporarily or permanently resident in the foreign lands treatment of equality before the law which democracy promises to all men." Nevertheless, the editorialist concluded, when "our emigrants" are "exploited and reviled" in the United States, it is of such importance "from the moral view point" that Mexico must do all it can to protect its citizens for the sake of national prestige.[29]

American consuls throughout the Mexican north provided a sense of how many Mexicans departed the United States during the repatriation crisis. William Blocker, the American consul at Ciudad Juarez, reported in November 1930 that 13,140 Mexicans repatriated to Mexico through that port of entry during the first ten months of 1930.[30] Two months later, in January 1931, Blocker reported that for the past several months an average of nearly 70 Mexicans, including women and children, had passed through Ciudad Juarez on their way to the interior. Of this amount, Blocker estimated, only 10 percent of *repatriados* were financially able to provide themselves transportation to the interior. Within that 10 percent, *repatriados* relied on cars for transportation, which were loaded with all of their belongings, including bedding and furniture. The local municipal government, in response to the poverty of *repatriados*, provided free food to returning Mexicans stranded along the border. In Ciudad Juarez the food prepared for inmates at the local prison was given to *repatriados* for free. *Repatriados* would head to the prison at mealtime for the food. Blocker estimated that about 300 persons were fed daily in this manner.[31]

In May 1931 the American consul at Nuevo Laredo, Oscar Harper, reported that almost 30,000 Mexicans had passed through that port of entry since the previous July and that almost 8,000 had passed through since January.[32] Four months later Everett Drumright, the American vice consul at Ciudad Juarez, reported that Mexican government statistics showed that over 67,000 Mexican nationals repatriated to Mexico during 1930, and he believed the rate of repatriation would only increase during 1931. Judging by the inflow of *repatriados* through his port of entry during the first eight months of the year, Drumright estimated a 50 percent increase in repatriation figures from the year before. *Repatriados* who arrived at Juarez returned from all parts of the American Southwest: predominantly California, but also Texas, New Mexico, Arizona, and Colorado.[33]

Between 1930 and 1933 Paul Foster, the American consul at Piedras Negras, Coahuila, provided quarterly reports on immigration and repatriation through his port of entry. These data provide a sense of how repatriation waxed and waned at the local level and serve as a case study to show how the mass return of Mexicans to Mexico during the early 1930s affected the border region. Before the onset of the Great Depression, Foster wrote poetically about the benefits of immigration for Mexican nationals. He claimed to detect a "more awakened, intelligent expression" in Mexicans who had spent time and worked in the United States, in contrast to those who had not and were, presumably, not yet enlightened. Additionally Foster argued that Mexico itself benefitted from the return of Mexican migrants. The infusion of *repatriados* into Mexican society would help the nation modernize. The "modern ideas of standards of living and political behavior" migrants acquired in the United States, Foster stated, "would act as a leaven to the great mass of their backward fellow citizens," and would help toward the economic modernization of Mexico.[34] Foster's perspective on repatriation was not dissimilar to that of Manuel Gamio and the Mexican government during this time—that the advanced labor skills Mexicans gained in the United States could be applied to the development of the Mexican economy. Such sentiment underscored the Mexican government's attempts to help resettle Mexicans within the nation during the repatriation crisis.

By mid-1930 Foster was no longer philosophizing about the socioeconomic benefits of immigration and repatriation. Rather he was focused on recording the increasing wave of *repatriados* who passed through his consular district. Repatriation rates via Piedras Negras gradually increased throughout 1930; they took a sudden dive in 1931, but spiked dramatically in late 1931 to early 1932. Another sharp decline in repatriation occurred between January and April 1932; repatriation rates stabilized by the spring of 1933.

Foster's explanation for this fluctuation in repatriation patterns through Piedras Negras and its vicinity reveals the various reasons why Mexican immigration shrank during the early 1930s, and helps explain why the congressional quota effort died during the same period. First, the onset of the Great Depression in the United States after October 1929 caused an unemployment crisis that resulted in the mass exodus of Mexican immigrants and Mexican Americans to Mexico. Second, the concomitant problem of unemployment, compounded by the long-term problem of underemployment, in Mexico forced many *repatriados* to seek reentry into the United States. Third, administrative restriction, which was implemented in March 1929, drastically curtailed Mexican immigration, preventing many Mexicans from doing what they had done for generations—migrating for work. The net result was a massive burden on the Mexican labor market. This chain of causation explains the fluctuation of repatriation through Piedras Negras.

As early as July 1931 Foster reported that *repatriados* had applied for immigration visas in order to return to the United States. No visas were issued to these applicants, Foster explained, because their poor financial positions marked them as LPCs (likely to become a public charge).[35] In April 1932, just after he had described what would be the highest peak of repatriation in January through Piedras Negras and its vicinity (more than 5,000 persons between October and December 1931), Foster credited the sudden decline in repatriation between January and April 1932 to Mexico's unemployment problem and to news that the stricter enforcement of immi-

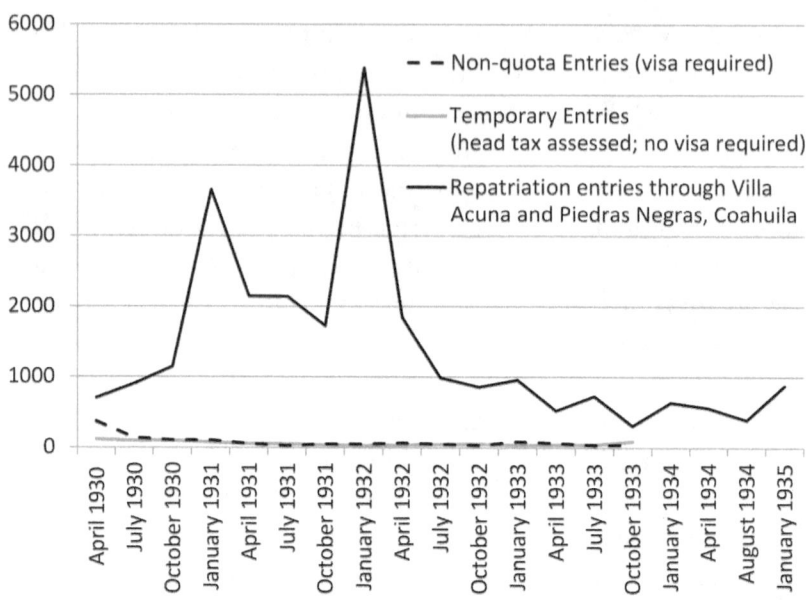

Rates of emigration and repatriation from Piedras Negras and vicinity. *Source*: As recorded in quarterly reports regarding Del Rio, Texas; Eagle Pass, Texas; Piedras Negras, Coahuila; and Villa Acuña, Coahuila, by U.S. consul Paul Foster at Piedras Negras, Coahuila, Mexico, to U.S. State Department. Foster to State Department, April 6, 1929, NARA, RG 59, 811.111 Mexico/192; September 27, 1929, 811.111 Mexico/276; February 6, 1930, 811.111 Mexico/321; April 10, 1930, 811.111 Mexico/349; July 8, 1930, 811.111 Mexico/408; October 14, 1930, 811.111 Mexico/491; January 27, 1931, 812.5511/105; April 13, 1931, 812.5511/113; July 14, 1931, 811.111 Mexico/656; October 9, 1931, 812.5511/122; January 20, 1932, 812.5511/132; April 7, 1932, 811.111 Mexico/798; July 11, 1932, 812.5511/143; October 10, 1932, 811.111 Mexico/898; January 21, 1933, 811.111 Mexico/947; April 19, 1933, 811.111 Mexico/1005; July 11, 1933, 811.111 Mexico/1051; October 11, 1933, 811.111 Mexico/1076; January 20, 1934, 812.5511/153; April 12, 1934, 812.5511/157; August 15, 1934, 811.111 Mexico/1150; January 16, 1935, 812.5511/167. Created by author.

gration laws by American consular officials made it difficult to reenter the United States. Almost daily, he stated, his office received visa applications from *repatriados* who sought to (re-)migrate northward. Practically all applications were refused because of many applicants' likelihood of becoming public charges. This trend continued into the summer.[36] Foster's quarterly reports for the latter half of 1932 reported similar findings: repatriation declined rapidly as news spread of the unemployment situation in Mexico and the disruptively efficient U.S. implementation of administrative restriction.[37] The case study of Piedras Negras reveals that the repatriation crisis was more than simply a headlong exodus of Mexican nationals in response to the Great Depression. Instead it was a period of furious repatriation tempered by individuals' efforts to salvage their livelihoods in the midst of a transnational economic crisis.

An *Excelsior* editorial from August 1930 commented on Mexico's socioeconomic shortcomings that accounted for the same fluctuations in repatriation observed by Paul Foster in Piedras Negras two years later. Commenting on the "fraternal and sympathetic" reception of over one thousand *repatriados* in Torreón, the editorial was pessimistic about how the nation would provide for its returned nationals in the midst of Mexico's economic troubles and underdevelopment. Despite the outpouring of charity from the residents of Torreón to the "numerous and afflicted" *repatriados*— the local chamber of commerce distributed coffee, canned goods, other food, and clothing to the returned Mexicans—a permanent place needed to be found for *repatriados*. The only fitting welcome the nation could give its *repatriados*, the writer continued, was a developing economy that could offer them work—where money circulated, credit was sound, machinery operated, and fallow lands were irrigated. Otherwise *repatriados* would only contribute to the nation's unemployment problem. Perhaps, the writer hoped, repatriation would inspire a change in Mexico's socioeconomic situation. Or perhaps the *repatriados*' presence could lead to a "reorganization of the national economy; a revision of procedures and 'ideologies' that have had such lamentable results; a renewal of the broken threads in the delicate warp of production." Until then, the editorialist concluded, Mexico's embrace of its returned nationals would not represent the return of the Prodigal Son, since at present "there is no fat calf to kill."[38]

Foster was overly optimistic about *repatriados*' ability to reintegrate into Mexico's shattered economy. He believed modern labor skills acquired by Mexicans who had migrated to the United States would ensure them work upon their return southward and would benefit the modernization of Mexico's economy. "It is noted," Foster wrote, "that all of these returning emigrants bring with them a practical knowledge of more modern farm and shop work which will not fail to be of value not only to themselves but to the district in which they take up their residence and to [Mexico] at large."[39]

The reality of *repatriados*' return to Mexico was quite different. According to Tim Henderson *repatriados* returned to Mexico to find ongoing hardship in their home country, and contributed to the nation's labor glut. *Repatriados* were received with ambivalence by their compatriots. While some Mexicans encouraged the return of migrants as a patriotic gesture that could benefit the nation, because of migrants' earnings, property, and new labor skills, others viewed *repatriados* as traitors who had abandoned the homeland and whose return undermined Mexico's political stability. Ambitious, government-led colonization projects that sought to settle returning migrants on fallow lands were often bedeviled by poor planning and government corruption.[40] Most *repatriados* were forced to scramble for work alongside their countrymen or compelled to attempt reentry into the United States.[41]

In April 1932, as Paul Foster reported a steep decline of repatriation through Piedras Negras, the *Los Angeles Times* published an editorial that seemed to mark the crest of Mexicans' return immigration to Mexico. Entitled "The Repatriados," the editorial stated that 200,000 Mexicans, or 14 percent of all Mexicans residing in the United States, had left the country during 1931.[42] The editorial called it the greatest immigration ever seen in the Western Hemisphere, but distinct within the history of great mass exoduses.

"The Mexican immigration was not a movement of people like the Greeks leaving Asia Minor after the World War—they were forced out; nor like the great Boer trek in South Africa; nor the Huguenots' departure from France; nor the barbarians who swept down from the North upon the Roman Empire to conquer. . . . The Mexican exodus as a great immigration was more like that of the Children of Israel when they left Egypt although in this instance the Promised Land lay behind rather than ahead."

The *Times* recounted how the Great Depression hit Mexicans hard in the United States. They lost work, became burdens to public charities, and were hounded by federal immigration authorities. Mexicans left the United States by car, train, or foot. Many left behind most of their possessions and sold their property cheaply. And yet, despite some pains of re-acclimation, they had the ability, the editorialist concluded, to (re)settle in Mexico and find work. No unemployment problem in Mexico was recognized, much less the desire of many *repatriados* to return to the United States. Instead the mass exodus of Mexicans back to Mexico was portrayed as a great benefit both to them and their home nation, which would benefit from (what Paul Foster called) the "more awakened" modern spirit and labor ability of *repatriados*.[43]

It is not clear how many Mexican immigrants and Mexican Americans repatriated to Mexico from the United States during the early 1930s. National figures provided by the U.S. Embassy in August 1932 confirm fluctuations witnessed by Paul Foster in Piedras Negras, while depicting numbers provided by the *Los Angeles Times* as exaggerated. Fernando Saúl Alanís Enciso, in an article on repatriation, presents more comprehensive figures. According to Enciso, the flow of repatriation was massive initially, lasted for only a brief period, and soon subsided.

Table 6. Nationwide repatriation to Mexico from the United States, October 1930–June 1932

	1930	1931	1932
January	—	6,657	9,394
February	—	6,216	6,501
March	—	7,719	6,229
April	—	7,448	8,594
May	—	7,616	7,925
June	—	9,959	—
July	—	8,465	—
August	—	8,624	—

September	—	9,398	—
October	8,610	17,092	—
November	9,679	21,055	—
December	9,927	14,742	—
Total	28,216	124,991	38,643

Source: Cummings to State Department, September 8, 1932, NARA, RG 59, 812.5511/144, 1; Cummings to State Department, February 19, 1932, NARA, RG 59, 812.55/179.

Table 7. Nationwide repatriation from the United States to Mexico, 1930–1934

1930–1931	From 70,127 to 138,519 (biggest year of return)
1932	From 138,519 to 77,453 (44% decrease from previous year)
1933	From 77,453 to 33,574 (57% decrease from previous year)
1934	From 33,574 to 23,934 (29% decrease from previous year)

Source: Enciso, "Repatriation of Mexicans from the United States and Mexican Nationalism, 1929–1940," 58.

Cities throughout the United States organized campaigns to drive out Mexican workers from their communities: New York City and Pittsburgh in the Northeast; Gary, Detroit, Kansas City, and Chicago in the Midwest; San Antonio and New Orleans in the South; El Paso, Texas, on the U.S-Mexico border and Phoenix in the Southwest; Denver in the Mountain West and Fairbanks in the Alaskan Territory; and all along the Pacific Coast—San Diego, San Francisco, Seattle, and Portland. According to historian Camille Guerin-Gonzales, U.S. authorities directed their repatriation efforts toward permanent residents of Mexican descent—both immigrant and citizen—rather than Mexican workers temporarily in the country. By seeking to remove the permanent Mexican population in the United States, Guerin-Gonzales argues, "authorities underlined the widely held belief that Mexican Americans had no legitimate claim to the U.S. as their home country."[44] Los Angeles County, which had the nation's highest concentration of Mexican immigrants, was considered the "hotbed" of the repatriation effort. By the mid-1930s well over twelve thousand Mexican immigrants and Mexican Americans had been shipped out of that county alone.[45] Charles Visel, the director of the Los Angeles Committee on Coordination of Unemployment Relief, believed the removal of immigrants from U.S. society was the surest way to resolve the nation's unemployment crisis. The local police chief, Roy Steckel, took Visel's reasoning one step further by arguing that the removal of immigrants would solve the city's crime problems. Visel used a scare tactic that he called "scareheading." According to historian Tim Henderson, this strategy involved having several men from the U.S. Department of Labor come to Los Angeles and preside over a few arrests, ensuring that those arrests received ample publicity. By early 1931 the Bureau of Immigration had sent agents to Los Angeles to assist in the removal process. Immigration agents and local police carried out a string of well-publicized raids that detained and questioned thousands of persons suspected of being in the country illegally. The majority of those apprehended and deported were Mexicans. Immigrant removal practices like scareheading created a social environment so hostile to immigrants that many Mexicans voluntarily left the United States.[46]

It is worth reiterating that most Mexicans who repatriated were not formally deported but coerced into returning to Mexico. Deportation proceedings involved cumbersome and time-consuming administrative procedures that the U.S. Department of Labor and Border Patrol, local welfare agencies, and other government bodies were not willing to undertake. Deportations, historian Dorothee Schneider shows, required hearings, background checks, and the opportunity for immigrants to prove their innocence. From the perspective of the Immigration Bureau, this was too slow a process to expel tens of thousands of suspected illegal immigrants. Instead the Bureau instituted a "fast track" system to deport men and women found to be in the United States illegally.

These de facto deportations occurred without hearings or appeals and were based on the premise that immigrants *volunteered* to leave the United States at their own expense. Fast-track deportations had advantages for the Immigration Bureau because it saved time and effort in the expulsion of undesirable immigrants from U.S. society, and it benefitted immigrants because voluntary departure did not classify illegal immigrants as deportees allowing them to apply for legal readmission to the United States once they were on the other side of the border.[47]

Instead social coercion, David Gutiérrez argues, was the preferred method.[48] According to Henderson federal, state, and municipal leaders used coercion to make living situations in the United States so intolerable for Mexicans that they decided to leave.[49] In addition to the lack of work and social prejudice, many Mexicans voluntarily left the United States because they hoped to receive aid from Mexico City and expected to be transported to farmlands in the interior in need of their labor or to their home villages.[50] In reality assistance was hampered by Mexico City's limited financial resources and many *repatriados* were simply left north of the border.[51] Circumstance often determined the fate of *repatriados*. Some aggravated Mexico's unemployment problem; some were able to slip back across the border into the United States. Others were absorbed into the traditional economy, while some actually benefitted from the land-redistribution programs.

The repatriation crisis did nothing to foster good relations between the United States and Mexico. The coerced deportation of Mexican nationals from the United States demonstrated how American racism undercut any spirit of Pan-Americanism of the time. As Josefina Vázquez and Lorenzo Meyer explain, Mexican newspaper accounts of *repatriados'* arduous journeys back to the *patria* hurt Mexico's national pride and deepened even further the ever-present sense of anti-American feeling among Mexicans.[52]

The striking curtailment of Mexican immigration to the United States through administrative restriction during the early 1930s coincided dramatically with the repatriation of Mexicans. American consuls, after March 1929 when the State Department implemented administrative restriction as official consular policy across Mexico, began to strictly enforce existing immigration laws as a way to reduce Mexican immigration without relying on new congressional legislation. Administrative restriction had the added benefit of cutting Mexican immigration without inciting Mexican ire. The quota was considered bad for U.S.-Mexican relations, and the State Department believed a reduction in officially recorded immigration would dampen calls for a quota. This goal was achieved, and quickly. By the spring of 1930 common laborers were no longer issued immigration visas necessary to enter the United States legally and Mexican immigration had been reduced by almost 90 percent compared to yearly averages between 1925 and 1929.

The Mexican government raised no objection to administrative restriction. Compared to the volume of rhetoric opposed to quota proposals in the United States from the late 1920s, the documentary evidence reveals no open, official Mexican opposition. This lack of opposition may be attributable to the fact that while administrative restriction drastically curtailed legal immigration, it did nothing to reduce temporary immigration and hardly stemmed illegal immigration (and perhaps encouraged it).[53] In this way the Mexican government's socioeconomic goals for the nation were abetted by U.S. immigration law: permanent immigration of Mexicans to the United States represented a permanent loss of laborers from Mexico, while the sustained (and growing) stream of temporary labor still allowed Mexico to rely on immigration as a safety valve for its Mexican economy. Even though administrative restriction complemented Mexico's development goals, it is surprising that the Mexican government raised no objection to U.S. efforts to curb its immigration. Economic slowdown had caused an unemployment crisis in Mexico after 1930. The repatriation crisis exacerbated this burden on the national labor market by saddling the already burdened labor market with hundreds of thousands of *repatriados* seeking work. In many ways administrative restriction worsened Mexico's socioeconomic troubles. And yet there was no significant protest. On the contrary some Mexican observers of the immigration problem viewed administrative restriction as an impetus to correct Mexico's problem of underdevelopment, which was viewed as the underlying reason why Mexicans chose to migrate in the first place. Mexico did not protest against administrative restriction because it occurred at the individual or local level, whereas the quota proposed to restrict Mexican immigration at the collective, national level.

Restrictionists relied on race as a prime justification for placing a quota on Mexico. These justifications upset the national pride of Mexicans and risked harming amicable relations between the United States and Mexico. By contrast the stricter enforcement of U.S. immigration laws by American consuls removed the prospect (and reality) of restriction from a national context and instead situated it at a regional and local level. Such restriction, while highly effective, was incremental and individual. Instead of facing restriction because of their nationality, Mexicans were restricted individually for not meeting the immigration requirements of the United States. Additionally administrative restriction entailed the enforcement of *existing* immigration laws; it did not require the passage of new legislation. As such, Mexicans were spared the national embarrassment they feared if Congress were to amend the Immigration Act of 1924 to remove Mexico from the list of non-quota nations. Furthermore, Mexicans could hardly criticize immigration laws that were applied broadly and across the world. Finally, administrative restriction gave the consular service flexibility in enforcing immigration laws. Just as easily as it ratcheted up its strict exclusion of Mexican immigrants, it could relax the strict exclusion of Mexicans if time and economic needs required it. In short, administrative restriction would defuse much of the immigration problem by the early 1930s and made the application of a quota unnecessary.

George Winters, the American vice consul in Mexico City, articulated clearly the State Department's preference for administrative restriction and described the legislation that underlined the legality of such a curb on immigration. In an address before the Seminar of the Committee on Cultural Relations with Latin America in July

1930, Winters said that the State Department opposed the Harris bill, which called for a quota on Mexican immigration, because it was "not necessary," and that existing immigration laws could adequately limit Mexico's immigration to "a reasonable figure." The Immigration Acts of both 1917 and 1924 formed the basis for administrative restriction, Winters argued. Section 3 of the 1917 act provided up to thirty classes of aliens that were inadmissible to the United States. Immigrants who were laborers were often affected by restrictions against contract labor, LPCs, and illiterates. Section 2(f) of the 1924 act stipulated that a consular official had the authority to refuse a visa to any applicant who—whether by observation, interview, or paperwork—seemed not to comply with U.S. immigration law standards. Winters demonstrated that the strict implementation of these laws had an immediate effect on Mexican immigration to the United States. Between fiscal years 1927–1928 and 1929–1930 (the first fiscal year during which administrative restriction was implemented) visa issuance to Mexicans was reduced by 80 percent. Not only had this new policy drastically reduced the rate of Mexican immigration, he argued; it also resulted in "a decided improvement" in the class of Mexicans to the United States: students, wives, and children, as opposed to common laborers. During fiscal year 1929–1930 only 1,199 visas were issued to common laborers who had not previously resided in the United States, and not a single visa was issued to a common laborer between April and June of 1930.[54]

In the months that followed the Senate's passage of the Harris bill in May 1930, the U.S. consul service began to report that administrative restriction was so effective that Mexican immigration was no longer a problem for the United States. During the summer of 1930 consuls from across Mexico reported the effectiveness of administrative restriction. According to A. Dana Hodgdon, chief of the Visa Office, only 370 Mexicans had received visas for entry into the United States during June 1930, and only 3,674 Mexicans immigrated to the United States during the first six months of 1930. At that rate, Hodgdon reported, only 7,348 Mexicans immigrated to the United States yearly compared to an average of 56,747 (an

Table 8. Visas issued to Mexican nationals,
FY1927–1928, FY1929–1930, FY1930–1931

Month	FY1927–1928	FY1929–1930	FY1930–1931	Percent Decrease, 1927–1928 to 1930–1931
July	6,583	1,950	324	95%
August	5,897	1,623	406	93%
September	4,548	1,429	438	90%
October	4,030	1,263	236	94%
November	3,963	1,024	188	95%
December	3,743	832	217	94%
January	3,425	864	157	95%
February	4,175	772	84	98%
March	6,081	726	113	98%
April	6,334	540	84	99%
May	5,001	400	101	98%
June	4,393	370	108	98%
Total for year	58,173	11,793	2,456	
Monthly average	4,848	983	205	

Source: Dwyre to Stimson, July 21, 1930, NARA, RG 59, 811.111 Mexico/416, 3; State Department Press Release, "Immigration from Mexico," August 19, 1931, NARA, RG 59, 811.111 Mexico/660, 2.

87 percent decrease) during the previous five years. Hodgdon did not believe this cut in immigration was due solely to economic decline since 1929, pointing to evidence that the actual demand for visas had not diminished. Instead he attributed the sharp decline in Mexican immigration to the effectiveness of administrative restriction. Hodgdon concluded his report by stating that Mexican immigration was "no longer a problem," a statement that would be repeated by consular and State Department officials for the next couple years.[55]

A year later, in August 1931, a State Department press release declared that the "problem of new immigration from Mexico through legal channels [seems] to be definitely solved." Figures reflecting the reduction in visa issuance seemed to confirm such statements.

Table 9. Mexican immigration to the United States following passage of 1924 immigration act

Year	Number
1925	50,602
1926	58,012
1927	77,162
1928	58,456
1929	39,501
Total	283,733
Average per year	56,747
Average per month, FY1925 to FY1929	4,729
Average per month, FY1930–1931	205

Source: State Department press release "Immigration from Mexico," August 19, 1931, NARA, RG 59, 811.111 Mexico/660, 2.

The American consul at Guadalajara, Raleigh Gibson, provided a local example of the drastic reduction in visa issuance. During the second quarter of 1930, 112 Mexicans were issued visas (an average of 37 per month) compared to 142 visas issued during the first quarter of 1930 (an average of 47 per month) and 392 during the second quarter of 1929 (an average of 131 per month). In other words between spring 1929 and spring 1930 the rate of visa issuance through Guadalajara was reduced by 71 percent.[56] Similarly Grover Wilmoth, the district director of the U.S. immigration office at El Paso, reported a drastic decline in Mexican immigration through his vicinity from the mid-1920s to the end of June 1930. In 1924, 49,142 Mexicans crossed into the United States via El Paso; in 1926 that figure was 34,175; in 1927 it was 40,877; in 1928, 32,346; and 18,225 in 1929. By the middle of 1930, however, only 6,911 Mexicans had entered the United States via El Paso.[57]

By the latter half of 1930 it seemed the State Department had succeeded in its endeavors to block the effort to place a quota on Mexican immigration. Public opinion was turning against the quota drive in favor of a continued reliance on administrative restriction. William Blocker, the American consul at Ciudad Juarez, gave the State Department a sense of the "pulse" of opinion toward the quota in El Paso and its vicinity in September 1930 by providing quotes from an editorial of a local paper:

Forget that Exclusion Business

"The State Department at Washington has announced that the immigration of Mexicans into the United States has been so drastically reduced that it is no longer a problem."

"In July [1930] only 324 Mexicans received immigration visas, none of them common laborers without previous residence in the United States."

"There has been a very great drop in the number of Mexican immigrants. . . . This can be attributed to a more strict interpretation of regulations and a more careful selection by the authorities."

Such low immigration figures "should be an effective silencer to those misdirected congressmen who know little about border conditions and who would urge the passage of an immigration act of special privilege which would be tantamount to an unjust, discriminating and good will–disrupting exclusion act so far as Mexico is concerned."[58]

A week later Blocker conveyed another sample of public opinion from the *El Paso Herald* when he referred to an editorial that argued that the decrease in numbers of Mexican immigration should end the "unnecessary fuss" that has been made in Washington regarding Mexican immigration.[59]

The following month Maurice Altaffer, the American consul in Nogales, reported similar sentiment from southern Arizona. In an editorial entitled "Better than a quota law," the *Arizona Daily*

Dispatch declared that administrative restriction had prevented an oversupply of labor at a time when unemployment was on the rise in the United States. The newspaper stated administrative restriction had accomplished the objective of reducing Mexican immigration without offending Mexico. Administrative restriction had worked because it was implemented immediately, instead of having to run a legislative "gamut" in Congress, with the risk of defeat or getting sidetracked, and risking presidential veto if passed by Congress.[60]

Significantly in November 1930 the *New York Times* quoted Secretary of State Henry Stimson as saying what by that time had been commonly accepted by quota opponents, particularly the State Department—that Mexican immigration had declined to such an extent that it was "no longer a problem." Of the few hundred Mexicans who had received immigration visas during previous months, Stimson informed a press conference, none of the recipients were common laborers who had never resided previously in the United States.[61]

The following year Everett Drumright, the American vice consul at Ciudad Juarez, summarized the reasons why administrative restriction had effectively reduced Mexican immigration and essentially defused the need for a quota on Mexico. His report of September 1931 to the State Department, entitled "Mexican Immigration," first described reasons why Mexicans were attracted to the United States during the 1920s. Mexican labor was in high demand because of quota restrictions on European immigration after 1924. Consequently Mexican immigration grew constantly between 1925 and 1929; Drumright estimated that 62,000 Mexicans entered the United States during the latter half of the 1920s, though it was "impossible to compute" the extent of illegal Mexican immigration of the same period. Drumright then went on to describe the effort to place a quota on Mexico in the wake of the 1924 immigration act and the debate that arose from that effort. Quota advocates believed a restrictive quota was the only way to avert a "race problem," he stated, since most Mexicans were "unassimilable, nomadic, [and] altogether unfit-ted" to become part of the American nation. While restrictionists justified a quota by arguing that Mexicans were no more desirable than European races excluded by the 1924 act, quota opponents argued that Mexican labor was indispensable and that a quota would harm political, social, economic, and diplomatic relations between the United States and Mexico. "Time," Drumright believed, had proved both sides of the debate wrong. Restrictionists were wrong when they assumed a quota could be placed on Mexico as it had been on European countries. Instead the strict enforcement of existing immigration law had resulted in an "amazing reduction" in the number of visas issued to Mexicans who sought permanent admission into the United States. And there had been no significant protest against administrative restrictions from quota opponents who feared that southwestern industries of the United States would suffer labor shortages if Mexican immigration was curtailed. Since the onset of the economic depression two years ago, Drumright stated, American workers had taken work they once scorned during times of prosperity. In sum, Drumright argued, no application of the quota basis "could be more successful in reducing immigration from Mexico than the efforts and accomplishments of consular officers, who have conclusively established that the application of a quota restriction law in order to diminish immigration from Mexico would be indeed superfluous."[62]

May 1930 proved to be the highpoint of the effort to place a quota on Mexican immigration. The State Department's unrelenting opposition, administrative restriction's drastic curtailment of Mexican immigration, and the repatriation crisis's removal of hundreds of thousands of Mexicans from U.S. society so eroded support for a quota that the effort finally died in February 1932. Sporadic attempts by restrictionists to place a quota on Mexico would occur after 1932; yet none of these efforts came close to achieving the diplomatic notoriety, public support, and congressional attention garnered by the Harris bill.

It was generally believed that the House would quickly approve the Harris bill after it passed the Senate in mid-May 1930.⁶³ Armed with a whole range of quantitative data reflecting the effectiveness of administrative restriction, however, the State Department renewed its opposition to the quota. In June 1930 it argued that administrative restriction had effectively reduced Mexican immigration: only four hundred Mexicans received visas during the previous month, and none of the recipients was a common laborer, the "type objected to by the political restrictionists on Capitol Hill." The State Department declared that such reductions in immigration demonstrated that Mexican immigration was no longer a problem and that administrative restriction had effectively reduced immigration without causing offense to "our friendly southern neighbor." According to the *Los Angeles Times* this argument seemed "to sweep the ground" from under the "three or four" restrictionists (undoubtedly referring to Albert Johnson, John Box, and William Harris) who pressed the exclusion issue for "political effect" in their home states. These restrictionists, the newspaper continued, "wormed" the Harris bill through the Senate "by trickery and misrepresentation, and were trying to do the same in the House."⁶⁴

Throughout the summer of 1930, as consular officials in Mexico and visa officials in Washington DC, reported that the quota was unnecessary in light of administrative restriction, the opinion of the national press seemed to turn against the quota effort. The *Washington Post* stated that administrative restriction was preferable to "a rigid quota" because it could exclude undesirable immigrants without exciting the enmity of Mexico. The *Los Angeles Times*, in a report reflecting State Department figures that showed that Mexican immigration was down almost 90 percent from previous years because of administrative restriction, reported that congressmen were declaring a quota for Mexico no longer necessary. Mexican immigration figures continued to decline precipitously throughout 1930 (see table 8). By the following summer the *Los Angeles Times* reported that the State Department had declared "the problem of new immigration from Mexico through legal channels to be definitely solved." In July 1931 administrative restriction had reduced Mexican immigration to "the vanishing point"; not a single common laborer had gained legal admittance into the United States for over a year.[65]

The quota effort sustained a huge setback after the passage of the Harris bill, however. In July 1930 John Box was defeated in the electoral primaries in the second district of Texas. As one of the three pillars of the "anti-Mexican triumvirate," Box had been a champion of the restrictionist cause. During his eleven years in Congress he had consistently pressed for a quota on Mexico's immigration. Throughout much of the 1920s he was the lone voice in the wilderness who believed Mexican immigrants just as dangerous to U.S. society as immigrants from eastern and southern Europe. His effort had gained appeal as his fellow lawmakers and the public grew increasingly concerned about the constant growth of Mexican immigration to the United States after 1924. The campaign to place a quota on Mexican immigration, to which John Box had contributed so much, culminated in the Senate's passage of the Harris bill in May 1930. Paradoxically two months later his constituents rejected him for reelection to Congress.

In the midst of the Harris bill's greatest success, John Box's loss at the local level portended the demise of the quota campaign against Mexico. Albert Johnson and William Harris, the other two pillars of the anti-Mexican triumvirate, ran close races in their electoral districts and often had to de-emphasize the quota issue for fear of exasperating their constituents. Reports on Box's failed reelection effort stated that the "Mexican question" aroused little interest among voters and that his call for a quota fell on deaf ears. Harris and Johnson carefully pitched their campaign planks to avoid Box's electoral fate. When arguments for a quota failed to excite constituents of his district in Georgia, in what the *Los Angeles Times* called "the heart of the Ku Klux belt," Harris instead extolled the merits of diplomatic isolationism to shore up voter support. According to press reports Harris's quota drive had lost momentum with the public because of administrative restriction. His electoral opponents relied on facts and figures that showed how Mexican immigration had been reduced to such an extent that a quota on Mexico was no longer necessary and would only serve to wound Mexican pride. Johnson faced similar difficulty during his reelection campaign. In the third congressional district of Washington State, his opponents strove to expose the Mexican problem as "a purely political attempt to get votes by prejudicing the people over a false issue."[66]

Unlike Box, both Harris and Johnson were reelected to Congress in November 1930. By that point, however, the Harris bill was in the doldrums, despite assurances from Senator Harris that he would renew his efforts to place a quota on Mexican immigration. In October 1930 Harris claimed that the Hoover administration had done little to enforce immigration law toward Mexican immigration until his quota measure passed the Senate months before. And while he recognized that administrative restriction enforced existing immigration laws, Harris feared that if his measure did not pass the House, the administration would "become lax in enforcement." If administration leaders had not prevented his bill from reaching the House floor for a vote during the last congressional session, Harris argued, the bill would have passed Congress, although he doubted that President Hoover would have signed it into law.[67] Despite Harris's protests the *Congressional Record* bears no evidence that the Harris bill elicited significant debate during the third session of the Seventy-First Congress (from December 1, 1930, to March 3, 1931). The bill proposal expired at the end of the session.

Interestingly, during the same time that the Harris bill floundered in Congress, the State Department stiffened its restriction of global immigration to the United States. In early September 1930 President Hoover ordered American consuls throughout Europe and Latin America to implement administrative restriction. In tandem with the quota and national origins approach established by the 1924 immigration act, European immigration came to an almost complete standstill during the early 1930s. Even

Latin American immigration, which was unregulated by the 1924 act, was reduced by administrative restriction.

Hoover's executive enforcement of administrative restriction was meant to relieve the U.S. unemployment situation caused by the Great Depression. Before the economic downturn, it was argued by Undersecretary of State Joseph Cotton (who composed a report about administrative restriction for Hoover), it was customary to grant visas to able-bodied workers who meant to find work and who had sufficient funds to support themselves. Now that the unemployment rate was so high, it had become necessary to restrict the entry of workers for whom there was no work in the United States and who were likely to become public charges.[68]

Importantly it was administrative restriction's success in curbing Mexican immigration that lay at the root of its broader implementation. Administrative restriction had effectively reduced Mexican immigration without having to make an exception of Mexico among all other Latin American nations by placing a restrictive quota on it.[69] It was hoped the strict enforcement of existing immigration laws by American consuls in Mexico would achieve similar results when applied by their counterparts throughout Latin America and Europe.

Administrative restriction quickly reduced European and Latin American immigration. In December 1930, just three months after Hoover implemented the policy, the chief of the Visa Office reported to Congress that 130,000 aliens who otherwise would have entered the United States during fiscal year 1930–1931 had been disallowed by American consuls.[70] The Labor Department asserted the following spring that the rate of arrivals of European immigrants had decreased by over 80 percent from the previous fiscal year.[71] Finally, in a letter to Hoover on September 17, 1931, Henry Stimson noted that administrative restriction had drastically reduced global immigration to the United States during the previous twelve months. According to Stimson, 146,000 European immigrants who normally would have entered the United States under existing immigration restrictions during the previous fiscal year were barred by administrative restriction. Only 48,528 of the total 153,714 annual visas allotted by the 1924 quota to Europe were distributed. In other words almost two-thirds of annual visas were not issued during fiscal year 1930–1931, and over half the visas that were issued were given to relatives of American citizens.[72]

A small sample of State Department statistics on the immigration of *non-preference* aliens from across Europe, the category in which common laborers were often classified by American consuls, indicates the extent to which administrative restriction sharply decreased European immigration to the United States. Immigration visas were under-issued to non-preference aliens by 72 percent in Denmark and 75 percent in Sweden. Both Czechoslovakia and Poland had under-issue rates of over 98 percent; Lithuania was not much better, with an under-issue rate of 93 percent. Russia and Greece witnessed relatively high percentages of immigration visa issuance to non-preference aliens (45:55 and 37:63, respectively), yet regional neighbors Yugoslavia and Hungary had lower rates (30:70 and 20:80, respectively). And as it did in central-eastern European nations, administrative restriction sharply curtailed immigration from southern Europe. Only 11 percent of the allotted immigration visas available for non-preference immigrants in Italy were distributed; in Portugal that figure was zero.[73] Finally, administrative restriction curbed immigration from non-quota countries (principally of the Western Hemisphere); 19,815 non-quota immigration visas were issued during fiscal year 1930–1931, down from 62,441 the previous fiscal year, a decline of 68 percent.[74]

The success of administrative restriction at the global level eroded further the argument for a quota on Mexican immigration. American consuls' strict interpretation of U.S. immigration law had effectively reduced Mexican immigration since administrative restriction's implementation toward Mexico in March 1929. And after the last quarter of 1930, administrative restriction demonstrated that it could curtail other streams of immigration to the United States. In this context congressional attempts to place a quota on Mexico's immigration seemed increasingly superfluous.

Despite administrative restriction's countervailing objective to the quota, the mood of restriction that was in full force by the latter half of 1931 momentarily revitalized the quota effort—especially after President Hoover, during his annual message to Congress on December 5, recommended that immigration restriction "now in force under administrative action be placed upon a more definite basis by law."[75] Four days after Hoover's address the Harris bill was reintroduced in the Senate Committee on Immigration and Naturalization. On January 15, 1932, it was (re)passed by the Senate Committee on Immigration and Naturalization.[76] It was then reported to the Senate, where it languished. Senators deferred action on the Harris bill until they learned the opinion of the State Department. According to the *Los Angeles Times* there was no reason to believe that the State Department would reverse its opposition to the Harris bill: singling out Mexico for quota restriction among all other countries of the region would undermine U.S.-Mexican relations, and administrative restriction's sharp reduction of Mexican immigration during the past couple of years seemed to make a quota proposal for Mexico obsolete. Additionally, despite his call to ratchet up immigration law, it was doubtful that President Hoover would support immigration law aimed solely at Mexico.[77]

Predictably, during the following weeks of the legislative session, business groups lobbied against the Harris bill. Like the State Department, they argued that a quota was unnecessary since administrative restriction had effectively curtailed the rate of Mexican immigration. Additionally business representatives before Congress argued that their need for Mexican labor would increase as the American economy improved. In late February 1932 representatives from various California business groups (the Western Growers' Protective Association, the California Statewide Committee on Agricultural Labor, the California State Chamber of Commerce, and the Central Chamber of Agriculture and Commerce) lobbied the House Committee on Immigration and Naturalization to leave Mexican immigration in its "flexible state." While American business sympathized with Congress's desire to keep out migrant labor, the representatives testified that they expected Mexican labor would be "sorely needed" after the nation's business depression ended. One representative, R. N. Wilson, urged the House Committee on Immigration and Naturalization not to create permanent legislation to remedy a temporary economic downturn. Newer and stricter immigration laws could complicate the procurement of labor when flush times returned. Wilson even pointed to Mexico's proximity and its citizens' ability to repatriate during the economic depression as an incentive to not excessively regulate Mexican immigration. "If we had been hiring Porto [sic] Ricans, Northern Negros or Filipinos we would be feeding them now."[78]

Secretary of State Henry Stimson struck the deathblow to the Harris bill in February 1932. In a letter dated February 5 to Henry Hatfield (R-WV), chairman of the Senate Committee on Immigration and Naturalization, Stimson summarized arguments that State Department officials had made against the quota since the late 1920s. Also, he reiterated the department's belief that administrative restriction's reduction of Mexican immigration rendered the quota unnecessary.

Stimson wrote his letter in response to Senator Hatfield's inquiry from January 28, which asked about the State Department's position on the reapproved Harris bill. Stimson wrote that an immigration quota on Mexico

> would be undesirable for the reason that such legislation is believed to be unnecessary and would be harmful to the best interests of the United States and its relations with Mexico and Latin American countries. In this connection it may be stated that the object of the proposed legislation, namely, the restriction of Mexican immigration through legal channels to a satisfactory minimum, has already been attained through the enforcement by consular officers of existing provisions of law.[79]

A restrictive quota on Mexico, Stimson continued, would be "a radical departure" from traditional U.S. policy toward Latin American "neighbors," which have "common problems, interests, and aims." Also, by singling out Mexico for immigration restriction, Stimson wrote, a quota would risk aggravating anti-American sentiment throughout the region. Such ill feelings would not only hurt diplomacy but also risk impairing trade relations, as foreign competitors could take advantage of the animosity to increase their commerce in Latin America at the expense of the United States. Finally, a quota on Mexico's immigration could jeopardize the negotiations of "many very important questions" in U.S.-Mexican relations, such as the protection of American property and interests in Mexico.[80]

A. Dana Hodgdon, in testimony before the House Committee on Immigration and Naturalization on February 25, 1932, provided the *coup de grâce* to the Harris bill. Chief of the Visa Office in Washington, Hodgdon argued that a quota would have the paradoxical effect of allowing a higher rate of Mexican immigration than administrative restriction and that the department opposed any effort to single out Mexico for immigration restriction. "The Department of State," said Hodgdon, "has felt that the placing of a quota on countries of the Western Hemisphere would be unfortunate, [and] that it would react unfavorably on our international relations and commerce." At the present time, Hodgdon continued, administrative restriction limited Mexican immigration to three to four hundred Mexicans annually. A quota would allow a higher rate of Mexican immigration—perhaps 1,500 to 2,000 annually. Therefore, Hodgdon concluded, "should quotes be placed on the Western Hemisphere, they should be placed on all countries and no individual country should be singled out. I am referring especially to bills placing a quota on Mexico."[81]

The Harris bill, and the restrictionist drive against Mexican immigration that had spawned it, were effectively dead after 1932. In a striking coincidence to the demise of his effort to place an immigration quota on Mexico, Senator Harris died of a heart attack in Washington DC, on April 18, 1932.[82] Rep. Albert Johnson, the last pillar of the "anti-Mexican triumvirate" in Congress was defeated for reelection that same November.

Although efforts to place a quota on Mexico continued beyond 1932, no measure came as close as the Harris bill to actually becoming law. In late February 1932 Rep. Thomas L. Blanton (D-TX) called for a five-year plan to exclude all aliens. His measure was directed primarily at the importation of cheap Mexican labor to Texas.[83] It went nowhere. In March 1934 Rep. William T. Schulte (D-IN) proposed a quota that would have capped Mexican immigration at 1,500 a year, claiming that Mexicans were aggravating the unemployment problem in border towns and taking jobs from Americans in industrial centers such as Gary, Indiana. The measure died in the House Committee on Immigration and Naturalization.[84]

The quota drive was defeated in Washington DC, just as repatriation crested in Piedras Negras, Coahuila. Both the quota effort and the repatriation crisis were entrenched in the racial prejudice of U.S. society. The quota campaign was a movement rooted deeply in the social politics of the United States. Broadly speaking, the attempt to place a quota on Mexico was simply an extension of the decades-long campaign to regulate immigration. Racism was the primary foundation of the quota effort against Mexican immigration. It explains why the quota campaign originated in the late 1920s as the United States experienced the full benefit of postwar prosperity and continued throughout the early 1930s, despite the massive repatriation of Mexicans during the Great Depression. Repatriation was in part a reaction against adverse economic conditions in the United States after October 1929. Although there were precedents for repatriation during the economic recessions of 1907–1908 and 1921–1922, the episode during the 1930s was unrivaled in duration and extent. Racism was the main reason why Mexicans departed the United States voluntarily during the early 1930s.

Administrative restriction was the third aspect of the political phenomena of Mexican immigration. Alongside repatriation this policy greatly reduced Mexicans' presence in the United States. Despite the Great Depression, when any measure to curb immigration in the face of rising unemployment would be expected to succeed, the Harris bill foundered in Congress and was staunchly opposed by the State Department. Diplomatic, not economic, considerations explain the bill's failure. Administrative restriction neutralized the quota effort by drastically cutting Mexican immigration without offending Mexico diplomatically. This method of restriction proved so successful toward Mexico that the Hoover administration, after September 1930, applied it to other immigration streams from Latin America and Europe. By 1932 the failure of the Harris bill, the effectiveness of administrative restriction, and the consequences of repatriation confirmed the State Department's argument that the revision of U.S. immigration law toward Mexico was unnecessary because the problem of Mexican immigration had been resolved.

Conclusion

Immigration regulation had a major impact on relations between the United States and Mexico during the 1920s and 1930s. An examination of the U.S.-Mexican debate over immigration demonstrates how immigration mattered to the history of U.S. foreign policy in several key ways: how racist rhetoric during domestic policy debates can have repercussions for U.S. relations with foreign states; how immigration, as a transnational phenomenon, inherently concerns the diplomatic relations between nations; how the divergent national views about immigration—its causes and potential solutions—between the United States and Mexico precluded a bilateral solution to the Mexican immigration problem; how a nation's internal considerations of economic development and employment can shape its diplomatic response to another country's immigration policy, and how the prospect of immigration restriction can have a concrete effect on the foreign relations between countries; how economics is not sufficient to explain why nations take legislative action to restrict immigration; and how bilateral, if not multilateral, negotiations between sender and receiver nations are necessary to forge permanent solutions to problems of immigration.

This historical treatment also asks why the congressional effort to place a quota on Mexico's immigration failed between 1928 and 1932. There was clearly a strong desire by restrictionists to curb Mexican immigration. For many quota advocates, Mexican immigration was equally, if not more, undesirable than European and Asian immigration. Mexican immigration was perceived as more dangerous because of the long, contiguous, lightly guarded international border. And there was a precedent for placing quotas on immigration; just a few years earlier, Congress had legislated a quota for all European immigration. Still, the restrictionists campaign for a specific quota on Mexican immigration failed.

The desire to preserve amicable diplomatic relations with Mexico, and to a certain extent the rest of Latin America, explains why the quota effort against Mexican immigration was not successful. Singling out Mexico among all other Latin American nations hurt U.S. relations with its southern neighbor. Attempts to restrict all of the Western Hemisphere threatened U.S.-Latin American relations more generally in the same way, since (as with Mexican immigration) justifications for a quota on Latin America rested on racist rhetoric. Eventually efforts to extend a quota to all of the Western Hemisphere failed because of what Albert Johnson called "consolidated opposition," or a region-wide critique of U.S. efforts at immigration restriction. Congress then focused its efforts on Mexico. As the Latin American nation with the largest rate of immigration to the United States, Mexico was the obvious target for immigration restriction. Yet this concentrated attempt to place a quota on Mexico did not alleviate Latin American opposition. Consolidated opposition pressured the U.S. State Department to oppose the quota for Mexico because such a policy would have had repercussions across the hemisphere.

Economics was not the prime motivation behind the effort to place a quota on Mexican immigration. Rather, contemporary concerns about Mexicans' presence in U.S. society and the racism that suffused these debates explain why policymakers wanted to place a quota on Mexico. The quota debate about Mexico took place against the backdrop of the passage of the 1924 immigration act, which placed a quota on Europe's immigration. The prime justification for such legislation was the alleged negative social impact European immigration would have had on the United States if it were allowed to continue unregulated. Economic arguments—while always present in restrictionists' statements against unrestricted immigration—were of secondary importance during a decade of noteworthy prosperity for Americans.

Instead it was the social basis for a quota that made it so consequential to U.S.-Mexico relations. If the restriction of Mexican immigration had been proposed as strictly an economic measure to protect the United States from a labor glut, Mexico may not have opposed the quota with such vehemence. Mexico had its own reasons for favoring the restriction of Mexican immigration to the United States, namely, the maintenance of a workforce that would help the nation's economic reconstruction after years of internal violence. Congressional debates over national immigration policy took on international import when restrictionists justified the quota on the basis of Mexicans' alleged inferiority. The quota effort destabilized U.S.-Mexican relations, despite quota advocates' assertion that the formulation of U.S. immigration policy should not be burdened by its potential consequences on U.S. foreign relations.

Consequently the State Department took actions to obviate the need for a quota. Initially it argued that the rate of Mexican repatriation exceeded the rate of Mexican immigration to the United States. This argument failed to dissuade policymakers from trying to place a quota on Mexico because statistics on Mexican immigration were unreliable and it did not diminish the social risks Mexicans posed to U.S. society. In response the State Department began to enforce strictly existing immigration laws that excluded the entry of immigrants into the United States who were illiterate, diseased, or likely to become public charges. This policy, known as administrative restriction and implemented in March 1929, precluded the need for a restrictive quota on Mexico because it sharply reduced the number of Mexicans immigrating to the United States. Administrative restriction proved the best method to curb Mexican immigration without harming diplomatic relations between the United States and Mexico. Although it should be noted that administrative restriction did not take account of illegal immigration.

The debate over the restriction of Mexican immigration to the United States illustrates how domestic developments, international factors, and foreign policy influence one another. While immigration is an inherently transnational phenomenon, it has domestic roots. Studying the social, economic, and political conditions driving Mexican immigration helps us understand why Mexican officials opposed the quota effort. Not only was it a matter of national disgrace, but it was argued by experts on immigration that the quota—by threatening to stop suddenly the flow of Mexican migrants northward—endangered the stability of the nation-state.

Conversely this book shows how external (read: international) pressures explain the internal (read: domestic) causation of Mexican immigration to the United States. Earlier chapters studied how Mexican immigration was a multipoint, transnational process of movement. Mexicans, most of whom derived from the southwestern and southcentral states of Mexico, often migrated to and worked in Mexico's north before eventually migrating to the United States. Numerous considerations explain why Mexicans chose to migrate to the United States: lack of work, lack of food, lack of political security in Mexico. While the push northward was local—even individual—in origin, the pull for migrants was transnational. A supply-and-demand curve linked the southwestern Mexican state of Jalisco with the southwestern American state of Arizona, for example. This intricate economic chain of workers responding to employers' demand for labor bonded the two nations in a social and economic process that had political repercussions for U.S.-Mexico relations.

Another recurrent theme of this book is the centrality of the state in immigration; it demonstrates how the state wielded real power in the regulation of immigration. Just as important this book shows that the *perceived* power of the state to regulate immigration had real consequences for diplomatic relations between the United States and Mexico. Also, the codification—or the prospect—of laws to restrict immigration not only influenced diplomatic relations but also shaped a nation's self-perception and identity.

At the same time, this book reveals the limitations of state power to control immigration. The United States was hard pressed to regulate the two-thousand-mile border it shared with Mexico. It was constantly bedeviled by Mexicans' illegal immigration, and its efforts to curb Mexican immigration were often undermined by American employers' insatiable need for migrant labor. Mexico was even less able to stop its immigration northward, nor were Mexican leaders much inclined to do so. The relative paucity of work within the national economy would have been exacerbated if Mexican immigration northward were greatly curtailed. Therefore Mexico's attempts to limit its immigration were often reduced to propaganda that sought to dissuade Mexicans from migrating. Even the not-so-altruistic endeavor of paying for *repatriados*' return to Mexico was hampered by shortages in the Treasury. In this sense immigration was a transnational, socioeconomic problem that transcended unilateral solutions prescribed by individual nations.

A related theme was the lack of bilateral negotiations between the United States and Mexico on immigration. Both nations advocated some type of restriction on Mexican immigration, yet their motives were different. Restrictionists in the United States believed Mexican workers menaced U.S. society and its labor market. Mexico wanted to curb its immigration northward in order to preserve its national labor force. Mexico's goal to stanch its immigration was a long-term objective, however; officials realized that Mexican immigration was necessary in the short term because the national economy could not provide work for all citizens. Mexico's officials begrudgingly argued that Mexican immigration to the United States should be allowed to continue unregulated until the nation's internal industries were developed to provide enough work to eliminate the need for immigration northward.

Within this argument for the continuation of the safety valve by Mexican officials was a criticism of the United States. Mexico resented how Mexican migrants were ill-treated north of the border. Experts on immigration warned Mexicans that abuse awaited them if they migrated. Also, Mexico resented migrant abuse because of the instrumental role Mexican laborers had played in the development of industries throughout the American Southwest. Many Mexicans believed quota advocates were hypocritical: Mexican immigration was welcomed as American industry grew in the Southwest from the late nineteenth century to the early twentieth century.

Once such regional industries were developed, so the argument went, Mexico's immigration was no longer needed and Mexicans themselves were castigated as undesirable. Finally, Mexican officials resented how Mexican migrants were abused because it exposed Mexico City's inability to protect its citizens abroad.

Mexico hoped to negotiate a bilateral solution to its immigration problem with the United States; the latter rejected such overtures. American diplomats feared bilateral or multilateral discussions about immigration would call into question Congress's sovereign right over U.S. immigration policy. American delegations' actions, or inactions, at international conferences, convened to examine the global significance of immigration, confirmed this fear. The Americans' unwillingness to discuss immigration bilaterally crippled Mexico's hope that a solution could be found to its immigration problem. This lack of negotiation did more than anything else to perpetuate the acrimonious debate over the quota during the late 1920s and early 1930s. Also, the failure to negotiate helps to explain why Mexicans opposed U.S. efforts to resolve the immigration issue unilaterally by placing a quota on Mexico.

The lack of bilateral negotiations was also attributable to the different ways in which the Mexican immigration problem was viewed in the two countries. Mexican observers viewed immigration as a transnational movement of workers who responded to demand from American business owners in the United States. In other words Mexican immigration was simply supplying workers to industries that required a large amount of cheap labor. Since immigration itself was a phenomenon rooted in the transnational supply of national demand, so solutions to the Mexican immigration problem required bilateral negotiation between the United States and Mexico. On the other hand many U.S. policymakers did not dwell on how Mexican immigrants had provided the labor supply demanded by industries across the United States. Nor were they persuaded by the potential negative effect a quota on Mexico's immigration would have on U.S. foreign relations with its southern neighbor. Instead they focused on how Mexicans' alleged inferiority made them undesirable for entry into the United States. In tandem with the fundamental belief that immigration policy was the sovereign right of Congress, congressional quota advocates believed no bilateral, much less multilateral, pressures should steer how the U.S. government legislated immigration restriction.

The failure to find a bilateral solution to the immigration problem between the United States and Mexico demonstrates the U.S. defense of a Westphalian conception of national sovereignty versus a Wilsonian approach to U.S. diplomatic relations. Congressional attempts to extend a restrictive quota to Mexico's immigration were part of a larger global, postwar trend that saw nations protecting the integrity of national boundaries and societies by regulating immigration. State Department officials defended Congress's sovereign right to formulate U.S. immigration policy during the quota debate, even as U.S. diplomats took steps to soften congressional efforts to regulate Mexican immigration. They warned lawmakers that a quota would harm U.S.-Mexican relations because it contradicted the U.S. goal of harmonious inter-American relations. They attempted to dissuade quota advocates by showing a predominant return movement of Mexicans to Mexico. And finally, they administered a type of immigration restriction that effectively curbed the amount of Mexican migrants entering the United States without having to place a quota on Mexico.

These actions reveal a contradiction between how the State Department viewed immigration generally and Mexican immigration particularly. This contradiction is explained by the State Department's Wilsonian approach to relations with Mexico and, to a certain extent, with Latin America as a whole. Wilsonianism influenced how diplomats attempted to preserve good relations with Mexico. There are fallacies to such an interpretation, to be sure. President Woodrow Wilson ordered multiple interventions into Mexico during the 1910s in an attempt to steer the course of the Mexican Revolution. Yet other aspects of Wilsonianism—a belief in upholding the law and spreading democratic values throughout the world, a recognition that the world was becoming more interdependent, and the expansion and preservation of commercial relations abroad—explain why the State Department opposed the quota by arguing that it could alienate Mexico. In this context administrative restriction was the perfect compromise between a Westphalian sense of national sovereignty and a Wilsonian notion of more cooperative diplomatic relations. Administrative restriction curbed Mexican immigration according to the sovereign immigration laws of the United States without offending Mexico with a quota.

No semblance of a bilateral solution to the immigration problem was brokered until 1942, when the United States and Mexico established a temporary worker program in which Mexican workers filled the labor shortage caused by U.S. participation in World War II. Attempts to implement such a scheme had failed before 1942. William Cochran Jr., an American vice consul at Mexico City, explicated the reasons for this failure in a report sent to Washington in December 1932. Entitled "Mexican Immigration after the Depression," Cochran's forecast provided a concise synopsis of the immigration debate up to 1932 and gave a sense of why a temporary labor scheme between the United States and Mexico was problematic.

Cochran looked to the past to predict the best way to mitigate problems endemic to Mexican immigration. He declared that the efforts since the 1920s to extend a quota to Mexico would have deeply wounded Mexican sensibilities because they rested on the implication that Mexicans were racially inferior. In addition the United States would have alienated its southern neighbor if it applied a quota to Mexico alone among all other Latin American nations. Cochran argued further that a quota would not have been flexible; it would have been difficult to alter restrictive legislation if (or when) demand for Mexican labor increased. Finally, administrative restriction had, by 1932, made the implementation of a quota unnecessary. For the time being, Cochran stated, administrative restriction was preferable to "sweeping legal change."

Cochran addressed one potential problem with administrative restriction: its continuation after the eventual recovery of the U.S. economy. Would thousands of *repatriados* be barred from reentry into the United States because of their reliance on public charities during the early part of the decade? Were Mexicans,

Cochran asked, "to be held liable to become a public charge and refused visas when they wish to return to the United States, as many undoubtedly will, because they were public charges during the depression?" A consistently strict application of administrative restriction during the depression could have the opposite effect when prosperous times returned. It could so stymie Mexican immigration that a labor shortage would result in the United States. Nevertheless Cochran believed administrative restriction was preferable to a quota.

Cochran's report also warned of the potential pitfalls that could underlie the entry of seasonal contracted laborers into the United States. His analysis stemmed from assertions by Manuel Gamio, that a temporary labor scheme would resolve the immigration problem between the United States and Mexico. According to Gamio's proposal, which was discussed among his multiple studies of Mexican immigration between 1926 and 1930, Mexican migrants could contract their labor to American employers, work in the United States for a fixed amount of time annually, and return to Mexico after the completion of their contracts.

Cochran identified several problems with the temporary labor scheme. First, the establishment of such a system would require changes to U.S. immigration law that disallowed the importation of foreign contract labor. Second, Cochran asked if it would be fair to apply this approach to Mexico only. United States immigration law was built on equal treatment among all nationalities, he argued; discrimination against any one nation had been avoided. A temporary labor arrangement with Mexico could undermine that tenet of equality. American labor unions—especially the American Federation of Labor (AFL)—would resent competition from Mexican workers, and employers of migrant labor could chafe at the requirement to provide return transportation for Mexicans. Also, employers could lower migrants' wages as a way to recoup the expense of worker transportation, thereby depressing U.S. wage scales and drawing the ire of American labor unions. The Mexican government might reject a scheme that led to the loss of their most enterprising and most ambitious workers. And the socioeconomic cost of reintegrating temporary workers into Mexican society each year could undermine the continuity necessary for the modernization of Mexico's economy. Moreover Mexican laborers themselves might not comply with the requirements of the temporary worker approach. They could break their work contracts, leave their place of employment, and not return to Mexico. Finally, the process of arranging contracts, managing the flow of migrants, and other administrative aspects of the scheme could invite corruption, abuse, difficulties, and neglect.[1]

Between 1928 and 1931 the Council on Foreign Relations published a multivolume analysis of U.S. foreign relations entitled *Survey of American Foreign Relations* (SAFR). The volumes focused on various topics that concerned the United States at that time, including collective security, disarmament, and postwar finance. The second volume of the series devoted considerable attention to immigration. It discussed the history of immigration to the United States, provided an explanation of the restrictive laws of 1917, 1921, and 1924, and analyzed the effects of U.S. exclusion laws, particularly in regard to Japan. The second volume—in a point that is relevant to this book—ended its discussion by commenting on the international implications of U.S. immigration restriction. Despite the United States' declaration that immigration policy was the sole domain of Congress, the volume stated, "the assertion of the right to sole national control [over immigration policy] does not dispose of the international consequences of national action, and it is likely that the immigration question, like tariffs, will in the future continue to occupy part of the field of international problems."[2]

The last volume of the series provided detailed analysis of U.S.-Mexico relations. Among issues of oil, monetary claims, and Mexico's debt, the volume provided an in-depth treatment of the Mexican immigration problem. Like all contemporaneous accounts, the SAFR's analysis of Mexican immigration and its bearings on the larger context of U.S.-Mexico relations was limited. The SAFR chapter was written during spring 1931 (published later that year), as administrative restriction massively curbed Mexico's immigration and the repatriation movement reduced the number of Mexicans who resided in the United States. Not surprisingly the SAFR account focused primarily on administrative restriction and how it had reduced Mexican immigration to such a degree that the immigration problem seemed resolved.

The SAFR survey confirms many of the key points argued in this book regarding administrative restriction and the quota issue generally. First, administrative restriction was a compromise: "an effort to meet popular demands for restriction [of Mexican immigration], and at the same time to avoid the giving of offense [to Mexico]."[3] The State Department feared a quota would undermine the "new era" in U.S.-Mexican relations. Second, Mexico would have resented a quota applied to it alone among all other Latin American nations. Third, administrative restriction was more legally flexible than a quota. Administrative restriction could be—and was—applied to Latin American nations without causing diplomatic or national insult. Implicit in this "certain flexibility" of administrative restriction was consuls' ability to reduce the strict enforcement of existing immigration laws if social, political, and economic conditions warranted it. By contrast a quota would become established U.S. immigration law and would require a herculean legislative effort to repeal it. Finally, the "quiet unheralded policy" of administrative restriction could help forestall the discriminatory rhetoric used by restrictionists to justify a quota that was so "distasteful" to Mexico.[4]

The SAFR chapter then proceeds to describe attempts by Albert Johnson, John Box, and William Harris (the anti-Mexican triumvirate) to restrict Mexican immigration. The SAFR confirms that the success of administrative restriction did not quell all restrictionists' hope that a quota would be applied to Mexico's immigration. They believed a legislated quota was the only permanent solution to the Mexican immigration problem. While the account explains the features of proposed restriction bills introduced by the triumvirate, it does not consider how these proposals affected U.S.-Mexico relations. Instead the author cuts off his analysis because

Conclusion   253

he believed such an in-depth treatment was not necessary since none of the bills had become law.

A broad analysis of immigration within the context of U.S.-Mexico relations demonstrates the importance of diplomacy and reveals what the SAFR author did not appreciate in 1931, namely, that proposals to restrict Mexican immigration provoked diplomatic controversy between the United States and Mexico during the late 1920s and early 1930s. The diplomatic debate sparked by quota proposals for Mexico touched on themes of race and racial ascription and racism, immigration law, national development, national identity, economic pressures, bilateral and multilateral relations, national sovereignty, and Mexico's postrevolution state making.

Immigration restriction was a perceived danger based in reality. Had not the United States placed a restrictive quota on Japanese immigration in 1924, despite prior bilateral agreements and Japan's vehement protest against a quota before and after the law's passage? Did not the poor treatment of Mexican immigrants in U.S. society portend a fate similar to that of excluded Chinese and Japanese peoples and restricted southern and eastern Europeans? Had not some of the same congressional figures who railed against Mexican immigration just a few years before successfully steered through Congress a new comprehensive immigration law that placed all of Europe's immigration on a permanent quota basis? And had not the United States shown unwillingness to consider the bilateral or multilateral consequences of its immigration policy?

The perceived and real issue of immigration restriction destabilized U.S.-Mexican relations between 1928 and 1932. Eventually the quota effort was defeated by a policy of immigration restriction that did not rest explicitly on the alleged inferiority of an immigrant's national identity. Alongside an economic depression that initiated a massive repatriation of Mexicans to Mexico, administrative restriction resolved the immigration problem and helped to preserve harmonious relations between the United States and Mexico during the interwar era.

Epilogue

There have been various efforts to resolve the immigration problem since the early 1930s. In the early 1940s the Mexican and American governments brokered a bilateral agreement that allowed U.S. employers to recruit Mexican workers on short-term labor contracts (less than a year in duration). After the contract was fulfilled workers were required to return to Mexico, at the expense of their U.S. employers. Most laborers worked in agriculture. The impetus for this agreement was a shortfall in labor as the United States entered World War II. The program existed from 1942 to 1964, eventually bowing to pressure that such labor agreements were no longer necessary, but especially because Mexican migrants were not returning to Mexico per the labor agreement. The misgiving of "surreptitious" entry of Mexicans into the United States morphed into a fear of "illegal" immigration by Mexican migrants. Long before the Bracero program was ended in 1964, the Dwight Eisenhower administration (1953–1961) took efforts to counter what was considered an increasingly large wave of illegal Mexican immigration. The most notable example was Operation "Wetback" of 1954, during which the Border Patrol worked alongside local and state officials from California to Texas to eventually deport as many as 1.3 million Mexican nationals.

A year after the Bracero program was allowed to expire in 1964, the U.S. government abolished the discriminatory quota-based immigration law that had been in place since the 1920s. The Immigration and Nationality Services (Hart-Cellar) Act of 1965 created hemispheric ceilings for the numbers of visas issued on an annual basis (170,000 for persons from without the Western Hemisphere, and 120,000 for persons from within), with no consideration of nationalities. The new law also stipulated that no more than 20,000 persons could come from any one country each year.

It will be recalled that despite restrictionists' efforts during the 1920s, Latin American immigration was never blocked by the quota regime of the Johnson-Reed Act. By contrast Asian immigration, which had essentially been blocked in one form or fashion since the 1880s, rose dramatically after 1965. The irony for Mexican immigration after passage of the Hart-Cellar Act was that the new law, passed during the Lyndon Johnson administration (1963–1969) in a spirit to redress the past wrongs of discriminatory immigration restriction toward peoples of Europe and Asia, codified a de facto limit on Latin American immigration. This cap of immigration number ceilings by the Hart-Cellar Act inaugurated a wave of illegal immigration to the United States.

By the 1980s public pressure was mounting for the U.S. government to stem the tide of illegal Mexican immigration to the United States, which had reached well over one million by the middle part of the decade. This pressure upon the administration of Ronald Reagan (1981–1989) eventually resulted in the Illegal Immigration Reform and Control Act (IRCA) of 1986. Significantly the IRCA broke from past legislative efforts regarding immigration by attempting to resolve the immigration problem at the demand side instead of the supply side. It was hoped that by imposing fines on U.S. employers who knowingly hired undocumented workers, increasing funds for the Border Patrol, and granting amnesty to undocumented workers who could show they had been living and working in the United States since 1982, the wave of illegal immigration would dissipate. Such hopes were met in the short term. Between 1987 and 1990 undocumented immigration declined. In the long term, however, the IRCA failed in its objectives. Restrictions on employers were poorly enforced, and amnesty as a method to deter illegal immigration was unsuccessful as well.

Undocumented immigration numbers equaled their pre-IRCA numbers by the mid-1990s. By the end of the decade it was estimated that there were more than 3.2 million undocumented workers in the United States, most of whom were Mexicans. Utilizing approaches similar to those used by U.S. leaders in the 1920s and 1930s, the administrations of Bill Clinton (1993–2001) and George W. Bush (2001–2009) tried to resolve the immigration problem by cutting off the supply of undocumented immigrants through stricter border enforcement and deportation standards. Between 1993 and 2004, spending on the Border Patrol quintupled from $750 million to $3.8 billion, and the size of the agency tripled to over 11,000 border agents. Some of these measures grew out of the Illegal Immigration Reform and Immigration Responsibility Act (IIRIRA) and the Anti-Terrorism and Effective Death Penalty Act, both passed in 1996, which toughened penalties against immigrants who overstayed their legal visas (making them ineligible to reapply for another three years) and broadened the categories of illegal activities that would trigger detention and deportation. Consequently new rounds of deportations took place. In addition to this new legislation, the Clinton administration attempted to plug key border crossing areas in Arizona, California, and Texas with border fortifications, surveillance equipment, and more patrols. Billions in federal dollars were expended to increase the size of the Border Patrol, whose sole task seemed to become the apprehension of undocumented migrants.

Such efforts continued under President Bush, as federal funding continued to increase the size of the Border Patrol as well as provide it with new surveillance tools: cameras, underground sensors, blimps, and later unmanned drones. In 2006 the Bush administration even took steps to build barriers on the border. The Secure Fence Act of that year authorized the construction of border fencing along the U.S.-Mexico border.

These efforts to stem the inflow of undocumented immigrants worked in apprehending a lot of people; over a million a year by the mid-2000s. Yet these robust border enforcement efforts did not stem the overall tide of illegal immigration to the United States. Another 3.2 million undocumented immigrants entered the United States between 1995 and 2004. In fact the largest deterrence of immigration of all kinds was the most recent recession that began in 2008. During the administration of Barack Obama (2009–2017), immigration numbers were at historic lows because of a depressed job market, not because of strict border enforcement, not because the Obama administration regularly deported undocumented workers, and certainly not because of the sharp rhetoric depicting immigrants as a threat to U.S. society.

At present the Trump administration has offered a border wall as a solution to the immigration problem. Neither this nor the approaches of previous administrations offer long-term solutions to the immigration problem, as indicated by the fact that the problem persists. The most recent focus on a border wall is the least constructive of all the approaches deployed by the U.S. government. Rooted more in heated rhetoric than rational legislative policy, the plan for a wall ignores the fact, blatantly so, that immigration is a transnational phenomenon. To resolve the immigration problem requires addressing both the supply and demand sides of the issue. The Mexican state has long suffered from a combination of burgeoning demography and stagnant job creation. Added to these problems are newer issues of drug cartels and the violence they bring down upon Mexican society. On the demand side Mexico has always had the (mis)fortune of bordering the most dynamic capitalist economy in the world. When one considers the chronic difficulties of the Mexican economy, it should come as no surprise that hundreds of thousands of Mexican citizens choose to migrate to the United States annually. It should be recognized, however, that these migrants just as much as they are fleeing relatively poor economic conditions in their home country, are in demand in the United States by employers in everything from the hotel industry to agriculture. Despite the overblown rhetoric coming out of the Trump administration, there is a little evidence to show that Mexican immigrants are predominately criminal and pose a threat to U.S. society. Just as restrictionists of the 1920s used blatant racist rhetoric to galvanize support for a quota scheme, such similar language is once again deployed ninety years later to galvanize a racist nationalist view of the United States.

As with most problems in U.S. diplomatic history, the only real solution lies in bilateral, even multilateral, coordination and cooperation. The political capital expended on a border wall would be better directed establishing an agreement between the United States and Mexico that responds to the labor needs of American business, relieves the labor glut of Mexico, and respects the human rights of Mexican nationals. Overblown accusations of Mexicans as threats to the United States subsumes the broad macro-economic forces and distinct internal issues of Mexico that underline the impetus for immigration: an insatiable demand for cheap migrant labor from American businesses, a Mexican state that chronically suffers from poor job growth relative to population growth, the reduction of trade barriers and improvements in communication attributed to the larger phenomenon of globalization that actually facilitates the increase of immigration, and Mexico's more recent trouble of violence associated with the drug war. Taking a hard look at the underlying factors of immigration would help Americans understand that the phenomenon is tied to other bilateral issues between the United States and Mexico. For example, if Americans were more aware of how the proliferation of guns in U.S. society satiates the demand of weapons from drug cartels, they might have a better sense of the importance for gun regulation.

The current political climate leaves one discouraged about the prospect of a solution to the immigration problem. Issues underlying immigration have only become more complicated, and the likelihood of negotiation and compromise seems further away than ever. If the quota debate of the 1920s shows us anything, it is that racist rhetoric used to justify harsh border enforcement actually undermines, not resolves, efforts to solve immigration problems.

Notes

Introduction

1. Rankin and Berger, "Peculiarities of Mexican Diplomacy," 539.
2. Sánchez, *Becoming Mexican American*, 21.
3. Grayson, *The United States and Mexico*, 139–40.
4. Grayson, *The United States and Mexico*, 139–40.
5. Ngai, *Impossible Subjects*, 10; Ngai, "Nationalism, Immigration Control, and the Ethnoracial Remapping of America in the 1920s," 12.
6. Ngai, *Impossible Subjects*, 10; Ngai, "Nationalism, Immigration Control, and the Ethnoracial Remapping of America in the 1920s," 12.
7. And, it should be mentioned, American investment wealth in Mexico *increased* after the end of major revolutionary conflict (1917) in Mexico, and in the face of stubborn Mexican revolutionary nationalism during the early 1920s.
8. Council on Foreign Relations, *Survey of American Foreign Relations*, 224.
9. Louria, *Triumph and Downfall*, 4.
10. Joseph et al., *Reclaiming the Political in Latin American History*, 7.
11. Fitzgerald, *A Nation of Emigrants*, 17.
12. Fitzgerald, *A Nation of Emigrants*, 18.
13. Fitzgerald, *A Nation of Emigrants*, 18–20.
14. Fitzgerald, *A Nation of Emigrants*, 19.
15. Bean et al., *At the Crossroads*, 4; Sánchez, *Becoming Mexican American*, 18.
16. Gutiérrez, *Between Two Worlds*, xiii, and *Walls and Mirrors*, 45; Barkan, *From All Points*, 199. According to an American consular report from October 1927, Mexican census information reported the following figures for Mexico's total population: 12,632,477 (1895 census); 13,545,462 (1900 census); 15,160,369 (1910 census); 14,234,799 (1921 census). The report stated that the decline in Mexico's population between 1910 and 1921 was attributable to the revolution and to the influence of immigration. NARA, RG 59, 812.5011/15.

17. Massey et al., *Return to Aztlan*, 42. Gutiérrez gives a substantially lower figure for annual Mexican immigration to the United States during the 1920s, at 25,000. Gutiérrez, *Walls and Mirrors*, 69.
18. Gutiérrez, *Walls and Mirrors*, 69.
19. Bean et al., *At the Crossroads*, 4; Barkan, *From All Points*, 251, n12, and 321.
20. Bean et al., *At the Crossroads*, 4; Sánchez, *Becoming Mexican American*, 18. Utilizing Mexican statistics, which he argues are more reliable because Mexicans had to register with immigration authorities when exiting and returning to Mexico, Jaime Aguila estimates that 853,038 Mexican emigrants entered the United States between 1910 and 1928. Aguila, "Mexican/US Immigration Policy Prior to the Great Depression," 211.
21. McMahon, "Toward a Pluralist Vision," 37.
22. McMahon, "Toward a Pluralist Vision," 49.
23. Oyen, "Allies, Enemies, and Aliens," iii.
24. Lee and Yung, *Angel Island*, 6.
25. Schuler, *Mexico Between Hitler and Roosevelt*, 3.
26. Grieb, *The United States and Huerta*; Smith, *The United States and Revolutionary Nationalism in Mexico*; Katz, *The Secret War in Mexico*; Grayson, *The United States and Mexico*; Vázquez and Meyer, *The United States and Mexico*; Knight, *U.S.-Mexican Relations, 1910–1940*; Hall, *Oil, Banks, and Politics*; Gilderhus, *Diplomacy and Revolution, PanAmerican Visions*, and *The Second Century*; Buchenau, *In the Shadow of the Giant*; Schuler, *Mexico Between Hitler and Roosevelt*; Spenser, *The Impossible Triangle*; Raat and Brescia, *Mexico and the United States*. General histories of Mexico that touch on U.S.-Mexican relations include the following: Ruiz, *The Great Rebellion* and *Triumphs and Tragedy*; Knight, *The Mexican Revolution*; Hart, *Revolutionary Mexico*; Gilly, *The Mexican Revolution*; Joseph and Buchenau, *Mexico's Once and Future Revolution*.
27. Vásquez and García y Griego, *Mexican-U.S. Relations*; Roett, *Mexico and the United States*. And in some cases treatments of Mexican migration history are incorrect. Contributors to *At the Crossroads* focus on Mexican migration to the United States to address its importance to U.S.-Mexican relations. Typically these scholars are concerned only with a recent history of Mexican immigration's effect on U.S.-Mexican relations, discussing migration in the immediate wake of NAFTA. Specifically, the scholar who addresses the topic incorrectly states that restrictions against Mexican migration came as a direct consequence of the Great Depression. Bean et al., *At the Crossroads*, 267.
28. Mitchell, *Western Hemisphere Immigration and United States Foreign Policy*, xi. They argue that for two different reasons "domestic" U.S. pol-

icymaking on immigration may enter the realm of international relations. First, the governments of sending states may come to play a part in the outcomes of U.S. immigration policy, influencing how many migrants are received or retained, under what conditions, and over what span of time. Second, there may be a "feedback" effect, in which U.S. immigration policy comes to influence U.S. foreign policy toward a specific nation.

29. Aguila, "Mexican/US Immigration Policy Prior to the Great Depression," 207–26.
30. Gabaccia, *Foreign Relations*; Cohen, *Braceros*.
31. Reisler, *By the Sweat of Their Brow*, 198–226.
32. Reisler, *By the Sweat of Their Brow*, 218.
33. Natalia Molina provides a cursory treatment of the quota debate in her article, " 'In a Race All Their Own': The Quest to Make Mexicans Ineligible for U.S. Citizenship," 188–89. Her account is based on Mark Reisler's analysis of the issue and, therefore, subject to all the shortcomings of that 1976 study. Also, she incorrectly states that the State Department implemented administrative restriction in 1928, when it in fact did so in 1929. Elliott Barkan mentions administrative restriction in a footnote but does not discuss how the policy fit within a broader effort to curb Mexican migration and why it was employed by the U.S. State Department (Barkan, *From All Points*, 251, n13). Michael Calderón-Zaks gives a more recent treatment of the quota effort against Mexico. Disturbingly, many of his key points on the topic are unsubstantiated, especially by Mexican archival sources. Also, he mistakenly attributes the quota drive to the "eugenics movement," instead of recognizing that not all opponents to Mexican immigration were eugenicists, nor did all eugenicists call for a quota on Mexico. Finally, like Reisler, Calderón-Zaks does not consider how Mexico's role in the debate resulted in the failure of the effort to place a quota on Mexican immigration. Calderón-Zaks, "Debated Whiteness amid World Events," 325–59.
34. Refer to Rosenberg, "Considering Borders," 176–93, and Zeiler, "The Diplomatic History Bandwagon," 1053–73, for centrality of the state in diplomatic history. Refer to St. John, *Line in the Sand*, for an example of borderlands history. S. Deborah Kang's *The INS on the Line* provides an understanding of how immigration law is enforced and negotiated at the local, national, and international levels. Finally, refer to Martínez's *Troublesome Border* for a foundational study of borderlands historiography.
35. Fitzgerald, *A Nation of Emigrants*, 4.

1. The Basis for the Quota Drive

1. Vázquez and Meyer, *The United States and Mexico*, 72–73 and 84.
2. Raat and Brescia, *Mexico and the United States*, 107–8.
3. Vázquez and Meyer, *The United States and Mexico*, 90 and 92.
4. Raat and Brescia, *Mexico and the United States*, 114.
5. Vázquez and Meyer, *The United States and Mexico*, 98–101.
6. Vázquez and Meyer, *The United States and Mexico*, 114.
7. Raat and Brescia, *Mexico and the United States*, 127.
8. Gilderhus, *Second Century*, 51.
9. Raat and Brescia, *Mexico and the United States*, 127.
10. Vázquez and Meyer, *The United States and Mexico*, 122.
11. Gilderhus, *Second Century*, 55; Vázquez and Meyer, *The United States and Mexico*, 124. Refer to Robert Smith for the political and legal underpinnings of the Carranza Doctrine. First, *the Drago Doctrine*. Promulgated in 1902 by Luis Drago, Argentina's foreign minister, this doctrine stated that powerful nations did not have the right to collect by force the foreign debts owed to their citizens. Drago hoped this doctrine would become a corollary to the Monroe Doctrine. The U.S. secretary of state at the time, Elihu Root, did not want to antagonize Latin American nations by completely rejecting it, so he persuaded the Second Hague Conference to adopt a modified version, which still sanctioned intervention as a last resort (Drago voted against this modified version). The United States was able to maintain the "right" to police Latin America. Second, *the Calvo Doctrine*. This was more extensive than the Drago Doctrine, as it was concerned not only with intervention but also with the basic question of the rights of resident foreigners. This doctrine was a nationalistic assertion of equal sovereignty and the right of a state to control its own internal situation. Carlos Calvo, an Argentine diplomat and commentator on international law (this doctrine was developed through his scholarly work over a period of years from 1868 to 1896), argued that foreign residents were subject to the same laws and to the same judicial processes as the citizens of the country. Foreign businesses had no right to appeal to another legal system—known as the principle of extraterritoriality—and instead should be treated as if they were owned by citizens of the country. All questions of economic policy involving foreign resident business would be domestic questions only, not subject to interference by foreign governments. The international rules of the developed nations would no longer be the overriding mechanism through which they controlled the treatment of their citizens by underdeveloped countries. Until the Mexican Revolution,

discussions about these doctrines were largely academic. No country had attempted a major implementation of them, and leaders of Latin American nations still accepted the basic premises and policies of capitalism. Smith, *The United States and Revolutionary Nationalism in Mexico, 1916–1932*, 27–29.

12. Schoultz, *Beneath the United States*, 273.
13. Car ownership among Americans increased by 80 percent between 1914 and 1920, from 1.8 million cars to 9.2 million cars. Knight, *U.S.-Mexican Relations*, 127; Schoultz, *Beneath the United States*, 273.
14. Schoultz, *Beneath the United States*, 274.
15. Schoultz, *Beneath the United States*, 274–75, Sheffield quoted on page 275. A year and a half later, in November 1927, after Sheffield left his post, he reemphasized similar points to his successor to the ambassadorship to Mexico, Dwight W. Morrow. "I am sure you will not take amiss my saying that there are principles at stake in our relations with Mexico which affect vitally our interests in Central and South America. If we yield on the principles in Mexico, we have got to yield elsewhere." Dwight W. Morrow papers, box 4, folder 100, Archives and Special Collections, Amherst College Library, James R. Sheffield to Dwight W. Morrow (letter), 17 November 1927, 1.
16. Gilderhus, *Second Century*, 63–64; Vázquez and Meyer, *The United States and Mexico*, 132; Schoutlz, *Beneath the United States*, 277; Langley, *Mexico and the United States*, 17. The Bucareli agreements represented the eventual denouement of the claims issue between the United States and Mexico. Few claims were settled during intermittent meetings of the 1920s. The total figure of $750 million was talked down to a mere 3 percent of the original. Finally, in the midst of World War II, the whole claims issue was concluded in 1941 with a package deal amid a mood of wartime détente and collaboration. In the words of Alan Knight, what was a "burning issue of one decade [became] the dusty files of the next." Knight, *U.S.-Mexican Relations*, 132.
17. Hall, *Oil, Banks, and Politics*, 7, 174, and 178.
18. Spenser, *The Impossible Triangle*, 129.
19. Langley, *Mexico and the United States*, 17–18.
20. James Rockwell Sheffield Papers (MS 446, series III, box 20, folder 118, autobiography, n.d., 34). Manuscripts and Archives, Yale University Library.
21. Schoultz, *Beneath the United States*, 277–79.
22. James Rockwell Sheffield Papers (MS 446, series III, box 20, folder 118, autobiography, n.d., 48). Manuscripts and Archives, Yale University Library.
23. Knight, *U.S.-Mexican Relations*, 133.

24. Schoultz, *Beneath the United States*, 280.
25. Schoultz, *Beneath the United States*, 260–62.
26. Schoultz, *Beneath the United States*, 262–63.
27. Knight, *U.S.-Mexican Relations*, 133 and 137; Langley, *Mexico and the United States*, 18.
28. Knight, *U.S.-Mexican Relations*, 133 and 137; Langley, *Mexico and the United States*, 18; Morrow quoted in Schoultz, *Beneath the United States*, 281.
29. Langley, *Mexico and the United States*, 18; Schoultz, *Beneath the United States*, 281–82.
30. Knight, *U.S.-Mexican Relations*, 137–38; Schoultz, *Beneath the United States*, 281–82.
31. Meyer, *The Cristero Rebellion*, 54.
32. Raat and Brescia, *Mexico and the United States*, 148–49.
33. Dwight W. Morrow papers, box 5, folder 123, Archives and Special Collections, Amherst College Library, 1–9; Langley, *Mexico and the United States*, 18.
34. Dwight W. Morrow papers, box 5, folder 123, Archives and Special Collections, Amherst College Library, 3.
35. Dwight W. Morrow papers, box 5, folder 123, Archives and Special Collections, Amherst College Library, 1–9.
36. Dwight W. Morrow papers, box 5, folder 123, Archives and Special Collections, Amherst College Library, 6.
37. Dwight W. Morrow papers, box 5, folder 123, Archives and Special Collections, Amherst College Library, 1–9; Langley, *Mexico and the United States*, 18; Hart, *Revolutionary Mexico*, 346.
38. Knight, *U.S.-Mexican Relations*, 133; Dwight W. Morrow papers, box 4, folder 100, Archives and Special Collections, Amherst College Library, James R. Sheffield to Dwight W. Morrow (letter), October 3, 1927, 2.
39. Dwight W. Morrow papers, box 1, folder 84, Archives and Special Collections, Amherst College Library, 1–2.
40. Two noteworthy studies on this period in U.S.-Mexican relations include Stephen Niblo's *War, Diplomacy, and Development* and Friedrich Schuler's *Mexico Between Hitler and Roosevelt*.
41. Knight, *U.S.-Mexican Relations*, 137 and 143.
42. See Nelli, *From Immigrants to Ethnics*. Katherine Benton-Cohen suggests that up to 50 percent of Italian immigrants re-migrated to Italy. Benton-Cohen, "Other Immigrants," 38.
43. Acuña, *Corridors of Migration*, xii, 47, 171–72, and 215; Barkan, *From All Points*, 196; Sánchez, *Becoming Mexican American*, 41 and 47.
44. Massey, *Return to Aztlan*, 169.

45. Gilderhus, *Second Century*, 38–39.
46. Hart, *Revolutionary Mexico*, 158.
47. Hart, *Revolutionary Mexico*, 162.
48. Hart, *Revolutionary Mexico*, 162.
49. In 1880 Mexico's total railroad trackage was 1,052 kilometers (654 miles); four years later that total had reached 5,898 kilometers (3,665 miles). By 1896 the Mexican rail network had expanded to 11,500 kilometers (7,146 miles). In 1900 the total railroad trackage was 14,573 kilometers (9,055 miles); ten years later, on the eve of the revolution, Mexican railroads comprised 24,560 kilometers (15,261 miles).
50. Gilly, *The Mexican Revolution*, 21.
51. Gilly, *The Mexican Revolution*, 22.
52. Hart, *Revolutionary Mexico*, 131–34.
53. Hart, *Revolutionary Mexico*, 141–44.
54. Hart, *Revolutionary Mexico*, 145–47 and 156.
55. Ruiz, *The Great Rebellion*, 85–86.
56. Ruiz, *The Great Rebellion*, 13. Adolfo Gilly argues similar points earlier in his landmark book on the Mexican Revolution by saying that railroads "radically altered local markets and prices structures; [they] redrew the parameters of landed property by raising the value of land near the railway; [they] greatly increased the mobility of both goods and labor; [they] implanted the railway industry as a modern sector, free of artisan encumbrances, at the very heart of national economic activity; [they] proletarianized peasants and artisans for work on the construction and operation of railways; and [their] progress through the country sharpened the regional inequality of Mexico's development." Gilly, *The Mexican Revolution*, 22.
57. Weber et al., *Manuel Gamio*, 122.
58. Raat and Brescia, *Mexico and the United States*, 106; Hart, *Revolutionary Mexico*, 361, who earlier in his work argues that by 1900 fully one-half of all U.S. foreign investments were in Mexico (177); Ruiz, *The Great Rebellion*, 13–17.
59. Mora-Torres, "Los de casa se van, los de fuera no vienen," 22.
60. Mora-Torres, "Los de casa se van, los de fuera no vienen," 22.
61. Mora-Torres, "Los de casa se van, los de fuera no vienen," 39–40.
62. Henderson, *Beyond Borders*, 8 and 16; Gonzalez, "Mexican Labor Immigration," 43. Refer to Foley, *White Scourge*, for an example of how small American farmers were displaced by commercial agriculture in Texas, their labor largely replaced by Mexican migrant workers.
63. Sánchez, *Becoming Mexican American*, 48.
64. Mora-Torres, "Los de casa se van, los de fuera no vienen," 22.

65. Hall and Coerver, *Revolution on the Border*, 11–13.
66. A recent criticism of the push-pull model for understanding Mexican immigration to the United States (which states that Mexico's poverty and lack of opportunity pushed workers out of Mexico while the possibility of work, opportunity, and higher wages pulled Mexican workers to the United States) argues that this schema "fails to incorporate the critical role of U.S. imperial economic expansion into Mexico and its far-reaching social consequences." What the author fails to emphasize is that Mexico was less acted upon than an actor in its own economic dependence on the United States. Porfirian leaders tapped into a Mexican liberal scheme dating back to Benito Juarez, at least, which believed foreign direct investment was the surest and quickest way to develop Mexican industry. The neocolonial relationship between the United States and Mexico during the Porfiriato was more complicit than imperial. An indicator of this can be found in the Mexican Revolution. Anti-Americanism was not nearly as powerful a social current as was popular backlash against native landowners and industry owners, who were viewed as the true oppressors of the people during the Porfiriato. Gonzalez, "Mexican Labor Immigration," 30. See also Knight, *The Mexican Revolution*, for the minimization of anti-Americanism.
67. James Rockwell Sheffield Papers (MS 446, series III, box 20, folder 118, autobiography, n.d., 45). Manuscripts and Archives, Yale University Library.
68. Hall and Coerver, *Revolution on the Border*, 6 and 126; Henderson, *Beyond Borders*, 16; Martínez, *Fragments of the Mexican Revolution*, 214.
69. Hall and Coerver, *Revolution on the Border*, 127; Martínez, *Fragments of the Mexican Revolution*, 308.
70. Knight, *The Mexican Revolution*, 2: 523–24.
71. Gonzalez, "Mexican Labor Immigration," 29; Sanchez, *Becoming Mexican American*, 41.
72. See Ignatiev, *How the Irish Became White*, and Smith, *Civic Ideals*, for discussions of how European immigrant groups acquired American whiteness by subscribing to social prejudice toward African Americans.
73. Jacobson, *Barbarian Virtues*, 97.
74. Sánchez, *Becoming Mexican American*, 61. Refer to Bodnar, *The Transplanted*, for the groundbreaking study that discusses the symbiosis between immigration and industrial capitalistic development in the United States from the 1880s to the 1920s.
75. King, *Making Americans*, 52–53; Dawley, *Changing the World*, 114.
76. Jacobson, *Whiteness of a Different Color*, 77–78.
77. Dawley, *Changing the World*, 90 and 115.

78. Jacobson, *Barbarian Virtues*, 61.
79. The Alien Contract Labor Law of 1885, also known as the Foran Act, forbade the importation of "contract laborers," i.e., anyone who had contracted to do a particular job before emigrating. The reality was that employers routinely circumvented this law by drawing not upon contracts per se but upon existing informal ethnic networks and family ties of workers. Jacobson, *Barbarian Virtues*, 67.
80. King, *Making Americans*, 11–13 and 51–52.
81. Jacobson, *Whiteness of a Different Color*, 77.
82. These points are informed by myriad works on the construction of American whiteness in the midst of mass immigration to the United States. Notable books within the historiography include Gerstle, *American Crucible*; Jacobson, *Whiteness of a Different Color*; Van Nuys, *Americanizing the West*; Ignatiev, *How the Irish Became White*; Smith, *Civic Ideals*.
83. LeMay and Barkan, *U.S. Immigration and Naturalization Laws and Issues*, 80–81.
84. LeMay and Barkan, *U.S. Immigration and Naturalization Laws and Issues*, xxxiii and 96.
85. LeMay and Barkan, *U.S. Immigration and Naturalization Laws and Issues*, xxxiii–xxxiv and 106–7.
86. Gerstle, *American Crucible*, 96.
87. Gerstle, *American Crucible*, 96.
88. LeMay and Barkan, *U.S. Immigration and Naturalization Laws and Issues*, 110.
89. Sánchez, *Becoming Mexican American*, 55.
90. Hall and Coerver, *Revolution on the Border*, 132–34.
91. Foley, *White Scourge*, 53.
92. United States Congress, Committee on Immigration and Naturalization, *Imported Pauper Labor and Serfdom in America: Hearings* (Washington DC: Government Printing Office, 1921), 9.
93. Barkan, *From All Points*, 211–12.
94. Foley, *White Scourge*, 45–46 and 52–55.
95. Hall and Coerver, *Revolution on Border*, 140–41; Henderson, *Beyond Borders*, 30–32.
96. Wilson justified his action by saying that the exemption made for Mexican labor staved off the need to import Asian migrants. Benton-Cohen, "Other Immigrants," 44.
97. Foley, *White Scourge*, 58.
98. Gerstle, *American Crucible*, 97; LeMay, *From Open Door to Dutch Door*, 71.
99. Reisler, "Always the Laborer, Never the Citizen," 241.

100. Hall and Coerver, *Revolution on the Border*, 133; Henderson, *Beyond Borders*, 33 and 35; Sánchez, *Becoming Mexican American*, 57.
101. LeMay, *From Open Door to Dutch Door*, 82; LeMay and Barkan, *U.S. Immigration and Naturalization Laws and Issues*, xxxiv; Barkan, *From All Points*, 216.
102. "One Hundred Years of Immigration," by James J. Davis, Secretary of Labor, *New York Times*, February 17, 1924, xxi.
103. "One Hundred Years of Immigration," *New York Times*.
104. *Papers Relating to the Foreign Relations of the United States* (hereafter FRUS), 1924, vol. 1: The Romanian Chargé (Nano) to the Secretary of State, February 2, 1924, 213.
105. FRUS, 1924, vol. 1: The Secretary of State to the Chairman of the Committee on Immigration and Naturalization of the House of Representatives (Johnson), February 8, 1924, 218.
106. FRUS, 1924, vol. 1: The Salvadoran Chargé (Castro) to the Secretary of State, January 4, 1924, 212.
107. FRUS, 1924, vol. 1: The Cuban Ambassador (Torriente) to the Secretary of State, January 14, 1924, 212–13.
108. Henderson, *Beyond Borders*, 39; "Hughes Criticizes Immigration Bill," *New York Times*, February 21, 1924, 19.
109. King, *Making Americans*, 207.
110. "Rush to Scale Immigration Bars Emphasizes Alien Problem," *New York Times*, July 29, 1923, xxiv.
111. "Rush to Scale Immigration Bars Emphasizes Alien Problem," *New York Times* (emphasis mine).
112. "Exodus of Mexican Laborers to the United States," Harper to the State Department, September 17, 1925, NARA, RG 59, 812.5611/1, 2 and 4.
113. "Mexicans Reported Streaming in Here," *New York Times*, March 1, 1927, 3; "English Races Gain in Immigrant Ranks," *New York Times*, September 12, 1927, 25; "Unskilled Labor in Immigration Gain," *New York Times*, August 23, 1926, 17; "Sees Annual Labor Loss," *New York Times*, October 10, 1927, 34.
114. Sixty percent of Cristeros were manual laborers and came from the rural class. "Immigration to the United States from the Consular District of Nogales, Mexico," Damm to the State Department, October 22, 1927, NARA, RG 59, 812.5611/7; Meyer, *The Cristero Rebellion*, 85 and 93.
115. Meyer, *The Cristero Rebellion*, 111.
116. Meyer, *The Cristero Rebellion*, 112. An American consular official in Piedras Negras, Oscar Harper, surmised reasons why Mexicans emigrated to the United States: lack of work and insufficient wages in Mexico, and rumors from relatives in the United States that salaries were better north of the border. Added to these standard reasons for

immigration were religious dissension and "the desire that the emigrant has of bettering his condition [in the United States] and political conditions [in Mexico]." "Mexican Emigration," Harper to the State Department, July 20, 1926, NARA, RG 59, 812.56/7, 2–3.
117. Meyer, *The Cristero Rebellion*, 112; Martínez, *Fragments of the Mexican Revolution*, 308.
118. Records of the Bureau of Foreign and Domestic Commerce (hereafter RG 151), Dye to Department of Commerce, box 1767, folder 2, March 11, 1924, NARA, RG 151, 1.
119. "Immigration Drops 68 Percent in the Year," *New York Times*, September 8, 1925, 23.
120. "Adjusting Immigration," *New York Times*, August 24, 1926, 20.
121. "Where Immigrants Come From," *New York Times*, December 8, 1926, 26 (emphasis mine).
122. "Wants Quota Law Applied to Mexico," *New York Times*, May 19, 1927, 7.
123. "Urges Extension of Quota to All," *New York Times*, June 24, 1927, 11.
124. "Immigration from Mexico," *New York Times*, August 3, 1927, 22. In reply to the foregoing article in the *New York Times*, an editorialist stated there is no common sense or fairness in a system that "excluded the full-blooded Spaniard, Portuguese or Italian, and admits any Latin American who elects to come in and live with us. The people of Southern Europe are capable of filling the specifications for a potential American citizen just as well as those Latins who happen to be living on this side of the water." "The Immigration Problem," *New York Times*, August 6, 1927, 12.
125. Gutiérrez, *Walls and Mirrors*, 53–55.
126. Quoted in Dawley, *Changing the World*, 100 and 367, n38; Gutiérrez, *Walls and Mirrors*, 54–55.
127. Gutiérrez, *Between Two Worlds*, xii, and Gutiérrez, *Walls and Mirrors*, 46–49.
128. Morrow to Kellogg, November 8, 1927, NARA, RG 59, 812.5611/10; Dye to Kellogg, November 22, 1927, NARA, RG 59, 812.5611/16.
129. Dawley, *Changing the World*, 290.
130. Fitzgerald, *A Nation of Emigrants*, 3; Henderson, *Beyond Borders*, 32.
131. Henderson, *Beyond Borders*, 32.
132. Fitzgerald, *A Nation of Emigrants*, 40–41; Smith and Bakker, *Citizenship Across Borders*, 28; Hernández, *Migra!*, 84.
133. Aguila, "Mexican/US Immigration Policy Prior to the Great Depression," 215.
134. Fitzgerald, *A Nation of Emigrants*, 42; Aguila, "Mexican/US Immigration Policy Prior to the Great Depression," 215–17.

135. Smith and Bakker, *Citizenship Across Borders*, 28; Fitzgerald, *A Nation of Emigrants*, 43.
136. Aguila, "Mexican/US Immigration Policy Prior to the Great Depression," 220 and 224; Fitzgerald, *A Nation of Emigrants*, 43; Hernández, *Migra!*, 84.
137. Aguila, "Mexican/US Immigration Policy Prior to the Great Depression," 224.

2. Singling Out Mexico for Restriction

1. *Congressional Digest*, "Immigration Problem—1928," May 1928, Archivo Histórico de la Secretaría de Relaciones Exteriores (hereafter AHSRE): LEG 782, exp. 16, 152.
2. "Urges New Check on Immigration," *New York Times*, February 14, 1928, 38.
3. King, *Making Americans*, 201.
4. Brandt to Carr, February 25, 1928, NARA, RG 59, 811.111 Quota, 10/104, 1; Brandt to Carr, February 14, 1928, NARA, RG 59, 811.111 Quota, 10/100, 3.
5. "Quota for Canada Meets Opposition," *New York Times*, February 22, 1928, 38; Brandt to Carr, February 21, 1928, NARA, RG 59, 811.111 Quota, 10/102.
6. "Statement of Henry de C. Ward," 1928, AHSRE: LEG 772, exp. 5, 37.
7. "Statement of Henry de C. Ward," 1928, AHSRE: LEG 772, exp. 5, 44–45.
8. Balderamma and Rodríguez, *Decade of Betrayal*, 18.
9. "Such a system would break down because of its administrative impossibility," Box argued in the early 1920s, "and would be ruinous in its effects upon the country."
10. U.S. House of Representatives, Committee on Immigration and Naturalization, *Temporary Admission*, 302–3; U.S. House of Representatives, Committee on Immigration and Naturalization, *Imported Pauper Labor*, 17.
11. "A few men can make more noise in Washington than a million men can make at home," he declared before the House Committee on Immigration and Naturalization in late February 1928.
12. Statement of the Hon. John C. Box, a representative from the state of Texas," 1928, AHSRE: LEG 772, exp. 5, 53.
13. "Quota for Canada Meets Opposition," *New York Times*, 38; Brandt to Carr, February 21, 1928, NARA, RG 59, 811.111 Quota, 10/102, 2–3; *Congressional Digest*, "Immigration Problem—1928," May 1928, AHSRE: LEG 782, exp. 16, 157.

14. Italian and Japanese reactions to the 1924 immigration act will be discussed in the next chapter.
15. Brandt to Carr, February 21, 1928, NARA, RG 59, 811.111 Quota, 10/102, 4; *Congressional Digest*, "Immigration Problem—1928," May 1928, AHSRE: LEG 782, exp. 16, 161.
16. Brandt to Carr, n.d., NARA, RG 59, 811.111 Quota, 10/104.5, 1.
17. *Congressional Digest*, "Immigration Problem—1928," May 1928, AHSRE: LEG 782, exp. 16, 161–64.
18. "Statement of Fred H. Bixby," 1928–1930, AHSRE: LEG 761, exp. 2, 26–27; *Congressional Digest*, "Immigration Problem—1928," May 1928, AHSRE: LEG 782, exp. 16, 161–64; Brandt to Carr, n.d., NARA, RG 59, 811.111 Quota, 10/104.5; "Oppose Bill to Bar Mexican Immigrants," *New York Times*, February 25, 1928, 33; Balderamma and Rodríguez, *Decade of Betrayal*, 17.
19. Brandt to Carr, February 14, 1928, NARA, RG 59, 811.111 Quota, 10/100, 3–4 (emphasis mine).
20. Brandt to Carr, February 23, 1928, NARA, RG 59, 811.111 Quota, 10/103; *Congressional Digest*, "Immigration Problem—1928," May 1928, AHSRE: LEG 782, exp. 16, 157.
21. "Statement of Hon. John N. Garner, Representative in Congress from the state of Texas," 1928–1930, AHSRE: LEG 761, exp. 2, 23–24.
22. "Statement of Hon. Frank B. Kellogg, Secretary of State," 1928–1930, AHSRE: LEG 761, exp. 2, 156–69; "Kellogg Opposes Davis Quota Plan," *New York Times*, March 6, 1928, 13. Compare United States Senate, Committee on Immigration and Naturalization. *Restriction of Western Hemisphere Immigration: Hearings*. 70th Congress, 1st Session (Washington DC: Government Printing Office, 1928), 155–72.
23. "Statement of Hon. W.W. Husband, Second Assistant Secretary of Labor," 1928–1930, AHSRE: LEG 761, exp. 2, 173–79. Compare United States Senate, Committee on and Naturalization. *Restriction of Western Hemisphere Immigration: Hearings*. 70th Congress, 1st Session (Washington DC: Government Printing Office, 1928), 172–80.
24. "Asuntos de interes, Febrero 23, 1928, 2.10 M.," 1928, AHSRE: LEG 772, exp. 5, 2 pages (2).
25. United States Congress, Committee on Immigration and Naturalization, *Temporary Admission of Illiterate Mexican Laborers: Hearings* (Washington DC: Government Printing Office, 1921), 10–11.
26. United States Congress, *Temporary Admission of Illiterate Mexican Laborers: Hearings*, 13.
27. United States Congress, *Temporary Admission of Illiterate Mexican Laborers: Hearings*, 13.

28. United States Congress, *Temporary Admission of Illiterate Mexican Laborers: Hearings*, 16.
29. United States Congress, *Temporary Admission of Illiterate Mexican Laborers: Hearings*, 299.
30. United States Congress, *Temporary Admission of Illiterate Mexican Laborers: Hearings*, 302.
31. United States Congress, *Temporary Admission of Illiterate Mexican Laborers: Hearings*, 303; United States Congress, Committee on Immigration and Naturalization, *Imported Pauper Labor and Serfdom in America: Hearings*. 67th Congress, 1st Session (Washington DC: Government Printing Office, 1921), 17.
32. United States Congress, *Imported Pauper Labor*, 17.
33. United States Congress, *Imported Pauper Labor*, 17.
34. United States Congress, *Imported Pauper Labor*, 18.
35. "Asuntos de interes, Febrero 23, 1928, 2.10 M.," 1928, AHSRE: LEG 772, exp. 5, 2 pages (2); Brandt to Carr, 811.111 Quota, 10–103, February 23, 1928, 2.
36. Suástegui to Téllez (letter), February 17, 1928, AHSRE: LEG 772, exp. 5, 3 pages (1).
37. Suástegui to Téllez (letter), February 17, 1928, AHSRE: LEG 772, exp. 5, 3 pages (2).
38. Suástegui to Téllez (letter), February 17, 1928, AHSRE: LEG 772, exp. 5, 3 pages (2).
39. Suástegui to Téllez (letter), February 17, 1928, AHSRE: LEG 772, exp. 5, 3 pages (3).
40. Morrow to Secretary of State, in Dwight W. Morrow papers, box 5, folder 124, Archives and Special Collections, Amherst College Library; Morrow to Kellogg, February 16, 1928, NARA, RG 59, 811.111 Mexico/7.
41. "Obregon Attacks Havana Conferees," *New York Times*, March 6, 1928, 7.
42. Schoenfeld to Kellogg, July 8, 1927, NARA, RG 59, 812.5611/5, 2; Morrow to Kellogg, November 7, 1927, NARA, RG 59, 812.5611/9. A typical call for Mexican labor appeared in *Excelsior* during December 1925. In the article entitled "Farm Hands Wanted in the United States" ("Solicitan Braceros Los Estados Unidos"), the paper reported that American farmers in Texas needed to clear 47,000 acres of land within thirty days. A "great number" of Mexican laborers were needed, and they "will find steady employment throughout all the winter. The average wage that a worker may earn runs between fifteen and twenty dollars a week. From one thousand and fifteen hundred Mexican laborers will be needed on these clearings, who, besides being employed for quite a while, will be able to maintain themselves until the coming cotton season." Three themes stand out from this

advertisement alone: the promise of immediate work, a high rate of remuneration, and the possibility of future seasonal work. According to the American consul at Guadalajara, Dudley Dwyre, who forwarded this advertisement to the Labor and State Departments, "as a rule" such announcements for laborers stimulated the immigration of Mexicans to the United States. "Emigration of Mexicans to the United States," Dwyre to the State Department, December 21, 1925, NARA, RG 59, 812.5611/3, 1–4. A comparable advertisement titled "We Need Laborers" was published in *La Prensa*, a Spanish-language newspaper in San Antonio, Texas, which announced the following in September 1928: "Pipe line work [at] $3.25 for nine hours[,] magnificent food. Permanent and assured work. A great opportunity to make money with the company better known and recommended by the Mexicans" [*sic*]. Within two days of this advertisement the American consul at Nuevo Laredo reported a noticeable rise in applications for nonimmigrant visas for Mexican laborers. There was "no doubt," the consul Richard Boyce believed, that such announcements attracted a "great deal of attention in Mexico, apparently far in the interior where most of the aliens who apply at this office come from." Boyce to Kellogg, September 19, 1928, NARA, RG 59, 811.111 Mexico/100, 1–2.

43. Gutiérrez, *Between Two Worlds*, xxii–xxiii.
44. Sanchez, *Becoming Mexican American*, 113. Such an economic scheme for development was reflected in a Mexican deputy's statement to *Excelsior* upon returning to Mexico from California. Mexico, Deputy Alfonso Francisco Ramirez argued, should undertake a campaign to maintain influence over its migrants in the United States and recall them. Mexico should seek to turn the training and experience gained by Mexican migrants in the United States "into a source of wealth for Mexico itself." Morrow to Kellogg, February 21, 1928, NARA, RG 59, 811.111 Mexico/10, 2.
45. Morrow to Kellogg, February 10, 1928, NARA, RG 59, 812.5611/19, 1.
46. "Mexicans Watching Quota Move Here," *New York Times*, March 5, 1928, 8.
47. Morrow to Kellogg, February 10, 1928, NARA, RG 59, 812.5611/19, 2.
48. "Proposed Quota Ban is Shock to Mexico," *New York Times*, March 11, 1928, 30.
49. "Mexicans Resent Box Bill," *New York Times*, March 13, 1928, 2; Morrow to Kellogg, March 3, 1928, NARA, RG 59, 811.111 Mexico/14, 1–2.
50. "Proposed Quota Ban is Shock to Mexico," *New York Times*, March 11, 1928, 30.
51. Kellogg to U.S. Embassy in Mexico City, February 25, 1928, NARA, RG 59, 811.111 Mexico/8; Morrow to Kellogg, February 29, 1928, NARA, RG

59, 811.111 Mexico/11; Dawson to Kellogg, December 13, 1928, NARA, RG 59, 812.5611/24, 3; Manuel Gamio, "Quantitative Estimate of Mexican Immigration to the United States," September 1926, AHSRE: LEG 761, exp. 1, 7. Annual repatriation statistics for the years immediately prior were as follows: 64,620 (1920); 106,242 (1921); 50,171 (1922); 85,825 (1923); 105,834 (1924); 77,056 (1925); 67,970 (1926); 69,125 (1927).
52. Kellogg to Morrow, April 18, 1928, NARA, RG 59, 811.111 Mexico/43.
53. Kellogg to Morrow, April 18, 1928, NARA, RG 59, 811.111 Mexico/43.
54. Manuel Gamio, "Quantitative Estimate of Mexican Immigration to the United States," September 1926, AHSRE: LEG 761, exp. 1, 8.
55. Manuel Gamio, "Quantitative Estimate of Mexican Immigration to the United States," September 1926, AHSRE: LEG 761, exp. 1, 8–9.
56. Manuel Gamio, "Quantitative Estimate of Mexican Immigration to the United States," September 1926, AHSRE: LEG 761, exp. 1, 8.
57. Téllez to U.S. House Committee on Immigration and Naturalization, February 14, 1928, AHSRE: LEG 772, exp. 5, 2–3.
58. Consulates from Mexico City, Ciudad Juarez, Nuevo Laredo, Nogales, Piedras Negras, Matamoros, Acapulco, Guayamas, Manzanillo, Progresso, Puerto Mexico, Salina Cruz, and Saltillo.
59. According to this data, there were only three years in which emigration exceeded repatriation: 1913, 1916, and 1919. Eaton to State Department, April 20, 1928, NARA, RG 59, 811.111 Mexico/61.5, 4, 7, 20–21, and 23.
60. Walsh to Kellogg, March 14, 1928, NARA, RG 59, 811.111 Mexico/16.
61. Jones to State Department, April 30, 1928, NARA, RG 59, 811.111 Mexico/66 (emphasis mine).
62. The American consul at Nuevo Laredo gave a sense of how Mexican immigration followed a seasonal pattern of circular immigration that dodged any attempt to tabulate accurately the rate of repatriation to Mexico. Between February 1 and May 31 of each year there was a "heavy definite movement of Mexican workers to the United States . . . and that for the last half of the year there is a corresponding return movement from the United States." Walsh to Kellogg, March 14, 1928, NARA, RG 59, 811.111 Mexico/16, 2.
63. Winters to State Department, April 19, 1928, NARA, RG 59, 811.111 Mexico Reports Inst., 5.
64. Winters to State Department, April 19, 1928, NARA, RG 59, 811.111 Mexico Reports Inst., 9.
65. Manuel Gamio, "Quantitative Estimate of Mexican Immigration to the United States," September 1926, AHSRE: LEG 761, exp. 1, 1 and 10–11. Kelly Lytle Hernández details the expense of migration for poor

Mexicans during the 1920s in her work *Migra!*, 91. Train fare from central Mexico to the northern border averaged $40–$50. Along the way migrants had to purchase food. Once at the border migrants had to secure lodging in preparation of crossing the border.

66. Manuel Gamio, "Quantitative Estimate of Mexican Immigration to the United States," September 1926, AHSRE: LEG 761, exp. 1, 1 and 10–11.
67. By way of example, plugging in low and high estimates of illegal immigration into the consular figures for Mexican a.) immigration, and b.) repatriation during 1926 when a.) represented 61,982, and b.) represented 73,063. Such figures demonstrate a 118 percent rate of repatriation. Accounting for the low estimate of illegal immigration gives us the following: a.) 61,982 + 20,000 = 891,982, and b.) 73,063 equals a 112 percent rate of *not returning* to Mexico. Accounting for the high estimate of illegal immigration gives us the following: a.) 61,982 + 50,000 = 111,982, and b.) 73,063 equals a 153 percent rate of *not returning* to Mexico.

3. International Pressure against the U.S. Effort

1. FRUS, 1928, vol. 1: The Secretary of State to the American Delegation, January 5, 1928, 561–62.
2. FRUS, 1923, vol. 1: The Italian Embassy to the Department of State, April 9, 1923, 115–16.
3. FRUS, 1923, vol. 1: The Italian Embassy to the Department of State, April 9, 1923, 116–17 (emphasis mine).
4. FRUS, 1928, vol. 1: The Secretary of State to the American Delegation, January 5, 1928, 561–62; FRUS, 1923, vol. 1: The Department of State to the Italian Embassy, May 10, 1923, 117.
5. Hirobe, *Japanese Pride, American Prejudice*, 4–5.
6. Hirobe, *Japanese Pride, American Prejudice*, 4.
7. Hirobe, *Japanese Pride, American Prejudice*, 7–8.
8. Hirobe, *Japanese Pride, American Prejudice*, 8–9; FRUS, 1924, vol. 2: The Japanese Ambassador (Hanihara) to the Secretary of State, April 10, 1924, 372–73. Izumi Hirobe argues that Hanihara's use of the phrase "grave consequences" had the unexpected result of convincing legislators that they should pass the bill to restrict Japanese immigration.
9. Hirobe, *Japanese Pride, American Prejudice*, 9–10.
10. A formal protest letter from the Japanese government to the United States stated that sovereign nations have sole power over their immigration policy, "but when, in the exercise of such right, an evident injustice is done to a foreign nation in disregard of its proper self-respect, of international understandings or of ordinary rules of

comity, the question necessarily assumes an aspect which justifies diplomatic discussions and adjustment." FRUS, 1924, vol. 2: The Japanese Ambassador (Hanihara) to the Secretary of State, May 31, 1924, 401; Council on Foreign Relations, *Survey of American Foreign Relations*, 1929, 512.

11. FRUS, 1924, vol. 2: The Japanese Ambassador (Hanihara) to the Secretary of State, May 31, 1924, 398; *Survey of American Foreign Relations*, 1929, 512 (emphasis mine). The same note also addressed restrictionists' argument that Japanese immigrants were a menace to U.S. society because they did not assimilate. The Japanese response to this accusation offers interesting insight into reasons why Mexican immigrants did not assimilate into U.S. society, a fact for which restrictionists believed a quota on Mexico's immigration was justified. "It has been repeatedly asserted in defense of these discriminatory measures in the United States that persons of the Japanese race are not assimilable to American life and ideals. It will however be observed, in the first place, that few immigrants of a foreign stock may well be expected to assimilate themselves to their new surroundings within a single generation. The history of Japanese immigration to the United States in any appreciable number dated but from the last few years of the nineteenth century. The period of time is too short to permit of any conclusive judgement being passed upon the racial adaptabilies of those immigrants in the matter of assimilation, as compared with alien settlers of the races classed as eligible to American citizenship. *It should further be remarked that the process of assimilation can thrive only in a genial atmosphere of just and equitable treatment*. Its natural growth is bound to be hampered under such a pressure of invidious discriminations as that to which Japanese residents in [the United States] have been subjected, at law and in practice, for nearly twenty years. *It seems hardly fair to complain of the failure of foreign elements to merge in a community, while the community chooses to keep them apart from the rest of its membership*. For these reasons the assertion of Japanese non-assimilability seems at least premature, if not fundamentally unjust." FRUS, 1924, vol. 2: The Japanese Ambassador (Hanihara) to the Secretary of State, May 31, 1924, 399 (emphasis mine).

12. FRUS, 1928, vol. 1: The Secretary of State to the American Delegation, January 5, 1928, 564; FRUS, 1924, vol. 2: The Japanese Ambassador (Hanihara) to the Secretary of State, April 10, 1924, 370.

13. Council on Foreign Relations, *Survey of American Foreign Relations*, 1929, 512–13.

14. "Statement of Hon. Frank B. Kellogg, Secretary of State," 1928–1930, AHSRE: LEG 761, exp. 2, 170–71.

15. FRUS, 1928, vol. 1: The Secretary of State to the American Delegation, January 5, 1928, 564–66. Incidentally Robinson added that the host country had an obligation to protect immigrants and provide for their welfare, by stating that "it follows that the country in which the immigrant takes his abode has the right and owes the duty to protect him and to promote his advancement and best interests in common with the citizens of the country as distinguished from immigrants, and that the country of origin cannot claim . . . the right to control him after he has taken up his residence in a foreign land."
16. FRUS, 1928, vol. 1: The Secretary of State to the American Delegation, January 5, 1928, 566.
17. The delegation included former secretary of state Charles Evans Hughes, former chargé to Mexico Henry Fletcher, and the acting U.S. ambassador to Mexico Dwight Morrow.
18. FRUS, 1928, vol. 1: The Secretary of State to the American Delegation, January 5, 1928, 561, 566, 573.
19. The other four commissions to the conference discussed several matters pertaining to the Pan-American Union, Inter-American Law, Problems of Communication, Intellectual Cooperation, and various social problems. FRUS, 1928, vol. 1: The Secretary of State to the American Delegation, January 5, 1928, 536–38.
20. Vol. 5, 1928, AHSRE: L-E 209, items 75–1 to 77–2.
21. Slight, yet important, modifications to these three acts between the two conferences will be discussed below (emphasis mine).
22. Vol. 5, 1928, AHSRE: L-E 209, items 115–3 to 115–4.
23. Vol. 5, 1928, AHSRE: L-E 209, items 78–1 to 78–2, 80–1 to 80–3, 114–3 to 114–5; "Acta Final de la Segunda Conferencia Internacional de Emigración e Inmigración, La Habana, 31 de Marzo–17 de Abril de 1928," AHSRE: III-32–3, folder II, 32 (emphasis mine).
24. The following *sixteen* national delegations to that conference approved the Mexican proposal: Argentina, Austria, Belgium, Chile, Costa Rica, Cuba, Dominican Republic, Ecuador, El Salvador, Guatemala, Haiti, Mexico, the Netherlands, Panama, Paraguay, and Uruguay. AHSRE: III-32–3, folder II, 32.
25. The following countries sent delegations to the Second International Conference on Immigration and Emigration: Argentina, Austria, Belgium, Bolivia, Chile, China, Colombia, Costa Rica, Cuba, Czechoslovakia, Free City of Danzig, Dominican Republic, Ecuador, Egypt, El Salvador, France, Guatemala, Haiti, Hungary, Italy, Japan, Latvia, Mexico, the Netherlands, Norway, Panama, Paraguay, Peru, Poland, Portugal, Romania, San Marino, Spain, Switzerland, United States, Uruguay, and Venezuela. The following countries sent observers to the confer-

ence: Australia, Germany, Great Britain, South Africa, and Sweden. "Acta Final de la Segunda Conferencia Internacional de Emigración e Inmigración, La Habana, 31 de Marzo–17 de Abril de 1928," AHSRE: III-32-3, folder II, 7–12.

26. FRUS, 1928, vol. 1: The American Delegation to the Secretary of State, August 25, 1928, 520. The American delegation to the Second International Conference on Immigration and Emigration was comprised of W. W. Husband (assistant secretary of labor, and chairman of the delegation), Norval Nichols (commissioner of immigration in Puerto Rico), Drs. John W. Kerr and John D. Long (both of the United States Public Health Service), Leo J. Keena (American consul general in Havana), and Henry Carter (the State Department's plenipotentiary at the conference).

27. FRUS, 1928, vol. 1: The American Delegation to the Secretary of State, August 25, 1928, 514–15. Drs. Kerr and Long were assigned to the first commission; Mr. Nichols and Dr. Long were assigned to the second commission; Undersecretary Husband and Consul General Keena were assigned to the third commission; Consul General Keena and Carter were assigned to the fourth commission; and Carter and Commissioner Nichols were assigned to the fifth commission.

28. FRUS, 1928, vol. 1: The American Delegation to the Secretary of State, August 25, 1928, 512, 515–17. After Long's statement Carlos Brebbia of the Argentine delegation, and Argentina's inspector general of immigration, stated that it was "hardly necessary to say that all of us who are working together here do not propose to compromise in any way the sovereignty of the countries we represent, their laws or their regulations. . . . It is simply a meeting of . . . men of business, who are thoroughly familiar with immigration problems and who have met in assembly to contribute . . . the lessons from his experience so as to harmonize as far as possible the conflicting interests of the immigration and emigration countries, all inspired with the wish of being useful" (517).

29. The following *twenty-eight nations* approved this measure: Argentina, Austria, Belgium, Chile, Costa Rica, Cuba, Czechoslovakia, Free City of Danzig, Dominican Republic, Ecuador, Egypt, El Salvador, France, Guatemala, Haiti, Hungary, Italy, Japan, Mexico, the Netherlands, Panama, Paraguay, Peru, Poland, Romania, San Marino, Spain, and Uruguay. "Acta Final de la Segunda Conferencia Internacional de Emigración e Inmigración, La Habana, 31 de Marzo-17 de Abril de 1928," AHSRE: III-32-3, folder II, 24–28.

30. The following *thirty nations* approved this measure: Austria, Belgium, Bolivia, Chile, Costa Rica, Cuba, Czechoslovakia, Free City of Danzig,

Dominican Republic, Ecuador, Egypt, El Salvador, France, Guatemala, Haiti, Hungary, Italy, Japan, Mexico, the Netherlands, Norway, Panama, Paraguay, Peru, Poland, Romania, San Marino, Spain, Switzerland, and Uruguay. "Acta Final de la Segunda Conferencia Internacional de Emigración e Inmigración, La Habana, 31 de Marzo–17 de Abril de 1928," AHSRE: III-32-3, folder II, 24–28.

31. The following *nineteen nations* approved this measure: Austria, Costa Rica, Cuba, Czechoslovakia, Free City of Danzig, Egypt, El Salvador, France, Haiti, Hungary, Italy, Japan, Mexico, the Netherlands, Poland, Romania, San Marino, Spain, and Switzerland. "Acta Final de la Segunda Conferencia Internacional de Emigración e Inmigración, La Habana, 31 de Marzo–17 de Abril de 1928," AHSRE: III-32-3, folder II, 24–28.

32. The following *twenty-two nations* approved this measure: Austria, Chile, Costa Rica, Cuba, Czechoslovakia, Free City of Danzig, Dominican Republic, Ecuador, Egypt, El Salvador, Hungary, Italy, Japan, Mexico, the Netherlands, Norway, Panama, Paraguay, Peru, Poland, Romania, and San Marino. "Acta Final de la Segunda Conferencia Internacional de Emigración e Inmigración, La Habana, 31 de Marzo–17 de Abril de 1928," AHSRE: III-32-3, folder II, 24–28.

33. The following *thirty nations* approved this measure: Argentina, Austria, Belgium, Bolivia, Chile, Costa Rica, Cuba, Czechoslovakia, Free City of Danzig, Dominican Republic, Ecuador, Egypt, El Salvador, France, Guatemala, Haiti, Hungary, Italy, Japan, Mexico, Norway, Panama, Paraguay, Peru, Poland, Romania, San Marino, Spain, Switzerland, and Uruguay. "Acta Final de la Segunda Conferencia Internacional de Emigración e Inmigración, La Habana, 31 de Marzo–17 de Abril de 1928," AHSRE: III-32-3, folder II, 24–28.

34. The following *twenty-eight nations* approved this measure: Argentina, Austria, Belgium, Bolivia, Chile, Costa Rica, Cuba, Czechoslovakia, Free City of Danzig, Ecuador, Egypt, El Salvador, France, Haiti, Hungary, Italy, Japan, Mexico, the Netherlands, Panama, Paraguay, Peru, Poland, Romania, San Marino, Spain, Switzerland, and Uruguay. "Acta Final de la Segunda Conferencia Internacional de Emigración e Inmigración, La Habana, 31 de Marzo–17 de Abril de 1928," AHSRE: III-32-3, folder II, 24–28 (emphasis mine).

35. The following *twenty-four nations* approved this measure: Argentina, Austria, Chile, Costa Rica, Cuba, Czechoslovakia, Free City of Danzig, Ecuador, Egypt, El Salvador, France, Guatemala, Haiti, Hungary, Italy, Japan, Mexico, Panama, Peru, Poland, Romania, San Marino, Spain, and Uruguay. "Acta Final de la Segunda Conferencia Internacional de Emigración e Inmigración, La Habana, 31 de Marzo–17 de Abril de 1928," AHSRE: III-32-3, folder II, 30 (emphasis mine).

36. "Acta Final de la Segunda Conferencia Internacional de Emigración e Inmigración, La Habana, 31 de Marzo–17 de Abril de 1928," AHSRE: III-32-3, folder II, 31–32 (emphasis mine). The following *seventeen nations* approved this measure at the Second International Conference on Immigration and Emigration, also in Havana, between late March and mid-April 1928: Argentina, Austria, Belgium, Chile, Costa Rica, Cuba, Dominican Republic, Ecuador, El Salvador, Guatemala, Haiti, Mexico, the Netherlands, Panama, Paraguay, Peru, and Uruguay. A final version of the proceedings from the Sixth Pan-American Conference sent by the Mexican delegation to Mexico City in mid-March 1928 contained interesting disparities from the final versions of the acts approved at the Second International Conference on Emigration and Immigration. Originally the second part of Article 5 read as "any offense" instead of "any limitation" of a nation's sovereignty. A press account of the document reflects the same difference in verbiage. That draft can be found in "Conferencia Internacional sobre Emigración e Inmigración, celebrada en La Habana," AHSRE: III-32-3, folder I, 4–6; the press account can be found in vol. 5, 1928, AHSRE: L-E 209, item 114–4, under the following article title: "Resuelto al fin el problema relativo a la inmigracion." Additionally the third part of Article 5 originally did not contain the phrase "from other continents." A version of the original act can be found in vol. 5, 1928, AHSRE: L-E 209, item 115–4. Parts marked in bold signify modifications from the original versions of these three articles.
37. Vol. 5, 1928, AHSRE: L-E 209, item 114–6 and items 115–1 to 115–2.
38. Archival records of the Salvadoran proposal can be found in vol. 5, 1928, AHSRE: L-E 209, items 80–3 and 114–5; "Conferencia Internacional sobre Emigración e Inmigración, celebrada en La Habana," AHSRE: III-32-3, folder I, 6; FRUS, 1928, vol. 1: The American Delegation to the Secretary of State, August 25, 1928, 522–23, which has the translation as "No one of the American States may place obstacles in the way of immigration and emigration of the other American States nor limit it to a determined number of citizens of another American State." The Mexican delegation was led by Carlos Trejo y Lerdo de Tejada and featured Dr. Manuel Gamio, former subsecretary of education and expert on Mexican immigration. Chapter 4 will discuss in detail his work on Mexican immigration.
39. "Conferencia Internacional sobre Emigración e Inmigración, celebrada en La Habana," AHSRE: III-32-3, folder I, 20.
40. "Conferencia Internacional sobre Emigración e Inmigración, celebrada en La Habana," AHSRE: III-32-3, folder I, 11.

41. It will be recalled from chapter 2 that the Alien Contract Labor Law of 1885, also known as the Foran Act, forbade the entry of contracted laborers into the United States.
42. "Conferencia Internacional sobre Emigración e Inmigración, celebrada en La Habana," AHSRE: III-32–3, folder I, 11–17.
43. "Conferencia Internacional sobre Emigración e Inmigración, celebrada en La Habana," AHSRE: III-32–3, folder I, 11–17. In his later work Gamio would refer to the United States as a "marvelous incubator" for the modernization of Mexicans. Hernández, *Migra!*, 87–88.
44. "Conferencia Internacional sobre Emigración e Inmigración, celebrada en La Habana," AHSRE: III-32–3, folder I, 11–17.
45. "Conferencia Internacional sobre Emigración e Inmigración, celebrada en La Habana," AHSRE: III-32–3, folder I, 11–17.
46. FRUS, 1928, vol. 1: The Secretary of State to the Cuban Chargé (Altunaga), September 14, 1928, 527 (emphasis mine).
47. "Septima Conferencia Internacional Panamericana, efectuada en la ciudad de Montevideo, Uruguay, del 3 al 26 de diciembre de 1933," AHSRE: L-E 218, 110–11.

4. Advantages, Disadvantages, Risks, and Rewards

1. Balderamma and Rodríguez, *Decade of Betrayal*, 18.
2. Those hurdles were the Senate, the House, and then the president. *El Paso Post*, December 14, 1928; Records of the Immigration and Naturalization Service, Series A, Part 2—Mexican Immigration 1906–1930 (hereafter RG 85), NARA, RG 85, folder 55598–459C; "Harris Bill is Approved," *El Paso Post*, December 14, 1928; Kellogg to U.S. Embassy in Mexico City, December 14, 1928, NARA, RG 59, 811.111 Mexico/128.
3. "For Quota Rates in this Hemisphere," *New York Times*, December 6, 1928, 24; "Changing Immigration Quota," *New York Times*, December 7, 1928, 28.
4. "For Quota Rates in this Hemisphere," *New York Times*, December 6, 1928, 24.
5. Visa Office to State Department, December 6, 1928, NARA, RG 59, 811.111 Mexico/127.5.
6. Davis to Carr, January 8, 1929, NARA, RG 59, 811.111 Mexico/148.5.
7. NARA, RG 85, folder 55598–459C; "Half Million Mexicans in United States Says Davis," *Arizona Daily Star* (Tucson), January 6, 1929; Davis to Carr, January 8, 1929, NARA, RG 59, 811.111 Mexico/148.5; "Immigration Laws," AHSRE: LEG 761, exp. 2. In early February 1929, John Box proposed a bill that attempted to regulate migrants entering on a temporary basis. Temporary entrants would be barred if they violated the Foran Act of 1885, which stipulated that contracted foreign labor was

not allowed to enter the United States. Box's bill stated that persons entering the States temporarily for reasons of business would not do so if they were under any prearranged labor contract, "unless specifically exempted from the contract labor provisions of the immigration laws." Since no migrants were exempted from the Foran Act, this bill would have applied to all Mexicans temporarily in the United States. "Bill Would Curb Alien Commuting," *New York Times*, February 6, 1929, 21.

8. "Mexicans Divided on the Harris Bill," *New York Times*, December 18, 1928, 26.
9. Visa Office to State Department, November 20, 1928, NARA, RG 59, 811.111 Mexico/133, 1–4.
10. Visa Office to State Department, November 20, 1928, NARA, RG 59, 811.111 Mexico/133, 7–8.
11. Schoenfeld to Kellogg, January 18, 1929, NARA, RG 59, 812.5611/31.
12. "The Mexican Migration Problem" (newspaper clipping), February 1928, NARA, RG 59, 812.5611/18.
13. "The Mexican Migration Problem" (newspaper clipping), February 1928, NARA, RG 59, 812.5611/18.
14. "The Mexican Migration Problem" (newspaper clipping), February 1928, NARA, RG 59, 812.5611/18.
15. Schoenfeld to Kellogg, December 17, 1928, "La Migración y Protección de Mexicanos en el Extranjero," NARA, RG 59, 812.5611/25, 15–16 and 29.
16. Schoenfeld to Kellogg, December 18, 1928, NARA, RG 59, 811.111 Mexico/138.
17. Schoenfeld to Kellogg, January 17, 1929, NARA, RG 59, 812.5611/30, 5–6; Schoenfeld to Kellogg, January 9, 1929, NARA, RG 59, 811.111 Mexico/148.
18. Dawson to Stimson, April 27, 1929, NARA, RG 59, 811.111 Mexico/216, 2; Schoenfeld to Kellogg, December 17, 1928, "La Migración y Protección de Mexicanos en el Extranjero," NARA, RG 59, 812.5611/25, 26.
19. Schoenfeld to Kellogg, January 17, 1929, NARA, RG 59, 812.5611/30, 4–5.
20. Hernández, *Migra!*, 93–97.
21. Hernández, *Migra!*, 93–97.
22. Balderamma and Rodríguez, *Decade of Betrayal*, 131.
23. Schoenfeld to Kellogg, December 17, 1928, "La Migración y Protección de Mexicanos en el Extranjero," NARA, RG 59, 812.5611/25, 14–15.
24. Schoenfeld to Kellogg, December 17, 1928, NARA, RG 59, 812.5611/25, 25.
25. Schoenfeld to Kellogg, December 17, 1928, NARA, RG 59, 812.5611/25, 25.
26. Hernández, *Migra!*, 90.
27. Schoenfeld to Kellogg, December 17, 1928, NARA, RG 59, 812.5611/25, 5–6. One of the main objectives of this report was to describe how the

Mexican government was making efforts to halt illegal immigration and to protect its citizens in the United States.

28. Boyce to Kellogg, September 19, 1928, NARA, RG 59, 811.111 Mexico/100, 2–3. It is not clear how much the Mexican government spent on repatriating its citizens relative to Mexico's national budget. The SRE's report on the protection of Mexicans abroad from December 1928 states that from July to December 1927 the Mexican government spent over $31,300 on repatriation and protection efforts for its citizens in the United States. How much of the Mexican national budget was consumed by such expenditures is also unknown. Schoenfeld to Kellogg, December 17, 1928, NARA, RG 59, 812.5611/25, 33.

29. Morrow to Kellogg, February 25, 1929, NARA, RG 59, 811.111 Mexico/172; Dawson to State Department, March 25, 1929, NARA, RG 59, 812.5611/35.5, 8. The Mexican states solicited for reports on immigration were Coahuila, Guanajuato, Jalisco, Michoacán, Nuevo Leon, San Luis Potosí, Tamaulipas, and Zacatecas. It will be recalled from earlier chapters that historically most migrants derived from Guanajuato, Jalisco, and Michoacán.

30. Hernández, *Migra!*, 85.

31. Schmidt, "Mexicans, Migrants, and Indigenous Peoples," 164–66. Gamio began his study in July 1926 and presented his initial findings—the "Preliminary Report on Mexican Immigration in the United States"—at the council's conference in September 1926 at Dartmouth College in Hanover, New Hampshire (excerpts of which are referred to in chapter 2). The Mexican government agreed in November 1927 to share the financial costs of Gamio's research at a rate of $500 a month, but because of poor economic conditions in Mexico, Calles's government ceased payments in June 1928 (the SSRC only funded the U.S.-based part of the study). Thereafter Gamio personally funded his research in Mexico and the additional expenses he accrued in the United States. In this situation Gamio approached Dwight Morrow, the U.S. ambassador to Mexico, and asked him to persuade the Mexican government to resume funding the project. Not wanting to interfere in the interpersonal affairs of Mexican officials, Morrow thought it best not to bring the matter up to the Mexican government. Instead, believing Gamio's study of immigration particularly important, Morrow personally funded Gamio's work at $500 (1000 pesos) per month. Despite a tepid response to Gamio's larger plans for his study of Mexican immigration, the SSRC helped subsidize the publication of *Mexican Immigration to the United States: A Study of Human Migration and Adjustment* in 1930. "Why the Social Science Research Council Favored the Study of Mexican Immigra-

tion into the United States and commended it to Dr. Manuel Gamio," in Dwight W. Morrow Papers, box 2, folder 63, Archives and Special Collections, Amherst College Library; Schmidt, "Mexicans, Migrants, and Indigenous Peoples," 168. If Morrow's financial support of Gamio seems unusually generous, it should be noted that in 1929 Morrow also funded Diego Rivera's completion of his murals at the Palace of Cortés in Cuernavaca. Ruiz, *Triumphs and Tragedy*, 369.

32. Schmidt, "Mexicans, Migrants, and Indigenous Peoples," 167.
33. Hoover, "Our Mexican Immigrants," 99–107.
34. Schmidt, "Mexicans, Migrants, and Indigenous Peoples," 172.
35. Schmidt, "Mexicans, Migrants, and Indigenous Peoples," 175, n11.
36. Dawson to Kellogg, December 13, 1928, NARA, RG 59, 812.5611/24, 1–2. Gamio estimated that while the average Mexican household needed $123.74 monthly to live above the poverty line, the average Mexican head of household earned only $17.67 per month. Hernández, *Migra!*, 86.
37. Vázquez and Meyer, *The United States and Mexico*, 139; Buchenau, *Plutarco Elías Calles and the Mexican Revolution*, 151–52.
38. Dawson to Kellogg, February 9, 1929, NARA, RG 59, 811.111 Mexico/166.
39. "Why the Social Science Research Council Favored the Study of Mexican Imigration into the United States and commended it to Dr. Manuel Gamio," in Dwight W. Morrow Papers, box 2, folder 63, Archives and Special Collections, Amherst College Library, 6.
40. "Why the Social Science Research Council Favored the Study of Mexican Imigration into the United States and commended it to Dr. Manuel Gamio," in Dwight W. Morrow Papers, box 2, folder 63, Archives and Special Collections, Amherst College Library, 6.
41. Manuel Gamio, "Quantitative Estimate of Mexican Immigration to the United States," AHSRE: LEG 761, exp. 1, 101.
42. Manuel Gamio, "Quantitative Estimate of Mexican Immigration to the United States," AHSRE: LEG 761, exp. 1, 99.
43. Manuel Gamio, "Quantitative Estimate of Mexican Immigration to the United States," AHSRE: LEG 761, exp. 1, 16–17.
44. This point, initially presented in September 1926, was developed further by Gamio in his later work when he discussed the Cristero Rebellion, which had begun only a month before he gave his "Preliminary Report" at Dartmouth College. The conflict zone of that rebellion was southcentral Mexico, from where many Mexican migrants historically derived. Gamio argued that a good way to relieve political pressure on the central government would be to encourage the mass emigration of displaced and unemployed peasants from that conflict zone, thereby solving the twin problems of economic grievances and political animosity toward Mexico City. Hernández, *Migra!*, 87.

45. Manuel Gamio, "Quantitative Estimate of Mexican Immigration to the United States," AHSRE: LEG 761, exp. 1, 103–4.
46. Toy, "The Survey of Race Relations on the Pacific Coast in the 1920s," 37–38 and 40. Notable sociological publications that stemmed from other projects funded by the institute included the following: Robert S. Lynd and Helen Merrell Lynd, *Middletown* (1929), G. E. E. Lindquist, *The Red Man in the United States* (1923, 1924), H. Paul Douglass, *1,000 City Churches* (1926), T. J. Woofter, Jr., *Negro Problems in Cities* (1928, 1929), and Edmund de S. Brunner and J. H. Kolb, *Rural Social Trends* (1933).
47. "Interest Found in Race Survey," *Los Angeles Times*, May 13, 1924, A5.
48. "Eliot G. Mears, 'The Survey of Race Relations,' *Stanford Illustrated Review*, 1925," Survey of Race Relations, box 22, folder 12, in Hoover Institute Archives, Stanford University, Palo Alto CA.
49. Toy, "The Survey of Race Relations on the Pacific Coast in the 1920s," 56.
50. Toy, "The Survey of Race Relations on the Pacific Coast in the 1920s," 38 and 59.
51. Toy, "The Survey of Race Relations on the Pacific Coast in the 1920s," 48.
52. "International and Interracial Factors in the Mexican Situation in the Southwest," Survey of Race Relations, box 20, folder 3, in Hoover Institute Archives, Stanford University, Palo Alto CA.
53. "The Future of Mexican Immigration: A Story on the Outside Looking In (Based in Large Part on an Actual Life Story)," Survey of Race Relations, box 20, folder 5, in Hoover Institute Archives, Stanford University, Palo Alto CA.
54. "The Future of Mexican Immigration: A Story on the Outside Looking In (Based in Large Part on an Actual Life Story)," Survey of Race Relations, box 20, folder 5, in Hoover Institute Archives, Stanford University, Palo Alto CA.
55. "The Future of Mexican Immigration: A Story on the Outside Looking In (Based in Large Part on an Actual Life Story)," Survey of Race Relations, box 20, folder 5, in Hoover Institute Archives, Stanford University, Palo Alto CA.
56. Sheridan, "Contested Citizenship," 8–18.
57. "Interview No. 50" and "*The Essentials of Mexican Culture*," Survey of Race Relations, box 20, folder 4, in Hoover Institute Archives, Stanford University, Palo Alto CA.
58. Foerster, *The Racial Problems Involved in Immigration;* Molina, "In a Race All Their Own," 181–82.
59. Foerster, *The Racial Problems Involved in Immigration*, 1–2, 7, 8, 10, and 11.
60. Foerster, *The Racial Problems Involved in Immigration*, 13.
61. Foerster, *The Racial Problems Involved in Immigration*, 11, 13–14.

62. Foerster, *The Racial Problems Involved in Immigration*, 53.
63. Foerster, *The Racial Problems Involved in Immigration*, 53 and 55.
64. Foerster, *The Racial Problems Involved in Immigration*, 56–57.
65. Foerster, *The Racial Problems Involved in Immigration*, 60.
66. Davis to Brandt, April 10, 1928, NARA, RG 59, 811.111 Mexico/36.5, 1; Davis to Carr, September 10, 1928, NARA, RG 59, 811.111 Quota 10/59.5, 5.
67. Davis to Carr, September 10, 1928, NARA, RG 59, 811.111 Quota 10/59.5, 5–7; Davis to Carr, December 28, 1928, NARA, RG 59, 811.111 Mexico/140.75, 1.
68. Davis to Carr, September 10, 1928, NARA, RG 59, 811.111 Quota 10/59.5, 4.
69. Dye to Davis, November 16, 1928, NARA, RG 59, 811.111 Mexico/120.5, 1–2.
70. Davis to Carr, April 10, 1928, NARA, RG 59, 811.111 Mexico/36.5, 7. In February 1929 a conference was held in Mexico City for American consular officials. The primary goal of the conference was to ensure that consuls in Mexico were enforcing U.S. immigration laws and exclusions in an equal fashion to standards set by consuls in Europe and elsewhere. Consuls at the conference believed that the best way to reduce Mexican immigration was not through the strictest law (a quota) but rather an equal application of enforcement laws across the world. Dawson to Kellogg, February 21, 1929, NARA, RG 59, 811.111 Mexico/171, 2.
71. Kellogg to Morrow, July 5, 1928, NARA, RG 59, 811.111 Mexico/82, 6–9.
72. Kellogg to Morrow, July 5, 1928, NARA, RG 59, 811.111 Mexico/82, 6–9.
73. Kellogg to Morrow, July 5, 1928, NARA, RG 59, 811.111 Mexico/82, 1–5; Davis to Carr, April 10, 1928, NARA, RG 59, 811.111 Mexico/36.5, 3–4.
74. Kellogg to Morrow, August 16, 1928, NARA, RG 59, 811.111 Mexico/92, 4–5. As early as April 1928, in the midst of seeking reliable Mexican repatriation statistics, Kellogg considered the passport scheme an alternative to the quota. In a telegram to Morrow, Kellogg stated that he was contemplating issuing instructions to consular officials in Mexico "to [e]nsure the enforcement of regulations under which all Mexican emigrants would be required to present passports" to enter the United States. "Some reduction in total immigration," Kellogg stated, "will no doubt result from a more exacting application of the provisions of existing legislation." Kellogg to Morrow, April 18, 1928, NARA, RG 59, 811.111 Mexico/43, 1–4.
75. Schoenfeld to Kellogg, December 15, 1928, NARA, RG 59, 811.111 Mexico/129, 1.
76. Morrow to Kellogg, August 24, 1928, NARA, RG 59, 811.111 Mexico/94; Schoenfeld to Kellogg, December 15, 1928, NARA, RG 59, 811.111 Mexico/129, 1.

77. Schoenfeld to Kellogg, December 16, 1928, NARA, RG 59, 811.111 Mexico/130, 1–2.
78. Morrow to Kellogg, March 1, 1929, NARA, RG 59, 811.111 Mexico/174, 2.
79. Division of Mexican Affairs to Carr, January 14, 1929, NARA, RG 59, 812.5611/28A, 3.
80. Kellogg to Morrow, August 16, 1928, NARA, RG 59, 811.111 Mexico/92, 1–2.
81. Morrow to Stimson, April 5, 1929, NARA, RG 59, 812.5611/37, 4–5.

5. The U.S. Senate Passes a Quota

1. Dawson to Stimson, October 19, 1929, NARA, RG 59, 811.111 Mexico/282; Dawson to Stimson, November 1, 1929, NARA, RG 59, 811.111 Mexico/287.
2. Dawson to Stimson, October 19, 1929, NARA, RG 59, 811.111 Mexico/282.
3. Durand, *Migración México-Estados Unidos. Años Veinte*, 13.
4. Morrow to Stimson, "El Problema de la Emigracion de Obreros y Campesinos Mexicanos," August 16, 1929, NARA, RG 59, 812.5611/39, 21.
5. Morrow to Stimson, "El Problema de la Emigracion de Obreros y Campesinos Mexicanos," August 16, 1929, NARA, RG 59, 812.5611/39, 21 and 34. Also refer to chapter 2 of Durand, *Migración México-Estados Unidos. Años Veinte*.
6. Balderamma and Rodríguez, *Decade of Betrayal*, 131.
7. Santibáñez, *Ensayo Acerca de la Inmigracion Mexicana en los Estados Unidos*, 16. Also refer to chapter 3 of Durand, *Migración México-Estados Unidos. Años Veinte*. Each essay originally appeared in the editorial section (page 5) of *Excelsior* on the following dates in 1929: October 4, 7, 9, 11, 14, 16, 18, 22, 24, 26, 28, and 30; November 2, 4, 6, 9, 11, 13, and 15.
8. Santibáñez, *Ensayo Acerca de la Inmigracion Mexicana en los Estados Unidos*, 100.
9. Santibáñez, *Ensayo Acerca de la Inmigracion Mexicana en los Estados Unidos*, 98.
10. Santibáñez, *Ensayo Acerca de la Inmigracion Mexicana en los Estados Unidos*, 88.
11. Santibáñez, *Ensayo Acerca de la Inmigracion Mexicana en los Estados Unidos*, 93–96.
12. Santibáñez, *Ensayo Acerca de la Inmigracion Mexicana en los Estados Unidos*, 72–75.
13. Hoover, "Our Mexican Immigrants," 99.
14. Hoover, "Our Mexican Immigrants," 99–102.
15. Hoover, "Our Mexican Immigrants," 103.
16. Hoover, "Our Mexican Immigrants," 103 and 105.
17. Hoover, "Our Mexican Immigrants," 104.
18. Hoover, "Our Mexican Immigrants," 106–7.
19. Hoover, "Our Mexican Immigrants," 106.

20. Hoover, "Our Mexican Immigrants," 107. Curiously, the *New York Times* argued that Hoover's argument offered an objective take on the Mexican immigration problem, "marked by fairness and a desire to present the [immigration] problem fully and without prejudice," and that his points could benefit both sides of the quota debate. Like Hoover, the paper identified race as the chief component to the Mexican immigration problem. Most Mexican migrants were of Indian ancestry, whose ability to assimilate into U.S. society was questionable. Of main concern was that a new race problem would affect the nation if the population of Mexicans was allowed to grow continuously (the editorialist estimated that the 1930 census would show a Mexican population of near 2 million in the United States). The problem with quota legislation, whether one was opposed to it or not, was that the legislation could be negated by the fact that Mexicans could easily cross the border that was patchily regulated by the Border Patrol. "Mexican Immigration," *New York Times*, October 13, 1929, E4.
21. Races of petitioners who were barred the right to naturalize were: Chinese, Japanese, Burmese, Hawaiian, those who were half Japanese and half white, and those who were half Native American and half white.
22. Molina, "In a Race All Their Own," 170; Ngai, "The Architecture of Race in American Immigration Law," 88–89.
23. LeMay and Barkan, *U.S. Immigration and Naturalization Laws and Issues*, 79; Menchaca, *Naturalizing Mexican Immigrants*, 152–56.
24. Menchaca, *Naturalizing Mexican Immigrants*, 152–56.
25. Santibáñez, *Ensayo Acerca de la Inmigracion Mexicana en los Estados Unidos*, 85–86.
26. Santibáñez, *Ensayo Acerca de la Inmigracion Mexicana en los Estados Unidos*, 101–2.
27. Santibáñez, *Ensayo Acerca de la Inmigracion Mexicana en los Estados Unidos*, 103.
28. Santibáñez, *Ensayo Acerca de la Inmigracion Mexicana en los Estados Unidos*, 104–5.
29. At the end of one of his essays, entitled "El derecho de una nación de la vida" (or "The right of a nation to life"), Santibáñez defended a country's sovereign right over immigration policy. "Every nation has the right to make laws that guarantee the character, the independence, and customs of the nation[;] and it reserves the right to expel the foreigner if they do not assimilate to the ways of the land even after they have been hosted and given the opportunity to live well and happy." One is left to wonder if he believed the United States violated the latter half of this credo by its ill treatment of Mexican migrants.

30. Santibáñez, *Ensayo Acerca de la Inmigracion Mexicana en los Estados Unidos*, 50–51.
31. Santibáñez, *Ensayo Acerca de la Inmigracion Mexicana en los Estados Unidos*, 82.
32. King, *Making Americans*, 204, 206–7; "Immigration Curb on Mexico Urged," *New York Times*, December 5, 1929, 15; "Urges Limitation of all Immigrants," *New York Times*, December 9, 1929, 31. It should be noted that African Americans were not included in the total calculations. Such exclusion denied their place in the American polity and, conveniently, reduced the total population figure to which national quotas could be fixed for immigration.
33. "Would Cut Influx of Western Aliens," *New York Times*, January 14, 1930, 11; "For Quota of 76,064 from the Americas," *New York Times*, February 27, 1930, 14.
34. "Immigrants from the New World," *New York Times*, January 16, 1930, 22.
35. "For Quota of 76,064 from the Americas," *New York Times*, February 27, 1930, 14; "Opposes Any Quota for Latin-America," *New York Times*, February 28, 1930, 15; "Further Limits on Immigration," *New York Times*, February 28, 1930, 22.
36. "Opposes Any Quota for Latin-America," *New York Times*, February 28, 1930, 15; "Further Limits on Immigration," *New York Times*, February 28, 1930, 22.
37. "For Quota of 76,064 from the Americas," *New York Times*, February 27, 1930, 14; "Opposes Any Quota for Latin-America," *New York Times*, February 28, 1930, 15; "Further Limits on Immigration," *New York Times*, February 28, 1930, 22; Dawson to Stimson, March 15, 1930, NARA, RG 59, 811.111 Mexico/340.
38. FRUS, 1923, vol. 1: Treaty between the United States of America and Other American Republics, signed at Santiago, May 3, 1923, 308.
39. FRUS, 1923, vol. 1: The Minister of Uruguay (Philip) to the Secretary of State, February 23, 1923, 293–94.
40. Unlike the League of Nations, the U.S. Congress ratified the Gondra Treaty in April 1924. Most Latin American nations signed onto the treaty except for the three Guianan states, Costa Rica, Peru, Bolivia, and, notably, Mexico. Both Bolivia and Peru refused to attend the convention (though they sent delegations to the conference itself) because of separate bilateral conflicts with Chile. Mexico, while it would accept and ratify the treaty by the next Pan-American conference in spring 1928, not only did not sign onto the treaty but declined attending the conference at all. The primary reason why Mexico did not attend the conference was its fraught relationship with the United States, stemming from the ouster (and subsequent murder) of Venustiano Carranza from the Mexican presidency in May 1920,

and exacerbated by interminable discussions over the protection of foreign (read: American) property rights in Mexico vis-à-vis Álvaro Obregón's effort to protect Mexico's sovereign right to nationalize the Mexican oil industry (recently promulgated by the 1917 Constitution). The Mexican government feared the United States might place a Mexican delegation to the conference in an "embarrassing position" by making reservations to agreements or conventions because of U.S. nonrecognition of Mexico. Secretary of State Charles E. Hughes responded to such misgivings by saying that the United States desired good relations with Mexico and that the delay in achieving that end was attributable to the Mexican government, which had failed to give assurances that foreign property rights in Mexico would be respected. While the U.S. government welcomed Mexican participation in the conference, Hughes concluded, the United States should not be expected to enter into treaties with governments it did not recognize. FRUS, 1923, vol. 1: The Chargé in Mexico (Summerlin) to the Secretary of State, March 1, 1923, and The Secretary of State to the Ambassador in Brazil (Morgan), March 5, 1923, 295–96.

41. "Seeks Drastic Curb on Entry of Aliens," *New York Times*, May 18, 1930, 16.
42. President Herbert Hoover called the Harris bill "obnoxious" to Latin America.
43. "Senate Recommits Immigration Bill," *New York Times*, April 26, 1930, 5; "Pass Bill to Apply Quota to Mexicans," *New York Times*, May 14, 1930, 56; "Seeks Drastic Curb on Entry of Aliens," *New York Times*, May 18, 1930, 16.
44. "Immigration from Mexico: Hearings—Statement of Hon. Joseph Cotton. 71st Congress, 2nd Session (Washington DC: Government Printing Office, 1930)," in Dwight W. Morrow Papers, box. 5, folder 122, Archives and Special Collections, Amherst College Library.
45. United States House of Representatives, Committee on Immigration and Naturalization, *Immigration from Mexico: Hearings—Statement of Hon. Joseph Cotton*. 71st Congress, 2nd Session (Washington DC: Government Printing Office, 1930), 8–9.
46. "Immigration from Mexico: Hearings—Statement of Hon. Joseph Cotton. 71st Congress, 2nd Session (Washington DC: Government Printing Office, 1930)," in Dwight W. Morrow Papers, box. 5, folder 122, Archives and Special Collections, Amherst College Library (emphasis mine).
47. Vázquez and Meyer, *The United States and Mexico*, 86 and 98; "Immigration from Mexico: Hearings—Statement of Hon. Joseph Cotton. 71st Congress, 2nd Session (Washington DC: Government Printing Office, 1930)," in Dwight W. Morrow Papers, box. 5, folder 122, Archives and Special Collections, Amherst College Library.

48. "Opposes Quota on Mexicans Now," *New York Times*, July 3, 1929, 8; Simmons to Reed, December 5, 1929, NARA, RG 59, 811.111 Mexico/291.5.
49. Blocker to Stimson, January 7, 1930, NARA, RG 59, 812.5611/40, 1–3: of the 275 Mexicans who applied for visas in December 1929, 100 were refused. Altaffer to Stimson, January 24, 1930, NARA, RG 59, 812.5611/41, 1–3: of the 3,059 Mexicans who applied for visas, 1,117 were refused.
50. Davis to Simmons, February 27, 1930, NARA, RG 59, 811.111 Mexico/328.5.
51. "Pass Bill to Apply Quota to Mexicans," *New York Times*, May 14, 1930, 56; "Fewer Mexicans Enter," *New York Times*, June 14, 1930, 10.
52. Refer to chapter 4 for a fuller description of this debate.
53. Simmons to Carr, October 17, 1929, NARA, RG 59, 811.111 Mexico/280, 2; Simmons to Dawson, December 30, 1928, NARA, RG 59, 811.111 Mexico/305.5, 1–3.
54. Simmons to Dawson, February 4, 1930, NARA, RG 59, 811.111 Mexico/317.25, 2.
55. Blocker to Stimson, January 7, 1930, NARA, RG 59, 812.5611/40, 1–3.
56. Altaffer to Stimson, January 24, 1930, NARA, RG 59, 812.5611/41, 2–3.
57. Gamio, *Mexican Immigrant*, 10–11.
58. Hernández, *Migra!*, 92.
59. Ngai, "The Architecture of Race in American Immigration Law," 90.
60. Schneider, *Crossing Borders*, 120–21, 131.
61. "Border patrol agents," Molina states, "played a key role in defining Mexicans as outsiders through their harassment and denigration of Mexicans at checkpoints." Molina, "In a Race All Their Own," 187.
62. Ngai, "The Architecture of Race in American Immigration Law," 90–91, and Ngai, *Impossible Subjects*, 54–55. The Rio Grande, Ngai states, "was reproduced in the twentieth century as an ambiguous boundary line . . . where Mexicans were welcomed as cheap and disposable labor but not as members of the polity." Ngai, "Nationalism, Immigration Control, and the Ethnoracial Remapping of America in the 1920s," 14.
63. Dawson to Stimson, March 15, 1930, NARA, RG 59, 811.111 Mexico/340.
64. Dawson to Stimson, December 16, 1929, NARA, RG 59, 811.111 Mexico/301; Dawson to Stimson, January 9, 1930, NARA, RG 59, 811.111 Mexico/308.
65. Dawson to Stimson, January 30, 1930, NARA, RG 59, 811.111 Mexico/319; Dawson to Stimson, February 20, 1930, NARA, RG 59, 811.111 Mexico/328; Dawson to Stimson, March 15, 1930, NARA, RG 59, 811.111 Mexico/340. Compare "For Quota of 76,064 from the Americas,"

New York Times, February 27, 1930, 14; "Opposes Any Quota for Latin-America," *New York Times*, February 28, 1930, 15; "Further Limits on Immigration," *New York Times*, February 28, 1930, 22.

66. Dawson to Stimson, February 20, 1930, NARA, RG 59, 811.111 Mexico/328; Dawson to Stimson, March 15, 1930, NARA, RG 59, 811.111 Mexico/340.
67. Dwyre to Stimson, May 27, 1930, NARA, RG 59, 811.111 Mexico/386, 1–2.
68. Dawson to Stimson, March 15, 1930, NARA, RG 59, 811.111 Mexico/340; Dwyre to Stimson, April 21, 1930, NARA, RG 59, 811.111 Mexico/355, 1; Dwyre to Stimson, May 27, 1930, NARA, RG 59, 811.111 Mexico/386, 3.
69. Dwyre to Stimson, May 27, 1930, NARA, RG 59, 811.111 Mexico/386, 8–9.
70. "Protests Continue on Mexican Quota," *New York Times*, May 29, 1930, 10; Dwyre to Stimson, May 27, 1930, NARA, RG 59, 811.111 Mexico/386, 5–7.
71. Ramo Pascual Ortiz Rubio, 1930, Archivo General de la Nación, LEG 1, exp. 49, folios 8303, 8307, 8330, 8331, 8436, 8476, 8518, 8537, 8608, 8625; Ramo Pascual Ortiz Rubio, 1930, Archivo General de la Nación, LEG 2, exp. 49, folios 9377 and 9029.
72. "Chamber Chief Flays Box Bill," *Los Angeles Times*, May 20, 1930, 3.
73. Boyce to Stimson, May 26, 1930, NARA, RG 59, 811.111 Mexico/382, 6.
74. Ramo Pascual Ortiz Rubio, 1930, Archivo General de la Nación, LEG 1, exp. 49, folio 6676.
75. "Opposes Mexican Quota," *New York Times*, May 26, 1930, 2.
76. "Mexico Will Protest Immigration Measure," *New York Times*, May 21, 1930, 11; "Mexico Resents Bill to Curb Immigration," *New York Times*, May 28, 1930, 9.
77. NARA, RG 85, folder 55598–459E, "Barring Mexicans," *El Paso Herald*, May 14, 1930, "Mexican Discrimination," *El Paso Morning Times*, May 13, 1930, "Why Mexico?," *El Paso Evening Post*, May 16, 1930.
78. "Quantitative Estimate, Sources and Distribution of Mexican Immigration in the United States," NARA, RG 59, 811.111 Mexico/352, 9 and 16. Gamio estimated that between 1920 and 1928, 583,957 Mexicans entered the United States and 697,257 Mexicans returned to Mexico.
79. Gamio estimated that in 1928 the permanent Mexican population in the United States was 470,658.
80. "Quantitative Estimate, Sources and Distribution of Mexican Immigration in the United States," NARA, RG 59, 811.111 Mexico/352, 10–11.
81. "Quantitative Estimate, Sources and Distribution of Mexican Immigration in the United States," NARA, RG 59, 811.111 Mexico/352, 13–14. Gamio did not mention Escobar's Rebellion of March 1929. His data reflects immigration trends up through 1928.
82. "Quantitative Estimate, Sources and Distribution of Mexican Immigration in the United States," NARA, RG 59, 811.111 Mexico/352, 11.

83. Dwyre to Stimson, May 27, 1930, NARA, RG 59, 811.111 Mexico/386, 5–7.
84. Dwyre to Stimson, May 27, 1930, NARA, RG 59, 811.111 Mexico/386, 5–7.

6. Administrative Restriction, Repatriation

1. Enciso, "The Repatriation of Mexicans from the United States and Mexican Nationalism," 58–59.
2. Guerin-Gonzales, *Mexican Workers and American Dreams*, 87.
3. Balderamma and Rodríguez, *Decade of Betrayal*, 99.
4. Fitzgerald, *A Nation of Emigrants*, 47; Enciso, "The Repatriation of Mexicans from the United States and Mexican Nationalism," 77; Aguila, "Mexican/US Immigration Policy Prior to the Great Depression," 217.
5. Aguila, "Mexican/US Immigration Policy Prior to the Great Depression," 217; Enciso, "The Repatriation of Mexicans from the United States and Mexican Nationalism," 58–59.
6. Balderamma and Rodríguez, *Decade of Betrayal*, 101.
7. Enciso, "The Repatriation of Mexicans from the United States and Mexican Nationalism," 58 and 71.
8. Henderson, *Beyond Borders*, 45.
9. Balderamma and Rodríguez, *Decade of Betrayal*, 113.
10. AHSRE, IV-356-23, Repatriaciones, Kansas City Consulado, nos. 2633 and 7096.
11. AHSRE, IV-356-17, Repatriaciones, Galveston Consulado, nos. 16380 and 16379.
12. Martínez, *Troublesome Border*, 132.
13. Joseph and Buchenau, *Mexico's Once and Future Revolution*, 103; Ruiz, *Triumphs and Tragedy*, 340 and 387.
14. Joseph and Buchenau, *Mexico's Once and Future Revolution*, 103; Ruiz, *Triumphs and Tragedy*, 386–87.
15. Shaw to the Department of Commerce, 1930, NARA, RG 151, box 1767, folder 2, Records of Commerce and Industries San Luis Potosí, Mexico Quarterly Reports, June Quarter.
16. Shaw to the Department of Commerce, October 24, 1930, NARA, RG 151, box 1767, folder 2, Records of Commerce and Industries San Luis Potosí, Mexico Quarterly Reports.
17. NARA, RG 151, box 1767, folder 2, Review of Commerce and Industries for Chihuahua, October 8, 1930.
18. Copley to Department of Commerce, July 12, 1930, NARA, RG 151, Review of Commerce and Industries for Monterrey, June Quarter, 1930.
19. MacDonald to Department of Commerce, NARA, RG 151, box 1767, folder 2, Review of Commerce and Industries for Nuevo Laredo, for quarter ended September 30, 1930.

20. Dwyre to Department of Commerce, NARA, RG 151, Review of Commerce and Industries for Mexico City, June quarter, 1930, Mexico City, 1–6.
21. Balderamma and Rodríguez, *Decade of Betrayal*, 119.
22. Balderamma and Rodríguez, *Decade of Betrayal*, 119.
23. Frazer to Stimson, November 8, 1930, NARA, RG 59, 811.111 Mexico/503.
24. Frazer to Stimson, December 28, 1930, NARA, RG 59, 811.111 Mexico/526, 3–4.
25. Frazer to Stimson, January 28, 1931, NARA, RG 59, 812.5511/107, 2–4.
26. Frazer to Stimson, February 26, 1931, NARA, RG 59, 812.5511/108, 4.
27. Frazer to Stimson, July 14, 1931, NARA, RG 59, 812.55/156, 6 and 8.
28. Sokobin to Stimson, July 20, 1931, NARA, RG 59, 812.5611/51, 5.
29. Frazer to Stimson, January 28, 1931, NARA, RG 59, 812.5511/107, 7–8.
30. Blocker to Stimson, November 6, 1930, NARA, RG 59, 812.5511/98.
31. Blocker to Stimson, January 3, 1931, NARA, RG 59, 812.5511/102, 1–2.
32. Harper to Stimson, May 12, 1931, NARA, RG 59, 812.5511/117.
33. Drumright to State Department, September 4, 1931, NARA, RG 59, 811.111 Mexico/665, 7.
34. Foster to State Department, April 6, 1929, NARA, RG 59, 811.111 Mexico/192, 5; Foster to State Department, February 6, 1930, NARA, RG 59, 811.111 Mexico/321, 9.
35. Foster to State Department, July 14, 1931, NARA, RG 59, 811.111 Mexico/656, 5. Immigration historians have discussed how U.S. officials lied to *repatriados* when they told Mexicans they could easily reenter the United States. Officials persuaded many Mexicans to leave the United States voluntarily rather than risk deportation, which would have made their return to the United States a felony. These officials stamped Mexicans' exit visas with indications that they had relied on public relief up to their time of departure from the United States. An example of this stamp read "Los Angeles Department of Charities." Consequently American consuls could easily deny visas to Mexicans who sought to reenter the United States on the grounds that applicants had relied on public charities in the past and were likely to become public charges if allowed to reenter the United States. Guerin-Gonzales, *Mexican Workers and American Dreams*, 109; Hoffman, *Unwanted Mexicans in the Great Depression*, 32 and 116.
36. Foster to State Department, April 7, 1932, NARA, RG 59, 811.111 Mexico/798, 5; Foster to State Department, July 11, 1932, NARA, RG 59, 812.5511/143, 5.
37. Foster to State Department, July 11, 1932, NARA, RG 59, 812.5511/143, 5; Foster to State Department, October 10, 1932, NARA, RG 59, 811.111 Mexico/898, 5.

38. Dwyre to Stimson, September 23, 1930, NARA, RG 59, 811.111 Mexico/472, 4–5.
39. Foster to State Department, January 27, 1931, NARA, RG 59, 812.5511/105, 4.
40. Refer to chapter 5 of Guerin-Gonzales, *Mexican Workers and American Dreams*, for an account on the Mexican government's resettlement projects.
41. Henderson, *Beyond Borders*, 46–48.
42. According to the 1930 census, 1,422,533 Mexicans resided in the United States, whereas the 1920 census enumerated 700,541 (0.7 percent of the total U.S. population in 1920 as opposed to 1.2 percent of the total U.S. population in 1930). While every U.S. state registered a Mexican population, Texas, California, and Arizona had the largest number of Mexican residents (683,681; 368,013; 114,173, respectively). "Population analyzed," *Los Angeles Times*, August 5, 1931, 1.
43. "The Repatriados," *Los Angeles Times*, April 24, 1932, 13.
44. Guerin-Gonzales, *Mexican Workers and American Dreams*, 78.
45. Barkan, *From All Points*, 329; Gutiérrez, *Walls and Mirrors*, 72.
46. Henderson, *Beyond Borders*, 45.
47. Schneider, *Crossing Borders*, 121.
48. Gutiérrez, *Walls and Mirrors*, 72.
49. Henderson, *Beyond Borders*, 46.
50. Barkan, *From All Points*, 329.
51. Barkan, *From All Points*, 329.
52. Vázquez and Meyer, *The United States and Mexico*, 141–42.
53. Ngai, "The Architecture of Race in American Immigration Law," 90; Calderón-Zaks, "Debated Whiteness amid World Events," 335 and 340.
54. Dwyre to Stimson, July 21, 1930, NARA, RG 59, 811.111 Mexico/416, 1–3.
55. Hodgdon to Paul S. Taylor, August 6, 1930, NARA, RG 59, 811.111 Mexico/447.
56. Gibson to Department of Commerce, NARA, RG 151, box 1767, folder 2, Review of Commerce and Industries for Guadalajara, August 4, 1930.
57. "New Visa Plan Halts Mexican Rush into U.S.," *Chicago Daily Tribune*, September 13, 1931, D10.
58. Blocker to Stimson, September 6, 1930, NARA, RG 59, 811.111 Mexico/456, 1–2.
59. Blocker to Stimson, September 17, 1930, NARA, RG 59, 811.111 Mexico/462.
60. Altaffer to Stimson, October 6, 1930, NARA, RG 59, 811.111 Mexico/481, 1–2. Compare NARA, RG 85, fldr. 55598–459E, "Immigration Policy Sound," *Arizona Daily Despatch*, December 14, 1930.
61. "Mexican entrants fewer," *New York Times*, November 4, 1930, 3.

62. Drumright to State Department, September 4, 1931, NARA, RG 59, 811.111 Mexico/665, 1–8, quote from 5.
63. "Chamber Chief Flays Box Bill," *Los Angeles Times*, May 20, 1930, 3; "Move to Force House Vote on Mexican Quota," *Chicago Daily Tribune*, June 5, 1930, 5.
64. "Mexican Influx Shows Decline," *Los Angeles Times*, June 14, 1930, 3.
65. "Mexican Immigration," *Washington Post*, August 10, 1930, S1; "Mexican Influx Shows Low Ebb," *Los Angeles Times*, August 28, 1930, 9; "Immigrant Cut Shown at Border," *Los Angeles Times*, June 2, 1931, 3; "140,000 Aliens Kept Away by New U.S. Policy," *Chicago Daily Tribune*, June 28, 1931, 17; "Immigration Visas Decline," *Los Angeles Times*, June 28, 1931, 9; "Immigration Visas Show Heavy Decline," *Washington Post*, June 28, 1931, M4; "Flow of Alien Tide Changes," *Los Angeles Times*, July 31, 1931, 2. A caustic editorial laced with hyperbole from the *Chicago Daily Tribune* demonstrated, however, that there was still strong opposition to State Department attempts to obviate a quota on Mexican immigration. In an editorial entitled "Czardom in the House," the newspaper argued that Congress should pass the Harris bill into law regardless of the supposed effect a quota may have on U.S.-Mexican relations. "The [Harris bill] would put Mexico on a quota basis where it belongs. Unrestricted immigration is creating social, political and economic conditions which are injurious to the welfare of the nation and the argument that a proper check upon it must not be applied for fear of some imaginable effect upon our relations with the Mexican government will not bear free examination in the House or elsewhere. The purchase of good opinions by concessions injurious to the permanent interests of the nation in assimilation and quality of citizenship is a delusion and a cheat. Good relations with Mexico are highly desirable and important, but they are not to be bought at the price of such concessions. For years these relations have been the football of shortsighted expediencies varied by sentimental fallacies, and our conduct procured us nothing but the scorn and hostility of recurrent Mexican governments. *There is no chapter of the history of American foreign affairs less creditable to American diplomacy than this chapter, and it is time we put our policy under the control of consistency and self-respect.*" The editorial went on to argue that the progress made toward fostering good relations between the United States and Mexico did not have to be jeopardized by the quota. More importantly it argued that U.S. government officials—especially the State Department—were wrong to limit Congress's sovereign power over immigration policy because of fears of the quota's supposed diplomatic consequence. And even if the quota did harm relations, the editorial stated, Con-

gress should not hesitate to take the necessary steps to regulate Mexican immigration. "The price of what are vaguely referred to as good relations is exorbitant and Congress should insist upon its right and duty to protect the general and permanent interest of the nation." "Czardom in the House," *Chicago Daily Tribune*, June 18, 1930, 10 (emphasis mine).

66. "Box Bill Plank Mighty Shaky," *Los Angeles Times*, July 31, 1930, 8.
67. "Restriction Measure to be Revived," *Los Angeles Times*, October 3, 1930, 3.
68. "Cuts Immigration as Unemployment Aid," *Daily Boston Globe*, September 10, 1930, 19; "Hoover Acts to Bar Immigrants Coming for Jobs," *Chicago Daily Tribune*, September 10, 1930, 3.
69. "Labor Immigration Halted Temporarily at Hoover's Order," *New York Times*, September 10, 1930, 1; (Main title blocked) "Immigration Restrictions to be Enforced Rigidly in Exclusion Effort," *Los Angeles Times*, September 10, 1930, 1; "Immigration Ban to Aid Unemployment," *Washington Post*, September 10, 1930, 2; "Defends Alien Ban as Aid to Jobless," *New York Times*, December 7, 1930, 47.
70. "Bar 135,000 Aliens under Visa Ruling," *New York Times*, December 6, 1930, 4.
71. "Alien Curb Succeeds," *Los Angeles Times*, May 16, 1931, 1.
72. *Restriction of Immigration and Reduction of Quotas, Part I: Hearings*, United States House of Representatives, Committee on Immigration and Naturalization, 72nd Congress, 1st Session (Washington DC: Government Printing Office, 1932), 35–37.
73. *Restriction of Immigration and Reduction of Quotas, Part I: Hearings*, United States House of Representatives, Committee on Immigration and Naturalization, 72nd Congress, 1st Session (Washington DC: Government Printing Office, 1932), 38. These statistics are taken from data provided by Stimson to Hoover, which categorized visa issuance by "number of relatives of American citizens," "farmers," [skilled agricultural workers and their families], "number of relatives of aliens," [relatives of immigrants already granted admittance into the United States], and "non-preference." The data provided above is drawn from the statistics recorded for visa issuance toward non-preference aliens, in which category immigrant laborers were most-often classified. Refer to section 6 of the 1924 immigration act, "Preferences within Quotas," for definitions of the immigration preference regime.
74. *Restriction of Immigration and Reduction of Quotas, Part I: Hearings*, United States House of Representatives, Committee on Immigration and Naturalization, 72nd Congress, 1st Session (Washington DC: Government Printing Office, 1932), 35–37.

75. FRUS, 1931, vol. 1: Messages of the President of the United States to Congress, Message of December 8, 1931, xxii.
76. "Mexicans Put on Quota Basis by Senate Bill," *Chicago Daily Tribune*, January 17, 1932, 17; "Senate Bill Reported to Fix Mexican Quota," *New York Times*, January 17, 1932, 2.
77. "Mexican Quota Bill Deferred," *Los Angeles Times*, January 26, 1932, 6.
78. "State Against Mexican Bars," *Los Angeles Times*, February 24, 1932, 5.
79. *Restriction of Immigration and Reduction of Quotas, Part I: Hearings*, United States House of Representatives, Committee on Immigration and Naturalization, 28.
80. *Restriction of Immigration and Reduction of Quotas, Part I: Hearings*, United States House of Representatives, Committee on Immigration and Naturalization, 25–26.
81. *Restriction of Immigration and Reduction of Quotas, Part I: Hearings*, United States House of Representatives, Committee on Immigration and Naturalization, 4–5. Albert Johnson attended this hearing. While there is no evidence to suggest this, one has to wonder if Hodgdon's point recalled to Johnson his arguments four years before about "consolidated opposition," or hemisphere-wide opposition to his effort to place a quota on immigration from all Latin American countries. His response then was to focus his quota effort on Mexico alone and then to seek a broader quota as circumstances allowed. It must have been clear to him by this moment—February 1932—that both efforts, especially the one toward Mexico, had failed.
82. "Senator Harris of Georgia Dead," *Daily Boston Globe*, April 19, 1932, 17.
83. *"Six Members of House Plead Own Alien Bills," Washington Post*, February 24, 1932, 10.
84. "House Committee Kills Sharp Immigration Cuts," *New York Times*, March 13, 1934, 2; "Curbs on Aliens' Entry Rejected," *Los Angeles Times*, March 13, 1934, 1.

Conclusion

1. Cochran to State Department, December 30, 1932, NARA, RG 59, 811.111 Mexico/942, 1–9.
2. *Survey of American Foreign Relations*, Council on Foreign Relations, 1929, 518.
3. Although it was not a formal compromise between the State Department and restrictionists, as Michael Calderón-Zaks states. Calderón-Zaks, "Debated Whiteness amid World Events," 335.
4. *Survey of American Foreign Relations*, Council on Foreign Relations, 1931, 222 and 224. The SAFR author, perhaps unwittingly, confirmed many of the racial stereotypes Americans had of Mexican immigrants

within their midst. He also suggested how racism toward Mexicans perpetuated the immigration problem between the United States and Mexico. "The racial question is not the least of the problems sprouting from a growing Mexican population [in the United States]. Most of those coming to the United States are Indian, or mestizo with a large measure of Indian blood. They have little opportunity or inclination to embrace the customs or the language of their new home; many do not regard the United States as a home, but merely as a place to earn sufficient money to return to Mexico. Apathy on the part of Mexican immigrants is greatly accentuated by the American attitude. Assimilation is discouraged and American prejudice against social intercourse with Indians or colored peoples is increasingly noticeable in regard to Mexicans. The American workingman of Texas or California does not wish to associate with the brown laborers from Guanajuato, with their ignorant ways and their squalid manner of living. In the southern United States, Mexicans must travel in Jim Crow cars and are not allowed in white restaurants or white schools." *Survey of American Foreign Relations*, Council on Foreign Relations, 1931, 215–16.

Bibliography

Archives and Manuscript Collections: Mexico

Archivo General de la Nación, Mexico City
    Galeria 3, Fondo Presidentes
        Obregón-Calles
        Emilio Portes Gil
        Pascual Ortiz Rubio
        Abelardo Rodríguez
Secretaría de Relaciónes Exteriores, Mexico City
    Archivo Histórico
        Archivo Departamento Consular
        Archivo Departamento Diplomatico
        Archivo General
La Embajada de México en los Estados Unidos de América
    Archivo embajada mexico en los Estados Unidos de América, 1910–1912
    Revolucion mexicana embajada los Estados Unidos de América, 1910–1920, vol. 2
    Catálogo de las relaciones México–Estados Unidos del archivo de la embajada de México en los Estados Unidos de América, 1922–1965
Inventario del fondo Numeracion Corrida

Archives and Manuscript Collections: United States

Amherst College Library, Amherst MA
    Dwight Morrow Papers
Congressional Record
Hoover Institute Archives, Stanford University, Palo Alto CA
    Survey of Race Relations (digitized)
Library of Congress, Washington DC
    Manuscript Division
        Henry P. Fletcher Papers

Charles Evans Hughes Papers
Frank Kellogg Papers
Philander Knox Papers
Robert Lansing Papers
William McKinley Papers
Theodore Roosevelt Papers
Elihu Root Papers
Henry Stimson Papers
William Howard Taft Papers
Woodrow Wilson Papers

NARA: National Archives, Washington DC and College Park MD
  RG 59: General Records of the Department of State
  RG 76: Claims Commissions Records
  RG 84: Foreign Post Records of the Department of State, Mexico
  RG 85: US Immigration and Naturalization Records
  RG 131: Records of the Office of Alien Property
  RG 151: Records of the Office of the Bureau of Foreign and Domestic Commerce, Mexico

New York Public Library, New York City NY
  O'Shaughnessy Family Papers, 1899–1937 (Nelson O'Shaughnessy Papers)

Papers Relating to the Foreign Relations of the United States (FRUS)

Yale University Library, New Haven CT
  James R. Sheffield Papers

Published Works

Acuña, Rodolfo. *Corridors of Migration: The Odyssey of Mexican Laborers, 1600—1933.* Tucson: University of Arizona Press, 2007.

Aguila, Jaime. "Mexican/US Immigration Policy Prior to the Great Depression." *Diplomatic History* 31 (April 2007): 207–25.

Allerfeldt, Kristofer. "'And We Got Here First': Albert Johnson, National Origins, and Self-Interest in the Immigration Debate of the 1920s." *Journal of Contemporary History* 45, no. 1 (January 2010): 7–26.

Ambrosius, Lloyd. *Woodrow Wilson and the American Diplomatic Tradition: The Treaty Fight in Perspective.* Cambridge: Cambridge University Press, 1987.

———. *Wilsonianism: Woodrow Wilson and His Legacy in American Foreign Relations.* New York: Palgrave Macmillan, 2002.

Ayón, David R. "Mexican Policy and Émigré Communities in the US." Background paper presented at the conference "Mexican Migrant Social and Civic Participation in the United States," Woodrow Wilson International Center for Scholars, Washington DC, November 4–5, 2005.

Bailey, David C. *¡Viva Cristo Rey!: The Cristero Rebellion and the Church-State Conflict in Mexico*. Austin: University of Texas Press, 1974.

Balderamma, Francisco, and Raymond Rodríguez. *Decade of Betrayal: Mexican Repatriation in the 1930s*. Albuquerque: University of New Mexico Press, 1995.

Bantjes, Adrian A. *As If Jesus Walked the Earth: Cardenismo, Sonora, and the Mexican Revolution*. Wilmington DE: Scholarly Resources, 1998.

Barkan, Elliot Robert. *From All Points: America's Immigrant West, 1870s-1952*. Bloomington: Indiana University Press, 2007.

Bean, Frank D., et al., eds. *At the Crossroads: Mexico Immigration and U.S. Policy*. Lanham MD: Rowman and Littlefield, 1997.

Beezley, William H., ed. *A Companion to Mexican History and Culture*. Marlton MA: Wiley-Blackwell, 2011.

Bender, Thomas. *A Nation Among Nations: America's Place in World History*. New York: Hill and Wang, 2006.

Benton-Cohen, Katherine. "Other Immigrants: Mexicans and the Dillingham Commission of 1907–1911." *Journal of American Ethnic History* 30, no. 2 (Winter 2011): 33–57.

Berger, Mark T. *Under Northern Eyes: Latin American Studies and U.S. Hegemony in the Americas, 1898–1990*. Bloomington: Indiana University Press, 1995.

Blake, Casey N. *Beloved Community: The Cultural Criticism of Randolph Bourne, Van Wyck Brooks, Waldo Frank, and Lewis Mumford*. Chapel Hill: University of North Carolina Press, 1990.

Bliss, Katherine Elaine. *Compromised Positions: Prostitution, Public Health, and Gender Politics in Revolutionary Mexico City*. University Park: Pennsylvania State University Press, 2001.

Bodnar, John. *Immigration and Industrialization: Ethnicity in an American Mill Town, 1870–1940*. Pittsburgh: University of Pittsburgh Press, 1977.

———. *The Transplanted: A History of Immigrants in Urban America*. Bloomington: Indiana University Press, 1985.

Boghardt, Thomas. *The Zimmermann Telegram: Intelligence, Diplomacy, and America's Entry into World War I*. Annapolis MD: Naval Institute Press, 2012.

Brands, Hal. *Latin America's Cold War*. Cambridge MA: Harvard University Press, 2010.

Brenner, Anita, and George Leighton. *The Wind that Swept Mexico: The History of the Mexican Revolution of 1910–1942*. New York: Harper, 1943.

Brinkley, Alan. *The End of Reform: New Deal Liberalism in Recession and War*. New York: Alfred A. Knopf, 1995.

Brundage, W. Fitzhugh. *Lynching in the New South: Georgia and Virginia, 1880–1930*. Chicago: University of Illinois Press, 1993.

Buchenau, Jürgen. *In the Shadow of the Giant: The Making of Mexico's Central America Policy, 1876–1930.* Tuscaloosa: University of Alabama Press, 1996.

———. *Plutarco Elías Calles and the Mexican Revolution.* Lanham MD: Rowman and Littlefield, 2007.

Buffington, Robert M. *Criminal and Citizen in Modern Mexico.* Lincoln: University of Nebraska Press, 2000.

Burgoon, Brian, et al. "Immigration and the Transformation of American Unionism," *International Immigration Review* 44 (Winter 2010): 933–73.

Calderón-Zaks, Michael Aaron. "Constructing the 'Mexican Race': Racial Formation and Empire Building, 1884–1940." PhD dissertation, State University of New York, Binghamton, 2008.

———. "Debated Whiteness amid World Events: Mexican and Mexican American Subjectivity and the U.S.' Relationship with the Americas, 1924–1936." *Mexican Studies/Estudios Mexicanos* 27, no. 2 (Summer 2011): 325–59.

Calhoun, Frederick. *Uses of Force and Wilsonian Foreign Policy.* Kent OH: Kent State University Press, 1993.

Capozzola, Christopher. *Uncle Sam Wants You: World War I and the Making of the Modern American Citizen.* New York: Oxford University Press, 2008.

Cardoso, Lawrence A. *Mexican Immigration to the United States, 1897–1931: Socio-Economic Patterns.* Tucson: University of Arizona Press, 1980.

Chambers, John Whiteclay, II. *The Tyranny of Change: America in the Progressive Era, 1900–1917.* New York: St. Martin's Press, 1980.

Chasteen, John Charles. *Born in Blood and Fire: A Concise History of Latin America.* New York: Norton, 2001.

Cohen, Deborah. *Braceros: Migrant Citizens and Transnational Subjects in the Postwar United States and Mexico.* Chapel Hill: University of North Carolina Press, 2011.

Cohen, Lizabeth. *Making a New Deal: Industrial Workers in Chicago, 1919–1939.* Cambridge: Cambridge University Press, 1990.

Council on Foreign Relations. *Survey of American Foreign Relations.* Charles P. Howard, ed. Four Volumes. New Haven: Yale University Press, 1928–1931.

Dawley, Alan. *Changing the World: American Progressives in War and Revolution.* Princeton NJ: Princeton University Press, 2003.

De La Garza, Rodolfo O., and Jesús Velasco, eds. *Bridging the Border: Transforming Mexico-U.S. Relations.* New York: Rowman and Littlefield, 1997.

Denning, Michael. *The Cultural Front: The Laboring of American Culture in the Twentieth-Century.* London: Verso, 1996.

Domínguez, Jorge, ed. *The Future of Inter-American Relations*. New York: Routledge, 2000.

Ducey, Michael T. *A Nation of Villages: Riot and Rebellion in the Mexican Huasteca, 1750–1850*. Tucson: University of Arizona Press, 2004.

Dumenil, Lynn. *The Modern Temper: American Culture and Society in the 1920s*. New York: Hill and Wang, 1995.

Durand, Jorge, ed. *Migración México-Estados Unidos. Años Veinte*. Mexico, D.F.: Consejo Nacional Para la Cultura y las Artes, 1991.

Durand, Jorge, Douglas S. Massey, and Rene M. Zenteno. "Mexican Immigration to the United States: Continuities and Changes." *Latin American Research Review* 36, no. 1 (2001): 107–27.

Eckes, Alfred, Jr., and Thomas W. Zeiler. *Globalization and the American Century*. Cambridge: Cambridge University Press, 2003.

Enciso, Fernando Saúl Alanís. "The Repatriation of Mexicans from the United States and Mexican Nationalism, 1929–1940." In *Beyond La Frontera: The History of Mexico-U.S. Immigration*, edited by Mark Overmyer-Velázquez. New York: Oxford University Press, 2011.

Engerman, David C. *Modernization from the Other Shore: American Intellectuals and the Romance of Russian Development*. Cambridge MA: Harvard University Press, 2003.

Ervin, Michael. "Statistics, Maps, and Legibility: Negotiating Nationalism in Post-Revolutionary Mexico." *The Americas* 66, no. 2 (October 2009): 155–79.

Fink, Leon. *Progressive Intellectuals and the Dilemmas of Democratic Commitment*. Cambridge MA: Harvard University Press, 1997.

Fitzgerald, David. *A Nation of Emigrants: How Mexico Manages Its Immigration*. Berkeley: University of California Press, 2008.

Flores, John H. "On the Wings of the Revolution: Transnational Politics and the Making of Mexican American Identities." PhD dissertation, University of Illinois, Chicago, 2009.

Foerster, Robert F. *The Racial Problems Involved in Immigration from Latin America and the West Indies to the United States*, Report Submitted to the Secretary of Labor, Washington DC: U.S. Department of Labor, 1925.

Foley, Neil. *White Scourge: Mexicans, Blacks, and Poor Whites in Texas Cotton Culture*. Berkeley: University of California Press, 1997.

Gabaccia, Donna R. *Foreign Relations: American Immigration in Global Perspective*. Princeton NJ: Princeton University Press, 2012.

Gaddis, John Lewis. *We Now Know: Rethinking Cold War History*. Oxford: Clarendon Press, 1997.

Gamio, Manuel. *Mexican Immigration to the United States: A Study of Human Immigration and Adjustment*. Chicago: University of Chicago press, 1930.

———. *Mexican Immigrant: The Life Story of the Mexican Immigrant, Autobiographic Documents.* New York: Dover Publications, 1971.
Ganster, Paul, and David E. Lorey. *The U.S.-Mexican Border into the Twenty-First Century.* Lanham MD: Rowman and Littlefield, 2008.
García, Mario. *Desert Immigrants: The Mexicans of El Paso, 1880–1920.* New Haven CT: Yale University Press, 1981.
Gardner, Lloyd. *Safe for Democracy: The Anglo-American Response to Revolution, 1913–1923.* New York: Oxford University Press, 1984.
Gerstle, Gary. *Working-Class Americanism: The Politics of Labor in a Textile City, 1914–1960.* Cambridge: Cambridge University Press, 1989.
———. *American Crucible: Race and Nation in the Twentieth Century.* Princeton NJ: Princeton University Press, 2001.
Gilderhus, Mark. *Diplomacy and Revolution: U.S.-Mexican Relations under Wilson and Carranza.* Tucson: University of Arizona Press, 1977.
———. *PanAmerican Visions: Woodrow Wilson and the Western Hemisphere.* Tucson: University of Arizona Press, 1986.
———. *The Second Century: U.S.-Latin American Relations since 1889.* Wilmington DE: Scholarly Resources, 2000.
Gilly, Adolfo. *The Mexican Revolution.* New York: New Press, 2005.
Gonzales, Trinidad. "The World of México Texanos, Mexicanos, and México Americanos: Transnational and National Identities in the Lower Rio Grande Valley during the Last Phase of United States Colonization, 1900 to 1930." PhD dissertation, University of Houston, 2008.
Gonzalez, Gilbert G. "Mexican Labor Immigration, 1876–1924." In *Beyond La Frontera: The History of Mexico-U.S. Immigration,* edited by Mark Overmyer-Velázquez. New York: Oxford University Press, 2011.
Gonzalez-Murphy, Laura Valeria. "Change and continuity in Mexico's immigration policy: How civil society organizations influence the policy process." PhD dissertation, State University of New York at Albany, 2009.
Grandin, Greg, et al., eds. *A Century of Revolution: Insurgent and Counterinsurgent Violence during Latin America's Long Cold War.* Durham NC: Duke University Press, 2010.
Grayson, George. *The United States and Mexico: Patterns of Influence.* New York: Praeger, 1984.
Grieb, Kenneth J. *The United States and Huerta.* Lincoln: University of Nebraska Press, 1969.
Guardino, Peter F. *Peasants, Politics, and the Formation of Mexico's National State: Guerrero, 1800–1857.* Stanford CA: Stanford University Press, 1996.
Guerin-Gonzales, Camille. *Mexican Workers and American Dreams: Immigration, Repatriation, and California Farm Labor, 1900–1939.* New Brunswick NJ: Rutgers University Press, 1994.

Gutiérrez, David G., ed. *Between Two Worlds: Mexican Immigrants in the United States*. Wilmington DL: Scholarly Resources, 1996.

———. *Walls and Mirrors: Mexican Americans, Mexican Immigrants, and the Politics of Ethnicity*. Berkeley: University of California Press, 1995.

Hall, Linda B. *Oil, Banks, and Politics: The United States and Postrevolutionary Mexico, 1917–1924*. Austin: University of Texas Press, 1995.

Hall, Linda B., and Don M. Coerver. *Revolution on the Border: The United States and Mexico, 1910–1920*. Albuquerque: University of New Mexico Press, 1988.

Hamilton, Nora. *The Limits of State Autonomy: Post-Revolutionary Mexico*. Princeton NJ: Princeton University Press, 1982.

Haney-López, Ian. *White By Law: The Legal Construction of Race*. New York: New York University Press, 1996.

Hansen, Jonathan M. *The Lost Promise of Patriotism: Debating American Identity, 1890–1920*. Chicago: University of Chicago Press, 2003.

Hanson, Gordon H. "Illegal Immigration from Mexico to the United States." *Journal of Economic Literature* 44, no. 4 (December 2006): 869–924.

Harris, Charles H., and Louis R. Sadler. *The Secret War in El Paso: Mexican Revolutionary Intrigue, 1906–1920*. Albuquerque: University of New Mexico Press, 2009.

Hart, John M. *Revolutionary Mexico: The Coming and Process of the Mexican Revolution*. Berkeley: University of California Press, 1987.

Hartmann, Edward G. *The Movement to Americanize the Immigrant*. New York: AMS Press, 1967.

Henderson, Timothy J. *Beyond Borders: A History of Mexican Immigration to the United States*. Malden MA: Wiley-Blackwell, 2011.

Hernández, Kelly Lytle. *Migra! A History of the U.S. Border Patrol*. Berkeley: University of California Press, 2010.

Herring, George C. *From Colony to Superpower: U.S. Foreign Relations since 1776*. Oxford: Oxford University Press, 2008.

Higham, John. *Strangers in the Land: Patterns of American Nativism, 1860–1925*. New Brunswick NJ: Rutgers University Press, 1955.

Hirobe, Izumi. *Japanese Pride, American Prejudice: Modifying the Exclusion Clause of the 1924 Immigration Act*. Stanford: Stanford University Press, 2001.

Hoerder, Dirk, and Nora Faires, eds. *Migrants and Immigration in Modern North America: Cross-Border Lives, Labor Markets, and Politics*. Durham: Duke University Press, 2011.

Hoffman, Abraham. *Unwanted Mexicans in the Great Depression: Repatriation Pressures, 1929–1939*. Tucson: University of Arizona Press, 1974.

Hogan, Michael J., and Thomas Paterson, eds. *Explaining the History of American Foreign Relations*. Cambridge: Cambridge University Press, 2004.

Hoganson, Kristin L. *Fighting for American Manhood: How Gender Politics Provoked the Spanish-American and Philippine-American Wars*. New Haven: Yale University Press, 1998.

Hollifield, James F., et al., eds. *Controlling Immigration: A Global Perspective*, 3rd ed. Stanford: Stanford University Press, 2014.

Hoover, Glenn E. "Our Mexican Immigrants." *Foreign Affairs* 8 (October 1929): 99–107.

Hunt, Michael H. *Ideology and U.S. Foreign Policy*. New Haven: Yale University Press, 1987.

———. *The American Ascendency: How the United States Gained and Wielded Global Dominance*. Chapel Hill: North Carolina Press, 2007.

Hutchinson, Edward P. *Legislative History of American Immigration Policy, 1798–1965*. Philadelphia: University of Pennsylvania Press, 1981.

Ignatiev, Noel. *How the Irish Became White*. New York: Routledge, 1995.

Igo, Sarah. *The Averaged American: Surveys, Citizens, and the Making of a Mass Public*. Cambridge MA: Harvard University Press, 2007.

Iriye, Akira. *Power and Culture: The Japanese-American War, 1941–1945*. Cambridge MA: Harvard University Press, 1981.

Jacobson, Matthew Frye. *Whiteness of a Different Color: European Immigrants and the Alchemy of Race*. Cambridge: Cambridge University Press, 1998.

———. *Barbarian Virtues: The United States Encounters Foreign Peoples at Home and Abroad, 1876–1917*. New York: Hill and Wang, 2000.

Johnson, Robert David. *The Peace Progressives and American Foreign Relations*. Cambridge MA: Harvard University Press, 1995.

Jones, Richard C. "Immigration Reform and Migrant Flows: Compositional and Spatial Changes in Mexican Immigration after the Immigration Reform Act of 1986." *Annals of the Association of American Geographers* 85, no. 4 (December 1995): 715–30.

Joppke, Christian. "Why Liberal States Accept Unwanted Immigration." *World Politics* 50, no. 2 (January 1998): 266–93.

Joseph, Gilbert M., and Daniel Nugent, eds. *Everyday Forms of State Formation: Revolution and the Negotiation of Rule in Modern Mexico*. Durham NC: Duke University Press, 1994.

Joseph, Gilbert H., et al., eds. *Close Encounters of Empire: Writing the Cultural History of U.S.-Latin American Relations*. Durham NC: Duke University Press, 1998.

Joseph, Gilbert M., et al., eds. *Reclaiming the Political in Latin American History: Essays from the North*. Durham NC: Duke University Press, 2001.

Joseph, Gilbert M., and Jürgen Buchenau. *Mexico's Once and Future Revolution: Social Upheaval and the Challenge of Rule since the late Nineteenth Century*. Durham NC: Duke University Press, 2013.

Kang, S. Deborah. *The INS on the Line: Making Immigration Law on the U.S–Mexico Border (New York: Oxford University Press, 2017)*.

Katz, Friedrich. *The Secret War in Mexico: Europe, the United States, and the Mexican Revolution*. Chicago: University of Chicago Press, 1981.

Kennedy, David. *Over Here: The First World War and American Society*. Oxford: Oxford University Press, 1980.

———. *Freedom From Fear: The American People in Depression and War, 1929–1945*. New York: Oxford University Press, 1999.

Kennedy, Ross. *The Will to Believe: Woodrow Wilson, World War I, and America's Strategy for Peace and Security*. Kent OH: Kent State University Press, 2009.

King, Desmond S. *Making Americans: Immigration, Race, and the Origins of a Diverse Democracy*. Cambridge MA: Harvard University Press, 2000.

Knight, Alan. *The Mexican Revolution*. New York: Cambridge University Press, 1986.

———. *U.S.-Mexican Relations, 1910–1940: An Interpretation*. La Jolla: Center for U.S.-Mexican Studies, University of California, San Diego, 1987.

Knock, Thomas. *To End All Wars: Woodrow Wilson and the Quest for a New World Order*. New York: Oxford University Press, 1992.

Krauze, Enrique. *Mexico, A Biography of Power: A History of Modern Mexico, 1810–1996*. Translated by Hank Heifetz. New York: Harper Collins Publishers, 1997.

LaFeber, Walter. *The New Empire: An Interpretation of American Expansion, 1860–1898*. Ithaca NY: Cornell University Press, 1963.

———. *The American Search for Opportunity, 1865–1913*. Cambridge: Cambridge University Press, 1993.

Langley, Lester. *America and the Americas: The United States in the Western Hemisphere*. Athens: University of Georgia Press, 1989.

———. *Mexico and the United States: The Fragile Relationship*. Boston: Twayne Publishers, 1991.

Larson, Edward J. *Summer for the Gods: The Scopes Trial and America's Continuing Debate Over Science and Religion*. New York: Basic Books, 1997.

Lee, Erika, and Judy Yung. *Angel Island: Immigrant Gateway to America*. Oxford: Oxford University Press, 2010.

LeMay, Michael C. *From Open Door to Dutch Door: An Analysis of US Immigration Policy Since 1820*. New York, 1987.

LeMay, Michael, and Elliot Robert Barkan, eds. *U.S. Immigration and Naturalization Laws and Issues: A Documentary History*. Westport CT: Greenwood Press, 1999.

Link, Arthur, ed. *Woodrow Wilson and a Revolutionary World, 1913–1921*. Chapel Hill: University of North Carolina Press, 1982.

Louria, Margot. *Triumph and Downfall: America's Pursuit of Peace and Prosperity, 1921–1933*. Westport CT: Greenwood Press, 2001.

MacLean, Nancy. *Behind the Mask of Chivalry: The Making of the Second Ku Klux Klan*. New York: Oxford University Press, 1994.

Mallon, Florencia. *Peasant and Nation: The Making of Post-Colonial Mexico and Peru*. Berkeley: University of California Press, 1995.

Manela, Erez. *The Wilsonian Moment: Self-Determination and the International Origins of Anticolonial Nationalism*. Oxford and New York: Oxford University Press, 2007.

Martínez, John. *Mexican Emigration to the U.S. 1910–1930*. Berkeley: R. and E. Research Associates, 1972.

Martínez, Oscar J. *Fragments of the Mexican Revolution: Personal Accounts from the Border*. Albuquerque: University of New Mexico Press, 1983.

———. *Troublesome Border*. Tucson: University of Arizona Press, 1988.

———, ed. *U.S.-Mexico Borderlands: Historical and Contemporary Perspectives*. Wilmington DE: Scholarly Resources, 1996.

Massey, Douglas S., et al., eds. *Return to Aztlan: The Social Process of International Immigration from Western Mexico*. Berkeley: University of California Press, 1987.

McMahon, Robert J. "Toward a Pluralist Vision: The Study of American Foreign Relations as International History and National History." In *Explaining the History of American Foreign Relations*, 2nd ed., edited by Michael J. Hogan and Thomas Paterson. Cambridge: Cambridge University Press, 2004.

Mead, Walter Russell. *Special Providence: American Foreign Policy and How It Changed the World*. New York: Knopf, 2001.

Menchaca, Martha. *Naturalizing Mexican Immigrants: A Texas History*. Austin: University of Texas Press, 2011.

Meyer, Jean. *The Cristero Rebellion: The Mexican People between Church and State, 1926–1929*. Cambridge: Cambridge University Press, 1976.

Meyer, Michael. *Huerta: A Political Portrait*. Lincoln: University of Nebraska Press, 1972.

Mitchell, Christopher, ed. *Western Hemisphere Immigration and United States Foreign Policy*. University Park: University of Pennsylvania Press, 1992.

Molina, Natalia. "'In a Race All Their Own': The Quest to Make Mexicans Ineligible for U.S. Citizenship." *Pacific Historical Review* 79, no. 2 (May 2010): 167–201.

Mora-Torres, Juan. "Los de casa se van, los de fuera no vienen: The First Mexican Immigrants, 1848–1900." In *Beyond La Frontera: The History of Mexico-U.S. Immigration*, edited by Mark Overmyer-Velázquez. New York: Oxford University Press, 2011.

Navarro, Aaron W. *Political Intelligence and the Creation of Modern Mexico, 1938–1954.* University Park: Pennsylvania State University Press, 2010.

Nelli, Humberto S. *From Immigrants to Ethnics: The Italian Americans.* Oxford: Oxford University Press, 1983.

Ngai, Mae M. "The Architecture of Race in American Immigration Law: A Reexamination of the Immigration Act of 1924. *Journal of American History* 86, no. 1 (June 1999): 67–92.

———. *Impossible Subjects: Illegal Aliens and the Making of Modern America.* Princeton NJ: Princeton University Press, 2004.

———. "Nationalism, Immigration Control, and the Ethnoracial Remapping of America in the 1920s." *OAH Magazine of History* 21, no. 3, Reinterpreting the 1920s (July 2007): 11–15.

Niblo, Stephen. *War, Diplomacy, and Development: The United States and Mexico, 1938–1954.* Wilmington DE: Scholarly Resources, 1995.

Novick, Peter. *That Noble Dream: The "Objectivity Question" and the American Historical Profession.* New York: Cambridge University Press, 1998.

Nugent, Daniel, ed. *Rural Revolt in Mexico: U.S. Intervention and the Domain of Subaltern Politics.* Durham NC: Duke University Press, 1998.

O'Leary, Cecilia Elizabeth. *To Die For: The Paradox of American Patriotism.* Princeton, Princeton University Press, 1999.

Overmyer-Velázquez, Mark, ed. *Beyond La Frontera: The History of Mexico-U.S. Immigration.* New York: Oxford University Press, 2011.

Oyen, Meredith Leigh. "Allies, Enemies, and Aliens: Immigration and U.S.-Chinese Relations, 1940–1965." PhD dissertation, Georgetown University, 2007.

Passananti, Thomas P. "Dynamizing the Economy in a Façon Irréguliére: A New Look at Financial Politics in Porfirian Mexico." *Mexican Studies* 24, no. 1 (Winter 2008): 1–29.

———. "Nada de Papeluchos! Managing Globalization in Early Porfirian Mexico." *Latin American Research Review* 42, no. 3 (2007): 101–28.

Paz, Octavio. *The Labyrinth of Solitude.* Translated by Lysander Kemp et al. London: Penguin Books, 1985.

Pearlman, Michael. *To Make Democracy Safe for America: Patricians and Preparedness in the Progressive Era.* Chicago: University of Illinois Press, 1984.

Pestritto, Ronald J. *Woodrow Wilson and the Roots of Modern Liberalism.* Lanham MD: Rowman and Littlefield, 2005.

Piccato, Pablo. *City of Suspects: Crime in Mexico City, 1900–1931.* Durham NC: Duke University Press, 2001.

Pickus, Noah. *True Faith and Allegiance: Immigration and American Civic Nationalism.* Princeton NJ: Princeton University Press, 2005.

Raat, W. Dirk. *Revoltosos: Mexico's Rebels in the United States, 1903–1923.* College Station: Texas A&M University Press, 1981.

Raat, W. Dirk, and Michael M. Brescia. *Mexico and the United States: Ambivalent Vistas.* Athens: University of Georgia Press, 2010.

Rankin, Monica, and Diana Berger. "Peculiarities of Mexican Diplomacy." In *A Companion to Mexican History and Culture*, edited by William H. Beezley. Marlton MA: Wiley-Blackwell, 2011.

Reed, John. *Insurgent Mexico.* New York: International Publishers, 1974.

Reisler, Mark. "Always the Laborer, Never the Citizen: Anglo Perceptions of the Mexican Immigrant during the 1920s." *Pacific Historical Review* 45, no. 2 (May, 1976): 231–54.

———. *By the Sweat of Their Brow: Mexican Immigrant Labor in the United States, 1900–1940.* Westport CT: Greenwood Press, 1976.

Richmond, Douglas W. *Venustiano Carranza's Nationalist Struggle, 1893–1920.* Lincoln: University of Nebraska Press, 1983.

Rodríguez O., Jaime E., ed. *The Revolutionary Process in Mexico: Essays on Political and Social Change, 1880–1940.* Los Angeles: UCLA Latin American Center Publications, University of California, Irvine, 1990.

Roett, Riordan, ed. *Mexico and the United States: Managing the Relationship.* Boulder: Westview Press, 1988.

Romero, Robert Chao. *The Chinese in Mexico, 1882–1940.* Tucson: University of Arizona Press, 2010.

Rosenberg, Emily S. "Considering Borders." In *Explaining the History of American Foreign Relations*, 2nd ed., edited by Michael J. Hogan and Thomas Paterson, 176–93. Cambridge: Cambridge University Press, 2004.

———. *Spreading the American Dream: American Economic and Cultural Expansion, 1890–1945.* New York: Hill and Wang, 1982.

———. *Financial Missionaries to the World: The Politics and Culture of Dollar Diplomacy, 1900–1930.* Cambridge MA: Harvard University Press, 1999.

Rourke, John T. *Congress and the Presidency in U.S. Foreign Policymaking: A Study of Interaction and Influence, 1945–1982.* Boulder: Westview Press, 1983.

Ruiz, Ramón Eduardo. *The Great Rebellion: Mexico, 1905–1924.* New York: W. W. Norton, 1980.

———. *Triumphs and Tragedy: A History of the Mexican People.* New York: W. W. Norton, 1992.

Sadowski-Smith, Claudia. "Unskilled Labor Immigration and the Illegality Spiral: Chinese, European, and Mexican Indocumentados in the United States, 1882–2007." *American Quarterly* 60, no. 3, Nation and Immigration: Past and Future (September 2008): 779–804.

Sánchez, George. *Becoming Mexican American: Ethnicity, Culture, and Identity in Chicano Los Angeles.* New York: Oxford University Press, 1993.

———. "Race, Nation, and Culture in Recent Immigration Studies." *Journal of American Ethnic History* 18, no. 4 (Summer 1999): 66–84.

Santibáñez, Enrique. *Ensayo Acerca de la Inmigración Mexicana en los Estados Unidos.* San Francisco: R and E Research Associates, 1970 (originally published by Clegg Company of San Antonio TX, in 1930).

Schiller, Nina Glick, Linda Basch, and Cristina Blanc-Szanton, eds. *Towards a Transnational Perspective on Immigration: Race, Class, Ethnicity, and Nationalism Reconsidered.* New York: New York Academic of Sciences, 1992.

Schmidt, Arthur. "Mexicans, Migrants, and Indigenous Peoples: The Work of Manuel Gamio in the United States, 1925–1927." In *Strange Pilgrimages: Travel, Exile and Foreign Residency in the Creation of Latin American Identity, 1800–1990s*, edited by Ingrid E. Fey and Karine Racine. Wilmington DE: Scholarly Resources, 2000.

Schneider, Dorothee. "Naturalization and United States Citizenship in Two Periods of Mass Immigration: 1894–1930, 1965–2000." *Journal of American Ethnic History* 21, no. 1 (Fall 2001): 50–82.

———. *Crossing Borders: Immigration and Citizenship in the Twentieth-Century United States.* Cambridge MA: Harvard University Press, 2011.

Scholes, Walter V., and Marie V. Scholes. *The Foreign Policies of the Taft Administration.* Columbia: University of Missouri Press, 1970.

Schoultz, Lars. *Beneath the United States: A History of U.S. Policy towards Latin America.* Cambridge MA: Harvard University Press, 1998.

Schuler, Friedrich. *Mexico Between Hitler and Roosevelt: Mexican Foreign Relations in the Age of Lázaro Cárdenas, 1934–1940.* Albuquerque: University of New Mexico Press, 1998.

———. *Secret Wars and Secret Policies in the Americas.* Albuquerque: University of New Mexico Press, 2010.

Schulzinger, Robert D. *U.S. Diplomacy Since 1900.* New York: Oxford University Press, 2008.

Sheridan, Clare. "Contested Citizenship: National Identity and the Mexican Immigration Debates of the 1920s." *Journal of American Ethnic History* 21, no. 3 (Spring 2002): 3–35.

Sherman, Rachel. "From State Introversion to State Extension in Mexico: Modes of Emigrant Incorporation, 1900–1997." *Theory and Society* 28: 835–78.

Skocpol, Theda. *States and Social Revolutions: A Comparative Analysis of France, Russia, and China.* Cambridge: Cambridge University Press, 1979.

Small, Melvin. *Democracy and Diplomacy: The Impact of Domestic Politics on U.S. Foreign Policy, 1789–1994.* Baltimore: Johns Hopkins University Press, 1996.

Smith, Michael. "Carrancista Propaganda and the Print Media in the United States: An Overview of Institutions." *The Americas* 52, no. 2 (October 1995): 155–74.

Smith, Michael P., and Matt Bakker. *Citizenship Across Borders: The Political Transnationalism of El Migrante.* Ithaca NY: Cornell University Press, 2008.

Smith, Robert Freeman. *The United States and Revolutionary Nationalism in Mexico, 1916–1932.* Chicago: University of Chicago Press, 1972.

Smith, Rogers M. *Civic Ideals: Conflicting Visions of Citizenship in US History.* New Haven CT: Yale University Press, 1997.

Spenser, Daniela. *The Impossible Triangle: Mexico, Soviet Russia, and the United States in the 1920s.* Durham NC: Duke University Press, 1999.

Spiro, Jonathan Peter. *Defending the Master Race: Conservation, Eugenics, and the Legacy of Madison Grant.* Burlington: University of Vermont Press, 2009.

Stansell, Christine. *American Moderns: Bohemian New York and the Creation of a New Century.* New York: Metropolitan Books, 2000.

Stepan, Nancy Leys. *"The Hour of Eugenics": Race, Gender, and Nation in Latin America.* Ithaca NY: Cornell University Press, 1991.

St. John, Rachel. *Line in the Sand: A History of the Western U.S.-Mexico Border.* Princeton: Princeton University Press, 2011.

Toy, Eckard. "The Survey of Race Relations on the Pacific Coast in the 1920s." *Oregon Historical Quarterly* 107, no. 1 (Spring 2006).

———. "Whose Frontier? The Survey of Race Relations on the Pacific Coast in the 1920s." *Oregon Historical Quarterly* 107, no. 1 (Spring 2006): 36–63.

Traxel, David. *Crusader Nation: The United States in Peace and the Great War, 1898–1920.* New York: Knopf, 2006.

Tucker, Robert. *Woodrow Wilson and the Great War: Reconsidering America's Neutrality, 1914–1917.* Charlottesville: University of Virginia Press, 2007.

Turner, John Kenneth. *Barbarous Mexico.* Austin: University of Texas Press, 1969.

United States House of Representatives, Committee on Immigration and Naturalization. *Admission of Mexican and Other Alien Laborers into Texas and Other States: Hearings.* 66th Congress, 2nd Session. Washington DC: Government Printing Office, 1920.

———. *Temporary Admission of Illiterate Mexican Laborers: Hearings.* 66th Congress, 2nd Session. Washington DC: Government Printing Office, 1920.

———. *Immigration on the Mexican Border: Hearings.* 67th Congress, 1st Session. Washington DC: Government Printing Office, 1921.

———. *Imported Pauper Labor and Serfdom in America: Hearings.* 67th Congress, 1st Session. Washington DC: Government Printing Office, 1921.

———. *Immigration from Countries of the Western Hemisphere: Hearings.* 70th Congress, 1st Session. Washington DC: Government Printing Office, 1928.

———. *Western Hemisphere Immigration: Hearings.* 71st Congress, 2nd Session. Washington DC: Government Printing Office, 1930.

———. *Immigration from Mexico: Hearings—Statement of Hon. Joseph P. Cotton.* 71st Congress, 2nd Session. Washington DC: Government Printing Office, 1930.

---. *Immigration From Countries of the Western Hemisphere—Statement by Hon. Thomas A. Jenkins, Hon. John C. Box, and Prof. Roy L. Garis.* 71st Congress, 2nd Session. Washington DC: Government Printing Office, 1930.

---. *Restriction of Immigration and Reduction of Quotas, Part I: Hearings.* 72nd Congress, 1st Session. Washington DC: Government Printing Office, 1932.

United States Senate, Committee on Immigration and Naturalization. *Restriction of Western Hemisphere Immigration: Hearings.* 70th Congress, 1st Session. Washington DC: Government Printing Office, 1928.

---. *Suspension for Two Years of General Immigration to the United States: Hearings.* 71st Congress, 3rd Session. Washington DC: Government Printing Office, 1930.

Van Nuys, Frank. *Americanizing the West: Race, Immigrants, and Citizenship, 1890–1930.* Lawrence: University Press of Kansas, 2002.

Vásquez, Carlos, and Manuel García y Griego, eds. *Mexican-U.S. Relations: Conflict and Convergence.* Los Angeles: UCLA Chicano Studies Research Center Publications—UCLA Latin American Center Publications, 1983.

Vázquez, Josefina Zoraida, and Lorenzo Meyer. *The United States and Mexico.* Chicago: University of Chicago Press, 1985.

Waters, Mary C., and Karl Eschback. "Immigration and Ethnic and Racial Inequality in the United States." *Annual Review of Sociology* 21 (1995): 419–46.

Weber, Devra, et al., eds. *Manuel Gamio: El inmigrante mexicano: la historia de su vida; entrevistas completes, 1926–1927.* México, D.F.: Centro de Investigaciones y Estudios Superiores en Antropología Social, 2002.

Westad, Odd Arne. *The Global Cold War: Third World Interventions and the Making of Our Times.* New York: Cambridge University Press, 2005.

Williams, William Appleman. *The Tragedy of American Diplomacy.* New York: Dell Publishing Co., 1959.

Wood, Amy Louise. *Lynching and Spectacle: Witnessing Racial Violence in America, 1890–1940.* Chapel Hill: University of North Carolina Press, 2009.

Zeiler, Thomas W. "The Diplomatic History Bandwagon: A State of the Field." *Journal of American History* 95, no. 4 (March, 2009): 1053–73.

Zolov, Eric. *Refried Elvis: The Rise of the Mexican Counterculture.* Berkeley: University of California Press, 1999.

Index

administrative restriction: as concept, 3–4, 127–28, 157–58; criticism of, 159–60, 189–91, 250–51; effectiveness of, 184, 187–89, 227–32, 235–37, 299n73; Mexican support for, 184, 225–26; passport requirement, 159–63, 288n74; State Department support for, 226–27. *See also* quota
Aguila, Jaime, 14, 262n20
Alien Contract Labor Law (1885), 84, 269n79
Altaffer, Maurice, 189, 190–91, 192, 231
American Defense Society, 71
American Federation of Labor (AFL), 46, 251
American League of Good Will, 71
American Protective Association (APA), 45
Arizona Daily Dispatch (newspaper), 231
Article 27 (1917 Constitution), 21–30
Asian immigration, 44, 53, 104–6, 148, 171–72, 277n8, 277–78nn10–11
assimilation, 44, 46, 51–52, 278n11

Balderamma, Francisco, 207, 209
Barkan, Elliott, 9–10

Basic Naturalization Act (1906), 47
Bean, Frank, 9, 10
Bixby, Fred, 72–73, 78
Blanton, Thomas L., 240–41
Blocker, William, 189, 215, 230
Boas, Franz, 142, 143
Borah, William, 183, 198
borders: and practicality of regulatory enforcement, 86, 130–31; and state power, 16; and U.S. Border Patrol, 192–93, 293n61
Box, John, 70–72, 78, 85–86, 179–80, 234, 272n9, 272n11, 283–84n7
Boyce, Richard, 189
Brazilian immigration, 110–11
Brebbia, Carlos, 280n28
Brum Rodríguez, Baltasar, 182
Bucareli agreement, 25, 30, 265n16
Burke, John J., 31
Burnett, John, 50
Bustamante, Luis, 195
Butterworth, William, 198

Calderón-Zaks, Michael, 263n33
California History and Landmark Club, 71
Calles, Plutarco Elías, 26–30, 31–32, 33, 63, 142
Calvo, Carlos, 264n11

Calvo Doctrine, 24, 29–30, 264–65n11
Camarena, Pascual, 209
Canadian immigration, 70, 74, 76, 180–81, 183
Canales, Felipe, 169
Carranza, Venustiano, 21–22, 24, 62, 291n40
Carranza Doctrine, 21–22
Cartaya, Enrique Hernández, 109
Carter, Henry, 114, 280nn26–27
Catholic Church, 30–32, 152
Chinese immigration, 171–72
Cleveland, Grover, 46–47
Cochran, William, Jr., 250–52
Coerver, Don, 42
Cohen, Deborah, 14
Collar, Lindolfo, 110–11
Confederación Regional Obrera Mexicana (CROM), 27
Constitution (Mexico, 1857), 61–62
Constitution (Mexico, 1917), 21–30, 62
contract and temporary laborers, 62, 70–71, 83–87, 111–12, 120–21, 140, 250–52, 269n79, 283–84n7
Coolidge, Calvin, 28–29, 106
Copley, W. E., 212
Cotton, Joseph, 184–86, 236
coyotes (people smugglers), 98–99, 138
Cristero Rebellion, 30–32, 56–57, 144, 286n44
Cuban immigration, 53

Davila, José, 133–35
Davis, James, 51–52, 129–30
Davis, Monnett, 156–58
Dawley, Alan, 46
Dawson, William, 187
de la Huerta, Adolfo, 143–44

Díaz, Porfirio, 19–21, 35–42, 154, 207–8, 268n66
Dillingham, William, 47
diplomacy. *See* U.S. foreign relations; U.S.-Mexican relations
Drago, Luis, and doctrine, 264n11
Drumright, Everett, 216, 231–32
Dwyre, Dudley, 212–13, 275n42

economy, Mexican: decline in demand for Mexican products, 57, 210; Great Depression unemployment crisis, 210–13; harmed by northward migration, 89, 171, 177–78, 200, 201; as impetus behind northward migration, 143–46; oil industry, 22–23, 26–28, 29, 30, 37, 210; and opposition to quota, 88, 133; during Porfiriato, 19–20, 35–42, 268n66; railroad construction and transportation, 36, 38, 39–41, 267n49, 267n56
economy, U.S.: Great Depression unemployment crisis, 221–23, 236; and opposition to immigration restrictions, 48–49, 59–60, 72–73, 85, 134–35, 146; and support for immigration restrictions, 76–77, 129–30, 173–74
El Heraldo (newspaper), 213
El Paso Evening Post (newspaper), 199
El Universal (newspaper), 90, 91, 194–95, 196–97, 201, 213–15
Enciso, Fernando Saúl Alanís, 207, 221
Escobar Rebellion, 144, 177
Estrada, Genaro, 89, 129, 135, 140–41, 162
eugenics, 45–46, 50, 51, 59, 145

European immigration, 44, 52, 57–58, 102–3, 236–37, 271n124
Excelsior (newspaper), 91–92, 132–33, 164–65, 170, 171, 193–96, 213–14, 219, 274–75n42

Fabila, Alfonso, 170–71, 201
Fifth Pan-American Conference, 182, 291–92n40
First International Conference on Emigration and Immigration, 102–3
Fiske, John, 45
Fitzgerald, David, 16
Fletcher, Henry, 118
Foerster, Robert F., 153–55
Foran Act (1885), 84, 269n79
foreign relations. *See* U.S. foreign relations; U.S.-Mexican relations
Foster, Paul, 216–21
Frazer, Robert, 214

Gabaccia, Donna, 14
Gamio, Manuel, 118–21, 141–46, 199–201, 251, 282n38, 285–86n31, 286n36, 286n44, 294nn78–79
Garner, John, 74–75, 78, 83–84
Gentlemen's Agreement (1907–8), 104, 105, 106, 172
Gibson, Raleigh, 229
Gilly, Adolfo, 267n56
Gondra Treaty, 182, 291–92n40
Grayson, George, 2
Guerin-Gonzales, Camille, 222–23
Gunther, Franklin Mott, 27
Gutiérrez, David, 9–10, 224, 262n17

Hall, Linda, 42
Hall, Prescott F., 45
Hanihara, Masanao, 104–5, 277n8
Harper, Oscar, 216, 270–71n116

Harris, William J., 128, 234–35, 240
Harris bill: failure of, 235, 238–42; Mexican opposition, 132–37, 186–87, 195–200; Senate approval of, 183–85, 234; Senate Committee approval of, 128–32
Hart, John Mason, 36, 37
Hatfield, Henry, 239
Henderson, Tim, 42, 220, 223, 224
Hernández, Kelly Lytle, 138, 140, 191, 276–77n65
Hewitt, Edgar L., 152–53
Hicks, C. D., 198
Hirobe, Izumi, 104, 105, 277n8
Hodgdon, A. Dana, 228, 240, 300n81
Holmes, S. J., 174
Hoover, Glenn E., 172–75, 290n20
Hoover, Herbert, 198, 199, 235–36, 238
Hudspeth, Claude B., 83–85
Huerta, Victoriano, 21
Hughes, Charles Evans, 3, 52–53, 104, 292n40
Husband, W. W., 76–77, 114, 119, 280nn26–27

illegal immigration: anticipated with quota, 157, 159; arrests and deportations, 191–93, 223–24; and contract labor policies, 62; increased by administrative restriction, 159–60, 189, 190–91; Mexican attempts to curb, 138–39, 140–41; reasons for, 98–99, 139–40; statistics, 97–98, 99, 156, 173, 277n67
illiteracy, 46–48, 50, 53, 85, 86, 98, 120, 158

Index 321

immigration: host *vs.* sender nation views, 8–9; internal and external nature of, 11–13; and labor, overview, 7–8; restrictionist policy development, 46–54; U.S. ambivalence toward, 44–46. *See also* administrative restriction; Mexican immigration; quota
Immigration Act (1917), 48–50, 53, 102, 227
Immigration Act (1929), 191–92
Immigration (Emergency Quota) Act (1921), 50–53, 102
Immigration (Johnson Reed) Act (1924), 11, 53–55, 56, 102, 103–4, 106, 131, 227
Immigration Restriction League (IRL), 45, 46, 69–70, 71
Immigration Study Commission, 71
international immigration debates. *See* U.S. foreign relations
Italian immigration, 102–3

Jacobson, Matthew Frye, 44–45
Japanese immigration, 104–6, 148, 172, 277n8, 277–78nn10–11
Johnson, Albert, 52, 67–68, 87, 179–80, 183–85, 190, 198, 234–35, 240, 300n81
Johnson, Hiram, 68, 76–77
Johnson-Box bill, 179–82, 194
Johnson-Reed Act (1924). *See* Immigration (Johnson Reed) Act (1924)
Juárez, Benito, 154
Junior Order of Mechanics, 46, 71

Kang, S. Deborah, 263n34
Keena, Leo J., 280nn26–27
Kellogg, Frank: and article 27 disagreements, 26–28; defense of immigration policy as domestic policy, 103, 107, 108, 112–13; influenced by Wilsonianism, 3; on international quota debate, 102, 103; opposition to quota extension, 75–76, 89, 92–94, 107, 128–29; support of administrative restriction, 157, 187; support of passport requirement, 160, 162–63, 189–90, 288n74
Kerr, John W., 280nn26–27
King, Desmond, 68
Knight, Alan, 27, 43
Ku Klux Klan, 46

Landa y Piña, Andrés, 139
La Opinión (newspaper), 213
La Prensa (newspaper), 197, 213, 275n42
Latin American immigration, 52–53, 74–75, 108–12, 115–17, 180–83, 235–36, 279n24, 291–92n40
Lee, Erika, 12
Lerdo de Tejada, Carlos Trejo y, 119, 282n38
literacy tests and illiteracy, 46–48, 50, 53, 85, 86, 98, 120, 158
Lodge, Henry Cabot, 45
Long, John D., 73–74, 114, 280nn26–27
Los Angeles Times, 220–21, 233–34, 238

Macdonald, John, 212
Madero, Francisco, 177
Martínez, Oscar, 209–10
Massey, Douglas, 10
Maxey, Thomas, 175–76
McMahon, Robert, 11
Mears, Eliot G., 147
Mexican government: attempts to dissuade northward migration, 61, 90, 170–72, 177–78; bilat-

eral immigration negotiation attempts, 88–89, 111–12, 119–22, 161–63, 178; immigration regulation, 16, 61–63, 90–91, 136–41, 275n44, 284–85nn27–28, 288n70; opposition to quota, 60, 77–83, 87–92, 117–21, 132–37, 186–87, 194–200; repatriation management, 62, 63, 93–100, 207–10, 213–24, 277n67, 285n28, 296n35; support for administrative restriction, 184, 225–26. *See also* U.S.-Mexican relations

Mexican immigration: border-crossing experiences, 98, 150–51, 169–70, 191–92, 276–77n65; contemporary studies on, 143–56; and exemptions of 1917 act, 48–50, 51, 59; impacted by Porfiriato, 37–42, 268n66; impacted by Revolution (1910–1917), 42–43; Mexican government regulation, 16, 61–63, 90–91, 136–41, 275n44, 284–85nn27–28, 288n70; modern scholarship on, 13–15, 262–63nn27–28, 263n33; pattern of, 34–35, 276n62; post-1924 increase, 56–59, 63; statistics, 9–11, 43–44, 93–100, 261–62nn16–17, 262n20, 277n67, 294nn78–79, 297n42; temporary labor, 62, 70–71, 83–87, 111–12, 120–21, 140, 250–52, 269n79, 283–84n7; wages, 35, 40–41, 42, 55–56, 129–30, 270n116, 274–75n42. *See also* administrative restriction; illegal immigration; quota

Mexican Revolution (1910–1917), 21, 42–43

mining industry, 36–39

Mitchell, Christopher, 13–14, 262–63n28

Molina, Natalia, 175, 193, 263n33, 293n61

Mora-Torres, Juan, 39, 40

Morgan, Stokely W., 27

Morrow, Dwight W., 29–33, 89, 90–91, 93, 198, 285–86n31

Munro, Dana G., 27

National Origins Act (1929), 179

national sovereignty. *See* sovereignty

New York Times, 53, 56, 57, 180, 199, 231, 290n20

Ngai, Mai, 2–3, 192, 293n62

Nicaragua, 28

Nichols, Norval, 280nn26–27

Obregón, Álvaro, 24–25, 31, 62, 89, 144, 208

oil industry, 22–23, 26–28, 29, 30, 37, 210

Order of White Citizens of America, 71

Ortiz Rubio, Pascual, 197, 198, 208

Oyen, Meredith, 12

Pan-American Conference (Fifth), 182, 291–92n40

Pan-American Conference (Sixth), 108–12, 115–17, 279n24

passports and visas, 138, 159–63, 187–89, 227–29, 237, 288n74

Patriotic Order of the Sons of America, 46

Porfiriato, 19–21, 35–42, 268n66

Porter, Stephen, 198

Portes Gil, Emilio, 31, 32, 208

property rights, 21–30, 36, 185–86, 292n40

Public School Defenders of California, 71

Puig Casauranc, José M., 142

quota: and contemporary anthropological and sociological studies on Mexican immigration, 143–56; diplomatic concerns, 66–67, 73–76, 87–88, 92, 106–7, 185–86, 198–99, 239–40, 298–99n65; economic arguments against, 59–60, 72–73, 83, 85, 134–35, 146; economic arguments for, 76–77, 129–30, 173–74; failure of Harris bill, 232–35, 238–42; Johnson-Box bill, 179–82, 194; Johnson-Reed Act (1924), 11, 53–55, 56, 102, 103–4, 106, 131, 227; Mexican opposition to, 77–83, 87–92, 117–21, 132–37, 186–87, 194–200; National Origins Act (1929), 179; racial arguments for, 69, 70, 86, 98–99, 152–55, 172–75, 290n20; regulatory enforcement arguments for, 86, 130–31; and repatriation statistics, 93–100, 277n67; scholarship on, 14–15, 263n33; Senate approval of Harris bill, 183–85, 234; Senate Committee approval of Harris bill, 128–32; support for, overview, 58–60, 67–72; temporary worker program resolution, 83–87. *See also* administrative restriction

race and racism: and assimilation, 44, 46, 51–52, 278n11; contemporary sociological studies on, 146–56; employers' preference for Mexicans, 73, 134; and eugenics, 45–46, 50, 51, 59, 145; Japanese resentment of racial prejudice, 105–6, 278n11; Mexican resentment of racial prejudice, 87–88, 91–92, 135, 142–43, 172; and naturalization qualifications, 175–76; in quota debate discourse, 69, 70, 86, 98–99, 152–55, 172–75, 290n20; and SAFR report, 300–301n4; in James Sheffield's discourse, 27, 32

railroad construction and transportation, 36, 38, 39–41, 267n49, 267n56

raw materials industry, 23, 36–39, 210. *See also* oil industry

Recinos, Elisa, 191

Reed, David, 75, 129, 130–31, 187

Reisler, Mark, 14–15, 263n33

repatriation, 62, 63, 93–100, 207–10, 213–24, 277n67, 285n28, 296n35

Robinson, Joseph T., 107–8, 279n15

Robles, Juan, 191

Rodríguez, Abelardo, 208

Rodríguez, Raymond, 207, 209

Rodríguez, Ricardo, 175

Romanian immigration, 52

Root, Elihu, 264n11

Ruiz, Ramón Eduardo, 38, 211

Ruiz y Flores, Leopoldo, 31

Salvadoran immigration, 52–53, 118

Sánchez, George, 9, 10–11, 262n20

Santibáñez, Enrique, 171–72, 175, 176–79, 193, 201, 290n29

Schmidt, Arthur, 142

Schneider, Dorothee, 192–93

Schneider, George, 70, 223

Schuler, Friedrich, 12

Schulte, William T., 241

Second International Conference on Immigration and Emigration, 112–21, 279–82nn25–38

Shaw, G. P., 211–12

Sheffield, James R., 26–27, 29, 32–33, 43, 265n15
Sheridan, Clare, 152
Simmons, John Farr, 187, 190
Sixth Pan-American Conference, 108–12, 115–17, 279n24
Sons and Daughters of the American Revolution, 45–46, 71
sovereignty: Mexican, 21–28, 30; Pan-American, 109–11, 116, 117; U.S., 2–3, 6, 101, 103, 106–8, 112–14, 118–19, 122, 290n29, 298–99n65
Spenser, Daniela, 25–26
Steckel, Roy, 223
Stimson, Henry, 3, 231, 236, 239–40
Suástegui, Francisco, 77–83, 87–88, 177
Survey of American Foreign Relations (SAFR), 252–54, 300–301n4

Taft, William, 47
Téllez, Manuel, 77, 95
temporary laborers, 62, 70–71, 83–87, 111–12, 120–21, 140, 250–52, 269n79, 283–84n7
Toy, Eckard, 148

United Spanish War Veterans, 71
Urbina, Salvador, 111
U.S. foreign relations: European immigration dispute, 52, 102–3; internal and external nature of, 11–13; Japanese immigration dispute, 104–6, 277n8, 277–78nn10–11; Johnson-Box bill dispute, 180–81; Pan-American immigration dispute, 52–53, 74–78, 108–12, 115–17, 180–83, 279n24, 291–92n40; and Second International Conference on Immigration and Emigration, 112–21, 279–82nn25–38; and U.S. immigration policy as domestic policy, 103, 107–8, 112–14, 118–19, 122, 174
U.S.-Mexican relations: bilateral immigration negotiation attempts, 88–89, 111–12, 119–22, 161–63, 178; and Cristero Rebellion, 30–32; during Díaz regime, 19–21, 41; diplomatic concerns over quota, 66–67, 73–76, 87–88, 92, 106–7, 185–86, 198–99, 239–40, 298–99n65; post-1927 détente, 32–34; property rights, 21–30, 36, 185–86, 292n40; and SAFR report, 252–54, 300–301n4

Valenzuela, José A., 38
visas and passports, 138, 159–63, 187–89, 227–29, 237, 288n74
Visel, Charles, 223

wages, 35, 40–41, 42, 55–56, 129–30, 270n116, 274–75n42
Ward, Henry, 68–69, 78
Ward, R. D., 45
Washington Post, 233
Westphalian ideology, 3, 6–7, 121–22, 182, 249–50
White, Francis, 27
whiteness, 27, 46, 154–55, 173, 175–76
Wilmoth, Grover, 229
Wilson, R. N., 238–39
Wilson, William, 49–50, 269n96
Wilson, Woodrow, 3, 6–7, 47–48
Wilsonianism, 3, 6–7, 121–22, 182, 249–50
Winters, George, 97–98, 159–60, 190, 226–27

Yung, Judy, 12

Index

www.ingramcontent.com/pod-product-compliance
Lightning Source LLC
Chambersburg PA
CBHW021831220426
43663CB00005B/211